NOT
IN
THIS
FAMILY

POLITICS AND CULTURE
IN MODERN AMERICA

Series Editors
Glenda Gilmore, Michael Kazin, and Thomas J. Sugrue

Volumes in the series narrate and analyze political and social
change in the broadest dimensions from 1865 to the present,
including ideas about the ways people have sought and wielded
power in the public sphere and the language and institutions
of politics at all levels—local, national, and transnational.
The series is motivated by a desire to reverse the fragmentation
of modern U.S. history and to encourage synthetic perspectives
on social movements and the state, on gender, race, and labor,
and on intellectual history and popular culture.

NOT IN THIS FAMILY

Gays and the Meaning of Kinship
in Postwar North America

Heather Murray

PENN

UNIVERSITY OF PENNSYLVANIA PRESS

PHILADELPHIA · OXFORD

Published by
University of Pennsylvania Press
Philadelphia, Pennsylvania 19104-4112

Printed in the United States of America
on acid-free paper
10 9 8 7 6 5 4 3 2 1

Library of Congress Cataloging-in-Publication Data
Murray, Heather A. A.
   Not in this family : gays and the meaning of kinship in postwar North America /
Heather A. A. Murray.
      p.   cm.
   Includes bibliographical references and index.
   ISBN 978-0-8122-4268-3 (hardcover : alk. paper)
1. Gay men—United States—History—20th century.   2. Gay men—Family
relationships—United States—History—20th century.   I. Title.
HQ76.M87   2010
306.76′62097309045—dc22
                                                          2010012587

CONTENTS

INTRODUCTION

THROUGHOUT THE 1970s and 1980s, poet Elsa Gidlow, then an elderly woman, met a number of younger lesbians who considered her a lesbian icon. Gidlow had grown up in Quebec but had settled in San Francisco in the 1920s, and she extolled the gay community she came upon there throughout the early part of the century. "Before every half-informed person had learned to mouth the jargon of the sexologists and psychiatrists to homosexuals," she insisted, "[individuals] respected one another's privacies" in day to day life, no less so in their own families.[1] Gidlow's mother, in fact, had lived with her and her partner, something her lesbian visitors found intriguing, as many felt that their parents had rejected them to varying degrees. But Gidlow insisted that they see a paradox in seeking their parents' understanding. "Do we not," she would ask, "in challenging our parents' values, reject them?" She did not find it "fair to expect [a] continuance of unquestioning approval."[2]

Mocking a contemporary coming-out scene, she insisted that she never would have considered taking her mother aside and saying, "Have you understood that my love and friendship for the women I lived with included *sex*?" In her view, telling parents would only bring about heartache and confusion and even prurience. "We are not responsible for the fantasies of others," she wrote. "All we can do is not contribute to them."[3] Gidlow went further, decrying a sexual voyeurism in the society at large, a corollary of a repudiation of discretion that she discerned surrounding sexual matters. "Who has ordained, and on what authority, that we must supply the world with script and justification of our intimate interactions?" she asked.[4]

Elsa Gidlow's reflections offer an arresting assessment of both the revelation of the personal and the significance of sexuality within the family. Her call to privacy seems particularly out of sync with the relationships between gays and their parents in contemporary North America, when the coming-out moment seems taken for granted as a significant and necessary ritual. The polite reticence that she described seems to have long since shattered.[5]

How can this shift be explained, between the mid-twentieth century, when Gidlow saw a fundamental rupture, and our own times? How did gays and their parents conceive of family selves and gay selves, and how did this duality manifest itself culturally? How did it come to be that gays and their parents became particularly burdened with negotiating both conditional and unconditional love within postwar families? From the perspective of many cultural observers, gays have been largely orphans, adrift from relationships with parents and kinship ties as heterosexual families have known them. And yet, between the immediate postwar period and the 1990s, the family of origin, as both a lived relationship and a symbol, has been a central animating force and preoccupation of both gay culture and politics and has shaped gay thought more broadly. Gays also have shaped the sensibilities of their families, provoking an analysis of the meanings of family intimacy and family activist politics.

This is a study of the relationship between gays and their heterosexual parents in North America starting in 1945 and ending in the early 1990s. I acknowledge the depth and the subtlety of the family's influence not only on the intimate expressions and collective memories of these individuals but also on culture and politics, the realms in which gays and their families observed each other, represented each other, and imagined each other. The relationship between gays and their parents illuminates larger themes of intergenerational tensions between baby boomers and their elders, evolving notions of intergenerational obligation and caring, demeanors of revelation and discretion, and, perhaps most important, feelings surrounding the very purpose of family life in the post–World War II period.

Despite cultural ideas and images of gays "coming out" to their families, or being excommunicated, the family of origin surprisingly has not been widely acknowledged by historians as a shaping force of either gay or family consciousness. In her historical ethnography, anthropologist Kath Weston has explored the biological family as a contested concept for gays, arguing that gay kinship challenges procreation and biology; in her view, gay people have pioneered new meanings and practices of kinship, with the social on a higher plane than the biological. Here "chosen" families—of friends, partners, activist communities, and their own children—are considered to be the crucial, and sometimes the sole, source of emotional and political sustenance for gays.[6] Other gay historians have assumed an existence of a chosen family as well, insofar as the gay historiography of the American postwar period has emphasized the formation of gay communities, gay activism, and the development of gay identities, especially in relationship with broader social and intellectual discourses.[7] Yet the private, domestic lives of gays and contested visions of family life have been pronounced and unmistakable features of post–World War II gay life.

World War II accelerated a broad recognition of gays as a distinct social group that shaped how parents would see their gay children and how gay children would conceive of themselves. This is not to say that gay communities and identities did not exist prior to the war. Even though the category "homosexuality" did not exist until the late nineteenth century, some historians feel that same-sex acts even during the colonial era constituted a gay sexual identity or that the acceptance and prestige of intense same-sex friendships within middle-class, homosocial worlds of the early nineteenth century were verifiable gay communities of sorts.[8] As late nineteenth- and turn-of-the-century American scientists and sexologists increasingly scrutinized and uncovered homosexuals as a distinct human species, visible and widespread gay communities and subcultures formed in urban enclaves such as New York City, and they even made their presence known in domestic venues such as house parties.[9]

World War II, however, was unique in that it brought young men and women into same-sex environments in the military and in defense production and transferred them in their formative years from rural to urban worlds where peer relationships took precedence over intergenerational family relationships. At the same time, as historian John D'Emilio has shown, expanding job markets and the growth of consumer capitalism gave gay men and women the chance to live as single adults and form their own relationships outside their parents' homes.[10] Psychology and psychiatry, so important to the war effort, had offered a reevaluation of gays during this period, in their suggestion that homosexuality was a mental state rather than a biological condition, as late nineteenth-century and early twentieth-century sexology would have deemed it. Ironically, these pathologizing portraits of gays projected homosexuality further into the realm of the human imagination. Examples of homosexual life stories abound in the psychological works of this period, but also in the famous sexuality studies of Alfred Kinsey, as well as gay pulp fiction, and even McCarthy-era Senate investigations into gays in government, all of which suggested the existence of a community of gays, albeit a shadowy and unsavory one. This recognition set the stage for gay secrecy and discretion in their public, and at times in their private, lives. But it also kindled gay organizing during these years. The most prominent strain of the homosexual rights movement—called the homophile movement—during the 1950s and early 1960s argued that gays were mentally sound, respectable, normal, and in fact quite close to heterosexuals.

The tenor of gay activism and gay cultural formations was less integrationist and more unrepentant during the later 1960s and early 1970s. Shaped by the deepening rights consciousness of North American society, gays increasingly saw themselves as a minority deserving of these rights. Gay liberation developed a critique of heterosexuality, broadly conceived to include the nuclear family structure and the institutionalization of heterosexuality. In turn, a countercultural ethos suggested that traditional families curtailed self-fulfillment, and this was especially so for gays who saw themselves as differing quite dramatically from "straight" society. The ritual of "coming out" to fellow gays and to heterosexual society during this period suggested that gays could unleash the inhibitions generated in having to keep their sexuality a secret. At the same time, during the 1970s, many lesbians were challenging the sexism within the gay liberation movement, finding the very category "gay" to be wanting, denying their unique experience. Adapting the political framework of feminism, these lesbians offered their own critique of the limitations of love and personal relationships in a society dominated by heterosexuality and fashioned a perspective of lesbian feminism.[11]

The trauma and dislocations of AIDS in the 1980s prompted a significant reevaluation of obligations between gays and within gay communities, as gays organized in caring networks, pursued better health care, and sought possible cures for their dying friends and partners. In the midst of the AIDS crisis, the New Right political movements of the 1970s and 1980s and their attention to the traditional nuclear family, sexual morality, and traditionalism had put gays on the defensive. In the discourse of the New Right, and especially the Christian Right, gays were antithetical to the family—rejected by their parents and society at large. In the face of this, some gay activists felt a need to return to a strategy of respectability and increased attention to reformist rather than radical activism.

This story of postwar gay community, identity formation, and gay activism, however, neglects the fact that families were always integral to these developments. Parents had, in fact, taken the cue from their children's own attempt to gain civil rights, and the initial parents' movement of the early 1970s built on those efforts, organizing for the rights of their gay children. By the 1980s, as the formalized, national movement of Parents, Families, and Friends of Lesbians and Gays (PFLAG) took hold, parents' organizing was as much for the parents themselves as it was for their children, as a perception developed that parents too had suffered within a homophobic society intolerant of their children's difference.

But even outside of this specific organization, parents of gays had long animated their children's political causes, their cultural formations, and their self-conceptions. Fantasies of family permanence and the tensions of rejection, on the part of both gays and their parents, spanned the postwar period. The family remained a symbol of care, intergenerational ties, and eternal relationships that shaped the revelations of gay selves, even amid anxieties or ideas about family excommunications. Gays and their parents pondered and reevaluated ideas about sexuality and family love with an intensity that in fact rendered them perhaps even more enmeshed in their original families than heterosexual sons and daughters, in the sense that gays and their parents became particularly marked by a contemplation of their personal pasts, even if only seeking the source of their difference or alienation from one another. This attention to the personal past is especially striking during the postwar period when the immediate, collective past, shaped by memories of warfare, became difficult and frightening to contemplate. Perhaps in the shunning of collective pasts interior pasts became all the more important, and a fantasy about home and family life became intensified.[12] This observation is not to assert that biological families necessarily trump other social arrangements or chosen families but to recognize the weight of that personal past on gay life and culture and on gays' parents' own intimate and cultural expressions. Contemplation of family life, including emotions of longing, loneliness, nostalgia, and melancholy, were the driving force behind many of these expressions.

The postwar period honored and dramatized the nuclear, and presumably heterosexual, family. The family would come to take on a therapeutic function of sorts and become, in the words of religious historian Robert Orsi, "a theater of self-revelation" between its members. This sort of family style allowed gays a fascinating position within these family constellations both when they chose not to reveal their sexuality, as they were more apt to do in the early postwar period, and when they did reveal, as was more common in the later decades of the twentieth century. Families became inward looking, and relationships between parents and children more direct and less mediated by extended family relationships, mirroring a broader social trend of the decline of communal links and the growth of individualism. This was particularly the case for white, middle-class families.[13] On the surface, children and parents also had more privacy from each other in this family setting, as home ownership increased and larger living spaces for family life became more common. But much as they accommodated the individual, these family formations increasingly expected mutual intimacy as well as affectionate companionship. As historian Elaine Tyler May points out, even the consumer culture of the postwar period was often geared toward families and the fun that they might have together.[14]

Companionate family styles, of course, have a history that long predates the postwar period. The ethos of families that are economically useless and emotionally priceless, as Arlene Skolnick puts it, developed among the middle classes in the early twentieth century.[15] The term "companionate marriage" was coined by Ben Lindsey in the book by the same title during the 1920s. Yet the profound suffering, grief, and social disorientations of the Depression years and World War II had put this notion of family life on hold until the social changes of the postwar years allowed for higher incomes, younger marriages, and more children, and in turn a greater sense of parental investment and hope in those children.[16] When families reintegrated, especially after prolonged absences of fathers during the war, they could feel a strong sense of estrangement or a disquieting feeling that they did not know each other anymore.[17] During the postwar years, families may have been celebrated for their relationships based on affection, mutual interests, and expressive individuality, and yet these families often seem perched uncertainly between the expectations of newer, affectionate families and a more pragmatic style of family life that had helped see them through times of crisis.[18] What, then, did it mean to be a family member within an affectionate postwar family? The very concept of unconditional love, so poignant for both gays and their parents in understanding their relationship, was not a self-evident concept, especially in the early postwar period. In fact, some child care writers advised against it, fretful that the demands of the all-encompassing affection that had emerged during the postwar period were simply too high for most families to fulfill.[19]

This ambiguity about the purpose of family life endured throughout the postwar period. Family relationships in general were now fraught with an expectation—and failure—of parents and their children to know one another intimately. This sense is captured uniquely by gay children and their parents who pondered each other as family members quite consciously and thus provide a lens through which to explore the tensions and strains within these postwar affectionate families. Gays challenged not only parental investments in children but also the very symbolism of children as their parents' fantasy selves in this period.[20] If gays have carried the burden of orphanhood uniquely in the twentieth century, this was perhaps because they typified a lingering and broader cultural fear of family breakup. This anxiety had once been quite prominent and widespread in American culture, especially during the mid-nineteenth century, a moment when it was becoming more common for adult children to leave their parents behind and when the figure of the orphan and themes of child rescue loomed so poignantly, especially within women's cultural sources, dramatizing the uneasiness surrounding family leave-taking.[21] I argue that this fear of family breakup was given new life in the post–World War II period and in fact had transformed into a powerful longing for family togetherness in the wake of the forced family breakups during the Depression and war years. In turn, the deepening recognition of the private, affective lives of children, as well as more vast representations of gay selfhood throughout this period, would set the stage for family clashes and an ongoing negotiation about generational obligations and the meanings of family love. I suggest that gays and their parents embody a longing for an eternal family life in which parents and children understand each other, care for each other, and stay together indefinitely—a kind of early modern ideal for family life that endured into the postwar period and even into the late twentieth century. Amid a sense of family purposelessness in the postwar period, the simple act of knowing and loving children gave the family a new driving force, kindling both a fear of orphanhood and estrangement as well as an emphasis on internal curiosity that increasingly rejected discretion.

This kind of family ideal was particularly fraught because, even as World War II provoked a nostalgic response for the security of the home and the family, a sense of the unknown in fact seemed to reside at the heart of these postwar companionate families. The question "Who are you?"—implicitly posed between family members during this period—was illuminated most poignantly by parents with gay children. Gay writings and ideas of the family allow for a charting of a unique history of family communication, as it moved from metaphor and code in the immediate postwar years to direct revelations and knowledge of one another by the end of the century. This dynamic of communication placed gays and their families at the heart of the conflicts—and paradoxes—surrounding twentieth-century ideas about privacy and discretion, including the attempt to guard privacy fiercely and the deepening curiosity surrounding private realms. Gays and their parents often found themselves straddling these impetuses in a way that was quite urgent, as knowledge of each others' private lives became so tied to intimacy within postwar families.

This is not just a story of chasms between generations and the ways they interacted, however, but a story of chasms and the relationship between the cultures of heterosexuality and homosexuality. Historian George Chauncey has suggested that gays are parallel to an ethnic group, given the distinctive language, folklore, values, and sense of style that developed in gay subcultures.[22] My study suggests that many gays saw themselves as having an ethnic affiliation that their heterosexual parents did not share; thus gay children represent not only a generational separation but a cultural one. In a sense, their feelings paralleled the children of immigrants who gradually left behind the Old World as represented by their parents—in this case the Old World of heterosexuality—and came into the New World of homosexuality. Gays too registered the feeling of deracination that inevitably accompanies this transition and even feelings of homesickness or nostalgia for the Old World that their parents embodied. However, it is not only gays who are culture bearers; heterosexuality also has a distinct lore, one that was depicted and symbolized by gays in their political writing and artistic culture throughout this time period, just as homosexuality was by parents. External cultural observers likewise portrayed both gays and their parents, and families reacted to as well as shaped this set of observations.

The period from 1945 to the 1990s was a time in which a visible gay writing culture, publications, and politics emerged and a parents' movement and literature appeared. I recognize that historical periodizations can be somewhat arbitrary. Sensibilities can flow into each time period or be revived; individuals can become repositories for the past and have a sensibility that seems oddly out of place for their time and generation. I try to take these strains into account, but nonetheless I have developed a periodization based on broad articulations of both gay politics and culture, including homophile activism, gay liberation, and lesbian feminism, the PFLAG movement, as well as AIDS activism, tracing how it is that cultural expressions, activist politics, and even perceptions of disease and dying were motivated by family pasts. While this study examines both American and

Canadian sources, it is not a sustained comparison between the two nations. I do take an often different Canadian gay historical narrative into account, however, and I draw on some Canadian sources. In so doing, I wish to explore the continuities at an intimate level despite the starkly different national experiences and perceptions of national characters between Canadian gay writers and activists and their American counterparts. These examples underscore that gays experienced some collective emotions that were not always precisely attached to a geography or national character, but were based on shared emotional sensibilities rather than citizenship.

Historical, literary, sociological, psychological, and visual sources for this study reveal my central themes of privacy, the negotiations of gay selfhood, conceptions of family emotion and intimacy, and generational chasms. I explore private, introspective writings, particularly personal correspondences and diaries, as well as published memoirs, fiction, poetry, song lyrics, movies, visual and print media, and artistic representations. I distinguish between those personal writings that individuals have produced based on their experiences and memories as witnesses of a sort, taking into account the importance of such venues as diaries as refuges to help gays and their parents maintain a private grip on the truth outside of the dualities that might be presented for a larger, public, and heterosexual world. Yet I do think of both sets of sources—the reflections and the fictional accounts—as representations, ones that demonstrate common patterns, emotions, and perceptions. Because sexuality in general and homosexuality in particular were emerging, during the post–World War II period, as both private experiences as well as public concerns and symbols, I also examine the explicitly political dimensions of gay culture, particularly the literature and advertising of gay social movements, as well as PFLAG.[23] The period I explore documents an explosion of gay publications, especially with respect to gay periodicals and the gay press. Finally, these years also saw a proliferation in genre writing such as self-help literature.

This range of sources permits an exploration of the relationship between private and public gay (and heterosexual) cultures, as well as the shaping force of family realities and ideals, not just in the basic sense that gays and their parents often depicted each other and emotions from their family experiences, including feelings of loss and tensions surrounding family intimacy, and hopes for better family relationships and love. But these sources also demonstrate that gay social and political movements accommodated these emotions, especially in the sense that parents of gays often took on symbolization as the state, or they became the often unspoken forces from whom gays sought redress for feelings of isolation and alienation. In turn, within the parents of gays movement, gay children often took on a broader symbolization as a challenge to conditional love in families that parents must, ideally, transcend.

In all of these sources, my sample is necessarily a group of thoughtful, sentient observers of their lives, their families, and their societies. Many were writers, artists, and political activists, who perhaps were more experimental in their lifestyle and philosophical in their personality type. Similarly, many parents who have left written records of their reactions to their children's gayness, or who participated in activism on behalf of their gay children, may have been unusually observant and prepared to express their thoughts and feelings. What is put forth in these written and artistic media is not necessarily a reflection of how people lived. Moreover, these subjects are disproportionately white and middle class, at least in terms of their adult sensibility, even when this was not the case in their original families. Given this slant of the sources, I do not claim to look at a typical experience or ideas of gays and lesbians and their parents but rather a group of thinkers who allow me to examine subjects often left unspoken, censored, or unpreserved.

One way of thinking about these sources is to bear in mind that these were the reflections of those who maintained some sort of family relationship, in their consciousness if not in their daily lives. This study makes no attempt to establish that gays were or were not banished from their families in the postwar period. My research has been dependent upon archives that have been both revelatory and limiting, in the sense that those who wrote, and those who saved their reflections, might have been more likely to have maintained some level of family integration.[24] Thus the very source base might push my analysis in a direction that assumes an overlap between the lives of parents and their gay children. At times, a set of diaries or letters would show that a family relationship existed, but no commentary beyond that; thus it also would be fair to say that these sources are representative of those who felt some difference between the sensibilities of parents and children. Moreover, the individuals I write about here wanted their stories to be told, and perhaps wrote for audiences, even within private contexts. Those who wrote in more public and political venues also were particularly aware and interested in their sexual identities in a way that may set them apart from other gays and their family members.

What drives this study, and perhaps where this study departs from other cultural and intellectual histories, is a question of what brings individuals—in this case gays and their parents—to write, represent, or have fantasies about their family lives. Implicit here is the idea that gays have a uniquely urgent desire to express selfhood and comment upon family life. The individuals I have written about often expressed themselves at moments of profound transformation, for instance after an unexpected conversation or harrowing encounter with a family member. Or they have taken great note of seemingly insignificant moments from their past, imbuing them with meanings about family emotion. I have tried to approach my sources with the view that these representations could be responses to family longings and that imagination, symbols, and reality do not necessarily trump each other but are always commingled. Abstract as these questions are, they are central to this cultural and intellectual history and integral to the history of gays and their families. Not only figures who were necessarily estranged from each other, or who unconditionally accepted one another, gays and their parents have left behind more unexpected and nuanced stories and imaginings.

1

Daughters and Sons
for the Rest of Their Lives

N THE FALL of 1945, after finishing his tour of duty in Hawaii, a twenty-one-year-old William Billings wrote a long and momentous letter to his parents, in Arkansas City, Kansas, where he had grown up. Billings was contemplating coming home and going to college with funds from the G.I. Bill of Rights. But he needed to tell his parents something first. He began by saying that since he had been away from Kansas's "provinciality and small town-ness," he felt he now understood, whether his family "recognized it or not, [that] the world is emerging from the Victorian Era and beliefs."[1] Though he pointed out that his enlightenment about "the facts of life" did not come from his parents, he reassured them that "no, darlings, I don't blame you." Nonetheless, he asked them, "Didn't it ever occur to you that certain tendencies I possess pointed in only one direction long, long before I was aware of it?" If they *had* seen "what I was heading for, you didn't face it. You were afraid to face the *truth!* . . .Well, dearest ones, think again. The inevitable is there. If you haven't faced the truth, please do it now. Let's quit playing 'Blind Man's Bluff.' "[2] Billings trusted that his parents knew to equate his "certain tendencies" with being gay.

On the surface, this revelation was more practical than it was emotional. His central purpose was neither to invite his parents to know him better nor to share an intimate aspect of his life, but to discuss the matter-of-fact consequences. "[I]n facing facts, truths as they are, it has of course been necessary to arrive at certain decisions," he announced.[3] These words of finality—"facts" or "truths"—conveyed what he considered the fixed and unchangeable character of his tendencies. In his view, it would be pointless to try to "erase inborn (maybe hereditary) traits" or to "blot out environment (and mine was feminine from beginning to end)."[4] He assured his parents that he did not "intend to let it wreck my life nor warp the pleasing attributes of my personality" and reminded them that "the ancient Greek civilization" was "practically based on it and its civilization flourished."[5] Still, he told his parents that they should feel "perfectly free and at ease with this opportunity to change [my homecoming plans] for me. I mean that. No person loves his home and family more than I, but I am cognizant—too—that it is your home to say who shall enter. After all, you are much older and your opinions on life are set in concrete. You may not feel it within the realm of your principles, ethics, and standards to accept this that I have declared."[6] Though he did not call himself a gay man per se, by page 10 of his thirteen-page letter, he left no doubt: "To state it inviolably so there can be no question in your mind, the sum and substance of the whole thing is briefly this: I am strongly attracted to members of my own sex!"[7]

Billings seemed prepared to forfeit his family relationships and assume an utterly independent adulthood. He clearly would have preferred to have his family in his life, but he did not harbor specific ideas about what this "much older" generation owed the younger one, particularly when their children were gay. He equated his parents with the "principles, ethics and standards" of their generation that presumably could not countenance the possibility of a gay child.

A sample of gay writers who, like Billings, would become teachers, or figures in the arts or literary world, suggests that for these individuals the immediate postwar period was a time of self-awareness about same-sex attractions, including what those attractions revealed about the nature of their true selves. In turn, these gays had to negotiate how, or even whether, they would give expression to this often hidden self in the family context. This dilemma was complicated by a sense of ambivalence and uncertainty that surrounded the family not just as a place of self-disclosure but as a place of mutual intimacy and affection between parents and children, where one central commonality between them was a presumed heterosexuality. In a society attuned so readily to rumor and false appearances, one that suggested a broad sense of scrutiny for outsiders, the question of who family members really were was pressing.[8] The very fact of being gay during this era marked these writers as nonconformists not just within the family but within a broader American culture that increasingly suggested polarities between conformity and nonconformity, or between group membership and individualism. While World War II had promoted a focus on purposeful group commitment, many observers increasingly linked the notion of the group to mass culture and the mediocrity of the herd. In this intellectual context, nonconformity could be considered an individualistic rebellion. Yet gay adults in this period were more likely to represent their own nonconformity as deviance and estrangement and seek some form of integration not just with mainstream society but within the family.

During World War II and the immediate postwar period, Americans looked inwardly and examined their fellow citizens, their family members, and themselves for evidence of this deviance. Throughout the war the American military observed potential gay recruits, instituting mandatory screening and discharge policies regarding homosexuals. Nonetheless, for Billings, the war had spurred on self-understanding by demonstrating that being gay was a recognizable social condition. Even if gay men and women existed at the borders of military culture, the recognition of a gay potential within this homosocial context gave gay men and women a presence in social life.[9] In fact, a perceived consequence of a society at war was that sexual expression and relationships outside of the structures of marriage and family life could potentially recast sexuality and gender roles. Thus heterosexual desire, expressed between married couples, emerged more firmly as an ideal.[10]

At the same time, World War II provoked a more general sense of nostalgia and sentimentalism for the home and for the past as represented by the family.[11] The idea of the middle-class companionate or affectionate family, a family valued for the emotional rather than economic presence of its members, was a long-term historical development, having its roots at the turn of the century and throughout the early twentieth century, only to be disrupted, as an ideology and a reality, during the anxiety and grief of the Depression and war.[12] After World War II, however, kinship strategies, especially in white, middle-class families, were shifting definitively as the relationship with older parents, the extended family, and local community ties became more distant, and the relationship with this chosen, companionate family, reinforced by culture, became more intense.[13] Gay adults and their parents during the early postwar period were straddling these distinctive practical and emotional family styles in their relations to one another.

Billings wanted to have both a family of his own and an ongoing rela-

tionship with his parents. He thought he could ease his parents' disquiet
by exonerating them from causing his sexuality. He emphasized that his
"feminine" environment while growing up had merely reinforced his
"nature." He told his parents that they might be interested to know that
"almost invariably a person of my type is irrevocably attached to his mother
. . . from his earliest years. In the case of a girl, she is usually attached as
strongly to her father. Why this is, I don't know. Just Nature's way, I guess.
So you see, when I used to play with girls even then the future was being
formulated."[14] Still, he did not want his parents to rue their son's fate.
"Please don't go to pieces over this," he said. "It's not as bad as all that."
Then he gave his parents even more reason for hope: "I may . . . marry out
of duty, convention, and my love of children. If I cannot love my mate
romantically, I will at least have a deep and abiding admiration for her."[15]
He even perceived being gay as something of an advantage in finding a
woman to marry: "You know, it's almost a joke: girls, you're as safe with
me as with your own mother—*ha*. That's why they like fellas like me, we
aren't trying to feel them up and rape them all the time. Maybe that's a
consolation—*ha*."[16] His predictions about his chances with women were
not wrong. Billings was to marry and have three children.

The irreverent, somewhat cavalier, and humorous depiction of his own
sexuality was at times belied by Billings's reassurances in this letter. On the
one hand, his language seems inflected with a campy sense of fun, in referring to his parents as "darlings" and "dearest ones" and punctuating his
somewhat raunchy descriptions of "feeling up" and "rape" with a "*ha*."
Although the parodies and exaggerations of camp as gay culture and sensibility had seen their heyday in the 1920s and 1930s, traces of this theatrical
gay past lingered in the social milieu of World War II that Billings had just
experienced, and perhaps this way of communicating defused his revelation
to his parents.[17] Nonetheless, he recognized that his parents could go "to
pieces" over his revelation, demonstrating an understanding of just how
weighty, from their perspective, his disclosure must have been.

Other gay adults were considerably more reticent with their parents
during the immediate postwar years. Throughout the same period, Robert
Leach, a professor, Quaker, and peace activist, never told his mother about
his attraction to men, despite acknowledging these desires to himself.
Unlike Billings, however, Leach believed that he could manipulate these
desires and alter his self. He felt that he could make a go of heterosexuality,
and not simply in a platonic way. He would do so by seeking psychiatric

treatment for what he considered an inner predicament, not his unalterable being.

Leach's faith in self-alteration and rehabilitation mirrored not only more widely held postwar beliefs in the possibility of adjusting or radically altering personal presentation but also Freudian notions of homosexuality as a life stage.[18] According to Freud, everyone's sexuality was homosexual in part, and it was predominantly so during the early life phases.[19] Freud's famous letter to an American mother, written in 1935 but published widely to American readers in 1951, pronounced homosexuality neither an illness nor a crime, but quite simply a neutral variation.[20] But this observation was not representative of the psychiatric ideas on homosexuality that would take hold in North America, especially during World War II and the postwar period. As psychiatry gained respect and prestige in its wartime military function, North American followers of Freud refashioned his ideas.[21] Perhaps most relevant to gays was a rejection of a notion of universal bisexuality and an emphasis that a heterosexual drive, present in all individuals, could be summoned to the surface through analysis.[22] Upon the creation of the American Psychiatric Association's first *Diagnostic and Statistical Manual* in 1952 (the *DSM-I*), homosexuality was considered a sociopathic personality disturbance rather than an innate condition.[23]

While Freud only gestured to the family types most likely to produce homosexuals, including the notorious family figures of the distant, weak father and the overbearing, dominant mother, American psychiatrists were more likely to insist on them.[24] This family model even seemed to become part of a gay slang during this period. Billings's reference to his intense attachment to his mother and his feminine environment as a child indicates at least some cognizance of psychiatric types in this era. The idea of family environments as agents of homosexuality in fact spurred on Robert Leach's own analysis of his personal past and his mother's hand in shaping his sexuality. Though Leach had been a conscientious objector during World War II and therefore was not screened as a prospective soldier, he was intrigued by the opportunity for intellectual introspection that analysis seemed to provide and appreciated psychiatry as a means to analyze his family critically. Moreover, he was the beneficiary of a new, postwar intellectual environment in the United States that rendered psychotherapy commonplace rather than strictly for elites with substantial wealth or for the insane in institutional settings.[25] His psychiatric sessions would become a central subject of his letters to his mother.

In 1950, when he was in his early thirties, Leach found a psychiatrist who was "about my age." He considered his first session to be "a happy time."[26] Leach was a professor in North Carolina then, and during the summer of his first treatments he wrote to his mother, Mary, to explain why he would not be returning to his hometown of South Ashburnham, Massachusetts, for a long visit that year. He told her he was having some "psychiatric work done" because "I have a mental problem of many years standing, which is now ready for solution. I have been seeing the doctor twice weekly."[27] Such was his first halting explanation of his psychiatric treatments. This news might have brought his mother face-to-face with the idea that her son's private life was more complex than she had imagined, if indeed she had even imagined it. But let him have a private life she did. In her letter back to him, she wrote that she was disappointed she would not get to see him as soon as she hoped but "[y]ou are very wise to have treatments for whatever troubles you. I am very glad that you are finding the solution. Perhaps you will feel like telling me about it while you are here. But if you don't feel like it, I will understand."[28]

Even if homosexuality had been in her mind, her son did not give her much reason to suspect it and instead cast his therapy as treatments for a misbegotten childhood. Because Leach's mother admitted that she knew little about psychology, and the gap between them—in education, wealth, and experience—was so large, Leach became an authority on the subject with her. He was not shy about relaying what he felt were her parenting problems. One of the central handicaps in their family, as he and his psychiatrist perceived it, was Mrs. Leach's cloying gestures of love, including the "many pictures of me (and [sister] Mary) in the house [which were] of course evidence of such fixation." Then he told her that the consequence of this smothering love was "*dependency*—which for excellent but mistaken motive you have helped build in me."[29] Consciously or not, Leach had suggested an idea of momism, a characterization of a stifling mother with nothing in her life to preoccupy her but her children, popularized by such authors as Philip Wylie in his 1942 work *A Generation of Vipers*.[30] Raising children in the 1910s and 1920s, mothers of Mrs. Leach's generation were parents before these widespread cultural critiques of mothers. In an earlier letter in 1945, she had even admitted, on her son's twenty-ninth birthday, that she "wished that I had known about some of the modern ways of bringing up children" when her son was younger.[31] Without knowing the shibboleths or critiques of "modern" parenting, Mrs. Leach might not have drawn any connection between her son's suggestion of maternal dependency or certain mothering types and homosexuality.

Without making the topic of homosexuality explicit, however, Leach did veer into the sexual realm when discussing his psychiatrist's observations about his Oedipus complex. "I suppose the hardest thing to realize is the incestuous overtones in our relationship which neither of us have recognized, and which need to be redeemed (not ignored) if I am to really mature," he said.[32] Never directly confronting her son's charge, Mrs. Leach began her response tentatively, saying that she was glad the doctor "helped you and that you can now go forward to a more satisfying and normal way of life."[33] She then pointed out that "[y]ou have a great deal to be thankful for—health, strength and a reasonable amount of brains. . . . Do think on these things and be happy. And if you can find the right girl, get married. Don't worry about supporting me, I can get old age assistance."[34] Not only did she urge her son to take stock of the promising parts of his life, but she also relieved him of an obligation to get married and to look after her, recognizing a shift away from an economic reciprocity between parents and children, more characteristic of an earlier family form. By implication, she also might have been relieving him of the obligation to be heterosexual. He was not beholden to her or her expectations in any respect.

But her son seemed to hold her accountable to a reciprocity that was introspective or emotional rather than fiscal. She wrote that she realized she had made "many mistakes" in parenting, "but I did what I thought was right. I am sorry for whatever I did wrong. . . . But I didn't know that I made either of you feel dependent on me."[35] The mother's tone of pain and reticence and also a slight defensiveness perhaps speaks to the somewhat impossible situation she had been placed in, that of apologizing for ideas that simply were not in her bailiwick. What had been in her sphere of reference was another dimension found in religion, not psychoanalysis. She wrote that when she was growing up "life seemed so much more simple. We never thought about what we inherited from our folks. We just went ahead and did the best we could. Maybe it would have helped to understand more—but I found that faith in God . . . carried me through. Instead of too much introspection, I found peace [in religion]."[36] This comment suggests a chasm between generations in their interpretations of feelings and self-expression, as well as a chasm in the expectations about what one generation owes to the next. More pragmatic than her son, Mrs. Leach also might have cherished more intense feelings of privacy; she simply might

not have considered such deeply personal matters suitable for family conversation.[37] A woman of her Victorian generation, particularly one who
lived in a small town and did not have the opportunity for formal education, might have lacked a language to describe subconscious or unconscious
motivations, and she might have felt directly accused of something unfath-
omable. The entire conversation might have seemed confusing to her, precisely because Leach stated the source of his problems, his homosexual
attractions, only obliquely, couched in the vague language of dependency,
the past, and the family. Still, perhaps it was gratifying for Leach when his
mother promised in her next letter, "I shall get a good Psychology text and
read up on all these things."[38]

Leach saw his gay attractions as a barrier to his happiness and a family
life. He was not completely amiss in imagining this to be the case. During
the early 1950s, when Leach was writing to his mother, gays were emerging
as symbols of scandal and subversion in the public imagination or, at best,
nonconformity. Ironically, at the very moment when the conformity of the
"masses" was causing some disquiet among intellectuals who wished to set
themselves apart from the thoughtless throng, Leach was a gay intellectual
for whom feelings of nonconformity and freakishness were most troubling.[39]

The idea of the multitude distressed American intellectuals, particularly
those who contemplated the recent past of warfare and totalitarianism.
Hannah Arendt argued that the loneliness and rootlessness of the masses
made them vulnerable to totalitarian regimes.[40] Other American cultural
observers fretted that postwar America had more than its share of lonely,
estranged citizens, for whom the workplace was the only institution of
social life. George Tooker's chilling 1950 painting *Subway*, portraying terri-
fyingly uniform workers in a subway station, gave visual form to these
ideas. Still other observers fretted that the United States had become a
bland and insignificant sort of place. Throughout the 1950s some white,
middle-class intellectuals embraced novelist Norman Mailer's thought that
white men abandon the stultifying aspects of postwar life—the stifling
nationalism, the isolation of suburbanization, the shallowness of consumption and uniformity of tastes, the trend toward jobs in middle-class man-
agement positions, proliferating bureaucracies, and the tyranny of the
nuclear family itself—and embrace "hipsterism" by becoming an outsider,
embodied in his creation of the "White Negro." The Beats kindled a similar
desire for the authenticity that they too considered the province of non-

white people living outside of middle-class conventions. This in fact included homosexuality, and some Beats experimented with it as well. But as white—and often heterosexual—intellectuals looked to what they imagined to be more daring, more exciting others as models for social possibilities, nonwhites and homosexuals alike largely embraced a strategy of integration into, rather than alienation from, mainstream society.[41] As historian Martin Meeker points out, the United States Supreme Court decision in *Brown v. Board of Education* in 1954 suggested powerfully not just to blacks but to gays as well that social equality would derive from integration rather than an embrace of nonconformity.[42] It was not simply that gays actively repressed their true selves and tried to perfect a social self that fit into society more, but that they recognized the deep loneliness of life on those margins that other observers romanticized.

In fact, gays themselves were sometimes ennobled as symbols of nonconformity in American life: even the popular sociology of the 1950s did so.[43] In *Must You Conform?* (1956) Robert Lindner singled out homosexuals as embodiments of unorthodoxy, suggesting that society did not despise homosexuality because of its sinful nature but because of its uncommonness. Lindner found something admirable in homosexuality if only for its flouting of the conventions of the Mass Man.[44] In this vein, in widely read and powerful social critiques that used psychoanalytic concepts, such as David Riesman's *The Lonely Crowd* (1950), the "inner-directed" person who developed a deep, individual sense of character was exalted over the "other-directed" or peer-oriented persona of his age who constantly sought the affirmation of others. Postwar existential philosophers such as Jean-Paul Sartre also emphasized trusting deep, genuine feelings and convictions to attain a sense of authenticity. This quest for authenticity was particularly urgent in a society that had just witnessed and was contemplating how extreme circumstances and warfare hampered and marred the individual. Psychiatrist Bruno Bettelheim's works showed how authenticity was tainted in the concentration camps and how selves split into the real and the social, with the real here taking on a sort of sacred quality, as the true self that got preserved.[45] However, for gays, this real self or this "inner direction" might have been too painful to apprehend if they dared let themselves ponder it. Leach had indeed recognized his inner character but took refuge and solace in the idea of developing an appearance of heterosexuality.

In fact, in some senses the dissent of "inner direction" in 1950s American culture was an ideal rather than a reality, or it was expressed culturally—in psychological and sociological sources, or in movies and music—rather than politically or even socially.[46] Not inclined toward dissent in his social life even if he was sympathetic in his intellectual life, Leach, like Billings, would go on to marry and have children. Reflecting on his younger years, he declared that he had been "determined to try to marry" because "the psychological pressure on me from my parents and background was enormous."[47] His psychiatric treatment did not appear to ease his disquiet over his homosexual feelings. As historian Beth Bailey has pointed out, even when concepts of homosexuality changed from a moral to a therapeutic model, the therapeutic judgments tended to intertwine with the older conventional views of morality.[48] Accordingly, even when Leach spoke in psychiatric terminology, he might have viewed himself as having an immoral, rather than a deviant, streak. By 1959, married and with two children, he noted with satisfaction that he was "well situated in the middle, a solid conventional member of society."[49]

Leach might have felt that marrying and having a heterosexual relationship reflected a degree of conscientiousness and maturity; to stay homosexual would be to renege on the commitments of adult life.[50] His impetus to keep up an appropriate position in the life cycle was thus also a part of his desire to assume a conventional life. A celebration of the nuclear family model in the 1950s, a spirit that saw a physical expression in household zoning regulations in major North American cities to prevent "unrelated persons" from living together, fostered an idea that those living outside this family model, such as the unmarried and the childless, were selfish and potentially deviant figures.[51] As a married man with children, Leach could protect himself from these charges.

In fact, Leach's stance reflects a wider strain of gay thought and debates about the embrace of conformity versus a celebration of nonconformity. Those who began publishing *ONE*, an early gay rights magazine, in 1953, felt that a sense of gay difference and open rebellion from the rest of society was necessary and beneficial.[52] Others regarded the impetus toward nonconformity as something quite hollow and disingenuous, not to mention unattainable. Writing an essay on the benefits of gay integration with the broader society in a lesbian periodical in 1957, Barbara Stephens portrayed alienation as somewhat fashionable and shallow and urged gays to see why they should commingle with heterosexual families and neighborhoods, even in the face of "the reported . . . evil of conformity-worship among the masses."[53] Like Leach, Stephens called attention to an unacknowledged privilege in having the luxury to afford being different or choosing the subject position of uniqueness. These viewpoints were not simply examples of the so-called silent generation of the young during the 1950s, seemingly out of touch with larger political issues and concerned solely with popularity, appearance, and getting ahead financially, as some historians have suggested of this cohort.[54] Leach was hardly a thoughtless robot, passively absorbing the gloomy messages about gays and grasping at the trappings of heterosexual conventionality, yet he remained unwavering in his desire for integration by seeking to acknowledge his gay feelings only inwardly and creating a respectable, public self as a professor and family man. In so doing, Leach felt that he could lead more of a multifaceted life.

Even those gays, like William Billings, who were perhaps more keenly in touch with their sexuality and more enthusiastic about being gay, were not about to embrace their gay selves exclusively or wholeheartedly. At times the stigma of being gay was not simply imagined or observed in the culture at large, but became a tragic reality, as it did for Billings. While living in Denver, Billings was arrested in 1955 for having consensual sex with another man. Devastated by this charge against her son, Mrs. Billings wrote to the *Denver Post* from Kansas in 1955, as her son had been charged under the Sex Law of Colorado, part of a series of postwar "sexual psychopath" laws enacted by more than half of the United States during the postwar period. These laws allowed for gays to be legitimately arrested for having consensual sex in both public and private places and recommended time in mental institutions for the transgressor.[55] Mrs. Billings noted that her son's teaching career—a particularly precarious profession for gay men during this period—was over and his "whole future . . . absolutely ruined" owing to a sentence worse than what "criminals who *kill*, steal, mutilate, molest women and children" received.[56] As Estelle Freedman has pointed out, rapists who did not murder their victims could be taken as more natural than men who committed consensual and nonviolent sodomy in the postwar period.[57] In fact, postwar North American society had constructed the homosexual stranger as the figure most likely to be a pedophile, seducing youth into becoming gay, an account of molestation that was in keeping with notions of homosexuality as a symbol for a range of perversions during this era.[58]

In Mrs. Billings's estimation, adult-child sexual contact of any kind was the crime most worthy of punishment, and these cases, as she rightly pointed out, were often not homosexual. She had read in the Colorado paper of a man "molesting an 11 year old girl" who had been given a minor sentence and paroled. "Wasn't that a far worse crime than our son committed?" she asked. "Oh, it can't be justice!" Though the act her son had committed, sex with another man, was "as repulsive to me as you," she felt that her son merited "treatment" just as "any other afflicted person" did, instead of time in a penitentiary. She concluded by saying that she and her husband were "heartsick and heart broken" and "disgraced, hurt, and grieved." Already suffering from "severe heart trouble," her son's one fateful violation of this "unreasonable law" was going to "send us to our graves."[59]

As with Billings, many gays in this period were subject to random police arrests and crackdowns even in specific gay venues such as bars or cruising areas, and their names subsequently could be released to newspapers.[60] Moreover, private venues such as parked cars were fair game for a police arrest, as National Association for the Advancement of Colored People (NAACP) activist Bayard Rustin experienced in 1953.[61] Entrapment for solicitation or even loitering was so widely acknowledged that homosexual civil rights activists printed pamphlets titled "What to Do if You're Arrested."[62] Sometimes families were perceived as a part of this state and police surveillance. In "A Minneapolis Father Discovers His Son's Homosexuality" in the *Minneapolis Star* in 1955, readers were told of a father who followed his son and contacted the police in order to catch him in a homosexual act and attempt to reform him.[63]

Internal family exposure was in fact as prominent a fear as exposure before the broader community. Writer Marge McDonald feared friends and acquaintances within her own orbit more than law enforcers. Her most central burden was protecting her family from the unthinkable disappointment she perceived they would feel over her sexuality. After her father died when she was five years old, McDonald was raised by her mother and her deeply religious aunt, Dora. In fact, McDonald believed that her mother and Aunt Dora already felt ashamed of her because she was a divorcée. By 1953, when she was in her early twenties, McDonald embarked on a life as a single working woman and in 1955 became employed in an insurance company in Columbus, Ohio. She left behind a series of intense and heart-rending diaries about coming to terms with her sexuality during these years. She confided in one diary entry that "it would hurt [my mother and Aunt Dora] deeply . . . to know that their 'baby' was a homosexual."[64] Tellingly, she used the word "hurt" rather than "embarrass" or "shame"; she did not separate parental hurt and shame, nor did she challenge these responses as illegitimate perceptions. Imagining her family's heartache contributed to her fears that they might find her out. She feared, for example, that a spurned lover might reveal her sexuality; one ex-girlfriend had even threatened to expose their relationship by mailing all of their letters to her mother and Aunt Dora. Naturally, McDonald wrote in her diary, this threat "weighed heavily on my mind."[65]

Yet even these threats did not push McDonald to reveal her sexuality to her family. She imagined that her family, if told, would be appalled enough to orchestrate forceful and invasive psychiatric treatment. Unlike Leach, who had the financial and educational resources to choose or reject psychiatric sessions, McDonald felt more vulnerable as a divorced, working-class woman. In turn, she did not perceive psychiatry as an intellectual boon, but more a terrifying experience that included lobotomies. McDonald wrote passionately in her diary in 1959 that "[n]o one ever has the right to tamper with the human brain—to use the 'ice pick,' to slash it beyond repair—destroying emotion. . . . [I]t is monstrous and inhuman."[66] Throughout her adult life she had suffered from bouts of depression, at least some of which were incurred by the problems she faced in coming to grips with her sexuality and relationships. She was convinced that if she were ever committed to an asylum "my family . . . would give their permission [for a lobotomy] if they told them it would help me . . . [because] they do not know of such things."[67] McDonald also felt that her girlfriend's mother would get her daughter a lobotomy if she ever found out about their relationship and said that she could "see myself killing her mother for giving permission for such a monstrous thing."[68]

Before the advent of pharmacological treatments for depression, desperate family members were indeed willing to pursue lobotomies for their children; lobotomies still were performed—though to a lesser extent than in the 1930s and 1940s—throughout the 1950s in the United States for melancholia, and they were more frequently performed on women.[69] This reality, as well as widespread images of catatonia and invasiveness in 1950s North American popular culture, might have informed McDonald's imagination.[70] The early postwar period witnessed widespread dystopian fantasies that primarily feared the reshaping of human character, inflected by knowledge of totalitarian systems as well as by a broader notion of scientism.[71] McDonald's fear of becoming an emotionless automaton speaks to a desire to maintain individuality and a refusal to compromise her inner character, even if it had to be hidden.

These preoccupations and anxieties about the consequences of displaying homosexuality outwardly and getting caught resonated with broader emphases of gay activism during the 1950s and early 1960s, a moment of early postwar gay organizing, activism, and publications, often referred to as homophile societies. 'Homophile,' a name not readily identifiable to the general public or censors, denoted advocacy for homosexuals.[72] The earliest homophile activist societies, the Mattachine Society, for gay men, and the Daughters of Bilitis (DOB), for gay women, were founded in California in 1950 and 1955, respectively. Each produced its own periodical, primarily emphasizing advocacy and public education, while providing a forum for religious and psychiatric opinion pieces regarding homosexuality. They too tended to be integrationist in ethos, and as Martin Meeker shows, they were particularly interested in changing the way homosexuality was represented and conceived of in the American public sphere.[73] The earliest of these were Mattachine's bimonthly *ONE* (1953–68, 1972), the monthly *Mattachine Review* (1955–66), and the DOB's monthly magazine, the *Ladder* (1956–72).[74]

For the activists writing in these journals, the reaction of the family of origin to homosexuality was one of the central difficulties in gay life. Although homophiles in this period typically focused on public activities, including picketing and demonstrations, they also fostered "inner-directed" activities aimed at private life, in which gays were urged to be open about their sexuality and "drop the mask."[75] In this vein, homophiles recognized that identifying gays as family members was a potent political statement. In a common advertisement in the homophile periodicals of this era, a drawing of an angst-ridden man clutching his face in his hands, with the title "How Can I Ever Face the World?" declared, "This man . . . is cut off from his family, his country, and his God." Yet "there may be as many as 15 million other men and women like him in the U.S. . . . You undoubtedly know some of them. They could even be your own son or daughter."[76]

A central preoccupation of these homophile writers was a fantasy of gay banishment from the family, and from the polity, embodied in "How Can I Ever Face the World?" wherein the homosexual man was depicted as being cut off not just from his family but from his religion and his country.[77] Tellingly, a major documentary on homosexuality in this period was titled, quite simply, "The Rejected."[78] Homophiles placed this plight as a fundamental homosexual oppression in need of redress. As activist Ken Burns noted in his address at the Third Annual Convention of the Mattachine Society in 1956, "[I]f the homosexual cannot receive love and compassion from those who have given him his existence . . . then where must he turn?" He called this problem "tragic."[79]

The homophile notion of gay banishment in fact resonated with a more far-reaching cultural script of the family lives of gays during this period that essentially deemed gays orphans. Edmund Bergler was one psychoanalyst who contributed to this script. Bergler made it a project to criticize sexologist Alfred Kinsey for exaggerating the numbers of homosexuals in American society, given Kinsey's claim that incidences of homosexuality were far more pervasive than previously believed and his suggestion that homosexuality was simply a natural variation, on a continuum, in fact, with heterosexuality.[80] In Bergler's 1959 work, *1000 Homosexuals: Conspiracy of Silence, or Curing and Deglamorizing Homosexuals?* he wrote that a first response of parents was to throw their gay children out of the house or to disinherit them.[81] Gay fiction, particularly gay pulp fiction that marketed stories of gays as a taste of deviant life, frequently presented the theme of family leave-taking, with homosexual characters fleeing their families in rural towns or farming communities for the privacy and independence of large cities.[82] In departing for the city, some gay characters were depicted as lost to a shadowy, underground world of homosexual communities, such as Ben Travis's character, Ray, in *The Strange Ones* (1959), who becomes almost inadvertently gay after going to New York.[83] Other characters in gay pulp fiction were portrayed as more deliberately grasping at a gay life. In Gore Vidal's *The City and the Pillar* (1948), a teenager also abruptly leaves his tyrannical father, the "bitter old man he was forced to live with," to start a new gay life in New York.[84]

The potential need to embrace this kind of independent adulthood was another central subject of homophile periodicals, and it was even advanced by parents of adult gay sons and daughters who dispensed advice to families in similar situations. These mothers—and they were, for the most part, mothers—often advocated a certain sense of emotional pragmatism about banishment. In 1958, Leah Gailey, the mother of a gay son, offered in the pages of the *Mattachine Review* a practical approach to telling parents about homosexuality. For her insights, the *Mattachine Review* had nominated her as its choice for Mother of 1958. Having little forbearance for parental trauma and drama, she wrote that if "you're rejected and forced from the family bosom, then just tell them that you are accepting your problem and that they may well assume theirs. If mother has a heart attack, don't be alarmed. She will recover!" These displays of hysteria most likely only amounted to "a play on your sympathies." Further, "if father rants and raves and disowns you—let him! . . . These fireworks will probably upset you, but try not to show it. As calmly as possible, tell them that you intend to live your own life."[85] Such a practical approach divorced of the underlying emotions of these "fireworks" and "psychosomatic" heart attacks—the very words indicate that she had dismissed the notion of great upset over sexual orientation—suggested that gays may have to affably assume a separate existence from their families. Another mother, this time of a gay daughter, Anne Fredericks, advised in 1961 that parents "should try to keep in mind that [the gay child] has probably been going through a most confused and confusing period" and "that an attempt to understand or at least to withhold judgment will do more good than any amount of breast beating or hair-pulling."[86] Again, the emotional trauma potentially experienced by parents of gays was identified as something superfluous and ridiculous, such as "breast beating" or "hair pulling."

Mothers writing in these periodicals also acknowledged the primacy of their children's feelings over their own worries about homosexuality, suggesting that a postwar notion of homosexuality as a difficult, painful fate for children could engender family sympathy. Another mother of a gay son, L. R. Maxwell, wrote in 1957 that mothers needed to overcome their "shocked senses" and try to understand their gay children. Otherwise "you strike out in anger and cruelty. . . . You wring your hands and weep [because] your love for yourself is greater than that for your son."[87] Mrs. Maxwell even embraced explanations of homosexuality in children that implicated parents as the cause of homosexuality. But here again it was suggested that parental failures needed to be borne with good, practical sense. She argued that many of the indictments that psychiatrists made about the family of homosexuals were "probably true" and suggested that mothers may have protected their sons too much in their "expression of mother love." She even advised mothers to "read Philip Wylie on 'Momism.'"[88] Such emotional pragmatism seems curiously out of sync with an era in which emotional fulfillment was, at least ideally, found within the family. Yet these were mothers of adult children. Raising their children in the 1930s and 1940s, amid the calamities of the Depression and World War II, these mothers might have felt steeled by the shame they already had faced during these years. During the Depression, and to some extent during World War II, many middle-class North American families lost any sense of propriety and privacy as they faced the public humiliations of being evicted from their homes, taking on jobs or boarders, doubling up with relatives, depriving children of material needs, and having to go on the dole. From these experiences, mothers of this generation also learned a certain toughness, and therefore a strength, in the face of a range of family and life adversities.[89]

Yet the mothers writing in this genre might have enhanced their practicality. Perhaps they saw themselves as activists in the same vein as their children and sought to distinguish themselves from the domestic histrionics that were offered up in more conventional women's housewife magazines of this period.[90] By 1960, membership in homophile organizations was only 230 for the Mattachine Society and 110 for the DOB, and so the mothers of members were a small sample indeed.[91] Not all gays had a "mother of the year" in their family homes.

Even exceptionally sensitive, perceptive observers, such as novelist Laura Hobson, wrote of a trauma upon finding out a child was gay, and the emotionality she evoked contrasts dramatically with the emotional reticence of homophile mothers. Hobson wrote a fictional account of her son's disclosure of his sexuality in 1975, though the story was set when he was a teenager, in 1960.[92] *Consenting Adult* starts with the mother reading her son's revelatory letter. The shock that she describes the mother character feeling was unbearable: she was "tranced," "motionless," and then emitted a "roaring sobbing, of an animal gored." A central emotion for her was "horror at *it*," and a recurrent vision of her son, Jeff, "physically close to another boy."[93] Much as her novel advances a stance of protecting the sanctity of private life, the portrait also reveals a sense of voyeurism about gay sexuality. A prurient innuendo about gay sexuality was not uncommon during this era. As James Baldwin's central character, David, expressed it in the 1956 novel *Giovanni's Room*, the very idea of homosexuality was a "cavern" in his mind, "full of rumor, suggestion, of half-heard, half-forgotten, half-understood stories, full of dirty words."[94] Within mainstream culture, the Motion Picture Production Code only allowed for broad hints about homosexuality, also contributing to these vague and shameful conceptions during this era.[95] Indeed, for Hobson, the thought of sex between men, though perhaps too fraught and shameful for her to write about explicitly, even from the vantage point of 1975, became a preoccupation for her mother character. It even tainted a formerly active sex life with her husband. During one scene, after her husband had made some overtures for sex, he gave up, owning, "If I so much as think of sex . . . I think of two men and that kills it for good." She had to admit that she felt the same way.[96]

In this portrait these parents did not communicate about sex outside the realm of furtive overtures late at night. But knowing they had a gay son forced them to contemplate their own sexuality all too self-consciously and vividly. The idea that emerged was that a gay child's revelation could become an uneasy meeting point between homo- and heterosexuality within family consciousness.

The dilemmas of gays with respect to revelation cannot be depicted within a clear-cut spectrum of parents who were dumbfounded and rejecting and those who were tolerant and accepting. Some gays avoided these perceived extremes by embracing a more ambiguous strategy of discretion as a way of maintaining both their gay and their family relationships. This ambivalence about disclosure and the possibility of discretion itself illuminates the nature of revelations about the sexual lives of family members during the 1950s, a moment when there was not a widespread cultural expectation that sexual matters be divulged to parents.[97] Revelation might not have been seen as a confident proclamation of identity or persona, but instead as an almost excruciating personal burden.

Such was the case for painter Mary Meigs. With wealth and a sophisticated world experience, Meigs's upper-class Philadelphia family was nonetheless discomfited by any discussion or acknowledgement of sexuality. In her memoir, she noted that her mother had found the McCarthy trials during the 1950s "abominable," not solely because she saw him as a "demagogue," but "because it was rumored that there was a homosexual relationship between him and Roy Cohn."[98] This rumor was ironic, of course, as McCarthy's anticommunist investigations had coincided with the persecution of gays as civil service employees, who were seen as susceptible to communist blackmail or to communism.[99] McCarthy himself had a boorish, rough manner and no doubt appeared unsavory to the refined, yet for this mother the aversion expanded into an offensive sexuality as well. In turn, her daughter found it unthinkable to tell her that she too shared this sexuality. As an adult Meigs seemed protected from her mother's speculations about her sexuality perhaps because her mother did not conceive of sexual matters as elements of polite discussion. Still, Meigs could feel her "heart . . . thump with the old fear and sickness that came over me at the very thought of talking," suggesting that in her family talking intimately itself was fraught and anxiety laced, let alone participating in a discussion of an aberrant sexuality.[100] For Meigs, discretion held a liberating potential. She did not feel forcefully repressed or burdened in not telling her mother. In fact, what afflicted her more was imagining her mother's reactions. She "continue[d] to doubt" that she ever could have broached this topic with her mother and was "thankful that I lived those last years of her life in a dishonest shadowland," convinced that "its air was the only air she could breathe."[101]

Written in 1981, her retrospective portrait allows for a less neutral interpretation of discretion than the word suggests, as she would come to feel that her discretion approached dishonesty. Perhaps this perception took shape as she adopted a gay liberation and feminist consciousness in the 1960s and 1970s, which valorized the personal experiences of gays and women as minority groups. The impact of memory filtered through a more contemporary consciousness about the right of gays to make a more public claim to their sexuality is also prominent within Robert Leach's reflections on his journals, written well after he had become an openly gay man. In these, Leach identified his past discretions as deceptions. In 1950, for instance, Leach wrote to his mother that a friend, Daniel, had "in typical Italian style kissed me twice in saying goodbye. I never had that happen before!"[102] What he left out was that Daniel had kissed him slightly more romantically than that, on the lips. More than thirty years later, after he had acknowledged his sexuality, he reflected in a journal that "I did mention he kissed me twice 'in typical Italian style'—OK just a shade, only the important, shade off from the truth."[103]

In fact, the dilemmas of discretion as equivocation were recognized as part of the lot of a gay family member in this era as well and were becoming central themes in the more sympathetic gay psychology emerging in the 1950s. Donald Webster Cory feared that many gays harbored a sense of doubleness, and he wrote in his 1951 work *The Homosexual in America* that many "have constantly striven to perfect their technique of concealment" in their work and family lives.[104] The necessity of these concealments, and the gap between who the individual really was and the social face that he presented to the world, were thought to have a grueling psychological impact, a perception that was in keeping with an emphasis on the health benefits of confiding. In "Emotions That Destroy Your Health and Person-

ality," Alice LaVere warned other homophiles that the extra effort that goes
into camouflage could cause tension, peptic ulcers, heart failures, and
strokes.[105] This faith in confiding propped up a homophile movement that
would increasingly premise itself on revealing one's sexuality to others. The
call for honesty and disclosure asked gays to summon a particular sort of
fortitude in an era when cautiousness surrounded self-revelation, given the
wide-reaching anxiety about gossip, rumors, and strangers in the political
sphere, and when guarded, prudential values prevailed at the intimate level.
Moreover, closeness between friends and family members during this
moment was less likely to be defined through mutual confidences.[106] Perhaps adult gays of this period were negotiating family styles that were curi-
ous about their family members but not yet at the level of intimacy through
revelation.

In fact, perfecting a "technique of concealment" could bring about
rewards for the gays who mastered a more common heterosexual life. After
his marriage, Leach enjoyed a much less burdened relationship with his
mother. She sounded especially alive and perky when her son started seeing
a beautiful and distinctive-looking woman in Geneva, where he was pursuing his doctorate. In a 1952 letter, Mrs. Leach asked her son, "Who was the
pretty girl on your right? She looks like Elizabeth Taylor, the movie actress.
Is she the newest girlfriend?"[107] She became increasingly interested in this
girlfriend and asked about her often in the ensuing months: "What is your
Elizabeth Taylor girlfriend's name? Where does she live and what does she
do? I am interested in her!"[108] She started to refer to her affectionately as
"ET."[109] Having an ET in the family, a figure both familiar and exotic,
seemed to heighten her own sense of heterosexuality and perhaps alleviated
some banality from her life. She was thrilled when Leach announced his
engagement: "I'm very happy about the thought of your marrying a good
girl. Do let me know how you get along. My natural curiosity!"[110] Her love
and affirmation was not doled out just to her son now but to the couple,
as she began addressing letters "Dear Robert and Jean" and signing off
"love to you both."[111] Leach himself played into this fascination and affirmation by relaying ET's positive qualities, and especially her appearance:
"She has dark curly hair. She has grey eyes, classic features . . . is slender,
trim—an excellent horsewoman."[112] This example of a newfound congenial
and more relaxed relationship between mother and son suggests that there
were more elements at stake in striving for heterosexuality than shirking

off a stigma or attaining normalcy: Heterosexuality could be a crucial way to secure a parent's interest and empathy.

At times, however, the heterosexual public self presented to families became an outright fabrication. A song lyric that captures the contradictory dimensions of maintaining discretion and family contacts through a sham heterosexuality appeared in Ann Aldrich's 1958 pulp sociology study of lesbians, *We, Too, Must Love*:

> Raise your voice an octave,
> Wear a skirt around,
> Mother doesn't get the bit
> And she'll be in town.

> Call some faggots, darling
> Ask them by for drinks,
> Mother's on her way, my love,
> And I'm straight, she thinks.

> Push our beds apart, pet,
> Put our things away,
> Mother doesn't understand,
> She arrives today.[113]

This lyric demonstrates not only tremendous attention to obscuring the material, recognizable expressions of a child's private life but also the ways in which appearances, surfaces, and objects such as voices and clothing were interpreted as remnants of a particular sexual sensibility. Here these contrivances were playful, as if to suggest an element of drama or daring in simply being gay and pretending otherwise.

But heterosexual contrivances could be fraught with tensions and anxieties, as well. As in this song, McDonald and her girlfriend, Barb, tried to be discreet through a feigned heterosexuality, only here the counterfeit complicated and created jealousies in their relationship. Barb in fact confided to McDonald that the reason she had to play tennis and "date fellows" was to "hide this from my mother."[114] McDonald eventually broke up with this girlfriend to give her more "peace of mind" and to allow her to stop "contriving herself."[115] Yet, because leading a life of discretion was preferable to leading a life of solitude and celibacy, McDonald had to negotiate the dilemmas of discretion, and not solely these boundaries between keeping secrets and outright lying.

McDonald was in a quandary because to make her sexuality seem real— even to herself—she needed to express her sexuality outwardly. One way to do so was by assuming a butch role persona. Though butch-femme roles have been important to how lesbians have structured their sexual relationships, for McDonald becoming a butch—and she was ambivalent about whether or not she truly was one—was equally important simply for self-understanding.[116] She favored her yellow corduroy jacket on dates with women because it made her look "very butch" and seemed to make her more comfortable in assuming a gay relationship.[117] She wore the corduroy jacket on a particularly passionate date with her girlfriend Vera, where the two had kissed in the restroom of a diner until "limp," and then "smooched up a storm" in a drive-in.[118] The day after, McDonald's Aunt Dora had prepared supper for the couple. However, Aunt Dora then made it clear that "Mom didn't want Vera at her house. I asked Mom about it and she said Aunt Dora was going to write me a letter about it, too." Though neither her mother nor Aunt Dora gave forthright reasons for their discomfort, their responses spoke to something vaguely awry in their midst.

These unexplained reactions of disapproval seemed to prompt a feeling of desperation in McDonald, a feeling rooted in the permanence of both her sexual feelings and her family as simply facts of her life. She wrote in her diary that "sometimes I almost hate them, but not quite. They are my family."[119] This sense of the family as an unalterable entity in fact resonated with gay culture within such stories as Vin Packer's pulps, *Whisper His Sin* (1954) and *The Evil Friendship* (1958). Here the only way gay characters feel they can be together is to murder their parents.[120] This gay fantasy of patricide might not have been solely the consequence of a homophobic culture that depicted gays as murderous, but rather a proclamation of a collective gay longing to maintain their relationships unfettered by families, as though only through being parentless could individuals experiment with different forms of selfhood, including being gay.

Not only was the family permanent, but in some ways it was ever present. The intensity of gay relationships had the potential to breed an internal familial surveillance. McDonald's relationships with women did not go unnoticed by her girlfriends' families, either. One mother, for example, felt uncomfortable about what she considered an extravagant Christmas gift that McDonald had purchased for her daughter, Barb. McDonald confided in her diary that Barb had told her mother about the robe McDonald was buying her for Christmas. Her mother was "displeased. Said it was too much money to spend on a girl and that she shouldn't take it."[121] That a gift of a robe could become ascribed with so much significance about intent and affect indicates the degree to which self-expressive items such as clothing could be read as a romantic rather than a friendly, platonic exchange. The gay adoption of these elements of a consumer culture of heterosexual treating, while potentially liberating in allowing gays to structure their erotic relations, also had the potential to reveal, even if only obliquely, a potential sexual nature of relationships.

In fact, Barb's mother had begun to "suspect" her daughter's relationship with McDonald, because, as this mother had told her daughter, there was "something about" McDonald.[122] The comment is markedly similar to a memo that a secretary-clerk at the State Department wrote in 1953 regarding her vague suspicions about her boss, Miss McCoy. As historian David Johnson recounts, this secretary typed an anonymous memorandum to the head of the State Department of Security, saying that there was "something about" her boss that gave her an "uncomfortable feeling," and this charge, in an atmosphere of anticommunist persecutions, was enough to call into question her boss' sexuality.[123] Even military examiners during World War II relied on their own vaguely defined hunches as to who was homosexual and who was not.[124] Postwar culture offered no precisely defined concept of a gay person within an everyday context from which these observers and parents could draw, but it did offer models of interrogation and surveillance for those who were suspicious in their gender nonconformity. In turn, Barb's mother did not elaborate on her hunch about Marge McDonald. When Barb pressed for more details, her mother withheld specifics and instead pressed Barb for the reason that McDonald had phoned one evening at 2 AM.

This mother's wordless suspicion also poses some questions about the boundaries of friendships between young women during this period. Mothers often wished to help their daughters define these boundaries, and because they were entrusted with the task of instructing their children through the proper life stages, they might have viewed an intense attachment to a young woman friend as a developmental stage to outgrow, particularly if these friends appeared relatively late in life, during the daughter's twenties.[125] In a period when women were marrying young, and patterns of dating had been adapted early, intense friendships between adult women might have seemed deviant.[126]

Motherly anxiety about their daughters' unconventional affective lives and practices at times afforded their gay children little privacy in terms of any intimate or romantic gestures, including the act of letter writing itself. Writing to each other throughout the 1950s and early 1960s, poet Dorothee Gore and a friend and love interest, Smitty, discussed their military experiences as members of the Women's Army Corps during World War II, a segment of the military in which there was initially less hostility and suspicion surrounding gays, in part because Selective Services did not have a precise conception of lesbian sexuality.[127] Gore and Smitty maintained their friendship started in the Women's Army Corps (WAC), and although they were both middle aged by 1960, the nature of their relationship was still vulnerable to parental imaginings, particularly because Smitty lived at home with her aging mother and took care of her. Still, Gore had made her feelings plain for Smitty in her letters. When Smitty wrote to tell Gore that she had feelings for another woman, she also admitted that her mother had "been sort of bitchy with me since your last visit. She expects me to read every line of your letters."[128] Smitty admitted that she had to "tear up" each of Gore's letters because "I know she'll be going through every 'looking' place there is in the room the minute I'm gone."[129] Smitty's mother even made oblique, yet disparaging, comments about her daughter's relationships with women, such as "the nasty crack . . . 'I wonder what you do to these women that they're so crazy about you.'" To keep her mother at bay, Smitty painted the letters as perfunctory and boring: "I just tell her 'it's the same old crap.'"[130]

As in this case, when parent and child lived in such close quarters, attempts at discretion were not always returned. Both McDonald and Smitty may have found a greater sense of privacy, both spatial and psychological, to pursue a gay relationship in public spaces, such as the drive-in or diner, rather than in the home, where a parent might rummage through the premises for evidence of something untoward. Privacy was, and is, a value shaped by class and material circumstances. Single, working-class women who maintained close ties to their parents in this period faced significant encumbrances when expressing their love lives and had to tread lightly within the family home.

If conducting gay relationships while maintaining family connections was complicated for these adult gays, it was infinitely more so for adolescents and children during the early postwar period. The focus on nuclear families stepped up attention on the ways in which children were raised and socialized during this period. It is especially possible to see the role that the memory of feelings of alienation from parents plays in gay consciousness in the reflections and memoirs of those who were children during the 1950s and 1960s—baby boomer children and youth. Perhaps it is inevitable that memoir reflections necessarily focus on seemingly trivial moments of the past, but fleeting conversations and comments that highlighted the gay child's uniqueness from the family here take on a magnified significance in gay interpretations of their parents' observation of them, just as they did in family constellations that emphasized commonalities and togetherness. While parental discipline and attention often fell by the wayside during the war years, children in postwar families were much more vulnerable to familial surveillance, even if, ironically, it was domestic contexts that proved crucial for exploring an incipient gay sexuality. Opportunities for public gay meeting places flourished during the 1950s and 1960s, with the development of bars, bathhouses, and bookshops, but an equally important realm of gay socializing and relationships unfolded within household spaces, and this was particularly the case for the young in their bedrooms.[131] After the war, middle-class and working-class families alike sought to regain a sense of privacy by buying single, detached houses, reflecting a broad postwar desire for spacious dwellings after wartime conditions in typically more cramped quarters. In these houses, children more commonly than ever before had bedrooms of their own.[132] Perhaps for gays in particular, sexual experimentation within their own bedrooms took on a heightened importance if they were young in the 1950s, a moment when American high schools became more entrenched as places of heterosexual experimentation and drama.[133] Sexual expression among children and adolescents was at least permitted some opening if it was heterosexual, but gay young people might have sought out an individual refuge more zealously.[134]

The motif of the bedroom and parental mystique about what went on in there was particularly strong in depictions by gays recalling their childhoods during the 1950s and 1960s. Parents seemed unsure of how to recognize this realm: Should they honor its privacy or intervene to protect children from their own fantasies? Writer Paul Monette was particularly mortified when his mother caught him and his boyfriend in the midst of sexual experimentation in his bedroom. She later confronted him, wanting to know just what was going on between the boys. Monette was evasive, telling her it was "nothing." When she asked her son again forthrightly, he responded angrily, "I told you—nothing," and then "skitter[ed] away . . . toss[ing] it again, with bitter emphasis. Nothing."[135] Memoirist Arnie Kantrowitz's mother also caught him having a sexual experiment in his bedroom as a twelve-year-old with a boyfriend, only he could not deflect his mother so easily. As he recalled the incident in his memoir, Kantrowitz lied that he and his friend had just been wrestling, yet his mother asked the boy to leave and not to visit her son any longer. Then she commenced what he described as an "inquisition," especially wanting to know if they had touched each other's "private parts," indicating just what unseemly and covert connotations the word "private" could take on in reference to a child's body.[136]

Galvanized by fears of how children were being raised, as well as more widely circulated notions of aberrant families, parents raising their children during the 1950s and 1960s might have been more aware of psychiatry's potential helping hand in family life and more likely to consider psychiatry as an option. Mrs. Kantrowitz quickly found her son a psychiatrist in Newark, New Jersey. Arnie told him "everything, determined to make a clean breast of it and be cured, contrite before my confessor," suggesting that a session with a psychiatrist had the potential to be a cherished, if frightening, chance to confide things children dared not say to parents. To the astonishment of both mother and son, however, the psychiatrist pronounced that Kantrowitz had "just been experimenting in the ways boys his age all do." He even asked Mrs. Kantrowitz a more foreboding question: "Do you want him to be a street-corner hooligan?" He declared her son "sensitive and intelligent. All boys aren't ruffians."[137] In this way, psychiatry's mandate about diagnosing and rehabilitating juvenile delinquents and homosexuals in the postwar period had intersected, with the surprising result that cues of homosexuality in the young also could be seen as cues of a gentle, law-abiding disposition.[138] In this sketch, the doctor's pronouncements were not brutal directives but, in fact, offered the gay child protection from heterosexual parents and their imaginings and voyeurism. As Kantrowitz noted, "Who was [his mother] to question medical science?"[139]

This recollection seems a testament both to the importance of the domestic for gay subjectivity and expressions of gay sexuality and to the perception of parents, especially mothers, as guardians of children's corporal experiences in these interior realms.[140] Mrs. Kantrowitz, for example, examined her son's play life assiduously, because she was concerned about his "sissy" behavior. She even had her son try boxing lessons and hormone shots to become more manly.[141] Monitoring a child's behavior included a more subtle range of tensions than sexuality, just as the scrutiny took other forms than confrontation.

Parents were more likely to feel that they had a chance to intervene in the development of their adolescent children's sexuality, especially as post-war North American society became increasingly attuned, in the later 1950s and throughout the 1960s, to a link between unconventional gender behaviors and homosexuality.[142]

These links had been long embedded in gay culture and found an articulation in camp culture, which was rooted in hyperbolized gender expressions, including the embellishment and theatricalization of womanly figures, as though there was an inherent irony in being gay but not having this known or understood by the majority of heterosexual onlookers.[143] Cartoons within the gay press during this period had great fun with the prospect of parents' confronting their children's gender aberrations. A campy and somewhat apolitical Toronto gay periodical, *Two*, for example, featured a cartoon in 1964 showing a boy in a Cubs uniform shaving off his sister's hair, to her delight.[144] A perplexed and bemused mother in an apron and high heels looked on. The little boy's caption read, "Sara wants a sex change so she can join the Wolf Cubs!"[145] This cartoon reflects an emerging understanding of the biological components of gender, including the more widespread knowledge of sex change operations; gay writers and artists appeared to see some commonalities between their experiences and those of transsexuals. A more vehement parental disquiet was echoed in the cartoons of two other gay cultural periodicals of the same time period, the Los Angeles *Tangents* and the Philadelphia *Drum: Sex in Perspective*, which brought fathers and their gay sons to the forefront.[146] In the first, a mother in her armchair, with a dreamy, naive look, said to her husband, "Wilber's 16 already. Shouldn't he go out and maybe hit some baseballs?" Her husband's sarcastic response was, "With what, his eyebrow pencil!"[147] In the second, a father, in the armchair again, sat before what appeared to be a daughter, wearing a dress and stylized hair. He said, "It's time you and I had a long, long talk—son."[148] The portraits of parents here suggest an implicit, underlying connection of gender difference to a divergent sexuality.

Even if only an underlying tension, the observation of children's gender expressions could lead not only to efforts to change their tastes and habits but also to explicit gestures of friendship between the generations. In his memoir story "My Mother's Clothes," writer Richard McCann recalled hearing his father say of him one night to his mother in their bedroom, "'He makes me nervous,'" though his father did not say precisely what it was about his son that caused him to feel this way. McCann presumed it to be a reference to his gender style—as the title suggests, he liked to sample his mother's clothing.[149] His mother felt it would be wise to start encouraging father and son to spend more time with each other, characteristic of broader family trends and social critiques of families in the postwar period. These encouraged fathers, largely displaced from their children's lives during the 1930s and 1940s, to be an active part of their children's lives.[150] Fathers were to become playmates to their children by assuming a masculine domestic role in outdoor and adventure play.[151] When McCann was eleven years old in 1960, his father took him on a trip to Fort Benjamin Harrison in Indiana, where he did his annual tour of duty as a colonel in the U.S. Army Reserves. But father and son were often at a loss for conversation during the time they were supposed to have become closer. When they would watch television—a favorite was *Perry Mason*—his father would throw out comments such as, "That Della Street . . . is almost as pretty as your mother," and, turning to sports, would suggest that his son loved sports such as football that McCann Junior plainly did not love. McCann believed that "[i]t was my job . . . to reassure him that I was the son he imagined me to be."[152] Perhaps, however, in talking up Della Street and football his father might not have been making an explicit boost for masculinity—or heterosexuality. Perhaps these were merely forced fragments of conversations illustrative of the pain of family communication, the ways parents and children truly might not have known each other—even in a companionate family context—outside of these gendered and heterosexual commonalities.

Tensions over gender expression, then, might only have complicated a relationship between parents and children that was already in many respects ambiguous during this period. Gays seemed to become a symbol of the unknown surfacing within the intimate sphere of the family, just as they were a broader symbol for latency in North American society. That gays could pass by unnoticed had made them an ideal minority symbol for communism. Elaine Tyler May has argued that there was a domestic expression of the foreign policy of containment of communism, that is, in the containment of familial subversion, which included women's and gay sexuality.[153] Yet this uneasiness about the potential for deviance lurking within all individuals also had a more intensely private dimension, as the anxiety flourished from within family structures of the 1950s and 1960s and reflected a more intense consideration of family members as feeling beings rather than economic actors or duty-bound practical contributors.[154] Children could appear to be knowable through a presumed heterosexuality and then turn out to be foreign or mysterious.

This internal familial curiosity resonated with psychiatric and cultural attention to the kinds of families that were likely to produce these alien figures. The early 1960s in particular would see a renewed animation of the idea of the dominant mother and weak father as family types of homosexuals. In his 1962 work *Homosexuality: A Psychoanalytic Study*, Irving Bieber emphasized the figures of the detached father and overbearing, seductive mother as central contributing factors to homosexuality.[155] The image of the overbearing mother in particular took hold during these years, and it became a relationship that was depicted, pathologized, and parodied in a way that gay daughters' relationships with their fathers was not, in part because major studies such as Bieber's considered male homosexuals exclusively.[156] Thus the more central worry was a mother's hand in shaping her son. In 1961, Marvin Drellich, a psychiatrist at the New York Medical College, tried to typify the family lives of homosexual men. He observed that the mother in such families often "encouraged feminine pursuits in her sons, e.g. knitting," and sometimes even "burdened her son with unwanted feminine confidences . . . even going so far as to embarrass her son with secrets of the boudoir."[157] In these modern families where gender differences became blurred, mothers in particular were cautioned not to emasculate their sons.

The socialization of children in these psychiatric sources suggested that the consequences of an overbearing mother, including excessive female domesticity and an omnipresent housewife, could be a gay son. The theme of the pus under a respectable domestic skin had a broad expression in postwar culture, evoked and parodied in literary sources such as the stories of suburbanites in the works of John Cheever.[158] That a gay son could be lurking in a common household was an intriguing and fantastic theme for mainstream cultural sources to explore, including a 1966 *Good Housekeeping* article, " 'Our Son Was Different': When a Mother Discovers the Agonizing Truth," an account of the Alberton family's discovery that their seventeen-year-old son was possibly a homosexual.[159] Mrs. Alberton, we are told, came upon her son's possible sexuality on a "dismal winter morning" when going through his bedroom closet to select clothes for ironing.[160] There she found a note from a male friend of his, commenting that the school dance they were attending together was "cruddy" and suggesting that they cut loose from it, followed by "a suggestive sentence."[161] Presenting the evidence to a psychologist, Mrs. Alberton "winced as though struck a physical blow" upon his opinion that her son might "already" be a homosexual.[162]

Yet this was not just a story of domestic ruin and disgrace, but triumph, because the author assured the reader that, like any form of latency, homosexuality could be changed. If being gay was something an individual could be encouraged to become rather than something one simply was, parents could take it upon themselves to mold their children into heterosexuals. This author observed that though "the disclosure . . . that a son or daughter has become a sexual deviate is a family calamity . . . [that] brings to most households the same desolate feeling of loss as a child's death," this did not carry the finality of a real death because homosexuality was an "illness," having its origins in *faulty parent-child relationships in the very early, very crucial years of a boy's life.*"[163] Mrs. Alberton, then, bore responsibility for engulfing her son in the home, never allowing him "roller skates ('Oh Lord, he'll split his head!') or a tricycle ('I'd be petrified every second')." In fact, mother and son spent all their time together engaged in homemaker tasks, and the boy even absorbed his mother's "interests in antique bric-a-brac and develop[ed] a fascination for fabrics and fabric design."[164] Mrs. Alberton was also said to have found fault with all the girls her son ever brought home as a teenager: "One had 'absolutely dreadful' taste in clothes, another was 'too stupid for words.'" More menacingly, the affection between this mother and son could be seen as seductive: Mrs. Alberton ran "her fingers through his hair, addressed him endearingly, [and asked] his opinion on her clothes, even talk[ing] over some of her personal problems with him."[165]

Not only did this portrait give life to Irving Bieber's typology of the parents of homosexuals in depicting a seductive, "excessively possessive, overprotective mother" and a browbeaten, "detached, indifferent father," but it also accentuated a broader cultural response of male resentment toward female-dominated domestic zones and an antimaternal feeling embedded within postwar North American society and culture that coexisted with this era's celebration of motherhood.[166] John Updike's 1960 novel

Rabbit, Run, in which the father leaves his nagging, careworn wife and their brood, is a case in point. Barbara Ehrenreich has argued that Hugh Hefner's *Playboy* magazine also reflected an anger at the monotony of the domestic realm, one that would later inspire a generation of feminists.[167] In these sources, women seemed to embody a dreary dailiness and were held accountable for feelings of ennui and routine in their families.

Of course, *Good Housekeeping* was not about to support this sort of male disgruntlement or advocate that men feel free to run off and have affairs, but instead tried to illuminate what might happen when men were not given a chance to provide antidotes to day-to-day malaise. For example, when Mr. Alberton tried to provide his son with a refuge from his mother's world by asking him to "come down to his place of business on a Saturday," Mrs. Alberton "vetoed the idea—'it's too dirty there and he wouldn't be interested.'"[168] Ultimately, however, Mr. Alberton was praised for showing composure in light of his son's sexuality, including finding a sedative for his wife and finding a doctor to treat his son. He then began to spend more time with him, having man-to-man talks, and taking him for driving lessons.[169] This article ends with the Albertons' crying "happy tears" over their son's revelation, in a letter home from college, that he was now "going with" a girl.[170] In the eyes of *Good Housekeeping,* fathers played a pivotal familial role in child transformation, piloting their children away from the static, overly feminine dominions of their mothers, into the exterior world and heterosexuality.

The fear of being swallowed up by these motherly realms left an imprint not just on popular, heterosexual cultural sources but on gay ones as well. Representations of mothers and sons in gay cartoons of the early 1960s, for example, portrayed mothers with bouffant hair, jewelry, a petticoat under a full skirt, often harboring some sign of housework or item of leisure, a particular stereotype of a white, middle-class, almost sitcom-like, postwar mother that had become part of the popular symbolism of this era.[171] In this vein, a 1965 cartoon in *Gay* depicted an object of housewife culture. A decorative poster on the wall of a nineteenth-century milk maiden mother figure, with mouth wide open, cheeks red, and eyeballs bulging, shouted, "My son and your son were doing WHAT together?"[172] The idea of a household object coming to life as an outraged parent suggests one way in which gays might have conflated their mothers, ideas of home, and notions of the everyday with an ever-observant culture of heterosexuality during this era.[173]

My son and your son were doing WHAT together?

Figure 1. Cartoon in *Gay*, 1965.

The intensity of the feeling of household scrutiny and alarm surrounding sexual experimentation and gender nonconformity, however, varied according to other foreseeable vulnerabilities and oppressions children might face. African American ballet dancer Bill T. Jones noted in his memoir, *Last Night on Earth*, that as a child he was always known as a "sissy boy" in his family lore, but even still, as a young teenager, a more central preoccupation on the part of his parents was how he would be perceived sexually on account of his race, not his gender expression. As a fourteen-year-old in 1962, after his family had moved from Florida to western New York, Jones was asked to a sleepover at a white friend's house. When he requested permission, his mother expressed worries about the presence of this white boy's sister. She advised her son not to go walking around at night in his friend's house and to lock his bedroom door because "there's a white girl there and before you know it that girl will be screamin' that you done messed with her."[174] A traumatic legacy of lynching African American men for alleged sexual assaults here seemed to overshadow attempts to change unconventional gender traits.[175]

Nor were gender nonconformity and sexual experimentation as noteworthy for parents of girls as they were for boys during this time period. Parents and cultural observers alike appeared to fear lesbian sex the least; indeed, most often it was not even perceived as such. Intense relationships between girls and even crushes or fixations, in the opinion of experts, veered toward the abnormal only when they lasted beyond adolescence.[176] In this vein, Ann Aldrich's work of lesbian pulp sociology, *We Two Won't Last* (1963), relayed a story of one mother of a lesbian finding her daughter and her "roommate" in the "same bed, nude, and in an embrace" and responding with, "For heaven's sake! . . . You two girls are much too old for this sort of nonsense! Now you both better grow up!"[177]

Just as fathers were advised to take charge of their sons' gender expression, so too did mothers assume this role for their daughters. A dearth of femininity in girls seemed to cause parents, particularly mothers, some pause, but not solely because it could be linked to homosexuality. A sense of investment in personal appearances might have been felt more keenly between mothers and daughters in general, but women who grew up to be gay might have felt especially intensely this disparity between mothers' expectations of femininity and who they felt themselves to be.

A youth-oriented postwar consumer culture offered ways to both reinforce and redefine femininity, and it could become a symbolic locus of mother-daughter conflict or separation.[178] During the early 1970s, when Del Martin and Phyllis Lyon were on the cusp of writing their advice book, *Lesbian/Woman*, they received an outpouring of letters from lesbians who wished to contact them with retrospective stories about their initial feelings of sexual difference during their childhoods in the 1950s. One striking way that young protolesbians articulated an early feeling of difference was through these fragments of consumer culture. One woman wrote that she had been a "tomboy wearing boys' clothes until I was 12, playing army with the boys, and being the man of the house while other girls dressed up in frilly things. . . . I had my cowboy outfit too, but I think I was better at handling a gun. I never learned how to dance, or set my hair or put make-up on or anything like that."[179] In her reminiscence, girls' activities appeared as skills that require a certain adeptness, whereas boys' activities were simply fun. All of these games, objects, and clothes stimulated a fantasy life that often suggested differences in taste and sensibility between mother and daughter.

Though not invited to share in their children's play lives, mothers sought to shape a daughter's character through objects and appearances as well. These attempts might have been heightened for parents who had experienced the material deprivations of the Depression when they were children and now took part in a postwar culture of abundance.[180] In her piece "First Love," writer Karla Jay recalled her perception of her 1950s childhood in Flatbrush, Brooklyn. She noted that her mother "wanted a clean, pink, passive child, one who adored her sterilized apartment and pretty clothes." Yet even with her mother's campaign to "keep the world pale velour and crinoline for me . . . I was always brown as ice cream and dirt and red as cut knees and elbows."[181] While other little girls might have worn the "pink lace crinoline dresses and white patent leather shoes" that her mother favored, she preferred a cowboy outfit with its hat, boots, and "holster complete with shiny metal gun," a style more akin to that for little boys in this period, mimicking the heroic men in popular 1950s Western fantasies.[182] Because her mother failed to impart her tastes in clothing to her daughter, she instead "created a totally pink room for me, with pink French Provincial furniture, hand-made pink beds with posters and canopies, and a pink high-gloss toy cabinet."[183] Jay seemed to find her mother's passive character reflected in this emotionless, cloying room and to feel a sense of pride at renouncing her mother's heritage, owing to a retrospective, contemporary feminist reflection of having been a tomboy.[184] Perhaps, too, her tone speaks to an easier familial acceptance of fantasies of gender inversion in girls during this era, as these were more readily tied to quirkiness of character, even charming pluckiness, than sexuality.

Writer Terri de la Pena also recalled her mother's disquiet over her tomboyish ways, only here this worry was complicated by the mother's idea that her daughter, in assuming an unconventional gender expression, was also taking on a less respectable racial identity. Her mother placed much stock in the skill of being feminine, as she worked as a cosmetologist. As a twelve-year-old in 1959, de la Pena received a rather severe haircut from the little girl down the street, who was practicing to be a beautician. When de la Pena arrived home with her "Italian boy look," her mother was shocked at the "scalping." Her daughter speculated that her mother viewed the androgynous haircut as a "harbinger" of an aberrant sexuality.[185] However, her mother's foreboding was compounded by her daughter's rejection of the "sausagelike Shirley Temple curls" that this mother favored for her daughters. As a Chicana living in California, her mother would not hear of "'natural' hairstyles, those which highlighted our mestiza realities: black, straight tresses. . . . She did not want me to look like 'una india.'"[186] After the legal end of segregation of Mexican schoolchildren in American schools, and the Mexican contribution to World War II, many Chicanos living in California in the 1950s sought integration with mainstream American society, including middle-class job opportunities.[187] Understandably, her mother might have been troubled by the prospect of her daughter's projecting a resemblance to a devalued racial group. In this instance, becoming a tomboy might have seemed to add another layer of outward difference to a family that already felt exposed by ethnic discrimination.

Young tomboys and sissies alike, then, were vulnerable to parental scrutiny, intrigue, and punishment. Yet there was a certain privilege of individuality in being young and part of the baby boomer generation. A deepening recognition of the increased subjectivity of children contributed to a North American cultural ethos that suggested these children were special or significant, a separate species from their parents. In the prescriptive literature of Dr. Spock, democratic and permissive parenting styles emphasized that the children of this generation had unlimited potential, as well as unique personalities.[188] These changes in family life seemed to give postwar youth a more profound sense of entitlement to a private life within the family home, which included solitary, reverie-charged leisure. Surveillance was certainly a factor in the lives of these young people, but it was never all-

encompassing. Growing up in rural Indiana in the 1950s and 1960s, writer
Alan Helms noted in his memoir that it was in fact relatively easy to maintain his privacy in the face of his parents. He simply manipulated a cultural
expectation, suggested by popular youth cultures of this period, that parents and youth were worlds apart in sensibility. Thus when his mother
caught him poring over male physique, or "beefcake," magazines and asked
him why he found these so interesting, Helms responded, "Just because,"
with "the airy vagueness allowed the American teenager."[189]

Gay adults of the same period did not have this recourse of a culturally
sanctioned sense of generational distinction, and just by virtue of being
older, they were less protected by the idea that their sexuality was simply a
life phase or a moment. They also fretted more intensely over banishments
from their families than their younger counterparts. This fear remained an
unresolved conflict running through gay culture throughout the postwar
period. Yet this anxiety is only part of the story. Fantasies of gay familial
banishment often coexisted with depictions of family longing. As figures
who lived outside the structures of marriage and conventional trappings of
adulthood, gay adults also seemed, paradoxically, to be considered, and to
consider themselves, permanent and rooted family members if for no other
reason than they lacked a firm footing in the adult social rituals of the late
1950s and early 1960s. Ironically, gays were inscribed in their families for a
lifetime on account of being gay.

Adult gays could even feel suspended in a perpetual stage of youthful-
ness. In parental perceptions, an idea of childlike sexlessness seemed to
follow lesbians in particular into adult life. As adults, lesbian daughters
could be equated with spinsters and considered celibate and asexual. Much
as single women increasingly had opportunities to escape the restrictions
that traditionally had been imposed on daughters in the family economy,
the idea of family obligation might have weighed heavily on lesbian women,
whether or not they were partnered, even at a historical moment when the
state was said to have displaced the family in this respect.[190] Dorothy Lyle
wrote about this sense in the *Ladder* in 1966, a moment that had even seen
the advent of a greater availability of social assistance programs for the
elderly. In "The Family and Money Injustice," Lyle said that, because she
was seen as single in the eyes of the law, she was expected to "carry the load
traditionally dumped on the unmarried offspring," in her case, contributing to her mother's limited income, even though she herself had a partner
who needed economic support and there was another married daughter

who could have helped. In her view, growing up to be a heterosexual "doesn't relieve [a child] of responsibility toward parents."[191] She speculated that gays put up with this injustice owing to an "exaggerated debt felt by the homosexual offspring towards parents" to compensate for the perceived betrayal of growing up to be gay. Lyle considered this set of attitudes a "ridiculous injustice" internalized by many of her lesbian friends.[192] In her case, gayness heightened an already existing generational gap in familial expectations surrounding responsibility to the family of origin. Similarly, DOB activists Del Martin and Phyllis Lyon noted this pattern among some of their lesbian correspondents and members throughout the 1950s and 1960s. According to them, some unmarried lesbian daughters "live with her parent or parents until their death, at which time she is 'free.'"[193]

Gay sons also were perceived as figures who would remain within the family of origin into their parents' senescence. In fact, sometimes families and cultural observers of this era interpreted the relationship between gay sons and their parents as more congenial than most, owing to the son's different sexuality. In these accounts, a caricature of an artistically talented, polite, and cheerful gay son figure, reminiscent of an idealized daughter, became its own kind of family ideal. For example, in a 1962 edition of the *Mattachine Review*, parents of a young gay man said that they had often unintentionally referred to their gay son as "her" because "he seemed a girl, gentle and artistic."[194] For these parents, a positive sense of uniqueness seemed to mitigate the fretful aspects of being gay. Even in the often disparaging psychiatric literature about homosexuality, a gay son could be a figure who gave his mother in particular some comfort in maintaining family ties and even providing for the family in later years. Jess Stearn, whose 1961 book *The Sixth Man* spent three months on the New York bestseller list, found in many cases that a mother acquired "a solicitous, considerate companion for her declining years—her homosexual son."[195] He even recorded a set of parents who felt grateful for the new son they had gained in the form of their son's boyfriend. Here again the gay man was inscribed with a domestic affability, as these parents were particularly "mad about [the boyfriend's] cooking."[196] If sons were only sons until they took wives, gay men could be considered daughters for the rest of their lives.

These ideas of gay sons also had some imprint on and were shaped by gay culture. Affectionate gay son–mother relationships were archetypes of gay humor during this period. In the cartoons from the collection *My Son*, *the Daughter* (1964), a play on the expression of parental pride "my son, the doctor," the mother proclaimed enthusiastically that her son Freddie was an entertainer with "so many friends. . . . All of them . . . young and handsome!"[197] These unperceptive captions, always accompanied by exclamation points to heighten the innocence of her responses, as well as pictures portraying Freddie as slim and delicate with immaculate clothing, formed the narrative structure of these cartoons. One picture showed her son holding his umbrella over a handsome stranger, neglecting women getting drenched in the rain; another even showed Freddie holding up a telescope to ogle a naked man in a nearby apartment window, with the mother declaring, "Freddie's new hobby is astronomy!"[198] Though this depiction mocks the out-of-it mother figure, it also suggests a gay mythologizing of family closeness.

The feeling of being enduring family members contrasted dramatically with a gay preoccupation with being orphaned during the immediate postwar period. This preoccupation did not vanish in the later postwar period, but instead was defused in a realm of humor or fantasy. Yet this uneasy strain between banishment and permanence could be taken as an essential animating tension in gay culture, including more serious gay reflections. Writer Philip Bockman wrote one such recollection. In 1961, home for the weekend from college at his family home in Grand Rapids, Michigan, he contemplated telling his parents that he was gay. He vividly remembered eating at the kitchen table with his parents "under the plastic sunflower-head chandelier. I'd always hated the tacky kitchen with its green and orange flower motif, but now I kept following the patterns of leaves and daisies on the shiny tablecloth, miserable with the thought that I might be banished forever from the warmth of that awful chandelier and all the love this stifling room suddenly seemed to represent."[199] As his nostalgia and ambivalence suggest, gays could represent families with as much longing as humorous derision and feel haunted by a yearning for an unconditional, enduring family love.

These longings were also accompanied by a deepening impetus within gay activism to view both heterosexuality and homosexuality as broader sexual cultures with a distinct set of sensibilities. By the mid-1960s, the tenor of gay activism was beginning to shift. Homophiles had challenged heterosexual perceptions of gay sexuality and gender demeanor alike throughout the 1950s, but they were becoming more emboldened in this effort throughout the early 1960s. No longer was the *Mattachine Review* presenting a forum for Albert Ellis's "On the Cure of Homosexuality," a hopeful article that gays could be cured.[200] Strengthened by the civil rights movement, gaining more ground through a wider participation in organizations such as the Congress of Racial Equality (CORE) and the Student Non-Violent Coordinating Committee (SNCC), gay activists of this period increasingly identified with racial or religious minorities, seeing their own oppression in continuum with theirs. As Christopher Nealon notes, the "ethnicity model" of homosexuality offered gay activism an entirely different means of self-interpretation and communal organizing, one that rejected the sickness model or the tortured soul model of homosexuality that came before it.[201] Broader changes in the political temperament of activism in the early 1960s, including growing antiwar protests after 1965, also helped shape a more unrepentant homophile activist movement. Cultural dissent, too, was deepening, especially given the proliferation of folk music that accommodated a protest message, activist comedians, and fiction that celebrated the outsider during the early 1960s.[202] Historian Kirsten Fermaglich has called the period in the United States between the late 1950s and the early 1960s "the turn of the 60s," to suggest subtly changing sensibilities from the earlier postwar period, the resurgence of liberalism as an American political ideology, and a kind of bridge moment between the ostensible quietism of the early 1950s and the more overt radicalism to emerge in the late 1960s.[203] Gay writers and activists were registering and proclaiming a similar shift in sensibilities. In particular, gay activism of the early 1960s was marked by a heightened desire to see gays as a minority with complex emotional and psychological differences, in addition to the sexual ones, and this claim was one that could be made quite powerfully at the familial level.

The story of the deepening recognition of the private lives of family members during the postwar period, then, was mutual between the generations, and between heterosexuality and homosexuality as cultures. Both gay baby boomers and their older counterparts paid marked attention to the family's imprint on their individual characters, as well as the ways that they themselves shaped their families through their difference. Gay adults trod uncertainly between the obligations characteristic of the economic reciprocity in older families and a newer family ethos that was concerned with emotionality, self-fulfillment, and the recognition of children's desires. As families became a collection of individuals with no formal economic functions, an interest in children's psychic lives intensified. Thus young gays developed privacy strategies that almost paralleled the older generation's articulations of personal privacy and the upkeep of an interior gay self. In spite of these dilemmas, however, the claim to sexual selfhood and the idea of being family members were not entirely incompatible. Fundamentally, these were gay selves rooted in families.

2

Better Blatant Than Latent

THROUGHOUT THE 1950s and 1960s, writer and peace activist Barbara Deming never explicitly told her mother, Katherine Deming, that she was gay. For a period of more than twenty years, they wrote each other loving and supportive letters, Katherine Deming from the family home in New York City, and her daughter from various places while living abroad, as well as her own homes in Massachusetts and Maine. For both mother and daughter, a subtle, quiet knowledge of Deming's sexuality seemed quite a livable strategy. Mrs. Deming clearly knew about and accepted her daughter's relationships with women, signing her letters with "love to all your household," or, when her daughter was partners with Mary Meigs, "love to you and Mary."[1] In turn, her daughter acknowledged the primacy of her relationships with women, which seemed an extension of the closeness and intensity of emotion between them as mother and daughter.

This dynamic shifted as Deming developed a more political conception of gay selfhood. In 1969, while informing her mother that she and Meigs would be parting and splitting up their household, a fifty-two-year-old Barbara Deming sent her mother a letter that somewhat haltingly declared her identity as a lesbian. "Dearest Mother, I have news of myself that I should give you," she began and went on to explain the particulars of her living situation. Describing her new partner, Deming wrote, "[S]he too is of a radical turn of mind politically. I love her children and they seem to love me."[2] "A radical turn of mind politically" might encompass a breadth of causes and sensibilities, and her mother was left to discern what these were. A more unambiguous revelation of her sexuality was to come in 1974, upon the publication of Deming's new book *We Cannot Live without Our Lives*, which she had dedicated to "my lesbian sisters." A confrontation with her mother about this dedication ensued over the telephone, and they wrote about the phone call later to try to resolve the dispute. In this letter, Deming said to her mother, "You find [the dedication] disturbing because [it is] 'so personal.' Yet if [a married woman author] wrote a book and dedicated it to wives everywhere, this wouldn't be too personal, would it? I know that society . . . smiles on wives but not on lesbians and wishes us not to be so personal as to exist. But, as you know, we do exist." Perhaps to exist at all, Deming's sexuality needed to be declared publicly. In this same letter, she suggested that her previous discretion about her sexuality had been untruthful. She wrote that each time she fell in love with a woman and took on a new living partner, her life "had changed profoundly," and yet "I didn't even tell you, my mother, in honest words, and I didn't tell friends who were close, close to me. . . . I was sure [they] would rather not be told. . . . Or I wasn't always sure that they'd rather, but I didn't want to risk embarrassing or estranging them." According to her, role-playing—even lying—had come to suffuse collective gay consciousness. She explained, "As I tried to say on the phone, pretending not to be ourselves has made us all feel a little bit insane. Yes, we *are* a movement now—the Gay Liberation Movement."[3]

Not all gay daughters and sons adopted Deming's gay political consciousness, one that she herself only came to define during the late 1960s and early 1970s, a moment when gay politics was aligning with other emerging liberation movements of the period—the counterculture, women's liberation, the New Left, black nationalism, the student and peace movements—giving sexuality a prominent place in a wide-reaching critique of both American politics and American social life.[4] The year in which Barbara Deming had made her first tenuous statement of a gay identity to her mother, 1969, had witnessed some specific moments that gave coherence to gay activism, including the Stonewall riots in New York City and the criminal code reform to legalize homosexuality in Canada.[5] The riots in particular became a mythologized event in North American gay culture, history, and ritual: annual gay pride marches started in 1970 continue to commemorate this event.[6] Adapting its name from Vietnam's National Liberation Front, the Gay Liberation Front had also formed during this year, first in New York City, and then in other large North American cities. Representing both gay men and women, this movement attempted to build a gay counterculture while rewriting the norms surrounding personal behavior and sexuality.[7]

Gay liberation forthrightly claimed a social and political identity for gay individuals as a minority group. Gays would come to seek a more unapologetic understanding of their private experiences that their forebears likely would not have felt entitled to seek, either within the family or in broader society. In turn, the subtleties of the metaphors, codes, and hints once taken up in the communication of intimate matters were becoming displaced by unequivocal revelations. This repudiation of discretion mirrored and even stimulated a broader loss of reserve surrounding the personal in many areas of North American life during this period. By "coming out" of what was increasingly considered the secrecy and isolation of the earlier postwar period, gays declared themselves not just to their peers but to the heterosexual world—and their parents.[8] In turn, gay liberation writers of this generation imbued these parents with a symbolic significance as the ambassadors of a repressive society and banal sexuality. The irony of this portrait is that it highlights, in its vehemence, the abiding hold of the family and longing for family life that it seems to belittle or diminish.

Of course, parents of gays did not solely embody these images of a quaint, inhibited, clueless, early Cold War generation. In fact, they could be said to have exhibited a deepening awareness of their children's private, affective lives that paralleled their children's avowed embrace of their authentic selves during this period. With gays brought more prominently into the public and parental imagination, most especially through the student and social movements of the late 1960s and early 1970s, parents were more likely to perceive being gay as part of being a "hippy" and thus a political or even fashionable possibility for their children. Hippies were in reality a loosely formed collection of people, not always affiliated in ideology or in style, and might have included student protestors, mystics, and Vietnam War veterans among others. The image that many parents seemed to retain, however, was a more general impression of youthful exhibitionism, reflecting a broader public curiosity during these years about youth cultures.[9] Busloads of tourists gawked at hippy enclaves in the Haight-Ashbury neighborhood in San Francisco and on Yorkville Avenue in Toronto. North American media in particular took an interest in what appeared to be a foreign culture of the young—in personal demeanor and attire no less so than in their music, language, and art.[10] The valorization of the personal that youth culture promoted during this period helped incite a parental recognition of the meanings of their children's sexuality.

The relationship between parents and children was also a more far-reaching theme of observers of North American culture and family life during the later 1960s and throughout the 1970s, which was particularly poignant when generational consciousness and fragmentation seemed to be such a vivid part of the public and intellectual imagination.[11] As the baby boomer generation came of age and appeared, at least on the surface, to be developing a uniform ethos of restlessness and social protest, their parents came under scrutiny for spawning what many considered a bored, uncommitted cohort. In this context, Republican vice president Spiro Agnew and Reverend Norman Vincent Peale had even leveled public, often overstated, critiques against Dr. Spock for his hand in encouraging "permissive" parenting and abetting these generational trends. Many families, of course, did not adopt Spock parenting: working-class parents were much more likely to insist on obedience and corporal punishment.[12] Moreover, the student revolt was not strictly an American phenomenon but an international one. Nonetheless, Richard Nixon's 1968 presidential campaign played on the idea of generational rift, contrasting a generation of baby boomers with their elders, who had been raised with common sense and, in turn, differentiating a "silent majority" of nondissenting, "forgotten" Americans from hedonistic and nihilistic young rebels.[13] In intellectual circles, social critics such as Theodor Adorno who had previously criticized the parents of the baby boomers as an apathetic and conformist generation came to criticize the young social protestors even more vehemently. He noted that their attempt to live outside of social forms, such as a widespread rejection of consumerism or government structures, was a rebellion that could become profoundly narcissistic.[14]

These perceived generational fissures also coincided with a greater consciousness about the meanings of family life itself during this period, both by those seeking to bolster traditional family forms and by those encouraging their dissolution. In his 1969 work *The Future of the Family*, Richard Farson acknowledged that this was a particularly fraught period for families. Many did not exhibit, in his view, "the kind of intimacy that will be demanded most—the intimacy of shared feelings, of 'This is what it is like to be me. What is it like to be you right now?'"[15] The call for the family as an emerging expressive space for empathy illuminates a new value placed on this kind of emotion during this historical moment. The civil rights movement, for example, asked that whites empathize with blacks by calling forth feelings of remorse about white racism. In turn, the circulation and politicization of stories of the self and personal experiences in effect asked that individuals understand a broad stream of inner life, and families were central sites for this new consciousness.[16] Families were celebrated for their potential intimacy in the earlier postwar period, of course, but increasingly this was seen as a hollow intimacy, one for show only. Farson felt that most families simply did not know each other enough to live up to this kind of empathic interaction. However, spurred on by liberationist ideas, gays were in fact posing—and answering—these questions within their family lives, placing them and their parents among the forerunners of a more wide-spread impetus for a mutually enhancing family intimacy.

Barbara Deming and her mother were so intimate in their letters to each other that theirs seems emblematic of the kinds of intensely empathic and loving relationships evoked by historians describing nineteenth-century women.[17] Katherine Deming herself was not a baby boomer parent, but her daughter was adopting the activist causes associated with a younger cohort. Accepting of her daughter's partners and proud of her daughter as a pub-lished writer, Katherine Deming nonetheless did not relent on her position regarding the lesbian dedication in her daughter's book. In fact, she seemed to long for an earlier dynamic, when she and her daughter did not speak of such deeply personal matters, as exemplified in a comment she made in 1957. "[B]ecause I refrain from asking you many personal questions does not imply a lack of interest," she wrote to her daughter then, "[but] merely a profound respect for your personal privacy."[18] Born in 1891, Mrs. Dem-ing had come of age at the turn of the century. As an adult, she was an upper-class woman married to a successful lawyer. In keeping with this class and generational sensibility, she regarded personal privacy simply as a right.[19] The safeguarding of the right to privacy and an emerging impulse to protect individuals from excessive publicity had been prominent themes at the century's turn; Mrs. Deming seems very much shaped by this sensi-bility about the sacredness of the private realm. Thus, it was perhaps unthinkable to her that her daughter now was discarding her own right to privacy.[20] Knowing about her daughter's sexuality was not the same as writ-ing and talking about it, and Mrs. Deming registered this change, fretting about the vulnerable aspects of her daughter's private life now exposed to public attention and discussion.

Accordingly, Katherine Deming did not engage very much with her daughter's suggestion of the toll her discretion had taken, but instead undertook a debate about the meaning and rewards of privacy. As she wrote to her daughter, "I did not realize that you had felt so much distress. That is sad. As to the dedication—I still feel it is a very private thing—I was not worrying about insults—why should there be? I thought these things were accepted as part of life these days—except when they are flaunted—as I'm afraid some of the 'gay' boys enjoy doing." She went on to list a number of gay couples she knew who were "respected and liked in the community" and claimed that "as long as people live decent lives and go on about their own business, it seems to me their private lives are their own."[21]

As Mrs. Deming implied when she denounced "flaunting," without a sense of privacy, life could become shallow and excessively self-aware. Much as the language of discretion of an earlier period could veer into code or, at worst, something shadowy and unseemly, it also conveyed something deeply personal or interior that could get lost through revelations. In this vein, when Mrs. Deming wrote that she did not understand "the need for announcement or 'confession' or whatever," because her daughter had quite simply "lived a wonderful life" and her "private life is [no one's] business," she also seemed to be reacting against the very impulse of talking, and writing, about the inner self.[22] "I've never understood how writers could write of their own intimate lives. I don't mean in fiction—but in intimate description," she wrote.[23]

In fact, the distinction between art and intimate life was collapsing even within fiction during this period, in an emerging, prominent confessional genre that overlapped with journalism and autobiography in the seeming artlessness of self-disclosure. Some of these works offered an unprecedented sexual frankness, among them, Philip Roth's somewhat raunchy teenaged narrator in *Portnoy's Complaint* (1969) or the poetry of Anne Sexton, including her 1969 poems "The Ballad of the Lonely Masturbator" and "In Celebration of My Uterus."[24] These blunt fictional testimonies seem motivated by a desire to uncover creative newness in a broad stream of experiential dimensions during this period, in particular through a move away from symbolic allusions, especially regarding sexual matters, a kind of renewed celebration of sensuality within American culture.[25] Certainly confessional literary cultures had existed prior to this moment, even during the early twentieth century, but they were primarily aimed at the radical intelligentsia or working-class women and were more marginal genres such as experiments in the new theater or *True Confessions* magazine.[26] But by the late 1960s and early 1970s, a culture of sharing secrets was propelling new realms for discussion within a broad sweep of writing. Even some writers of the New Journalist tradition felt that news should read like a novel, as Thomas Wolfe famously put it, and thus reality should be just as interesting as fiction, or at least bound up with it.[27] Perhaps the boundary between revelation within fiction and the plain facts of book dedications was not as rigid as it seemed, or as Mrs. Deming felt that it should stay. Nonetheless, if gay liberation had encouraged this shamelessness, Mrs. Deming said, "I regret that this has become a movement. I don't see how it can do any good to anyone. But that seems to be the way things are these days."[28]

Though Mrs. Deming did not decry the younger generation—her own daughter was middle-aged by this point—a language of wariness of time and fads was salient in her descriptions of such movements "these days." The honesty that Barbara Deming craved with her mother instead seemed to inscribe her, from her mother's point of view, in a largely abstract generation of activists whom she found alien and exhibitionistic. Her reservations about gay liberation as a movement in fact anticipated what would become a larger body of criticism of the politicization of private life and public performance of selfhood, including Christopher Lasch's *The Culture of Narcissism* (1979) and Betty Friedan's critiques of a strain of feminist "naval gazers." Lasch would suggest that the radicalism of the late 1960s and early 1970s served as a form of therapy for those who embraced it for personal rather than political reasons, degrading politics to the level of self-discovery rather than social change. In a similar vein, Betty Friedan feared that the public goals of feminism—integrating women in the workplace or helping women achieve political power, for example—were becoming displaced by those who wanted to talk about their relationships, appearances, and their personal experiences of oppression.[29] At the base of their concerns was a fear of the diminishment of the public sphere. To see her daughter bound up with these trends appeared both disorienting and unsettling for Katherine Deming.

On the surface, then, Barbara Deming alienated Katherine at the very moment that she had invited her mother to know her and understand her more fully. There was something quite abstract about the way that Deming told her mother she was a lesbian, as it was embedded in a language of politics and seemed to breed a debate about the nature of the personal and the private in contemporary society rather than a discussion about Deming's affective life. And yet coming out and gay politics did offer a way to bring about intensely personal conversations that might otherwise, without this framework, simply have remained submerged.

The very idea of coming out of the closet was marked by peeling off the layers imposed by the family and society to attain an original or authentic self, a quest that itself could become a source of family friction. Coming of age during the early 1970s and adapting a gay liberation perspective then, writer and performer Michael Callen felt frustrated by his parents' refusal to acknowledge what he took to be his true self, including his sexuality. Throughout the 1970s, Callen was living in New York City, trying to make a career as a singer, writer, and performer. He would go on to write gay liberation songs, becoming a member of the gay male a cappella group *The Flirtations* and subsequently, during the 1980s, an important AIDS activist and writer.[30] As a twenty-five-year-old in 1979, not long after revealing his sexuality to his parents, he wrote to them in Hamilton, Ohio, where he had been raised. He recognized here that he had become more urban in his sensibilities than his family. He even let his parents know that there "is a New York City saying that roughly goes, 'Therapy hasn't been successful until you can tell your parents to go f——themselves.'"[31] Though he assured them that he did not subscribe to such a cavalier attitude, he noted that his primary purpose in this letter was to "*communicate*. . . . I feel, even post 'revelation,' that we aren't really talking. . . . I have been realizing over a period of time that it's not the frequency of calling that disturbs me, but the content of our conversations—or should I say lack of content. It seems to me that we've exhausted the weather and general health considerations."

He then called for more open emotional expression in his family. The problem with all of the Callens, as he perceived it, was that they were not "straightforward. We hint for love. We wait around hoping someone will sense we are deep in the need. . . . Then we withdraw because no one ever seems to be able to break the code." He noted that his father had trouble with the "physical expression of affection, i.e. hugging," though he praised his father, too, for "mellowing out at 66."[32] Finally Callen admitted to his parents that he wished he could "say I love you just plain out, without any qualifiers. However, we have both let this relationship coast on pilot for so long, that I just can't and mean it. . . . I want to mean it unequivocally"; his letter had represented "the first step on my part . . . towards a real, meaningful vital up-to-date relationship."[33]

Just as gays might have felt a forced sense of reticence within their families, in being asked to keep their sexuality to themselves, so might parents have felt that the intimacy their children called for was forced and self-conscious. Singled out the most in this letter, Callen's father chose to respond to his son, delineating what he felt was a more reasonable way of communicating feeling. Underlining to make his point, Mr. Callen firmly declared that *"all relationships must have reasonably defined parameters within the basic tenets of each other's philosophy."*[34] In this case, "parameters" perhaps referred to the very idea of revelations or the necessity to talk "meaningfully." In his view, his son's sexuality need not be discussed at all. Instead, they could talk about "many areas such as entertainment, travel, family, past shared experiences, future expectations, and . . . others," an itemization of family small talk rooted in both current events and the family's shared experiences. And, because they did not see each other very much, "I don't feel I'm asking for the moon for you to 'play it straight' when we are together."[35] In effect, his father asked him to create different selves according to the audience that his son might find himself before, a compromise—or strategy—that gays of the earlier postwar period seemed prepared to accept, perhaps because they were more likely to think of themselves as having multiple selves. In some senses, gays like Leach viewed their gay selves as psychological exhibits rather than as the gay subjects that Callen had claimed.[36]

Both Mr. Callen and Mrs. Deming extolled a more subtle means of communication with respect to sexuality, one that was implied or hinted at rather than expressed directly. Mr. Callen was much blunter in his suggestion that his son simply "play it straight," but both reflected, from their children's perspective, a failure to understand how pervasive gay sexuality was to self-expression, intimacy, and day-to-day life.[37]

In keeping with a central tenet of the gay liberation movements that located a fundamental oppression in the maintenance of silence around gayness, Callen, too, suggested that his father's exhortations about discretion implied merely shame. His criticism has a meaningful synchronicity with a particular historical moment when polite reticence about taboo matters seemed increasingly to be a repressed, disingenuous position. Personal writing and the performance of popular music during this period both might have shaped popular behavior that embraced exhibitionism. But it was not just cultural expressions that had grown weary of reserve. Abetted by an atmosphere of openness about feelings in this period as well as the rigorous questioning of the justice of Cold War military interventions, Vietnam War veterans were returning home and talking about their experiences in warfare in a way that World War II veterans had not.[38] Just as many observers rejected a duty-bound view of warfare, they also cast aside the notion of unthinking duty and blind loyalty as principles within personal relationships, especially within family life. Disruptions within personal relationships were becoming more open to discussion, especially as the start of no-fault divorce laws took some of the shame and stigma away from divorce, something that further highlighted themes of individual over family happiness.[39] In turn, deference and formality between the generations were eroding.

In light of these ruptures, open avowal and discussions of gay sexuality seemed not only less shocking but in a sense even needed to keep pace with the times. Openness was equated with recognition of full personhood. As liberation activist Martha Shelley, in the first of the series of *Gay Flames* pamphlets in 1970, put it, "The worst part of being a homosexual is having to keep it secret. Not the occasional murders by police or teenage queer-beaters, not the loss of jobs or expulsion from schools or dishonorable discharges—but the daily knowledge that what you are is something so awful that it cannot be revealed." She likened this enforced silence to an "internal violence," something that could be felt most acutely in the family context. [40] Like this writer, Callen used the example of heterosexual marriage as a counterpoint to gay expressiveness when he wrote back to his father, "You touch mother. You discuss your marriage. You mention that you live together. That you have children . . . No one accuses you of slapping your sexuality in everyone's face just because [mother] wears a wedding band."[41] Privacy was seen as a hypocritical standard applied only to gays.[42]

Self-presentation came to the forefront as another locus of family conflict in these meditations on privacy and closeness. Even parents who felt more comfortable with homosexuality could nonetheless feel circumspect about their children's expressions of it. When she found out her son was gay, for example, Mrs. Brass seemed to identify with his pain in being an outsider. Throughout the 1970s, her son Perry was a student at New York University, as well as a poet and gay liberation activist.[43] At the same time, Mrs. Brass, by then a divorcée, had started living in a retirement building in Savannah, Georgia, the city where Perry had grown up. He wrote of his mother in retrospect, "My homosexuality was a problem to her in that it revealed her own—she wanted throughout her life to be acceptable, and she was a big, mannish woman with a gay, not terribly manly son."[44] Brass's mother appeared to be struggling against her sexuality: she wanted to have sex with women but also maintain a sense of respectability and perhaps even southern gentility. In fact, Mrs. Brass was having an affair with a married yet "gay as they come" woman in her retirement complex, whom she criticized for being "geared to the system" and hiding the affair. Nonetheless, Mrs. Brass asked her son a favor upon his visits to her home. "The only thing I ask," she said, "is please leave off the make up and jewelry while you visit me. I live in a very conventional building. It would be a favor to me and I would appreciate it. You see after you leave, I've got to keep on living here and in this town. If I had my own home things would be different."[45] From her perspective, outward signs of an unmistakable gayness were not only embarrassing and gratuitous but potentially endangering. This mother might have felt all the more urgent about the protection of her son's identity, owing to her desire to protect her own ambiguous sexuality.

Parents, of course, fretted over both their children's welfare and their own when they considered public displays of gay sexuality. But their children's perceptions of the stunted candor of this older, heterosexual generation not only suggested a failure of intimacy in family life but also reverberated with gay liberation ideas and critiques of broader social restraints of sensuality and feeling, spurred on by the sexual revolution's emphasis on the pursuit of pleasure and new sexual arrangements during the late 1960s and 1970s.[46] Though the sexual revolution was largely heterosexual in scope, gays shaped it as well, and it had an impact on gay consciousness.[47]

The public performance of the sexual, including its commodification, dramatized sex for its own sake. Frankness about sexual explicitness might have suggested a corresponding frankness about sexual identity. Moreover, as historians John D'Emilio and Estelle Freedman have noted, greater opportunities for birth control tended to soften the association between sexuality and reproduction.[48] In turn, looser censorship laws abetted representations of gays. By 1968, the Motion Picture Production Code was abolished, giving way to more frank portraits of homosexuality in mainstream Hollywood films, including the 1970 film *Boys in the Band*, based on Mart Crowley's 1968 play of the same title. In turn, a landmark Supreme Court case in 1967, *Redrup v. New York*, had a profound impact on freedom of expression, including the obscenity judgments on gay pulp fiction.[49]

Though gay pulps remained marketed as exposés of a lurid world, their titles and plots had become more sexual and salacious throughout the later 1960s, including books such as Meredith Gorman's *Homo Playboy* (1969), Gene Evans's *Homo Hunt* (1969), and Thomas Aaron's *Gay Orgy* (1968). Pulp sociology such as Norm Winski's *The Homosexual Revolt* (1967) discussed today's "New Homosexual," or "Crusading Homo," who "sneered at relations between man and woman while glorifying their own."[50]

This increasing sexualization of the representations of gays to some extent replaced—though never fully displaced—gender nonconformity as a central code for gay sexuality. Two 1969 cartoons in the *Los Angeles Advocate*, a more consumerist gay magazine that surfaced during this period, portrayed gay sexual expression, not gender nonconformity, as the site of the chasm between gays and their parents.[51] Fusing a campy sensibility with gay sexual liberation, these featured ridiculous and larger-than-life family disclosures, such as the appalled mother and angry father who opened their son's closet to find his naked lover standing before them, declaring, "Mercy, I can't tell you how much I've looked forward to meeting Harold's parents!"[52] Another showed a well-coiffed and -dressed mother, accompanied by a brutish-looking husband, fists clenched at his naked son and his boyfriend whom he caught making out on his couch. Blasé, the mother says to her husband, "Oh cool it, Harry. At least Sonny won't get pregnant like his sister."[53] Unlike earlier campy portrayals, where the hint of sexuality was so exaggerated it was almost rendered asexual, in these cartoons, gay sex was depicted in a realistic way, with nakedness and bedroom scenes. Although these cartoon narratives, like those of the earlier postwar period, remained structured around getting caught, the image of direct confrontation suggests a building impetus for revelation, both within the family and more broadly.

An ethos of revelation informed by gay politics was a more salient theme within the more politically oriented publications of the gay liberation movement throughout the early 1970s. In these, writers and observers celebrated gay sexual expression and denounced what they saw as the repressed, rigid, and legalistic behavior of heterosexual parents.[54] Gone were the portraits of somewhat charming, oblivious parents that gays of an earlier generation had produced. Instead, liberationist images of parents seemed to combine with a bland, suppressive, and forbidding idea of 1950s family life, as though a broad sense of history, for these gay writers, was bound up with their individual family pasts and became a collective memory.

"MERCY, I CAN'T TELL YOU HOW MUCH I'VE LOOKED FORWARD TO MEETING HAROLD'S PARENTS."

Figure 2. Cartoon in the *Los Angeles Advocate*, 1969.

Generational cleavage and doubts about inherited wisdom merged with the new postures and reorientations of social and political life during this period and kindled gay evaluations and representations of family life. The student and peace movements, the New Left, and the women's liberation movement all offered a critique of modes of intimate life and emotional expression that was especially pertinent to the project of gay liberation. Many of those who identified themselves as gay liberationists were students during this period. Lacking the encumbrances of jobs or families, they felt freer to participate in emergent gay liberation and discussion groups surfacing on American campuses.[55] There they also could absorb a culture of student protest, not only against university bureaucracies that seemed aligned with an imperial American government, but against the banality of their studies.[56] Increasingly, students asked that they be taught something "relevant." Social critic Paul Goodman attested that chaotic student riots

Figure 3. Cartoon in the *Los Angeles Advocate*, 1969.

would not have erupted in the late 1960s and early 1970s if only university administrators could "speak like human beings."[57] This desire for interest, fulfillment, and spontaneity in day-to-day life and relationships was a pervasive emotional component in other social protest movements as well, and this longing perhaps most directly informed critiques of the family. In this vein, even the peace movement did not solely question the necessity or morality of the Vietnam War and other American foreign policy interventions, but perceived American cold war values in the broadest sense, as they manifested themselves both in those larger political undertakings and in the everyday.[58] Moreover, widespread images of carnage from warfare had challenged ideas of obscenity and sexual taboos; violence now defined obscenity, not pornography or homosexuality.[59] Indeed, the violence of Vietnam troubled not just concepts of obscenity but the notion of polite reticence itself. In this vein Robert Lowell attacked the critics of the student rebels by saying that they were more preoccupied with the paltry violence of student uprisings than they were the nation at war, or "napalm on human flesh."[60]

New Left leaders and thinkers interpreted the social trends of the early Cold War—suburbanization, bureaucratization, consumption, the growing military-industrial complex, and the containment of communism—as the consequences of the excessive uniformity and apathy of the period in which their parents had come of age. They, in contrast, could not live with the contradiction between their own comfortable lives and the rest of the world's turmoil. Thus Students for a Democratic Society called on youth to abandon their parents' social worlds and embrace creative, self-directed work, repudiating the older generation's "superfluous abundance."[61]

This scrutiny of the personal past and the family's questionable legacy was also a prominent theme of countercultural commentary and lifestyle experiments, as well as the observations of women's liberation. In a manifesto of the Yippies, or the Youth International Party, formed in the aftermath of the 1967 March on the Pentagon, *We Are Everywhere* (1971), Jerry Rubin condemned parents who pushed their religions, prejudices, and lifestyles on their children.[62] Some counterculturalists tried to amend this inevitable passing down of values by developing alternatives to nuclear family structures, such as the establishments of communes.[63] The analysis of the nuclear family as constraining the potential of women specifically was a central perspective of women's liberation. The feminist movement had farreaching interests and imperatives, including an analysis of male supremacy, wage labor, and women's exploitation in the media among others. Yet women's liberation also resonated perhaps most compellingly with gay liberation in its insistence that personal matters had political relevance and in its critique of the gender conceptions and roles that had confined women—and men—to narrowly defined social and intimate expectations.[64]

Gay liberationists, then, both adopted and refashioned the priorities of the other liberation and social movements in their midst and in the process elevated homosexuality to the level of the political. And yet with gays, perhaps, there was something even more trenchant about these social criticisms, particularly with respect to the family. It is true that increased college attendance and a later age of marriage during the late 1960s gave all young people, not just gays, more time and social space as individuals in between their original families and their eventual chosen families.[65] But the lingering sentiment or cultural ethos of banishment gave gay critiques of their family lives and social worlds an urgency and a sharpness that seems unique to gays during this period. In "The Family and Gay Oppression," a writer for *Come Out Fighting*, a gay socialist newspaper of the Lavender and Red

Union, denounced the family for stunting gays in their sexual quests and for sending them "away to be 'cured,' beaten, or cast aside."[66] Accordingly, a central animating force of gay liberation as a culture and social critique could be articulated as a need to seek reprisals or justice for a sense of alienation and rejection that gays felt acutely within intimate life. A well-circulated photo of a group of lesbians at a demonstration holding up a sign that read, "Here I Am, MOM: SURPRISE," typified the emerging sense that gays could reject the lifestyle and choices of their heterosexual parents as much as these parents could reject those of their gay children.[67]

One form that this rejection took was simply a disavowal of an array of internalized social norms that parents had placed upon their children, especially gender roles. In 1969, Red Butterfly, a Marxist cell of the Gay Liberation Front, singled out five "institutions of repression"—the educational system, organized religion, government, business, and the family—that acted together to repress gays. The "American family," they wrote, was perhaps the most insidious of these, as it was the "starting point for anti-gay attitudes" and suppressed gay selfhood by "stifl[ing] and crippl[ing] people's abilities to develop" while fostering "confining sex-typing of personality traits."[68] A cartoon in Canada's best-known gay liberation periodical, Toronto's *Body Politic*, reprinted in several American sources, substantiated this critique.[69] In this 1975 reprint, parents appear as disembodied voices, their strictness conveyed by the knifelike quality of their cartoon bubbles. A little boy and little girl appear in stages, with coffins growing up around them as they grow older. In panel 2, they sit in coffin frames while voices shout, "Only Sissies Play with Dolls," and "Girls Don't Climb Trees." By the time the parents declare, "Your Hair's Too Long—You Look Like a Girl," and "Why Don't You Wear a Skirt?" the coffins are almost fully built up around the children, burying them alive. In the final caption, the parental voices proclaim, "An Ideal Couple. They Were Made for Each Other."[70] Seldom did gays of a previous generation express their alienation in such an embittered way, even within homophile circles; this earlier generation of activists appeared to expect that their parents would fail to understand their gender interests and sexuality. This newer generation of gay activists, by contrast, was developing an expectation of a family intimacy that included an understanding of children's uniqueness even in their gender deviations.

Joan Larkin took up a similar theme of intergenerational tyranny in her 1975 poem "Rhyme of My Inheritance." Here she repudiated the notion of parental inheritance at the levels of both material comforts and character.[71] She wrote of parents who "took me to school where I learned to be cute: / I wore clean jumpers and washed my hands" and "did what girls were supposed to do. / I wore a white dress; I was photographed." Despite her parents' attention to her well-being, she was

> giving the gifts back, one by one.
> I'm tearing the pages of my past.
> I'm turning my back. I'm turning them down.[72]

This disavowal of both instilled gender behaviors and those material aspects of her childhood—her jumpers and dresses—suggests an additional rift between the generations in the interpretation of what constitutes affection. For her parents, the attention they took with the upkeep of her girlhood and the very abundance in which she came of age might have suggested a deep love for their child. For their daughter, these were cloying and burdensome and ultimately acted as barriers to her finding out who she really was. Still, hers is a poem with more of a sense of empowerment than the coffin cartoon; the final verse reads, "May I let go of these bitter rhymes; and may this burial be my last. . . . / Let this coffin of verses inherit my pain."[73]

The image of the coffin is poignant because the families of gays were often depicted as being dead in an emotional sense, a deadness that threatened to swallow up the children in their midst. Notably, these critiques were not advanced solely by American gay liberationists but by Canadian ones as well. But there were some important differences in the context of these critiques. Canadian activists, both within and outside of gay liberation, did not contend with the same imperial government that their American counterparts did, nor had they witnessed the level of violence and venom unleashed against American protestors and demonstrators during the student riots and the Democratic National Convention of 1968, to name just two examples. To be sure, Canadian New Left activists within such groups as Student Union for Peace Action (SUPA) valued participatory democracy, fought against poverty and racism, and sought a fulfilling education, just as their American counterparts did. Some Canadian activists even felt as though their government was complicit in the Vietnam War.[74] Nevertheless, the Canadian government was at least somewhat congenial to student activism, even funding a dissident youth group, the Company of Young Canadians (CYC).[75] Moreover, some observers saw Canada as a victim of American imperialism and considered Canadian nationalism, in the face of this, as itself a subversive political stance.[76] Thus, in Canadian gay liberation periodicals such as the *Body Politic*, writers did not indict the Canadian family as emblematic of a repressive state in the same way that American gay liberationists attacked the American family. And yet there were many continuities at an intimate level, suggesting a more intensely private and diffuse dimension to gay liberation not precisely connected to specific political activism, or even to a condemnation of war or racism, but to an indictment of private mores, boredom, stultification, and an inability to feel, in this case homosexual feelings. It is as though the 1950s, as a collective memory, became a marker of a generic story of repression regardless of the geography.

Parallel to their American equivalents, Canadian gay liberationists also denounced their families for instilling stifling gender roles and for a banality that went beyond personal plight to become a social condition. In a 1973 article in the *Body Politic* titled "Hetero-burbia," Amerigo Marras, a prominent activist in the Canadian gay movement, denounced "average, middle-class, Christian, suburbs" that led to an "enforced lack of socio-sexual contacts and individuality." The domination of the nuclear family within single family homes evoked for this writer "the pattern of prison cells sharing the same conformity and TV set."[77] White, middle-class family homes became impersonal factories in this portrait, engendering unthinking, automaton-like consumers.[78] Suburban affluence and status were seen as intertwined with a cold asceticism and the inability to feel vividly. The image of suburban neighborhoods would become another salient motif of these liberationist sources, calling into question a perceived heterosexual aesthetic or "straight"-ness that saw its expression within these sterile confines. Betty Friedan's oft circulated, chilling image of suburban "comfortable concentration camps" where 1950s housewives had let their talents and potentials lie fallow were given a gay life here.[79]

The portrait to emerge in both Canadian and American sources suggests that parents had led insipid, unremarkable lives, superficially attuned to conventions, in the benighted 1950s, while their children were living in a more socially significant and tumultuous time period. This rereading of the past fits into a broader countercultural atmosphere of a renunciation of the family image of innocence popularized in the television and other pop culture families of the 1950s. Satires of this kind of family were embodied in the comic strips of Robert Crumb, such as 1969's "Joe Blow." Allen Gins-

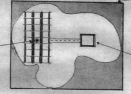

Figure 4. Cartoon in the *Body Politic*, 1973.

berg's poem "Howl," which proposed that the 1950s generation's god was the barren and engulfing "Moloch," was written—and censored—in 1956 but enjoyed enormous popularity by the later 1960s.[80]

In gay male liberationist portrayals in particular, these criticisms of the older generation and the family life they conducted often were focused on mothers, who appear as anachronisms. This emphasis suggests some ideational linkages between disaffected male intellectuals of the 1950s and 1970s: a continuity of notions of momism, only here with a gay twist.[81] In a 1974 cartoon in the series "Closetary Comix" that appeared in the Rochester gay liberation periodical *Empty Closet*, B. I. Groach parodied a housewife's afternoon social, calling it "Mothers in Agony Is Now in Session." In the cartoon, several mothers, drawn more like grandmothers, congregate around a woman who tearfully admits, after other testimonials, that her son is "queer." The mother confides that she does not know where she went wrong with her son—her husband played ball with him, she had spanked him every time she "caught him playing with my lipstick," but he still "turned out queer. Boo-hoo! And he refuses to get help. How could he be so cruel to his only mother?" Another member rushes over to give her some comfort, declaring, "You poor dear!" The mother then reveals that her sister had told her son he would have "a gay time" at college, which indicated that "she knows! Sob! I know she knows! And tonight she's probably telling everyone at her bridge party!" The cartoon strips ends with the women assuring her that her secret is safe with them. The epilogue reads, "Don't feel too sorry for these Mothers-in-Agony. With hubbie off winning the bread, they've nothing else to do but watch their own soap operas. Besides, at least M.I.A. gets them out of the house one afternoon a week! On second thought, pity them the problems they don't know they have."[82] The problems they "don't know they have" could entail, from this cartoonist's perspective, the boredom of their lives, their superficial preoccupation with propriety or potential shame, and their misapprehensions of the younger generation and gays specifically.

This apparent misogyny and negative mother image could have been informed by a cartooning tradition in which women often appeared as nags, sex objects, or opportunists, typical in male cartooning both predating and during the postwar period.[83] Such matrophobia oddly clashed with the valorization of women's experiences brought about through women's liberation. Ironically, too, mothers were sometimes blamed in the culture at large for instilling too much creativity and a questioning spirit in this

Figure 5. Cartoon in the *Empty Closet*, December 1974.

generation.[84] Yet these liberationists perceived their mothers as unenlight-
ened about liberation in the broadest sense and as complicit in some older
regime of heterosexuality. Perhaps there were even deeper, more personal
reasons to these indictments as well: a sense of hurt that these mothers
would turn on their gay sons for the very gender expressions that might
have made them potentially close to their mothers in terms of interests or
sensibility. In this way, negative images of mothers became another means
of gay vindication for feelings of family rejection.

However, this cartoonist, like the author of the "Hetero-burbia" piece,
also criticized mothers simply for their stifling domesticity. This criticism
might have been propelled by an intellectual context in which coming out
and revelation had taken on radical political connotations, a more public
act to be shared in broader political circles, one that stood in sharp contrast
to housebound mothers inhibited about sharing experiences even in the
narrow worlds of their families and friends. Coming out as an essential
aspect of personal and political integrity was prominent in many gay liberation interpretations of family relationships—and their disavowal—during
this time period. In 1971, the lesbian periodical *Focus*, by the Boston DOB,
asked its readers, "Is it important to have 'good' family relationships while
denying a part of yourself?"[85]

In some portraits, gays satirized both their parents and psychiatry,
deeming them complicit in an oppressive surveillance of gays that had crip-
pled gay selfhood. This was a period in which gay liberationists, in keeping
with an antiauthoritarian countercultural spirit, had in fact made some
important challenges to psychiatric tenets about homosexuality, including
the notion that families had a hand in causing homosexuality.[86] In 1970,
the Chicago Gay Liberation Front had urged fellow gays to get "Off the
Couches and into the Streets!" in their leaflet against the American Medical
Association.[87] It took radical activism and more mainstream lobbying by
progressive psychiatrists to win the 1973 decision removing homosexuality
from the American Psychiatric Association's (APA) *DSM*, in response to its
second revision in 1968, where homosexuality had been labeled a "nonpsy-
chotic mental disorder."[88] Consequently, sodomy laws in states that
depended on the medical opinion that homosexuality was a perversion
could no longer refer to the *DSM*; during the course of the 1970s, half the
states eliminated sodomy from the penal code.[89] But the APA's decision
also had some important consequences for gay daily and family life, as there
could no longer be such a glaring justification for the psychiatric cure of

gays.[90] In spite of these changes, the idea of homosexuality as a mental illness remained a touchstone for gay activists and writers. In a 1975 satirical piece, "The Heterosexual World: An Anthropological Study," Satya Klein turned this idea of sickness to heterosexuality, noting that it was "surprising that so many healthy gays have managed to come from sick het parents."[91] While heterosexual fathers were satirized as brutal and autocratic, the mothers of the "het" world were "forced to become a retarded form of adult. . . . Their main cultural outlets are cooking, talking on the telephone, and spraying Sani-flush into toilet bowls."[92]

In mocking the pathology of heterosexuality, this sketch evoked a broader gay impetus to displace external observers from their lives. The irony of this desire is that the intense scrutiny of gay lives was in fact a central aspect of gay liberation culture and perhaps a refashioning of this kind of observation. The questions that gay liberationists asked themselves about their past and their family lives even could be said to parallel psychoanalysis, including broader themes in the psychoanalysis of the 1970s, such as those offered in the works of Heinz Kohut, who placed the self and its genesis and development at the center of his studies.[93] Of course, liberationists were not asking themselves what was wrong with their sexuality, or even so much how they came to be homosexual, as this paralleled questions of etiology too directly, but they were in a sense taking life histories by recounting their life stories, with tremendous emphasis on their childhoods and their feelings of alienation and a view to uncovering the sense of forced conformity or false consciousness.[94] In this sense, liberationists became embroiled within individual pasts, just as, to some extent, countercultural movements more collectively were quite preoccupied with the historical moment in which they had experienced their childhoods. Liberationists perhaps even created a more formidable and pervasive influence of their parents than even psychoanalysis conjured through the very symbolization they gave them in gay culture.

While just as attentive to their family lives as their gay forebears were, liberationists nonetheless rejected the concept of parental obligation. If family duties could be cast as mere social constructions, then the deep burden of causing parents pain by virtue of being gay could be assuaged or at least muted. In 1967, Dick Michaels, the founder and editor of the *Los Angeles Advocate*, wrote that even "the most 'enlightened' parents are determined to inflict their own hangups on their children. Twenty years later they will sob on the shoulder of a cop or social worker, 'Where did we go wrong? We gave him everything.' Sure. Everything . . . including your own warped outlook."[95] It is not that gay critics like him wanted to see their parents sob, but they came to believe, through a gay liberation and pride analysis, that this sobbing had an illegitimate basis. According to psychologist Howard Brown, who observed a sample of gay men during the 1970s, the central reason that an earlier generation of gays did not tell their parents of their sexuality was to "spar[e] them the agony of having to think of us as sexual beings."[96] But this ethos of sparing the parents—which included the necessity of maintaining a secret self—had begun to fade. It was the family who now needed to change to accommodate their gay children, and not the reverse.

Still, parents did not necessarily see their children's homosexuality as immutable and deeply engrained during this period. Parents whose children came of age in the late 1960s and 1970s might have seen their children's sexual orientations as temporary sexual preferences subject to change, and not necessarily because they saw their children's homosexuality as a psychological stage. Rather, they came to see these sexual preferences as part of the fashions, demeanors, tastes, politics, and lifestyles of the youth cultures in their midst.

In his reflective prose poem of 1972, "Words on Mother," published in *Faggotry*, John Knoebel noted that his mother believed it was the appearance of female "hippies" that had made her son gay. Knoebel was an "effeminist" man, or a gay man who identified with femininity and believed that the oppression of gay men ensued because of their alignment to femininity. He had thought deeply about the relationship between gayness and feminine appearances. In this piece, he recalled his mother's telling him,

> "You sell us girls short. You just met the wrong kind, all those
> Long-haired, hippy types in college. You should come home and
> Meet a nice girl who'd cook your meals and keep house for you."[97]

Mrs. Knoebel apparently considered the natural look of young women during this period, including long, straight hair and a rejection of makeup and other feminine accoutrements, to be stark and unappealing, perhaps even unkempt and bedraggled.[98] Ironically she echoed the criticisms of appearance that some mothers would make toward their lesbian daughters. In Lisa Fenton's 1979 memoir piece "The Radical Home Haircut," the mother might have been relieved if her daughter had favored a hippy look, because at least then she would have had long hair. Fenton described her teenaged arguments with her mother over her appearance throughout the late 1960s, as being "locked in violent opposition. . . . We bickered daily over my usual garb of T-shirts, blue jeans, and size 4 boys' sneakers. The latest aggravation had been my acquisition of a faded *Lee Rider* denim jacket and my flat refusal to wear a bra." If this garb was not enough, Fenton then appeared before her mother with an extremely short hair cut, scrapping her shoulder-length "curly mass." She recalled her mother "let[ting] out something like a shriek, 'What have you done to yourself?! You look like a dyke!' "[99] Not only was the appearance of "hippy" women or "dyke"-looking daughters an affront to the femininity of these heterosexual mothers, but it also seemed to carry a more precise indicator of an unnatural sexuality than it had in years gone by.

Gay sons, too, felt scrutinized for their hair and clothes, which signified both a social and a sexual deviance. Many gay male writers of this period had insisted that they, like women, had been the victims of confining and brutish articulations of masculinity, including manly appearances. While homophiles in the early 1960s had taken up the gay cause through a strategy of respectability that included gender-appropriate clothing and dress-up clothes, increasingly gay liberation celebrated those more androgynous styles that were becoming more mainstream among the young.[100] But these revisions of masculinity were not limited to gay men. For some, long hair and the feminization of clothing styles, including flowered shirts and beads among other items, were not only gay codes but a conscious rejection of a masculinity that they associated with a militarized culture.[101] Mike Hippler, a gay writer who kept a diary during the early 1970s when he was a college student at Duke University, observed that traditional masculine appearances were still very much in vogue on his college campus, and thus his long hair made him feel a bit freakish. As a sophomore, he returned to his family home for a social function, where he was praised lavishly for a newly short hair cut. "I have never been so sick of hearing how *good* . . . I look now—I look terrible!" he complained. "I am embarrassed to be seen in public! Long hair is beautiful; these jerks have got to understand, styles change. Mrs. Winderwheedle said the favorite—'You look so good and wholesome and All American. Good for you—you're on OUR side.' "[102] "Our" side might have meant the "silent majority" of Americans, though it could just as easily have referred, implicitly, to the "side" of heterosexuals.

These appearance divisions reflected broader divisions in politics, class, sensibility, and sexuality in American culture during this period. Political debates took on this cultural dimension in the tremendous attention they paid to the demeanors and appearances among different "sides." A prominent example is the tumult after the Kent State and Jackson State student murders in 1970. As a response to these killings and to Nixon's policies in Cambodia, student protestors from several New York City colleges gathered in the financial district, only to be attacked by construction workers chanting, "All the way, U.S.A." Though on the surface this conflict concerned the support of the American government, it took on class and cultural dimensions as well, vividly demonstrating an antipathy between "longhairs" and "hardhats."[103] While some white, middle-class students did go to fight in Vietnam, it was more often working-class young men who saw the front lines of battle.[104] This knowledge fueled resentment against student protestors who might have appeared cavalier about social obligations and duties, both figuratively and literally. As historian James T. Patterson noted, it was not so much that working-class observers were in favor of the war, but they tended to be "anti-anti-war."[105] Even ostensibly political critiques of student protestors, such as diplomat George Kennan's 1968 speech at Swarthmore College, "Rebels without a Program," faulted them more for their untidiness and poor personal manners than for their lack of political decorum.[106] That Hippler could be viewed as a political radical on the basis of long hair, when in fact he was expressing a gay masculinity, shows just how much gay appearance codes had now become entangled in a range of ideas about students, hippies, and "flower people" during this period. Unlike the young rebels of the 1950s, who were more likely to be viewed as aggressively heterosexual, as "angry young men," the "rebels" during this time period were viewed as potentially homosexual.[107]

Seeing gay sexuality as simply a facet of a larger political sensibility, then, allowed some parents to consider their children's sexuality to be malleable. In her 1972 poem for *Come Out!* "Wow, I'll be really uptight if my family sees this," Emily Rubin Winer wrote that her mother felt she was "only / doing what was fashionable at the time," both in having a severe, short hair cut and in being gay.[108] Condescending and infuriating though this stance appeared to Winer, if gay sexuality could be understood as simply a political phase, children could be protected to some degree from parental disappointment, acrimony, and rejection.

Gay liberation thus left gays in a somewhat paradoxical position in their families. On the one hand, gay sexuality and individuals were more visible than they had ever been before and perhaps were more real to their parents.[109] But on the other hand, gay sexuality remained confined in a personal politics that likely seemed quite strange, even alien, to parents. It was rare for a gay person to talk to parents about sexuality unabashedly, as Marist College professor William Cannicott Olson did with his mother. An avid reader of gay literature and simultaneous absorber and critic of gay liberation, Olson told his mother about his sex life with boyfriends throughout the 1970s, including details about the sexual attractiveness of these men. In 1977, when he was in his thirties, he wrote to his mother that he "got it on for 1.5 hours in the car" with a twenty-one-year-old man who was "very cute" and also about another man "who is my current, 'Can I make him,' trick." He told her that "one of the advantages of having a gay son is that you never know what new surprises await you,"[110] perhaps including mentioning to her the year before that his anniversary sex with his boyfriend was "by far the best sex ever."[111] Even then, though, he was careful to place his sexuality as secondary to the practical, domestic aspects of his relationships. He told his mother that he and his partner were both "cooks, dishwashers, lawn mowers, swimming pool experts, wood sawyers, painters, cleaning persons, drivers and riders in cars" as the "spirit moves" them. He did not want his mother to believe that they had assigned roles and that one was "the wife." But most important, he told her, "we are persons, human beings, first, and sexuality is way down on the list."[112] He also acknowledged at other points that it took him some time, roughly ten years, to even tell his mother and other close people in his life that he was gay.[113] But his boyfriend's mother was not as understanding as Olson's, and he had separated from her for a time.[114] Even with the framework of politics to convey their sexuality and the presence of gay political organizations to ensure that gays had some place to turn, gay liberationists, too, exhibited an enduring, often underlying worry about family banishments.[115] Their disquiet was perhaps starker in this era than earlier time periods, because the impetus to reveal brought about concrete dilemmas about how parents would react.

Accordingly, gay liberationists offered advice to other gays about how familial revelations should be considered. In her 1975 piece "How to Come Out without Being Thrown Out," Jeanne Cordova, a former nun who went on to found and publish Los Angeles' *Lesbian Tide*, delineated five possible coming-out methods and discussed the merits and drawbacks of each one. The "Help Me, Help Me" method usually resulted in mutual tears and a

"visit to a psychiatrist, priest, doctor, or mental institution of your choice."
The "So There Approach" was marked by "extreme anger/hatred/bitterness
toward parents . . . always justified but sometimes careless," as well the one
most likely to result in being "thrown out" or "incarcerat[ed] in a mental
institution."[116] Next was the "Oops Approach," wherein a gay child left a
telling item, such as a letter from a lover, lying around the house that did
not leave much to the imagination, in order to provoke a conversation.[117]
This was deemed too apologetic, leaving the child vulnerable to the charge
that a wayward influence had seduced him or her into being gay. Finally,
the "Dear Mom/Dad Approach, a favorite of the 'They're in New York and
I'm in California so it's safe' live-away gay," was deemed too wishy-washy,
prompting Mother to "fall apart and run to 'Your Father' when she reads
the words." In Cordova's view, it was far better to educate parents, by
adopting the "Gradual or Naturalization Approach," which allowed for a
build-up to the revelation through gay politics, so that a gay child could
"come across honestly and proud," with the hope that "your parents will
think so too one day."[118]

While Cordova emphasized bringing about mutual understanding, she
was not so utopian as to believe that gays would be welcome within every
family. In fact, she recommended a kind of pragmatism about parental
intolerance and a theme of independent adulthood that curiously recalls
the practicality of the activist mothers of gay children in the 1950s. When
parents "refuse to speak to us for three years or say, 'You're no daughter/
son of mine!' it's not really us they're talking to! They are dealing with their
own sexual identity conflicts. A certain objectivity is necessary. When they
say these terrible things it is not . . . the 'end of the world.' For most parents,
this is merely a phase."[119] This statement, suggesting that a potentially
nightmarish moment of family rejection be taken as an instance of false
consciousness, to be borne calmly, shows that the story of gay liberation
and pride, at once so in touch with emotional expression and revelations,
could still lead to a kind of emotional detachment. Perhaps this disengage-
ment was the only way of not feeling the devastation of being "thrown
out." Just as their gay forebears placed images of excommunication within
the realm of fantasy or humor, these gay liberationists reinvented that dis-
tancing strategy, within a seemingly unwavering and staunch political rhetoric.[120]

But this sense of objectivity was not always within the grasp of even
those gays who subscribed consciously to a liberation perspective. In a per-

sonal piece in San Francisco's *Vector* in 1973, Robert Burke avowed that he was not coming out to his family members because "I simply don't know at this point whether or not I would be able to handle their rejection which is, I feel, a very real possibility."[121] Another column in the *Lesbian Tide* asked its readers in 1971, "have you ever . . . [c]ried because you saw your parents cry—when they discovered you were a 'Queer,' and told you that you would be better off dead?"[122] Even those portraits that appeared to be unrepentant denunciations of parents suggest an underlying pain at the prospect of being disowned or simply the pain of conditional love. In another *Closetary Comix* in 1974, B. I. Groach turned his attentions to the husbands of the Mothers-in-Agony characters, with his creation of John Q. Het, a Willy Lomanish character who decided to take out some insurance on his son, because he was worried his son "might turn out queer." Should this be the case, John Q. Het commented to his insurance agent that he would need extra money because the homosexual son would never get a job, and he and his wife would need to "pay for shrinks and electro-shock therapy." The insurance agent agreed that this was a "reasonable request." The epilogue reads, "Don't *You* Wish Your Parents Had Had Foresight?"[123] This cartoon plays on the notion of disowning in a literal way, casting children as parental possessions subject to ruin and disappointments, like a house or car. It also denounces a notion of parental hope and investment in their children by portraying it in these crass, literal terms.

Gay liberation culture, then, existed within a delicate balance between wrath and sadness over the idea of family banishment. The burden of fantasies of familial estrangement perhaps had not actually waned as drastically as even the most venomous of gay liberation portraits might have suggested. And the potent hold of the family's expectations certainly had not waned, even at a rhetorical level, for perhaps the majority of gay people living in this era, for whom gay liberation and culture were more remote forces. A sense of family obligation continued to be true for those who did not have the distance of living away from their parents. Throughout the 1970s, lesbians in the vulnerable position of living in the family home wrote often wistful letters telling of their loves and families to the self-appointed lesbian counselor of the New Jersey DOB, Julie Lee. She directed these women to lesbian meetings and reading resources, both sharing her own life story and commenting upon theirs.[124] While these letters are fragmentary and suggestive rather than definitive, a sample illuminates the feelings of gays who did not adopt an explicit gay politics during this era, as well

Figure 6. Cartoon in the *Empty Closet*, October 1974.

as some of the unspoken fears and family yearnings of gay liberationists themselves.

One book that Julie Lee advised her correspondents to read was the 1972 book of advice literature and personal lesbian stories, *Lesbian/Woman*, by DOB pioneers Phyllis Lyon and Del Martin. Martin and Lyon bridged the homophile and gay liberation movements and sensibilities, in light of their sympathies toward discretion and their desire to live openly as lesbians. They acknowledged that "today, with so many in the gay liberation movement advocating total openness, it is even more difficult to make the decision [about telling one's parents]. If you are a teenager and keep hearing older (and presumably wiser) homosexuals shouting, 'Tell your parents, tell your boss, tell the world—don't be ashamed!' the pressure can be fierce."[125] Martin and Lyon even helped unify families, prolonging the earlier postwar homophile emphasis on family reunification. They noted that they knew a young lesbian who had cut off connections with her parents because they were "nagging" her too much to get married. But when the mother of this lesbian got in touch with Phyllis Lyon, Lyon wrote, "Never underestimate the power of parental concern," and got in touch with the young woman to say, "Your mother is concerned. Please write her."[126] That they could write this after exhibiting some sympathy with the desire to cut off relations with parents, and after demonstrating the cruelties of parents toward gay children, indicates a tenacity of homophile emphasis on enduring parental bonds. The lesbians who wrote to Julie Lee seemed to straddle, in their own dilemmas, this perceived shift in presentations of the personal between two generations of gays.

In fact, gays living in the family home might have welcomed the very reticence about sexuality that gay liberation had come to disfavor. One of Lee's correspondents, a twenty-three-year-old woman living in rural Utah, had purchased *Lesbian/Woman* in 1972 upon Lee's advising. She found that she could create a buffer against parental inquisitiveness about her sexuality only by treating homosexuality as an intellectual question, and this was how she justified owning the book to her mother. However, she noted that her mother had griped, "'Why do you feel like you have to own it, why don't you just get it at the library?'"[127] Another sixteen-year-old lesbian complained to Lee in a 1973 letter that she enjoyed virtually no private life. What precipitated this thought was her mother's alarm upon noticing that her daughter had received a magazine about "our kind" in the mail. Her mother regularly "takes my mail and reads it or else she demands to know what I got in some box, etc! My God, I'll be seventeen this Thursday and if she doesn't think I deserve my privacy now then she's really mistaken. It's bad enough she goes through [my sister's and my] room when we're not home. I have to hide everything I don't want to her see."[128] That the central area of parental invasion was mail suggests a distrust of extrafamilial relationships on her mother's part; she wanted to know who was writing to her daughter and what was being said. If her daughter would not own up to this, then going through her daughter's things could become a material and spatial substitute for intimate conversation. But this daughter did not feel she could broach the kinds of personal topics that she could with Lee.

For some, even the question of leading a secret life was simply not on the table. One of Lee's correspondents was forty-eight years old, living alone in a small town in Pennsylvania near her parents' family home. She described the town as a place "where things like this are never mentioned and if they are it is with hate," and said of her family, "I don't think they know about my condition though some may suspect."[129] Here the discussion of being gay was framed with an underlying question of why she was like this in the first place, perhaps as a way to reverse her predicament, and this perception rendered discretion almost irrelevant. She was not asking Lee how to tell her family members but whether or not it was "true [that] conditions like this are caused by the way a person is brought up?"[130]

As an advisor, Lee herself might have reinforced this incompatibility of women's family identities and their gay identities. She felt that lesbian friends could become substitute families of sorts, alleviating the loneliness that many of these correspondents felt characterized the gay life.[131] Lee chastised this forty-eight-year-old correspondent heavily for maintaining such strong ties to her family at her age, which apparently included her parents' picking up her mail for her. "Now that's NONSENSE!" Lee exclaimed. "Don't you think it's time at 48 to start picking up your own mail, and EVEN if NOT, to tell your family that you want privacy?? . . . How about starting to pick up your own mail, for a change, or get your own box, if you share it with your family? . . . YES, YOU PICK YOUR LIFE THE WAY YOU WANT TO LIVE IT."[132] With her twenty-three-year-old correspondent, whom Lee also considered too isolated in rural Utah, Lee was even more unequivocal: "You are . . . no baby; you have two choices[:] either stay in Hicksville, and continue your present lifestyle, or leave Hicksville and live. I'm afraid it's as plain as that. Gay life—much like all life, only more so—requires commitments, and you cannot have your cake (living at home with your folks in their 'nest') and eat it too (living a gay life with gay relationships)."[133] Lee's theme of self-fulfillment over family obligation reverberated with liberationist advice to gays who lived in rural areas with their parents. An advice column in the New York City's *GAY*, a periodical that many considered to be the equivalent of an East Coast *Advocate*, for example, advised a struggling twenty-four-year-old who feared shaming his family in his small town: "The first loyalty you owe is to yourself, not your family or your town."[134]

Nonetheless, those gays who tried to proclaim their family loyalties and their sexuality could face the almost unthinkable circumstance of having to choose between their families and their loves. One young woman wrote to tell of her terrible dilemma of attempting to maintain a lesbian relationship her parents did not condone, while still living with them. This woman had met her girlfriend in nursing school in the New York City area, but she had been asked to leave the school on account of this relationship. Her parents subsequently tried to keep her apart from her girlfriend. She was still working out the logistics of going back to school to complete her degree, and commuting with her girlfriend, when she wrote to Lee in the winter of 1971 that "it'll work out 'cause we love each other so much and nothing's gonna stop it. . . . It's horrible to be so much in love and have to hide it."[135] This woman tried to become somewhat hard-nosed in her family dealings: "I just have to forget I have a family. . . . I have someone who I love and I'm not giving her up. . . . If I don't take this stand now, I'll be forever doomed to a life I would just be existing in."[136] However, in the summer of that same year, she wrote a more desperate-sounding letter. By this point, she had moved back home, on the condition that she never see her girlfriend again. Yet she had been seeing her girlfriend on the sly, and this girlfriend's mother had phoned her family to tell them of the situation. She weighed her predicament by pointing out, "If I leave, they said I wouldn't have any family at all (and you know the family guilt bit)." But the tone in the letter suggests that she did not find the "family guilt bit" a bit at all, but a genuine quandary. She was not worried about having to support herself, "but I can't leave with the guilt feeling on my mind, that I caused so much heartache and pain. So what do I do? . . . [T]here's no way out and I'm helpless in trying to decide. I love [my girlfriend] very much, yet I have a love for my family."[137]

Gays of this era, then, could be just as likely to ascribe themselves with tremendous power with respect to parental feelings: this woman perceived that her sexuality had caused her family heartache and pain, not their own distorted perspective, abetted by an unjust and intolerant society, on homosexuality. Her personal predicament might have been felt as more intensely personal—and painful—without the extra dimension that liberation politics provided to sexuality.

Lacking a political underpinning also left some gays more vulnerable to the ideologies and discourses that informed parental ideas of homosexuality, including, perhaps most powerfully, religion. Though the idea of homosexuality as a sin was being removed from the beliefs of certain denominations during the early 1970s, including some liberal protestant churches such as Unitarianism, this was not the case with all denominations, including the Baptist Church.[138] In a series of fictional works, Larry Duplechan created a black, gay character who came of age in the Baptist Church in Lancaster, California, during this period, named Johnnie Ray Rousseau.[139] The critique of the bourgeois nuclear family certainly did extend into the analysis of nonwhite individuals who had adopted a gay liberation political perspective, balancing a view held by some black power activists that homosexuality was a white man's weakness or illness. Yet the teenager that Duplechan created seemed too young to be attuned to these activist perspectives and debates.[140] His parents in turn did not see him as adapting a white sensibility or disease in being gay. Instead, his incipient gay sexuality clashed with his parents, owing most centrally to their strong faith.

In his novel *Blackbird*, Duplechan portrayed the parents of his protagonist as having a grim, though somewhat histrionic, reaction to their son's homosexuality. Johnnie Ray makes the mistake of confiding his gay feelings to the youth minister at his church who only reveals them to Johnnie's parents. Johnnie comes home one night to find his mother "wearing a look of complete and utter disgust; a look just a scream away from infanticide," and his father "weeping audibly, his massive shoulders shaking with sobs."[141] His mother confronted him first: "You probably think you're real cute . . . with this 'I think I'm a homosexual' crap." She then screamed out, "Lord, ha' mercy today! I don't know what I coulda done to give birth to a per*vert.*"[142] The conversation continues relentlessly in this vein; despite his repeated protests that being gay is something he simply is rather than something he has chosen, his mother insists that he could not love his family, given what he had done to them. These parents enjoin their son to fight his sexual predicament through religion; his mother pronounces with some certainty, " 'Jesus will help you,' " and wondered, " 'Have you asked him? Have you asked the Savior to help you?' "[143] His father adds to the conversation, " '[Y]ou just have to give girls a chance, son.' "[144] Johnnie was left bemused by his parents' solutions, likening his father's advice to the Beatles song "Give Peace a Chance": "All we are say-ing, is give girls a chance."[145] Duplechan's portrait is softened by these kinds of ironic comments, and yet this humor underscores a harrowing family scene, wherein a son had become more than simply alien to his family, but in fact a product of the devil. For gays who came of age in religious contexts, repudiating parental expectations could be a more profound quandary than for those who came out within the secular, more self-conscious ethos of gay liberation.

But the polarities of gay experiences during this period need to be balanced by taking into account that gay liberation, as a culture and politics, was sedimented. Voices of the gay past, like Martin and Lyon, as well as gays who were not expressly involved in the gay political movement, also formed a part of the liberationist sensibility. Though subtle and often only implicit, gay liberation, too, encompassed some of this sense of reverence for the family as an institution, or at least the potential closeness and intimacy that it represented. While neglecting the idea of primal family bonds, liberationists' insistence that their parents strive to understand them suggests its own veneration for companionate family life, an orientation toward the past, and a desire for family permanence. Dick Leitsch suggested this idea in his 1970 article, "Turning on to Daddy," in New York City's *GAY*, where he called for gay liberationists to see "the old guy as a human being." He noted that "youth culture" tended to look to figures such as Paul Goodman, Eldridge Cleaver, Dr. Spock, and Eugene McCarthy as father figures, but the real thing, in one's own family, deserved a chance. While observing that many "sons are basically strangers to their fathers," he still felt that "many of them are probably very groovy, even if they are over 30."[146] Dick Leitsch was by then the militant president of the New York Mattachine Society, sensitive to both a gay liberation perspective and the homophile one that preceded it.[147] Moreover, *GAY* supported the more moderate offshoot of the Gay Liberation Front, the Gay Activists' Alliance, or GAA, which advocated civil disobedience and "zap" actions, as opposed to revolution.[148] In his role at *GAY*, Leitsch had criticized the younger generation of gay liberation activists for their lack of historical perspective in gay activism; here this criticism took the form of what he saw as their shortsighted inhibitions regarding the entire older generation.

While the testimonies and portraits at the expense of mothers and fathers were at times scathing in these liberation era sources, the tremendous outpouring of support and respect for parents who were understanding and "groovy" about gayness in many of these same sources also indicates a yearning for parental love and understanding even during some of the most radical moments in gay political history. Gay liberationist periodicals in fact heaped praise upon parents who fought for their gay children's rights and gave extensive coverage to the early formations of what was to become the Parents, Families, and Friends of Lesbians and Gays (PFLAG) movement.[149]

To be sure, understanding from one's own peers was prized more highly within gay liberation culture than the understanding of outsiders, even these generous and tolerant members of PFLAG. If one desire seems to characterize gay liberation communities during these years, it is a desire to have the affirmation of an individual who has faced similar experiences: a sense of identification perhaps more than a sense of abstract empathy. The circulation of personal experiences and confessional stories that were so prominent in the gay liberation movement, as well as in other social movements, displaced, to a certain extent, the imaginative realms of sympathizing with another's experience at the same time as they sought to reinforce them. In effect, these movements did not ask individuals to sympathize with the lives of others but to tell their own stories. This longing for identification in fact illuminates some of the cleavages within gay liberation itself. For example, many lesbians observed the sexism of gay males who seemed to lack an understanding of what it meant to be a lesbian and called for a more specific lesbian feminist perspective.[150] In turn, many nonwhite gays noticed the insensitivities of a predominantly white gay liberation movement to race-specific issues, including the perhaps even greater burdens that they faced in coming out to their parents.[151] Separatism within gay liberation as an organizing strategy might have been pursued in order to feel a greater sense of mutual identification. Yet this identification and compassion were craved not just from political or chosen peer "families" but from parents and original families as well.

Within the family and outside of it, liberationists felt that the means to gay political consciousness, not to mention individual happiness, was by being public about inner lives. Collisions with parents on the basis of political ideas and trends might have provided gays in this period and in succeeding years with a means of opening up the family forum to sexual politics, and then talking to parents about intimate matters outside of the explicit realm of politics. They increasingly felt that what gays owed their parents was revelation, not decorum—for the sake of family intimacy, the expression of an authentic self, and even the rectification of the inhibitions of daily life. In turn, parents owed their children an intimacy in the form of truly knowing them. As historian, writer, and gay liberation activist Martin Duberman expressed so elegiacally in *Midlife Queer: Biography of a Decade, 1971–81*, upon his mother's death in 1977, "[O]ur entangled relationship had never gotten worked through; the emotional bond remained powerful but subterranean, felt but avoided." During his teen years, he had "stopped telling her anything important about myself. I didn't want to risk getting near the subject of my homosexuality and, more encompassingly, had grown to resent her intrusive, engulfing ways; to her onslaught of questions, I had returned monosyllabic replies." When Duberman realized his mother was dying, he "kept thinking we would, we must, have that final talk that would erase the long-standing tension and leave the love, uncontaminated, intact. But as is so often the way, that final talk never took place."[152]

Perhaps many gay liberationists, too, were motivated by a need for a final talk, hoping for it even within their daily family lives. The phrase "yet I have a love for my family" was not limited to the young lesbian, struggling at once to maintain her family and lesbian relationship, who expressed it so sorrowfully. There was an implicit "yet" at the heart of gay liberation culture.

3

What's Wrong with the Boys Nowadays?

THE GAY LIBERATION MOVEMENT marked a moment of hope that gay individuals would no longer just be faintly—or even pruriently—imagined figures in North American life. Insisting upon the recognition of a knowable gay self, liberation thinkers and writers sought to demystify gay sexuality and in turn urge a rethinking of ideas of personal and familial intimacy. By the 1970s, these alternative imaginings were transforming into a distinctive gay culture of intimacy, with coming-out rituals, writings, art, and street theater.

Lesbian writers and activists had embraced this emerging culture under the auspices of the gay liberation movement, which did attempt to represent both gay men and women. But many lesbians would come to feel that the gay liberation movement was dominated by the interests and needs of gay men, just as the feminist movement seemed dominated by the interests and needs of heterosexual women. One response of politically engaged lesbians was to set themselves apart by fashioning a lesbian feminist movement.[1] Thinkers and writers within this movement suggested that lesbianism was a logical, or at least a possible, outcome of feminism and that the two were basically intertwined. An outpouring of lesbian feminist writing and publications emerged during the early 1970s and continued into the early 1980s. Like gay liberation, the movement existed in tandem with other lesbian voices that highlight the braided tenor of lesbian experiences during this period.

As lesbian feminists problematized the borders between friendship, love, and sexuality, they also developed distinctive, generational ideas of selfhood and the relation of the self to others. As with the case of gay liberationists and the counterculture, lesbian writers and activists questioned the authorities in their childhoods and in their pasts, especially their parents, and their views on gender roles, sexuality, and emotional expression. Lesbian poet and scholar Minnie Bruce Pratt recalled a profound sense of having been lied to throughout her life, particularly as a young white southerner coming of age in the 1950s, given her realization that what the adults in her life had told her, especially about race but also about gender and sexuality, was so glaringly wrong. Her response was not just to reject the authorities in her midst but to make an authority of herself and extensively document her thoughts and experiences. This response was not unique to Pratt, however. Lesbian archivists have noted the need for preservation of women's lives so that lesbian stories were told by themselves rather than by medical, legal, religious observers or other experts.[2]

For some cultural critics, though, this emphasis on self-authority was not genuinely introspective or ethical but another example of a ubiquitous therapeutic culture, permeated with narcissism or massive self-absorption, particularly pervasive in the United States in the 1970s given the disenchantment that some observers felt with 1960s forms of radicalism. Elisabeth Lasch-Quinn has argued that the larger shift away from a religious to a psychological sensibility, charted by critics such as Philip Rieff in the *Triumph of the Therapeutic* (1966), had promoted "a belief in the primacy of personal authenticity, now associated with emotional disclosure."[3] According to her, when social movements like black civil rights lost hope in changing politics or economics in the external world, they retreated to seek psychic solace or self-help. In doing so, a therapeutic conception of the self triumphed over the idea of being a citizen.[4] But these critiques about narcissism neglect a vision of civil rights as an internal or an emotional one. Literary critic Lauren Berlant has characterized feminism as sometimes a "vehicle for the imaginative refusal of what in intimate and political life has not worked for women."[5] It is difficult to evaluate lesbian feminism in particular as a civil rights movement that was strictly interested in political or economic change or redress for injustices in those realms. Lesbian activists and writers sought a sense of intimate redress from society—including their parents—about experiences of emotional alienation.

The pronouncement of narcissism, an-all encompassing critique of the 1970s as an epoch, in fact dovetailed with how parents interpreted their daughters' lesbianism at this moment.[6] But this was not the only point of contention between lesbians and their parents. Unlike the narcissist caricature in these academic critiques that was incapable of analyzing the past, lesbian daughters were keenly attuned to the past, especially through their relationships with their mothers.[7] The debates between lesbian daughters and their heterosexual parents could even be said to exhibit, at a family level, some of the tensions and uncertainties within heterosexuality during these years, including both the hope—and the fear—that the distinction between heterosexuality and homosexuality was withering away. When lesbian daughters sought a revision of the very notions of women's life course and "nature" that presumed heterosexuality, they again disrupted the potential for commonality between them and the older generation, particularly their mothers. These family standoffs and exchanges illuminate a generational cleavage about the very purpose of relationships in women's lives, about the role of ideology within the intimate sphere, and what it meant to love. Contentious as these discussions were, it was as though companionate family styles actually resonated with what many lesbian daughters were seeking from their parents, especially a knowledge and understanding of their personal lives and choices.

Parents had to contend with lesbian writers and activists who articulated heterosexuality as an ideology, an institution, and a culture rather than an intimate imperative or conscious choice. Outside of the family context, this critique had provoked a split with the mainstream feminist movement and heterosexual women activists who did not necessarily see a lesbian feminist challenge as central to their aims. In the American context, the feminist movement did not accommodate lesbians at first. In 1970, Betty Friedan, president of NOW, the National Organization of Women, referred to the lesbian platform as the "lavender menace," suggesting that lesbians would hamper the movement and taint its publicity. This stance prompted the New York City collective, Radicalesbians, to issue a manifesto of lesbian feminist politics, titled *The Woman-Identified Woman*, which suggested that lesbians were crucial to feminism rather than peripheral, because it was lesbians who were uprooting patriarchy in not having relationships with men. This tract affirmed the idea of lesbianism as a subversive act: "Our energies must flow toward our sisters, not backward to our oppressors."[8]

As a political movement and culture, however, lesbian feminism had many different ideological strains and imperatives. Some of these did align with the goals of women's liberation.[9] Themes of legal, political, and workplace rights, for example, resonated with lesbian women no less than with heterosexual women. Lesbian theorist Charlotte Bunch has suggested that the issue that best symbolized the intersection between the interests of the women's movement and lesbian feminists was the individual's right to control her own body and thus her sexuality.[10] While women's liberation sought an increased public presence for women in the labor force and politics, it was also attentive to politicizing personal issues such as child care, birth control, and domestic labor. The expansion of women's choices in public and domestic arenas alike might have suggested some choice in the arena of sexuality, as well. Not only could women choose whether to get married, have a baby, or take a paid job, but they could also choose whether they even wanted to be heterosexual.[11] Moreover, women's liberation was attuned to women on a psychological level in its pursuit of more equitable personal relationships as well as less rigid gender roles, and these were vital concerns of lesbians.[12] As historians Verta Taylor and Leila Rupp have noted, many women came out as lesbians within the radical branch of the women's movement, which located women's oppression in a complex system of male domination.[13] But lesbianism also mingled with cultural feminism and its emphasis that women's culture and values were different from those of men and potentially more loving and pacifist.[14] In this vein, lesbian separatists conceived of a Lesbian Nation, with a distinctive women's economy, institutions, values, and music and writing culture.[15]

Perhaps the most provocative suggestion that lesbian feminists would make during the 1970s, however, was that if women felt drawn to their women friends they could be open to having sexual intimacy with them as well, an idea that for some scholars revived nineteenth-century women's romantic friendships.[16] As Adrienne Rich would write in a pathbreaking essay in 1980, heterosexuality was a cultural presumption, and women were conditioned into it without realizing that they might be able to choose to have loving, and sexual, relationships with women.[17] This way of thinking marked a fundamental break from any notion of innateness or inner compulsion in being lesbian.

Thus lesbian feminists had recast the idea of sexual orientation as an idea of sexual preference. This was reinforced by widely published testimonies from women about their sexuality and new research into women's sexuality during the early years of the 1970s that primarily sought to provide feminist alternatives to psychoanalysis.[18] At a more political level, research into women's sexuality was taken up to suggest that women could easily have sexual satisfaction without men. In her influential 1970 essay

"The Myth of the Vaginal Orgasm," Anne Koedt argued that women were better acquainted with each other's bodies and could potentially have more fulfilling relationships with each other than they could with men, an idea also suggested in what would become a best-selling feminist self-help book on women's health issues, *Our Bodies, Ourselves*, in 1973.[19]

This emerging impetus toward the disclosure of women's experiences—in both their sensuous and their emotional aspects—would also provide a context for lesbian revelations at the family level. Ironically, the idea of choice about sexuality provided a way for parents to contemplate—and often reject—the idea of their daughters as lesbians. If lesbianism was the practice to the theory of feminism, parents could urge their daughters to just stop practicing it.[20]

Such clashes between lesbians and their mothers in particular had themselves become popular items represented in North American lesbian feminist culture by the early 1970s.[21] Lesbian creative writing had been spurred on by the success of Rita Mae Brown's semiautobiographical lesbian coming-out story, *Rubyfruit Jungle*, first published in 1973. As of 1974, lesbian presses such as Naiad in Florida had started publishing lesbian literature at an unprecedented rate. Bonnie Zimmerman notes that, between 1977 and 1982, seven anthologies were published with lesbian first-person narratives, and these became part of a larger group of works that included lesbian feminist theory, music, and poetry.[22] In addition, lesbian periodicals became a central venue for personal writing. By 1975, there were roughly fifty lesbian periodicals with a circulation of about 50,000, many of which were published by lesbian collectives.[23] Most sought to valorize lesbian women's personal experiences and their creative sides, as well as provide analysis: they solicited journal entries, personal essays, poetry, letters, and book reviews.[24] Rejecting a conception of creativity that emphasized literary skill and technique, the editors sought a more authentic, raw, and unfiltered account of women's lives and stories, perhaps believing there was inherent creativity in relating a coming-out story.[25] These writings affirmed the status of simply telling one's story as art. Christine Stansell has noted that bohemian radicals in the 1910s talked about sex in such self-dramatizing ways that it was easy for it to be imagined onstage. Late twentieth-century lesbian culture deeply prized the honesty and rawness of a personal story and shaped a culture around its recounting.[26]

Lesbian anthropologist Ellen Lewin has noted that women's coming-out stories are more often concerned with aspects of intimacy and the choice of being lesbian, while men's seem more concerned with formative sexual experiences.[27] The coming-out letter during this period is a vital source for understanding these themes of intimacy, and particularly when they appeared in lesbian feminist periodicals, the political implications of being a lesbian.[28] In an issue of New York City's *Dyke* in 1976, one correspondent praised the periodical for the forum it had given to these letters: "It's so important for Lezzies to share the games played on us—and our mothers are a biggie—their hold can be so strong and subtle on the Dyke Daughter."[29]

"Linda" was one woman to donate a correspondence between her and her mother for publication. In 1974, she was a young, recently divorced lesbian from Niagara Falls, New York, living in Toronto and trying to make a career of being a painter. She gave the Toronto periodical the *Other Woman* a copy of a letter her mother had sent her, in response to Linda's coming out.[30] Her mother did not waste much time in giving her opinion on her daughter's "present situation," as she called it. "I think it stinks," she said. "I think you are making a big mistake—one which could affect your entire future. Look at this thing honestly, Linda. Is this really what you want of life?" Her mother claimed that she had "taken into account your disappointment and loneliness since the failure of your marriage—I suffer for you—believe me, but lesbianism is not the answer." If lesbianism was something Linda pursued on account of disappointment with men, her mother tried to talk up heterosexuality: "Men really aren't all that bad. I've known a few good ones in my time. They will be as bad or as good as you let them. . . . They are lovable and desirable with all their faults and very necessary in the scheme of things." She went on to declare that the "women in my family have always been liberated. This they gained through various methods—the most likely and obvious were probably in this order: good cooks, sense of humor, good housekeeping, and willing bed partners." While perhaps it might have been heartening for Linda to hear her mother enumerate "willing bed partner" as last on the list, her mother did not endear herself to her feminist daughter when she closed with, "the girls of today are their own worst enemy [who] let this sex freedom idea take over where their good sense used to be. . . . Please, Linda, come to your good senses and start thinking of a more normal life for yourself. Love, Mom."

Linda's mother was not done after signing off, however. In a postscript, she added: "A person has to be a person, true—but one has to fit into the accepted pattern or social structure to be really accepted into society as a

whole and that's what it's all about, isn't it? How can you be happy existing
in the fringes of society—being laughed at, mocked at, and insulted—that's
how it is where you're looking for happiness." And finally, in a post-postscript,
Linda's mother spoke on behalf of her husband: "I just have not had the
heart to let your father read the letter you sent me. You will have to tell
him yourself if you want him to know. Heart attack? No—but how about
Heart break?"[31]

Linda's mother spoke not only for her husband but for generations of
women in her family and for the patterns of empowerment within heterosexual marriages that, in her view, had served them all well. Her rendition
of power within her family and over her man is reminiscent of the subtle
technique of emotional manipulation that sociologists of the 1950s such as
Talcott Parsons had uncovered for women in families.[32] She seemed to suggest an enjoyable challenge in reforming or civilizing a husband, as though
lesbians were simply making too many demands for psychological compati-
bility on their male partners. The very fact that she felt she could sway her
daughter with the positive aspects of a heterosexual relationship indicates
that Linda's mother did not perceive her daughter's sexuality to be final or
unwavering. Linda came out to her mother through a specific lesbian politics, and her mother, accordingly, argued with her daughter on the basis of
ideas—the nature of men and marriage, sexual liberation, and nonconformity. It is not being lesbian that became the source of rupture, but choosing
it as "the answer" to a failed marriage or pursuing it as an aspect of feminism. The very nature of this revelation illuminates a particular generational conception of lesbianism: while lesbians of a previous era might have
viewed a disclosure of sexuality as a plea for self-knowledge, lesbian feminism during this era also articulated political commitments and an investment in self-identification.

Linda's response, perhaps tailored for its appearance in this feminist
publication, was indignant about her mother's blunt suggestion that being
a lesbian "stinks," and she was equally blunt in her response. "I don't think
Lesbianism 'stinks' at all," she said. "I think men stink." She believed that
she had never been "better . . . since I stopped thinking I had to impress
men." Being with women had "doubled [her] self-confidence," because
relationships with women did not "compromise" her the way her relationships with men had. She would not "waste any more time, energy, or love
on people who won't believe I am an equal human being. My faith is with
my sisters." In her sign-off she reiterated, "No, I don't think this 'stinks' at

all. I think it shows that love is not dead in this world. It lives on in *women loving each other*. Love, Linda."[33]

Ironically, Linda's mother's suggestion that sexual liberation had some contradictory effects and had actually hurt women was perhaps an implicit point of her daughter's, in the sense she conveyed of feeling "compromised" in her relationships with men. As affronted as Linda was by her mother's response, she did not appear to find her mother's presumption that Linda sought out lesbianism as an antidote to negative experiences with men offensive. It was more that she wanted to clarify why she could not be with men and still be an artist. In her claim of greater independence through lesbian sexuality, Linda exemplifies broader feelings of women's dissatisfactions and yearnings during these years, even in the wake of egalitarian social movements. Some women who had participated in New Left political organizing, for example, had noticed a profound contradiction between the egalitarian rhetoric that men within the movement had espoused and their actions. For many women, a more liberated sexual environment meant that they had lost the right to say no. A protest against this sexual exploitation was widely articulated in feminist arenas, both lesbian and heterosexual, for example in such works as Marge Piercey's popular novel *Small Changes*.[34] In fact, some otherwise heterosexual women became willing to consider lesbianism as an alternative to these "liberated" articulations of heterosexuality.[35]

Of course, Linda's mother probably also meant the "sex freedom idea" to refer to the very idea of becoming a lesbian. On this point, mother and daughter reflect differing judgments of happiness in women's lives. Her daughter's assessment of utopian possibilities for relationships between women contrasted starkly with her mother's acceptance of given realities. This sense was not unique to heterosexual women of her generation, but perhaps to some lesbian women in the same generation as well. One woman wrote to the Boston Women's Health Book Collective upon the publication of *Our Bodies, Ourselves* that she was a lesbian woman married to a man, a faculty member in a college in a rural town. She was quite secretive about her sexuality and did not "like being this 'un-free.' But I am fifty, have knowingly made my decisions and my choices. Perhaps sometime in the future I may choose differently and be willing to stand up and be counted. In the meantime, I will just support my homosexual friends . . . as best I can and accept [that] my own life cannot be as full and fulfilling as I would [like] it to be."[36] For heterosexual women, this acceptance of a given order actually might have included some degree of hierar-chy between men and women. The camaraderie that Linda suggested with her "sisters" might not have been easy for her mother to understand, given a greater sense of reticence on the part of women about their dissatisfac-tions—if indeed they had perceived them as such—throughout the earlier postwar period. As lesbian feminist writer Audre Lorde noted in her mem-oir, *Zami*, it seemed to her that "gay girls were the . . . only women who were even talking to each other [during] the 1950s."[37] Thus an extra burden to the barriers in communication and understanding between mothers and daughters during this period also might have been, in addition to ideas about the purpose of relationships, simply the ways these relationships got expressed. During this period, consciousness-raising methods that valued the sharing and analyzing of personal experiences between women as a vital part of political awareness shaped the language surrounding women's intimacy.[38] The deliberate, self-conscious language surrounding "sister-hood" might have seemed affected or overly ideological to their mothers.

However, if lesbian writers placed sexuality within the realm of choice and reason rather than nature, parents might feel that they could reason their daughters out of it. Such was the tactic taken up by the parents of a lesbian poet during this period. Like Linda's mother, her parents could see little point in choosing to become a lesbian unless a woman, through a hapless soul and biology, had to be one. Having grown up in the United States, this poet was living abroad throughout her thirties, during the 1970s, and becoming an active international feminist. She would go on to write several collections of poetry in the 1970s and 1980s. Her parents, both college professors, wrote letters to her there, discussing her writing career, their hope that she would attend grad school eventually, her sister and nephew, as well as their daughter's ideas about lesbian feminism. She was insistent that her parents try to understand her and her poetry, which con-tained her ideas about loving women and its feminist implications.

This lesbian poet was quite forthright with her parents about her choice to become a lesbian. Writing to her in 1975, her father conceded that his daughter had made "a strong case for [her] point of view" on this choice, yet his "unaltered [*sic*] conviction [was] that the path you are on leads to a dead end. I do not suggest that, for a woman, heterosexual marriage is the only goal"; however, he was suggesting that "heterosexual, monogamous marriage . . . despite aberrations, exceptions, failures, heartaches and bumps in the road . . . still leads to the greatest good."[39] This evocation of marriage failures did not offer a ringing endorsement of heterosexuality and was reminiscent of Linda's mother's comment that men were not "all that bad." Nonetheless, he portrayed heterosexuality as a necessary, natural life course whose good could not be simply disregarded.

Her mother's letters on the matter of choice, however, were more ambivalent, suggesting an awareness of lesbianism as a possibility for women even on the part of an unambiguously heterosexual woman who had raised her children during the war and immediate postwar period. Her mother watched as her daughter wrote poetry for lesbian magazines and became more involved with an international lesbian movement during the 1970s. In a letter of 1975, her mother wrote to say that she was "concerned" with her "daughter's new interests." In her view, "if some women prefer sexual relations with women they are entitled to do what they please. That is their misfortune in a world where the norm of mature people is hetero-sexual." She seemed to ascribe to a Freudian view of mature heterosexual-ity; homosexuality might be a life stage, but one exclusively for the young. Perhaps this conception refers directly to sexual acts themselves, as though mature sex was heterosexual, while everything else was simply cuddling.[40] She even admitted that she herself "[a]t the age of 11 . . . was in love with a girl of 13. But most of us grow up and discover that this is not the way the world goes round."[41] Thus she did not call her daughter's sexuality into question so much as her adulthood. That she lacked some notion of an idealized love that transcended gender perhaps indicates the degree to which these popularized Freudian ideas, which documented and legiti-mized a youthful lesbian stage, had taken firm roots, pervading the thinking of women's own life histories about same-sex attractions.[42] According to this mother, "if people are gaited that way, OK—that is their business. But I can't see why anyone would want to cultivate it. It is one thing to like, be friends with, and work with women. It is quite another to spend wild, wet nights with them." This mother's prurient, voyeuristic depiction of lesbians suggests that, for her, the sexual was not an extension of the closeness of the intense friendships that she herself had enjoyed. The sexual was more a matter of "being gaited that way," a matter of biology, which almost seemed to spoil that intimacy, by taking it to the "wild, wet" level. As far as her daughter's making this choice in her life, "I *would* want to talk about it," her mother affirmed.[43]

Part of the lesbian feminist challenge to dominant heterosexuality, how-ever, was to provide an awareness of love relationships that were on the

borders of heterosexuality: to see the importance of the relationships with
mothers and to see the vitality of friendship as a form of love, for example.
Somewhat contradictorily, this mother also understood this point from her
daughter, and she too was aware of the possibility of love between women.
In another letter in 1975, her mother conceded that "[t]heoretically" her
daughter "may be quite right" about lesbianism's being a more satisfying
option than heterosexuality for women to pursue. She discussed watching
a program on George Sand on public television where Sand was portrayed
as having had a mutually enhancing relationship with actress Marie Dorval.
This heterosexual mother was even willing to admit that "love is love
regardless of sex."

Yet her objections to lesbianism reveal a conception of life choice that
was more realistic and less sentimental, as well as more static and less experimental, than her daughter's. Despite appreciating this relationship between
women, and perhaps the social ease between women, she could "see no
point and much harm in your cultivating [lesbianism]. Life is hard enough
without complicating it." Like Linda's mother, she identified her primary
worry as her daughter's welfare. This mother's mind had a commonsense
and practical bent. She herself had not pursued a conventional path, as she
eventually pursued a Ph.D. Nonetheless she seemed shaped by a pragmatic
sensibility characteristic of the Depression and World War II era. The care-
fulness and vigilance of those times, including the senses of self-discipline,
self-sacrifice, and delayed gratification, might have been sensibilities that
she applied to all areas of life, including feelings.[44] The pursuit of choice in
the sexual arena might have seemed fanciful to her, or self-indulgent, an
artificial choice. When her daughter suggested that her mother might be
"personally somewhat frightened by the idea of lesbianism for yourself,"
her mother wanted to clarify that this was not the case, even subconsciously.[45] "I am not at all frightened about lesbianism for myself," she said.
"I never considered it and never will."[46]

Her daughter even cast herself as potentially more self-examined than
her mother in her lesbianism, proposing an emotional scheme for all
women that rejected heterosexuality as narrow-mindedness. She felt that
her own "feminist evolution" had caused her to "re-evaluate [her] past
life," realizing "things I had been refusing to see before about my previous
relationships."[47] Her feminism allowed for a huge continuum of women's
relationships, including "little old maiden ladies living together in previous
centuries in tranquil spinsterhood." She then pronounced that "*any woman*

can love other women," echoing a broader impetus among lesbian feminists to reclaim examples of lesbianism throughout history and assert a universal quality to lesbian love.[48] She expressed her choice as an emotional preference, not primarily a sexual one, perhaps owing to a larger lesbian feminist effort to remove lesbianism from the realm of voyeurism or pathology.[49] She even considered the relationship between mother and daughter to be inherently lesbian: "The only difference between lesbian lovers and a close mother/daughter is the part of the body they touch."[50]

Given these stances, her mother might have found her daughter proposing a confusing new order to the classification of relationships, feelings, and sexuality: How could one now distinguish between a sexual and a nonsexual relationship? Was it all simply a matter of intention, like an artist who declares an object art?[51] There is an intriguing synchronicity in this period between the kinds of conceptual art flourishing in the art world and the intentionality and rationality that gays, especially lesbians, ascribed to intimate relationships, as though these, and gay identities, were ever-evolving art forms themselves. Self-conscious experimentalism as demeanor in either art or personal relationships was not new to this era, and yet the merging of these two realms of experimentation does appear unique to the late twentieth century. Did one simply choose things now that used to be—or at least seemed to be—a matter of objective nature? Philosopher Martha Nussbaum has argued for a concept of emotions that have intelligence and intentionality and are not just "of the body."[52] Perhaps the poet's mother even felt a degree of uneasiness about having the leisure or the luxury of even thinking about such obligatory or self-evident areas of life as choices.

That lesbianism was an appealing theoretical idea that should remain in the realm of theory was a stance that seemed particularly illogical in mothers who had affective relationships with women but sexual ones with men. In 1973, a high school lesbian told Julie Lee, the lesbian counselor of the New Jersey DOB, that, upon her revelation of lesbianism, her mother said that she was "rushing things" and had plenty of time when it came to dating and sex.[53] While not advocating a lesbian relationship, her mother did not think that "lesbians are child molesters [sic] or crazy or *anything* like that at all." This mother would have preferred her daughter to "be straight." Yet, "as people, she thinks more of women than of men. She has told me many times she thinks they are better than men."[54] Even if this mother could understand emotional love and intimacy with other women, she most emphatically was not "attracted to women sexually. She says it's fine for women to love other women, but not in that way."[55] This mother appeared to separate sexual and emotional needs, proposing that women could get emotional but not sexual satisfaction from women friends, a prescription that lesbian feminism had attempted to complicate.

Sympathetic to lesbianism in the abstract, yet hostile to it when it played out in their daughters' lives, mothers during this period seemed concerned not simply with social censure but with a desire to maintain the boundaries surrounding platonic and sexual relationships as they had known them. Nancy Garden, a children's and teen literature writer whose books often dealt with gay relationships and homophobia, gave a portrait of this kind of mother-daughter conflict in her 1982 young adult book, *Annie on My Mind*. Her protagonist, Liza, and her friend Annie were involved in a scandal of making out at the household of one of their teachers, where they were supposed to be looking after the cat. Annie's mother brought the matter to the table by telling her a story of her own close friend when she was younger. She told her daughter that she and her friend had "loved each other very much" and then "blush[ed]" to reveal that one night when she slept in her friend's bed "we kissed each other. And then for a while we pretended one of us was a boy."[56] She assured her daughter that lots of girls did this kind of thing, and "it's normal to experiment." She then asked her daughter, in a more foreboding way, if there had been any more than the "usual experimenting" between her and Annie.[57] She was relieved when her daughter, lying, told her that there had not been. But this mother character never did say what exactly "the usual experimenting" entails. In this portrait, only experimental sex between women could be tolerated because it was seen, to a large degree, as adolescent play.

These vague parental depictions of lesbian sexuality speak to perhaps a larger vagueness about what a lesbian even was. Although lesbian feminism had insisted upon its validity as a movement alongside gay liberation, perhaps neither of these movements was widely known as such to the public. At the level of innuendo, it was gay men who were more a part of the public imagination than gay women, even throughout the liberation period. A 1967 documentary film produced for CBS television, *The Homosexuals*, for example, dealt solely with gay men, especially their perceived "promiscuity" and cruising habits. There was scarcely a mention of a gay woman.[58] In a feature on the family in *Look* magazine in 1971, a gay male couple was included, but they were there as a counterpoint to images of gay men who had "one-night stands in bathhouses, public toilets, or gay bars."[59]

For some parents, too, the gay male experience—or what they imagined it to be—became a template for lesbian experiences, especially in the sexual realm. This might have been particularly the case for those lesbians who came out to their parents without the additional perspective of feminism. In 1973, one teenager had hinted to her parents that she was gay and then wrote to Julie Lee, distraught, because her father called gay people "queers. He also says they are sick, and that they 'stake out their victims,' such as me, or young girls like me, to convert them." This myth of recruitment was deeply engrained in early postwar culture, though it usually exploited the sexuality of gay men.[60] And this father was indeed talking about stereotypical gay men, while warning his daughter away from older women. "My dad just loves to mimic gay people," this young woman noted, "the swish, the wrist-flapping, high-pitched voice, and all."[61] Another teenager claimed that her mother had asked her if "a few minutes of sexual gratification [were] worth being rejected by society?"[62] This image of gay sexuality as quick gratification was quite different from what lesbian feminists in particular had evoked in their emotional emphasis on love, but the image that many parents clung to was one of gay promiscuity and chance encounters that they imagined to be the province of gay men. Parental homophobia about gay men could thus play out in their daughters' lives. Some parents appeared to lose sight of their daughters as individuals and, when faced with a gay revelation, simply viewed them as part of a generic gay story.

What might have been clearer than lesbian sexuality to parents was simply the idea that lesbianism tarnished their daughter's womanhood. Indeed, for some parents, heterosexuality was a matter of effort and a kind of accomplishment. Thus even heterosexuality's downside—such as unwanted pregnancy—could be considered a relief in the face of lesbianism. Writer Judith Katz's mother felt this way. In 1972, Katz made the trip to her hometown of Worcester, Massachusetts, to tell her parents that an article about her appearing in her college newspaper at the University of Massachusetts would reveal that she was a lesbian. Because the revelatory article was about Katz as well as a prominent Massachusetts abortionist of this period who had been invited to speak at the university, Katz introduced the topic gingerly, first telling her parents that the article was about her and the abortionist. To this, her mother said, "The abortionist? You didn't have an abortion?" Katz detected some "hopeful" excitement in her mother's voice in asking this question. When Katz denied this firmly, her mother asked, "Are you pregnant?" with "[a]gain . . . a glimmer of hope in her voice."[63] After her disclosure, and her father's lament that he wanted nothing more than to give his daughter a wedding, Katz protested that she had never, in all her life, had a boyfriend, and so being a lesbian should not have come as a real surprise. Her mother pointed out, however, that her daughter "never tried very hard either," indicating that for her heterosexuality was a matter of effort, ability, and competence, something she had achieved and her daughter had not. Finally Mrs. Katz pronounced, "I want you to know . . . this is not my fault."[64] If heterosexuality was not precisely a virtue to this mother, it was at least a skill; having a lesbian daughter was perhaps a comment on this mother's failure to pass down a vital skill.

Mothers also fretted about a perceived lesbian assault on femininity. Penny House, editor of the lesbian separatist periodical *Dyke*, suggested that her mother's opposition to lesbianism stemmed most centrally from anxieties about her daughter's appearance. Challenging women's sexual objectification and rigid ideas of attractiveness, some lesbian feminists had in fact embraced a more unisexual look, rejecting not only the artifices of women in heterosexual culture but also the perceived artifices of gay culture, such as butch/femme appearances.[65] Penny House and the *Dyke* periodical, produced by a New York City collective, were no exceptions; this periodical explicitly eschewed makeup, long hair, feminine accoutrements, and clothing.[66]

In 1976, House donated her correspondence with her mother to *Dyke*. She included a letter in which her mother said that being a lesbian made her daughter "only *partially* a woman, and not a whole one." Mrs. House firmly believed that her daughter needed to look after the aesthetic aspects of her womanhood. She clarified that it was not her daughter's shapeless, sloppy clothes that distressed her, but "what seemed to me as your contempt for your own body: not what society calls feminine, but what nature, God . . . genes, hormones, etc. has determined for you, a woman's body." Her mother pointed out that her daughter's body was "born as a woman, to be lived as a woman (short of going to Dr. Money at Johns Hopkins)."[67] This reference to a doctor who performed sex reassignment surgery during these years suggests that she aligned her daughter's femininity with a sense of biology. Her daughter was therefore simply "hurting your own self, your birthright" by defiling the beauty of nature. She was not sure what offended her most about her daughter's "ambience": "Perhaps it's your weight, perhaps it's the cropping of your beautiful hair, or pushing down your breasts . . . the muscles unsupported [by a brassiere] will make them sag more and more." Whatever it was, this mother insisted that her objection had nothing to do with "fashion magazines" or "social habits" but instead "deep *self-respect*. . . . If Lesbianism is a celebration of womanhood, celebrate it!"[68]

Mrs. House's objections perhaps reflect the prominence and importance that physical beauty held for the mothers of the baby boom generation, as though not to cultivate beauty would be to curtail one's life opportunities. In the midst of feminist revisions to women's appearances during this period, social and literary critic Diana Trilling claimed that women of her generation, who came of age in the 1930s, had been made to think that "you had to conform to some impossible standard of advertising beauty in order to be in the running at all" for a sexual relationship. She noted that it was "wonderful . . . for us to be living in a period in which Dostoevski's statement that there was no such thing as an ugly woman was at last coming true."[69]

Penny House, however, might have been attempting to explore new possibilities for personhood and femininity by assuming a style and a body type that were in fact specifically intended to avert the male gaze, a strategy within white, middle-class lesbian feminist communities during this time period in particular.[70] At the very moment that this daughter thought she was being particularly honest and uncovering a truer self, or at least a truer embodied experience, than what her "birthright" allowed, her mother in some sense accused her of affectation.[71] The emphasis Mrs. House placed on her daughter's appearance and womanhood also suggests that lesbianism would not have been such a problem to her if it *had* involved a celebration of a more conventional femininity, including an emphasis on hair, body image, undergarments, and beauty. In a powerful way, the daughters of this generation seemed to represent a fantasy self, or a more beautiful self, than their mothers. By discarding a maternal fantasy of femininity, lesbian daughters appeared to be dashing parental hope.

For other mothers, this disavowal of femininity was a part of what they considered an affected rhetoric and public performance of the feminist movement more broadly. Like other intellectual women of her generation, the lesbian poet's mother often felt sympathetic with the intentions and some of the ideas of the feminist movement, but not so much with its rhetoric and symbols.[72] In fact, this mother was wary of any ideology or dogma, perhaps a generational sensibility that took shape for her, owing to the disillusionment with ideology that many intellectuals experienced during the 1930s and 1940s, in the wake of totalitarianism.[73] Fiercely protective

of private life, the mother felt that her daughter was allowing the politicization of emotions through the intrusion of ideology into the private realm.
Independent minded and individualistic, she told her daughter that it was
"highly unlikely" that she would "get into any 'movement,'" feminist or
otherwise.[74] In 1975 she wrote to her daughter to discuss a *New York Times*
article that fretted that the "strident voices" within the women's movement
were undermining efforts to pass the equal rights amendment. She affirmed
that "[t]he reason I can't get myself to work with the women's movement
is because of those 'strident voices.' Going without a bra when you need
one, and letting the hair grow on your chin when it looks ugly, and speaking rudely/sharply when you want to make a statement, turn people like
me off from active participation in a movement that I really believe can be
important."[75]

This concern over appearance and comportment shaped how she
viewed prominent figures within the feminist movement, and by extension
her daughter as well. Upon attending a guest lecture at her university in
1975 by lesbian writer and antipornography activist Andrea Dworkin, this
mother confided that, had her daughter not insisted that her mother pay
close attention to her ideas, she would have dismissed Dworkin as a "fat,
outlandishly dressed young woman. She wore denim overalls—the kind
you might look charming in with a size 7 or so—and a fluffy pink . . .
blouse. Her hair was [a] long and careless 'Afro,' as though she didn't give
a hoot about appearance."[76] For this mother, appearance was certainly not
a simple matter of vanity or an instance of the oppression of women; rather,
it was an obligation, or as Alice Munro put it, a kind of housekeeping.[77]
This interpretation was at odds with her daughter's view of beautifying as
social brainwashing. Her daughter even chastised her mother for succumbing to "self-devaluatory notions" by wearing makeup to cover up her wrinkles for her university lectures and declared, "You *earned* those wrinkles,
honey."[78] To this suggestion her mother was indignant, because she saw
"no reason why everyone should not try to look as well as they can. Who
likes to be around shlumps?" She felt she had accepted herself as she was,
"but who needs wrinkles. If I can hide them, I do, and from myself as much
as from the public."[79] Her justification mirrored Betty Friedan's exhortations to feminists within the movement—undoubtedly shaped by media
representations that declared all feminists unattractive—to try to look as
pretty as they could.[80] Friedan's reasons for this stance were both the public

and private ones that this mother had suggested: that prettiness was good not only for women's public role but for one's self-image.[81]

Even if their feminist daughters maintained a conventionally feminine or pretty appearance, anecdotal or cultural images of lesbian appearances could be troubling for mothers of this generation. In "My Daughter Is Different," a Long Island mother of a lesbian daughter confessed her assumptions about lesbians and their appearance in *Family Circle* in 1974. After Judith Ramsey realized her daughter was a lesbian, she reflected, "*Lesbian*. It was a frightening word to me. . . . I had a very stereotyped image of a lesbian; she was not only tough-looking, wearing mannish clothes and a 'butch' hairdo, but she was rough-acting and coarse." Yet her daughter, Kim, was "none of those things."[82] In addition, her daughter's first girlfriend was "slim, pretty, well-mannered, and extremely intelligent."[83] This impression of a lesbian, emphasizing coarseness, seems to have been informed by class in its evocation of a stereotypical tough, bar lesbian, quite different from the lesbian feminists who had self-consciously cultivated a disregard for conventional standards of feminine beauty.[84] Mrs. Ramsey's eye-openers about the diversity in lesbian appearances were related for their somewhat shocking human interest value and perhaps also as a way of reaffirming her own femininity. While "there are lesbians who are 'butch' types, there are also many, like Kim, who are highly feminine," she declared.[85]

Tensions about conventional beauty standards and femininity surfaced between lesbian daughters and their fathers as well. Writer and dancer Donna Allegra was a young black teenager living in Brooklyn, when in 1968 the New York public school system started allowing girls to wear pants to school. She was only too pleased that now she could start wearing "dungarees, man-tailored shirts, loafers, [and] round-toed sneakers," a preppy style more likely to have been embraced by black lesbians than white lesbian feminists.[86] However, her father took her aside to exhort her to "adopt a more feminine appearance." She recalled her father saying, "I fear you're taking on behaviors and attitudes that will stand in the way of having a healthy relationship with men." Allegra took this opportunity to confide that she was a lesbian. The talk did not go as well as she had hoped. Though he was not one to lose his temper, and she described him as wise and generally "liberal," he "showed no emotional presence that I can recall." However, she did remember that he argued for heterosexuality along the lines of "a man has a penis, his hands and a mouth, so there can be no contest about who can satisfy a woman."[87] His evocation of heterosexual desire contrasted sharply to mothers' reasons for being heterosexual, which instead embraced aspects of womanhood often not directly related to the sexual realm, such as femininity and married life. This emphasis spoke to the relative insignificance of, or perhaps simply reticence about, the sexual in mother/daughter assessments of relationships.

Still, the lesbian rejection of male sexuality was an implicit rejection of men that seemed a personal slight to some fathers. Like Donna Allegra's father, the lesbian poet's father came to feel that his daughter only expected and wanted intimacy from women, and that he was being shunned from the family. Given his daughter's "current orientation," he wrote, the "rapport that I thought existed between us" had gotten lost in her "absorption with the 'sisters,' which includes mother by definition, [and] leaves no room for your old dad." Continuing in this third-person vein, he regretted that "the best that you can say for him, apparently, [is] that he is not hostile to feminist ideas and can be classified as 'supportive' so he isn't as bad as most male chauvinists." Like his wife, this father resented being categorized as part of a broad stream of feminist ideas that characterized men as oppressive and women as submissive. He hoped that the feeling of being in a "family unit" would eclipse these dogmatic ideas.[88] In her defense, this poet said that her newfound, somewhat exclusive relationship with her mother in some ways "redress[ed]" an "old wrong" wherein her mother had felt "excluded from the special rapport you had with me for many years."[89] This poet did seek a greater affinity with her mother during these years, though she never lost her affection for her father. Like many lesbian feminists, she was not separatist in her daily life.[90]

Nonetheless, it was mothers who became more prevalent subjects and symbols within lesbian feminist writings. Lesbian writers and activists seemed to feel a deeper sense of ambivalence and even regret about the belittlement of their mothers and their domestic worlds so often evoked in gay liberation and, at times, their own depictions, perhaps because they appreciated the contradiction in embracing a love of women from which their own mothers were excluded. These contradictions and tensions about motherhood were lurking in the women's movement more broadly. Some critics have suggested that matrophobia was a preoccupation of second wave feminists, particularly expressed in the fear of becoming one's mother.[91] On the one hand, feminist critics such as Shulamith Firestone in *The Dialectic of Sex: The Case for Feminist Revolution* (1970) disavowed biological motherhood altogether. On the other hand, while acknowledging the contradictory dimensions of motherhood, Adrienne Rich also extolled and celebrated it, outside of patriarchy's constraints, in her work *Of Woman Born* (1976).

Lesbian feminists tended to embody these debates and contradictions about mothers and at times stood astride these two distinct sensibilities in their portraits. Lesbian feminist writers evoked an image of the 1950s as a benighted moment that paralleled broader countercultural and feminist conceptions of the era, such as the feminist art installation project "Womanhouse." In 1972, under the direction of Judy Chicago, artists refurbished an abandoned mansion into a model of a 1950s suburban home, featuring a "Bridal Staircase" that led into a kitchen of never-ending meals to be served and a woman performance artist chanting in a monotone voice the words, "I am waiting. . . ." She was waiting for many, ultimately unfulfilling, stages in a woman's life cycle, such as her body breaking down and visits from distant, thankless children and grandchildren.[92] In some senses, the creepy, ghostlike women of Womanhouse were marked by what J. David Hoeveler has called the "timelessness" and "eternal cycle of the home and family."[93] The lesbian feminist recapturing of this story of domesticity was to show the relentlessness of nurturing tasks and life cycle stages of women's lives during the 1950s, perhaps shaped by Betty Friedan's positioning of women's selfhood in the labor market. As one of Betty Friedan's interview correspondents in *The Feminine Mystique* avowed, "I can take the real problems; it's the endless boring days that make me desperate."[94] This idea of the domestic sphere as a zone of isolation, compliance, boredom, and the careworn rang true for lesbians no less so than for heterosexual women. In an article on lesbian culture in the 1950s appearing in the 1973 Boston lesbian periodical *Focus*, Kay Silk described the time period that her older lesbian sisters had to endure as a "bland and prissy time. The clothes and the social customs and interior decoration (beige on beige) were bad enough. Far worse was the public attitude: the repression of anything suspected of being 'different.' "[95] Strikingly, this era was depicted as a time most oppressive on account of the home, decoration tastes, and colors, as though these spilled into a general attitude.[96]

But many lesbian observers did not simply position themselves against an imagined heterosexual housewife and mother, as this perspective neglected any ambivalent or contradictory feelings on the part of these mothers.[97] Lesbian writers seemed marked by a desire to uncover the submerged longings and insights that they believed, or hoped, their mothers had cherished even amid these perceived repressive and confining circumstances.

If mothers were limited in their understanding and their experiences, lesbian writers tended to view this as the fault of cultural pressures of the time period in which these mothers came of age rather than their own incapacities or even complicity. In the poem "My Mother," which appeared in *Coming Out Rage* in 1973, Joy Scorpio suggests that her mother's desire was to "gain their acceptance / by fitting into their definition of normal behavior." Here "they" is an ambiguous though harmful entity:

They told her to be an innocent virgin
men worshipped her purity and competed
to be the first to possess her. Then they told her to be a sensuous
    woman
She had a thousand orgasms and faked the rest.

The assumption is that this mother never enjoyed her sexuality and simply played out a series of suffocating roles. The author encapsulates her mother's life by saying, "They told her to be a loving mother; nurture the man / be unselfishly concerned with his welfare." Accelerating her life to old age, as if to show how empty all the years of her life were, Scorpio writes:

When she became old, she lifted up her sagging smile
and went out to sit in the sun
wondering about her strange daughter,
how they do it to each other without a man.[98]

There is perhaps an irony in the mother figure's not being able to understand her daughter's sexuality in this poem, when the lesbian daughter finds her mother's own sexuality somewhat incomprehensible as well, or at least fake and lackluster. Heterosexual sexuality seemed conflated here with the banalities of family nurturing.[99] In this idealized comparison, lesbian writers saw a malaise and overriding disappointment when they imagined their mothers' sexuality, and perhaps a fracture between a supposedly duty-bound heterosexual love and an experimental lesbian love.

This disparaging portrait needs to be placed in a feminist and, in turn, a lesbian feminist context of anger during this period. Feminist and lesbian presses alike seemed to provide a theater in which women's collective anger, against parents, men, and sexist society, could be expressed unfettered. In *Our Bodies, Ourselves*, the Boston Women's Health Book Collective perceived that the venting of this rage was perhaps essential to a woman's health and mental balance.[100] But even in the angriest lesbian feminist sources, a lesbian impetus to educate their mothers and uncover their brainwashing by misogynistic society surfaced. A coming-out letter in this vein was published in a 1971 edition of Ann Arbor's *Spectre*, in the hope that it would "give some strength to revolutionary lesbians who read this."[101] Addressing her mother by her first name and accusing her of treating her daughter "like a mindless rag-doll," this lesbian admitted to having tried to kill herself as a young teenager and later entertaining some matricidal fantasies. She acknowledged that all of "this might hurt for you to hear," but it was necessary because "then maybe you'll try to change just a little."[102] Published in the political forum of a revolutionary lesbian separatist magazine, this letter might not have been precisely the one sent to her mother, or a letter that was sent at all, and its anger might have been enhanced. With an air of condescending sympathy, she invited her mother to disavow her present life: "I really feel for . . . [what] you have to go through as a working woman, wife, mother . . . obliterated by all the roles you have to fulfill."[103]

Another portrait appearing in a 1974 edition of Chicago's *Lavender Woman*, a lesbian separatist periodical, did not simply pity a mother's lot, but tried to demonstrate some feminist potentials and possibilities for her life. This cartoon showed "Agnes Molasses: A Mama" as a color-and-paste doll with bouffant hair, a girdle, and high-heeled shoes. Beside her are several color-and-cut outfits and accessories: one displaying a hippy style peace-sign jacket, a shirt that said "55 & Proud Woman," and some accessories such as a "Do It Yourself Kit" and wrench. These outfits seem to be juxtaposed against the more traditional outfits that a woman of this generation might have worn, such as a conventional dress, as well as a bouquet of flowers and a baking rolling pin for accessories.[104] Just as lesbian daughters could modify or recast femininity and womanhood by altering their own clothes and tastes, mothers were conceived as having the potential to do the same.

There was even a feeling among lesbians that they and their mothers could come to understand each other or at least have some common ground. Lesbian activists in New York City, for example, started sponsoring panels titled "Mothers of Lesbians" in 1973, an event that was written up in New York's *Gay Activist* as "Blessed Be the Mothers of Lesbian Nation."[105] A woman writing in the *Lesbian Connection* in 1978 wrote of her desire to share with her mother her newfound lesbian feminist realizations, thinking her mother could appreciate them too. In "How Do You Judge Me," "Ava" donated to this periodical a copy of a letter she had written to her mother, who had been "very freaked out" when her daughter confided she was a lesbian. In the letter, she emphasized to her mother that she was having "trouble understanding why you're so repulsed," as lesbian relationships, according to this woman, had "no power struggles." Further, "there is so much of my life I'd like to share with you—healing circles, festivals, music, magic, political work." Finally, she expressed her desire to "share our dreams and respect each other's differences."[106]

In fact, this lesbian fantasy of motherly empathy was a fundamental aspect of lesbian feminist culture. Lesbian daughters commonly did not give up on their mothers, but longed for mutual revelations. Indeed, lesbian feminism as a political and cultural movement could be taken as a movement of the revolutionary potential of personal honesty and soul bearing.

Under scrutiny here was the quotidian quality of familial relationships: many lesbian feminist writers pushed for something more emotionally satisfying and suggested that it was only through mutual disclosures that family relationships could be close. In her poem "family dinner" in a 1977 issue of *Focus*, Jo-Ellen Yale conveyed a bland family conversation, with her momentous personal revelation trying to break through the banality. She described the conversation through a stream-of-consciousness technique in her poem:

isn't this weather just
awful
you look well tonight, dear
i'm gay . . . pass the butter, dear
i'm gay
mary and john are having
problems
are you seeing, anyone, dear
i'm gay
we're glad you're so happy.[107]

The weather as a symbol for the utter poverty of emotional communication in families was a more far-reaching theme in these evocations of family life. In a similar piece, "Coming Out: Sooner or Later," which appeared in New York City's *Lesbian Feminist* in 1976, Susan MacDonald wrote of a colossally boring family dinner in which her mother talked about the weather and her father mentioned that he was worried about being laid off from work. She did not choose that moment to come out to them but fretted later that perhaps she used his impending layoff as "yet another excuse." On the bus back to her home, she had the sinking feeling that nothing was said, "nothing shared."[108]

Self-expression and revelations were not just perceived as crucial elements of family talk but also were a central element within lesbian personal and fictional writings. In fact, many canonized North American women fiction writers in this period were, in a parallel way, evoking women's coming-of-age experiences in day-to-day and domestic settings, perhaps to illuminate the experiential, biological, and psychological differences between men and women.[109] Adrienne Rich, too, has spoken of the profound shift that occurred for her when she started, in her poetry, to use the pronoun "I" rather than the pronoun "she," as her writing then became less dependent on allusion.[110] In coming out through writing for a public audience, lesbian feminists also sought to make a similar radical statement.

But lesbians who did so in public contexts faced an extra set of tensions with their parents. Some writers, like the lesbian poet, used a fictional form and metaphor to convey deeply personal "true" experiences. Her fiction seemed an extension of the kinds of conversations she was having—or wished that she could have—with her mother. Her mother had her own, very distinct set of ideas about what constituted fictional writing, however. At the moment that her mother mentioned she was rereading *Buddenbrooks* by Thomas Mann, a novel of social realism that captured nineteenth-century German bourgeois society, her daughter was urging her mother to read Kate Millett's *Flying*. This was an autobiographical work that Millett had published in the wake of the public controversy surrounding her coming out as a lesbian during the promotion of her most renowned work, *Sexual Politics*, in 1970; Millett herself had received censure for her open lesbianism, and her mother had been upset with her.[111] *Flying* provided a forum through which the lesbian poet and her mother first broached the issues of privacy within the arena of writing and, more implicitly, the presentation of the self.

After reading *Flying*, the lesbian poet's mother declared that "the real reason it is so popular is not that it is so good, but that it relates such personal experiences so openly. And so many 4 letter words! People just don't seem to be able to resist that." She then pronounced Kate Millett "one of those who wants instant gratification."[112] She even included a short, point form book report titled, *K. Millett: Flying*. "Revelation?" this mother asked. "More like indecent exposure." She noted, "Forever smoking pot, even on the bookjacket. And forever f——ing." If these graphic aspects of the book were not enough, she also objected to the writing style of this self-proclaimed "notebook," which she found to be more a "helter-skelter diary." She noted that the author herself asked, "Who will ever want to read this book, this collection of the clutter in my mind." On that point, this mother agreed with Millett: "That's what it is . . . clutter in her mind." She also noted that the author called her book a "record." "So everything that happens to her has to go in . . . even stuff about her friends, even if she thinks she may lose them by putting them in a book. WHY DOES EVERYTHING THAT HAPPENS TO HER have to be written. Who cares? She just wants to be a writer."[113] This attitude of "who cares?" in fact describes a broader stance that some women, both lesbian and heterosexual, took toward what they perceived as a culture of lesbian confessionals developing during these years. Joan Larkin, for example, had written an article that relayed her own coming-out experience in the March 1976 edition of *Ms.* magazine, and her piece received all sorts of responses, both positive and negative, in the forms of letters to the editor. One woman who did not reveal her sexuality to the magazine, nonetheless wrote in to say "who cares!!!" about Joan Larkin's "breast beater." This woman relayed that she felt quite "surfeited with all the groups and articles written by homosexuals, bisexuals, heterosexuals, in the presumptuous vein that their method of physical, psychological and emotional sexual relief is of earth shattering or mole hill crushing interest to anyone but themselves." Instead she wanted "some realistic articles on the 45 to 65 year old female and her successes (there are many of us) as well as failures."[114] Another lesbian woman wrote in to say, "Please, no more confessionals!" In her view, coming out was more properly the territory of gay men, and the magazine was not in fact "supporting the lesbian reader by reporting confessionals."[115] This viewpoint departed dramatically from a lesbian feminist belief that all women's stories were profound testimonies that could be transformed into cultural artifacts.[116]

In the wake of the discussion about Millett's confessional, the lesbian poet's mother told a story that she hoped would illustrate generational differences regarding privacy to her daughter. She then revealed that a relative had asked "Grandma when she married Henry whether they had 'sex' [beforehand]. . . . Grandma told her promptly to mind her own business. That's how that generation . . . settled the matter, and the daughters appreciated it." But "the trouble with this present generation," she said, "is that they think sex is everyone's business . . . theirs and yours."[117] Her mother appeared to find this curiosity and openness to be simply brazen. Perhaps her indignation was fueled by a different conception of hierarchy between the generations: she evoked a time when there was more formality between young people and older adults and when personal matters were more appropriately the province of peer interactions. Yet there also seems to be a firm stance here that her daughter, in breaking down the boundaries surrounding the personal, had failed to distinguish between secrets that gnawed away at their keepers—as keeping sexuality a secret might have— and secrets that individuals chose to keep. The poet's mother located this need to uncover and reveal in the general feminist writing culture but also would see it in the way that she communicated with her daughter, and in her daughter's own writing.

In 1975, this mother received a copy of her daughter's poem, "Coming Out":

Coming Out
the first person I loved
was a woman my passion
for her lasted thirty years
and was not returned
she never let me suck her nipples
she kept secrets between her legs
she told me men would love me
for myself she couldn't tell me
ways to love myself
she didn't know

I would like to help you
Mother, swim back against the foaming river
to the source of our incestuous fears
but you're so tired

out beyond the breakers
and I am upstream among my sisters
spawning[118]

Writing her daughter a response to this poem, she praised her for writing
a "very good poem" that was placed first in the magazine's order, "before
Adrienne Rich who seems to be making off with all the prizes."[119] However,
she objected to the line that referred to the "secrets between her legs."
"Hasn't it been overdone?" she asked her daughter. "I know that it is common nowadays to call a spade a spade, but in a poem one can be descriptive
metaphorically, whimsically, or some other pleasanter way than plain
English." Thus one of her concerns was simply the poem's blunt expression
of the personal, reflective of a more precisely defined aesthetic assessment
of writing. Subtlety and intrigue were essential to her ideas of even semiautobiographical fiction. Letting it all hang loose in this way simply seemed
to be dispensing with art or beauty altogether. She in part chalked up this
disparity in their feelings about personal writing to the different kinds of
people she and her daughter were: "I am a private person with no great
need for confidences and revelations about myself."[120] Finally, she perceived
a disparity between the old and the young in talking about sexual and
bodily matters: "There *has* been a sexual revolution, and it hasn't been easy
on parents brought up in another day."[121]

But this poem also illuminates different judgments about the elements
that make up familial love. The poet's mother noted this too and objected
to the depiction of her own reticence. She could not countenance the idea
that "I withheld love in any way. True you weren't breast fed, but . . .
bottles were the big thing anyway." She realized that her daughter "didn't
mean it in a literal sense but it really doesn't fit me or the mother I was. I
can't imagine anyone loving their first child more."[122] This mother's conception of love included other forms of intimacy that her daughter did not
mention, such as practical and physical care and a recognition of a mother's
time and bodily sacrifice.

But this daughter felt that her mother's response to the poem suggested
a fear of closeness between them. She clarified to her mother that the
"Coming Out" poem was about love, shaped by all lesbians'—and everyone
else's—first love of their mothers, a notion perhaps inspired by a broader
lesbian feminist cultural reclamation of primal images of mothers as well
as feminist rereadings of familial relationships.[123] During this period, psy-

chologists such as Nancy Chodorow had reevaluated the pre-Oedipal period, arguing that children are not, as Freud thought, originally bisexual, but instead were gynesexual or matrisexual.[124] The childhood experience of being cared for by a member of only one sex had far-reaching implications for human psychology, and as adults women in particular sought ways to re-create this mother-daughter bond.[125] This primal bond of intimacy and oneness between mother and daughter and the notion of a delicate ego boundary between mother and daughter were themes that dovetailed nicely with these lesbian feminist ideas. This daughter could not help but feel that her mother had been holding back love to her daughter "because of some secret fear." She was sorry that when she was growing up her mother "couldn't share my delight in the discovery of sex, nor talk about your own sex life by way of helping me learn to live mine. I always regretted that." She then asserted what seemed to be a guiding belief regarding the ways that she conducted her personal relationships: "Women need to talk to other women, and a daughter needs to learn from her mother's experience."[126]

Yet there was sometimes a contradiction displayed in the desire for intimacy that mothers themselves likewise requested of their lesbian daughters. This contradiction was wittily captured in a 1974 cartoon appearing in the *Gay Community News* titled "Mommy." Here a hippy-looking daughter with mammoth bell-bottoms, says, "Hi, Mom, Guess what? I'm gay!" The mother says, "You are? How come you never said anything before? That's the trouble with you! You're so secretive, you keep everything in. There's no communication between us!" The mother pauses and says, "Don't tell your father!"[127] Despite her own exhortations to keep the personal private, the lesbian poet's mother ultimately praised her daughter for the intensity they shared. In contrast, she felt somewhat cut off from her other daughter. As she described this daughter, "She always brushed me aside—she was writing 'things,' taking courses in 'things,' doing 'things.' She was never very communicative."[128] However, she praised her lesbian poet daughter for her efforts in thoughtfully describing her life choices: "What an essayist you are! [Your sister] would never take the trouble to explain herself to us the way you did."[129] In turn, her poet daughter always appeared affectionate toward her mother even amid their disagreements over the "Coming Out" poem. She loved the very fact that her mother was "willing to go at the issue of *Amazon Quarterly* with an open mind and a reasonable degree of interest."[130]

One way of thinking about these exchanges, then, is to explore the inherent closeness between parent and daughter in simply being able to write about and debate personal matters. Mothers and daughters themselves took note of this idea. In a collection of lesbian personal stories, one mother wrote that she struggled to come to terms with her lesbian daughter but felt that she knew her daughter better after the revelation. At first it was difficult for "Mrs. O'Keefe" because she "didn't know what to say" to her daughter: "I wanted to say something, but I wanted it to be the right thing."[131] However, she took heart in the thought that "neither one of my kids is perfect [and] they've never had to go around the corner and hide things from me." In this respect, "it pleases me immensely they feel enough confidence in my love that they can tell me." This stood in contrast to "a lot of parents" she knew "who know nothing about what their kids do."[132] Susan MacDonald's mother—the mother of the lesbian whose family talked about weather and her father's imperiled job at the supper table—also gave a positive, almost envious response to her daughter, urging her to tell her more about being a lesbian.[133] "Please Susan, feel free to talk to me," her mother wrote. "I've read a lot about it and I think you're better off than most couples that are bickering all the time like Daddy and me. When we see each other again we'll have a long talk."[134] Perhaps this sentiment reveals most centrally this mother's idealization of the way women relate to each other, unlike women and men, and her disappointment with her own marriage. Yet she did appear delighted and somewhat intrigued by the more intimate relationship she and her daughter seemed to be developing and more able to say what she felt was wanting in her own life. It was as if, once the taboo of lesbianism had been broken, a host of other intimate topics could be broached too.

Similarly, Mrs. Ramsey, the woman who wrote about her pretty lesbian daughter in *Family Circle*, came to appreciate a sense of intimacy with her daughter that she felt she had not known with her husband. Her daughter had revealed her sexuality only after her mother had found some suspicious literature while dusting her bedroom one day. Yet Mrs. Ramsey relished the close conversations that this discovery had brought about.[135] While she had married a "responsible husband," she owned that living with him was "a little like having a taciturn houseguest around. Even after 27 years of marriage, I still don't know what he is really thinking."[136] But she shared at least some of his reticence, for up to this point she had never really talked much about intimate matters with her daughter, Kim. She called Kim's sex life a "delicate matter" and had been worried primarily that her daughter would have sex too early with a young man. She owned that she "bowed out by not discussing sexual matters very much with her"; in turn, her daughter "certainly didn't confide in me."[137] After her daughter had come out to her, Mrs. Ramsey could no longer abide this reticence. She went to a counselor to talk about Kim's childhood and her lesbianism, but in so doing she reviewed her marriage and her "entire past." The counselor finally advised her that she seemed to have "no sense of [her] own identity as a woman separate from [her] relationships with [her] husband and children." As he told her firmly, "Stop brooding about your daughter . . . and face up to the facts of your own life." Mrs. Ramsey then joined a "consciousness raising group," mostly with other housewives, who met once per week to discuss their common problems and exchange experiences. Feeling more confident, she got a job for the first time, as a secretary in a large company. Her relationship with her daughter was much improved because "we know each other better, respect each other more."[138]

Though the *Family Circle* article reads as a mother/daughter success story, perhaps fitting the magazine's tone of both family voyeurism and celebration, this response to shattered family perceptions that could potentially shift to an exuberant new family closeness suggests an emerging need for parents to know their children, even in their aberrations. Lesbianism was, no doubt, contested terrain between daughters and their parents, especially between mother and daughter. The revelations were often anxious and uneasy. But as a movement, lesbian feminism was perhaps more pertinent to the family relationship than gay liberation, in that it was more explicitly about intimacy between women. Thus the mother-daughter relationship was inherently a part of it. The lesbian feminist call for closeness between parent and child was perhaps premature and fraught, even for those parents who were willing to discuss sexual preference at all. Yet it also seemed to kindle a desire for greater intimacy with gay children, perhaps a broader desire than many lesbian feminists ever appreciated, and one that would be responded to in a movement of the parents' own.

4

Out of the Closets, Out of the Kitchens

ESBIAN COUNSELOR Julie Lee was quite confident that most parents would not reject their gay children. To a teenager fretting about her parents' response to her lesbianism in 1974, Lee wrote, "If your family rejects you because of something like that, all I can say is that THEY need psychotherapy, not you!" And, she noted, this therapy was now available for parents: "There is a lovely Jewish couple in New York who have started an organization for families of people like us—so the parents . . . come together and discuss their problems."[1] This lovely Jewish couple was Jeanne and Jules Manford, who started discussion groups among parents of gays at a Greenwich Village church in New York City in 1973. "JOIN THIS DYNAMIC GROUP OF PARENTS. Learn from their experiences. Share with them your experiences," an early poster for the group announced. A "newly formed Discussion Group for mothers and fathers of Lesbians and Gay males" promised to address such questions as "How do I relate to my child? What should I say to friends and family? Did I make any mistakes? What can we do to help our daughters and sons?"[2]

The New York City group held several such meetings throughout the 1970s. By the later part of the decade and the early 1980s, local groups had sprung up in California, Arizona, Colorado, Illinois, Washington, Massachusetts, and other states and provinces. These groups presaged the national organization of what is now known as PFLAG (Parents, Families, and Friends of Lesbians and Gays).[3] At first, parents' groups in different locations knew of each other only through informal networks. A national organization was planned to coincide with the National Gay and Lesbian

March in Washington in 1979. Incorporated in 1982, there were about twenty North American chapters within the organization then.

Throughout the 1970s and the early years of the 1980s, organized parents of gays existed alongside other parents who were beginning to write about their gay children in advice literature and memoirs. Both these activist and literary responses suggested a more defined and perhaps even ritualized possibility of parental empathy with their gay children. If such children seemed unknowable or remote through their sexuality, parents' writings and gatherings could help reacquaint parent and child and reassure fretting parents about the family life they had conducted. Did I make any mistakes? If the broader culture answered yes and reinforced the feeling of family deficiency, the testimonies and meetings of fellow parents could provide a powerful counterdialogue.[4]

In sharp contrast to the lesbian feminists and gay liberationists of the 1970s who insisted that gender roles and sexual orientations were social constructions and personal choices, organized parents of gays attempted to reinscribe homosexuality in nature: their children had no choice in the matter, nor had their parents any hand in it. From this standpoint, it would also be against nature to reject their children. The script of gay family rejection was an idea that sounded deeply within parental organizations and loomed as a backdrop to parents' testimonies and activist rhetoric. But this script also provided parents with some moral leverage: the virtuous thing to do was not to reject gay children but to embrace them. During a political moment in the United States when the Left had all but ceded moral issues, at least at a rhetorical level, to the Right, the moral voice of a parents of gays organization that became pointed against the right's focus on family and social values was indeed powerful.[5]

The sympathetic testimonies of fellow parents even offered a forum for the repentance of parental failures in regard to their children, particularly the failure to know and understand their children's intimate lives. This was no doubt a shortcoming of many parents even in companionate family styles, but one that was highlighted most poignantly when children were gay. Organized parents of gays would come to suggest expanded meanings for family nurturance during this period, particularly ones that attempted to acknowledge the reality of their children's affective lives and sexuality.

As the movement was initially conceived, however, during the early and middle 1970s, these parental gatherings were not primarily therapeutic in purpose but activist. Parents who organized on behalf of their gay children during this period faced a specific dilemma: How were they to defend their gay children when homosexuality still symbolized sexual immorality and deviancy? The initial PFLAG and parent help movement was inspired by a gay activist son, Morty Manford, who had urged his mother, Jeanne, to start a support group for parents of gays. Morty Manford participated in gay liberation politics of a more reformist than revolutionary nature: he was a prominent student leader for gay rights at Columbia University and was an active member of the Gay Activists' Alliance (GAA), formed in 1969, alongside the Gay Liberation Front (GLF). Unlike the GLF, which had allied itself with the Black Panthers and the antiwar movement, the GAA eschewed violence and the rhetoric of insurrection. While the GLF never had a formal structure and consisted instead of a series of "cells," the GAA was a formal organization with a constitution and a system of committees, focused on attaining antidiscrimination legislation while pursuing activist tactics known as zaps.[6] Jeanne Manford was moved to become an activist for gay rights after she witnessed her son receive a particularly brutal beating during one such GAA protest at the Hilton Hotel in New York City, as the city's police looked on quietly. Having already participated in the civil rights movement, Manford had a political framework for her outrage. She started taking on an activist role herself by writing a letter of support for her son in the *New York Post* and hoisting a sign that read "Parents of Gays Unite in Support for Our Children" in the gay pride parade in New York City in 1972. The outpouring of emotion and praise she received for these simple acts of love for her gay child—and perhaps, by extrapolation, the declaration of the very existence of gay children within families—seemed to open the possibility for parents to have a potent role within the gay liberation movements of that period. As another early organized parent, Leonore Acanfora, said, once her son came out of the closet, it was time for her to "come out of the kitchen" to face his sexuality and agitate for his rights.[7]

For these early organized parents, gay oppression was located in a larger social context of oppression and injustice. Sarah Montgomery, another major early organizer, had, like Jeanne Manford, a social activist past in the civil rights movement. She had even been a suffragette as a very young woman. Lovingly dubbed "Grandma Lib" and "Everybody's Favorite Mother" in the gay press, Montgomery was seventy-five years old at the height of her activism on behalf of gays in 1974, just two years after her gay son and his partner had jointly committed suicide, which she attributed to the exhausting, cumulative effects of a life of homophobic discrimination. She had marched in the first New York Christopher Street Liberation Day parade in 1970, the only parent to have done so. Her son's suicide fortifying her sense of purpose, Montgomery felt it a parental duty to be open about gay family members and take up the cause of gay rights. She could not abide parents who wallowed in their own guilt for breeding a gay child, because "[i]t annoys me to see this guilt. . . . When a child has the courage to tell them about his homosexuality, then parents should feel pride and not sit around moaning, feeling sorry for themselves."[8] She was also wary of those parents who seemed to have an "I love my child . . . but" attitude.[9] To get rid of the "but," parents had to embrace homosexuality as well as their child.

The tenor of parental activism during the initial years of the movement tended to be set by activists of Montgomery's ilk, and they had little patience with parents who exhibited any kind of self-pity. Her attitude was shared by other early organized parents. In an interview in the *Advocate* in 1978, Bernice Becker, an "enlightened and proud" mother of two gay daughters, out of the closet since the mid-1960s, suggested that some of the parents she had met at Parents of Gays meetings "often don't seem concerned enough about their children." She felt that some were "looking for a shoulder to cry on. They want somebody to tell them they're really nice people."[10] In a message to Parents of Gay People of the Greater Bay Area in San Francisco in 1978, Becker insisted, "Don't cry about society's persecution of your child. Get out there and help change it."[11] Edith Perry, mother of Troy Perry, a gay activist who founded the Metropolitan Community Church in 1976, which had a specific outreach to gay Christians, concurred with this statement. She wrote in the foreword to her son's book *The Lord Is My Shepherd and He Knows I'm Gay* (1972) that she felt proud of her son for standing up "to be counted with his gay brothers and sisters" and affirmed the gay activist mission that "no one should live in a miserable world of shadows and be threatened with ruin and exposure." She chalked up parental shame to being "afraid of what others may say or think" and admonished parents for succumbing to such shallow thinking: "That's just plain silly, when it comes down to it."[12]

Parents also were advised not to dwell on their own sense of investment in children. In "What Parents of Gay Children Fear Most Is Their Children," Florida activist Jean Smith labeled parental laments about sons failing to carry on the family name or daughters failing to provide a grandchild "selfish."[13] Betty Fairchild, who authored one of the first official pieces of PFLAG literature in 1975, called *Parents of Gays*, sympathized with them, insofar as families of gays also "suffer in virtual silence."[14] Yet she came down hard on parents who were preoccupied with shame and their own feelings. Some parents, she observed, "seem more concerned with their own feelings, and the opinions of others, than with what their child is feeling—or really *is*, for that matter."[15]

For these activist parents, figuring out who the child really was offered the promise of an exciting family intimacy, even if what preceded this new terrain was family upheaval. As the poem included in the *Parents of Gays* pamphlet said,

> Telling Mom and Dad you're gay
> Is not an easy thing to say.
> And, where the folks are coming from,
> It's harder news to hear than some.
> But if your family is caring
> You'll gather closer, through this sharing.[16]

It was not enough simply to be supportive and selfless, seeking a sense of intimacy within the family. In a way, the promise of intimacy was fused with civil rights: parental activism laid the groundwork for that intimacy. Sarah Montgomery insisted that "if parents go into the closet it's in itself a condemnation . . . a parent must be prepared, just as any brave, valiant, young gay is prepared, to face an ignorant and bigoted world."[17] In this vein, an early PFLAG pamphlet of 1977, "Parents of Gays and Lesbians Speak Out," featured Sarah Montgomery's quotation, "I refuse to be a closet mother!" as well as the declarations "The Problem Is Silence" and "The Solution Is Speaking Out."[18]

As was the case for activist gay children, activist parents could hardly be discreet if they were to participate in the kinds of political endeavors for gay civil rights that they did. Jeanne Manford wrote President Gerald Ford in 1974, drawing on her moral authority as a mother when talking about political injustices to gays. The immediate purpose of her letter was to advocate for a bill in New York City to give civil rights to gay people in housing and employment, a bill repeatedly rejected by the city council. She then wished to press him to issue an executive order prohibiting discrimination on account of sexual orientation in the civil service, an order that would result in the Civil Service Commission's lifting its ban on the employment of gays in 1975.[19] While applauding him for saying in a recent speech that he supported all people, "regardless of political leanings, race, or religion," Manford pointed out that "if you really meant that you will be the president of all the people. . . . God will bless you if you extend a hand to over twenty million homosexuals in this country."[20] She explained that "as a mother and as a citizen I feel a vested interest in seeing the quality of life improved for twenty million Gay women and men."[21]

Casting gay activism as the concern of parents and citizens was both strategic and heartfelt. In some sense it seemed important for parents to distinguish themselves from gay radicalism or any expressions of radicalism that had so beguiled American ideas of law and order throughout the late 1960s and early 1970s. Jeanne Manford found it odd that she was, in fact, considered a radical in any sense of the term. For much of her married life, Manford had been an assistant to her husband in his dental practice, though by the 1970s she was training to become a primary schoolteacher. She considered herself an unremarkable, middle-class woman, living in Queens, New York, then known for its political and social conservatism.[22] Mainstream media presented her as a "prim, bespectacled woman" who lived in a "comfortable, three-story home," suggesting that the Manford family could be featured in a "Disney movie, rated 'G,'" as though something perverse or radical was to be expected of parents of gay children.[23] Remarking on her emergence as a gay activist, Manford wrote in 1973, "I, who have always been a quiet, retiring sort of person, have appeared on television, spoken on radio, and been interviewed by the *New York Times*. . . . Recently, my son discovered my picture . . . in a revolutionary calendar [after Mao Tse Tung and Martin Luther King]. I who never cross the street against a traffic light, have been called a revolutionist!"[24]

These activists affirmed not only that they were simply loving parents but also that they were, in fact, socially conservative: their heterosexuality, marriages, and families were intact, and they were not particularly left-leaning or sympathetic to radicalism. It was no wonder that when Larry Starr, a founder of Parents of Gays in Los Angeles (1976), wrote to Jack Kilpatrick in 1977, criticizing the commentator's ignorant and sensationalized portrait of gays in the CBS program *Sixty Minutes*, his letter did not start with a declaration of love for his gay son, but with this statement: "I have been happily married for over thirty five years and have five happy and healthy children, one of whom happens to be gay." He then discussed his education and professional activities: "I have a Master's degree and a C.P.A. certificate; my annual income is well above the average. I am by no stretch of the imagination a crusader for leftist causes."[25] Starr highlighted his education, class, and politics more than his role as a father.

This stance of respectability was becoming increasingly important as the decade progressed and a new conservative movement emerged. While the "old" right had a socially conservative bent, as a political movement it was primarily concerned with secular issues such as the maintenance of laissez-faire capitalism and the containment of communism. By contrast, the New Right paid focused attention to social issues and religious values, in addition to economic and defense issues, and it was shaped by a growing evangelical Protestant movement in the United States in the 1970s.[26] The New Right and Christian Right perspective gained ground as conservatives reflected upon the legacy of the 1960s, especially the divisive impact of the Vietnam War, feminism, and the civil rights movement, including broader rights consciousness.[27] As Susan Sontag has noted, the movement waged a Kulturkampf on vague ideas and images of the 1960s, not unlike the counterculture's own assault on ideas of the 1950s; both movements were animated by images of the past.[28] The New Right, however, tended to romanticize the 1950s and not disparage a supposed time of tradition. Uncertainty and disquiet about the tenor of social and private life were compounded by the instability of the economy, as both the American and Canadian economies, so intertwined, saw their worst decades since the 1930s, characterized by a diminished oil supply, excessive inflation, and high unemployment rates.[29] All of these promoted a socioeconomic desire for stability.[30]

For some conservative thinkers, the increasing visibility of gays was a signpost for all of the frightening and undesirable social changes of this period. While earlier conservatives of a laissez-faire or libertarian bent, as characterized by Barry Goldwater, tended to think of homosexuality as a strictly private matter, the New Right saw gays as an affront to traditional morals and families.[31] Gays were regarded as another antifamily force besieging American society, in the wake of feminism, abortion rights, and no-fault divorces. All of these private issues were elevated into matters of public discourse because, as Lauren Berlant has argued, a conservative coalition in a sense fostered the privatization of U.S. citizenship.[32] The antigay campaign was characterized by emerging leaders such as popular television evangelist Jerry Falwell, who, borrowing from Nixon's "silent majority," coined the term the "Moral Majority" for his organization.[33] He was explicitly hostile to gays, even denouncing effeminate portraits of Jesus that showed him with long hair and flowing robes.[34] This conservative discourse added another layer to the deeply embedded hostility to gays in mainstream culture and politics.

By definition, gays also posed a challenge to the maintenance of heterosexuality and biological reproduction. The debates surrounding the equal rights amendment (ERA) in particular demonstrate how fears of gender equality spilled over into fears of a broad social acceptance of gays, and even the idea of gay sexuality as a viable alternative to heterosexuality. Phyllis Schlafly, author of *The Power of the Positive Woman* (1977), founded an association called STOP ERA, appealing to housewives who felt denigrated by feminism. At anti-ERA rallies, she passed out homemade loaves of bread "from the breadmaker to the breadwinner."[35] In her speeches and in her reports, she suggested that the ERA would lead to a host of undesirable social changes, such as unisex washrooms, women in the military, cavalier abortions, as well as an easier social acceptance of gays, including gay marriages. She had been known to refer to ERA supporters as "pro-lesbian."[36] In this portrait, once the boundaries between the genders had broken down, and once there was too much choice in the sexual arena, even heterosexuals could become gay.

This notion of gay recruitment of those who were otherwise heterosexual, particularly children, was an especially pressing concern of the New Right. The individual who best embodies this idea of child saving in this period was former beauty queen Anita Bryant. Under the auspices of the Save Our Children campaign, Bryant sought to create a dichotomy between heterosexuals who procreate and homosexuals who recruit the young and innocent.[37] In 1977, this group lobbied successfully for the repeal of a gay rights ordinance in Dade County, Florida.[38] Bryant drew on Christian imagery, reasoning that if homosexuality were normal, God would have made "Adam and Bruce," and tried to suggest that treating gays as a minority group worthy of rights was simply a case of rights ideology gone too far.[39] In her view, if gays were a legitimate minority group, then so too were "nail biters, dieters, fat people, short people, and murderers."[40] The Pro-Family Rally at the International Women's Year Conference held in Houston in 1977 also evoked these concerns. In one of their advertisements, a doll-like little girl in an innocent-looking dress asks, "Mommy, when I grow up, can I be a lesbian?" The caption reads, "If you think this idea is shocking . . .

read what the IWY is proposing for your children."[41] In fact, many antigay
activists did not want gays in the presence of children, period. The Briggs
Initiative of 1978, the proposal of state senator John Briggs of Orange
County, California, to bar gays from teaching in California public schools,
was defeated but suggests a mounting fear of gays in everyday, intergenerational contexts.[42] Perhaps conservative thinkers were invested in marginal-
izing gays in more sensational contexts so that they could maintain the
notion of gays as abstractions freighted with salaciousness and nefarious-
ness, which was necessary to their rhetoric. Defense lawyers for Dan White,
the San Francisco supervisor who murdered his fellow supervisor, the
renowned gay politician Harvey Milk, in 1978, argued that White came
from a fundamentally different social background from Milk, that he was a
man of "family values" and therefore in a world apart.[43] These highly publicized campaigns animated conceptions of gays as a menace to the family.

Nonetheless, the New Right campaign could be said to have galvanized
gay self-representations as family members during this decade. The irony
of seeing gays at the heart of largely heterosexual conflicts such as abortion
and divorce was not lost on gay commentators. In New York City's *Gaysweek* in 1978, David Rothenberg stated most emphatically that as "a gay
male, I do not feel responsible for divorce, the abuse of children, runaways,
teenage addiction or prostitution—yet I constantly see homosexuality cited
as a problem concerning the American family."[44] In turn, gay activists and
writers appeared now to be claiming a much less ambivalent place in their
families than their liberationist forerunners had sought or perhaps consciously acknowledged. This move for family restoration coincided with
changing currents within gay activism. The gay radicalism of the late 1960s
and early 1970s was giving way, by the later 1970s, to activism that was
more liberal, institutional, and integrationist. In part, the reason for this
was that students and young people who had formed the bulk of the liberation movement were getting older and pursuing other goals.[45] Morty Manford felt that this period marked a definitive shift in gay organizing and
demonstrating: he noted that the response at gay demonstrations had
declined markedly in numbers by the mid-1970s.[46] In turn, more gay
reformist organizations were coming on the scene during the 1970s and
early 1980s, most notably the reconstituted GAA, which in 1973 had
become the NGTF. This new organization emphasized political lobbying,
legal changes, and community education through formal structures and
constitutions, a salaried staff, and a board of directors who already had

professional jobs outside of the organization.[47] The NGTF's 1977 "We ARE Your Children!" campaign typified the strategy of refuting the claims of the New Right and the Moral Majority through the same family rhetoric that the conservative movement took up.[48] In 1979, the NGTF proclaimed a "week of dialogue" between gays and American parents and families, featuring well-known individuals from both the gay and heterosexual communities.[49]

New Right portraits roused and shaped the parents movement as well, particularly by the end of the 1970s and the early 1980s. Organized parents now faced a formidable opponent in the New Right, and this influenced the parents movement to move away from the civil rights rhetoric and tactics of those organizers of the early 1970s toward an inward emphasis on the potentials of family love. Gradually parents began to see themselves as victims of homophobia, too, simply by having gay children. They emphasized the need to talk to each other and to make their way through layers of homophobia that had perhaps even pervaded their own family lives. Between roughly 1977 and 1983, the rhetoric of the parents movement began to shift.

One tactic that activist parents pursued was to attack a broad set of myths about homosexuality mobilized by the New Right, among them the idea that homosexuality was a conscious choice on their children's part. Organized parents conceived of homosexuality as a condition that simply existed. How could the Right, then, organize protests against or even disagree with something that just *was*?

This notion of a lack of choice also reflects a more unwavering parental belief in the rigidity of sexual categories, including heterosexuality. In a chapter in the book *Positively Gay* (1979), Betty Fairchild addressed parents, in a section titled "IT IS NOT YOUR FAULT! IT IS NOT A CHOICE!" by telling them to "ask yourself if you could change your sexual preference on request."[50] If choice was simply not a question, gay children could not be asked to change, and parents in turn would not have to engage in self-blame, as gayness could not have been prevented or attributed to them. In fact, when a new generation of American psychiatrists during the 1970s embraced a more biological notion of sexual orientation, their accounts were more likely to grant parents only a peripheral role as a contributing factor to homosexuality, and this is the sort of narrative that PFLAG parents encouraged.[51]

If children did not choose their sexuality, then they hardly merited pun-

ishment for it, an assumption that acknowledged a notion, whether by the
New Right or subconsciously by the parents themselves, that being gay by
choice was worthy of some kind of punishment. In an official PFLAG
audiotape of 1990, "Accepting *Your* Gay or Lesbian Child: Parents Share
Their Stories," a father recalled that his gay daughter and his gay son came
out in the late 1970s and reflected that if parents believe their children
chose it "then the best to be done is tolerate their presence, but if they
didn't choose it, then you can befriend them and love them."[52] The New
York City parents group likewise said that gays should never be seen as
"heterosexuals who have perversely chosen to behave as homosexuals. They
are attracted to those of their own sex because *their very nature inclines
them that way*."[53] The word "perverse" suggests that choice in the realm of
sexuality was indeed a perverse proposition, a stance that affirmed a parental rejection of the notion of sexual preference in favor of sexual orientation.

Organized parents, then, tried both to absolve themselves of having
caused their children's sexuality and to engender sympathy for gay sexuality
by casting it as a predetermined proclivity, refashioning, in a sense, the
sympathetic observations of sexologists at the turn of the twentieth century
and becoming themselves the benign observers of homosexuals.[54] Jean
Smith of Parents of Gays in Pensacola, in the particularly besieged position
of defending gays in the deeply divided state of Florida during this period,
was one mother to take up this tactic. In 1978, she wrote an indignant letter
to Ann Landers, upon reading Ann's column to a mother of a gay son who
wanted to know what caused his homosexuality. The mother in the column
had told Landers that she had a "beautiful marriage" and stressed that she
could not accept homosexuality, or her son. Though Ann Landers under-
scored, as her headline said, "Parents Shouldn't Reject Homosexual Son,"
and pointed out that homosexuals do not precisely choose it, she did enter-
tain speculation that homosexuality was the result of a psychological disorder caused by a number of problems, including a "smothering mother and
a tyrannical, weak, or absent father." Despite Landers's exhortations not to
disinherit gay children, this response was hardly satisfactory to Smith, who
wrote to say that "homosexuals and parents carry enough guilt without you
stating that it is a 'psychological disorder.'" She had to agree, however, that
"homosexuality is not a choice" and went on to give Ann Landers some
information about parents' discussion groups so she could have some more
appropriate information to give out for the next time.[55] She might have

been heartened by a "Dear Abby" response a few years later in 1981, which told a mother seeking the cause of her daughter's lesbianism not to blame herself because "sexual preference is not a matter of choice; it is determined at a very early age."[56]

Jean Smith attacked Anita Bryant's Save Our Children campaign on similar grounds. Here Smith attempted to provoke a reader's shame and empathy in her portrait of gay suffering at the hands of the New Right.[57] In her statement against Bryant, Smith blamed tragedies such as gay murders and suicides on Bryant's "vicious, unchristian-like campaign." This reaction was not unique to Smith or even organized parents of gays. A horrific stabbing murder of a gay man in the summer of 1977 in San Francisco prompted his mother to say that Anita Bryant had blood on her hands, an opinion shared by many gay activists who felt that Bryant had only stirred up a long-standing, seething hatred.[58] Even if Bryant's 1977 book, *The Survival of Our Nation's Families and the Threat of Militant Homosexuality*, did not sell well, and she had become something of a parody of herself in popular culture, gays and their families still saw her as a figure who could seriously harm their lives and cause.[59] Jean Smith affirmed, "I cannot believe homosexuality is simply a choice, when so many destroy themselves as the only means of ridding themselves of homosexuality."[60]

In this same statement, Smith countered Bryant's child-saving campaign by suggesting that organized parents of gays were engaged in their own kind of child saving. Reminiscent of the child-saving campaigns of the nineteenth century, her poem "The Key to the Closet" depicted piteous gay children crying, locked up in a closet.[61] Among them, she heard her own child's voice. She felt an "unbearable anguish" amid harsh, "Bible-toting" townspeople, who insisted that her child was deviant. However, while the townspeople cried out in ignorance, Smith set herself apart from this uproar, through assuming a godlike image herself: "I knew I was the one, to search for the key." One townsperson in particular, presumably based on Bryant and her testimonials for Florida oranges in those years, "shook the orange trees, and raised all sorts of Holocaust." But among these misled religious zealots, whom Smith considered to be participating in a kind of genocide, she spoke of seeing the goodness of gays as a religious moment of truth: "Mine eyes have truly seen the glory."[62] Her poem hints at a feeling of gratification, even holiness, in being parents who loved their gay children. It also suggests that at the level of representation, PFLAG parents

were preoccupied with portraying their gay children as victims—perhaps as
a way to see their children as human.[63]

Central to shedding myths about homosexuality was likening it to some
accepted, innate biological variation. While the recruitment myth suggested
that unwitting heterosexuals could be talked into homosexuality, the New
York City parents' group emphasized that a child could not take a turn
toward homosexuality, because this orientation was his path all along and
simply a variation akin, they wrote, to "black skin and left-handedness."[64]
Although this statement called attention to skin color and handedness, a
more common analogy to homosexuality during the late 1970s and early
1980s was one of health or mental condition. Seeking more publicity from
the editors of *Newsweek* regarding the parents of gays movement, Smith
emphasized that "no other generation of parents have done what we are
trying to do." Moreover, while there were "brochures for other families
regarding drugs, alcoholism, mental illness, handicapped children, etc.,"
there were "none for our families regarding homosexuality."[65] If gayness
could be seen as parallel to a deficiency or an illness, then surely these
parents of diseased children merited some support. These metaphors even
imply a kind of superiority in homosexual children, because these children's "addictions" were not as serious or socially harmful as drugs or
alcohol and merited sympathy rather than punishment.

The drug and alcohol metaphor also applied to parents, however, and
not coincidentally some parents suggested parallels between the formation
of a parents of gays movement and Alcoholics Anonymous and other
Twelve Steps programs of the postwar period.[66] Smith felt that it was just
as difficult for an alcoholic to admit his problem as it was for her to say,
"My name is Jean and I am the parent of a homosexual son."[67] This rhetoric of addiction presaged an enormous cultural emphasis on drug addiction
among youth during the 1980s, including Nancy Reagan's Just Say No campaign of 1985. Addiction was becoming viewed as just another in a series
of problems, like homosexuality, that could befall contemporary youth. The
somewhat sensationalistic self-help book *Mother, I Have Something to Tell
You* (1987) was said to give advice on "What to do when your child
becomes an alcoholic, a drug addict, a homosexual, a criminal, joins a cult,
gets pregnant. Required reading for parents."[68] This kind of portrait
inscribed gayness within the dreaded fantasies of parents in an era when a
renewed concern about juvenile delinquency or simply youth gone awry
was gaining force.

In another attempt to solicit compassion, gay children were portrayed as special-needs children. A New York City parental activist, Richard Ashworth, noted in 1979 that "even if you think homosexuality is something undesirable, [persecuting them] would be like being critical of someone for being mentally retarded."[69] Despite its connotations of impairment, evoking the image of a "retarded" child perhaps had a greater and more uncomplicated emotional resonance than the image of drug addiction.

These analogies of difference seemed to merge homosexuality with a disability or, most benevolently, specialness. Curiously, one strain of sympathy for gay children in the earlier postwar period was to see them as children who would stay within the family bosom well into their adulthood, because they could not marry and were less likely to have children of their own. PFLAGers did not endorse this idea of gay children as a family enrichment on this score but instead as a family condition in need of internal discussion and support. The organization even appeared to embrace gayness as an element of chance and potentially bad luck that characterized simply having children.[70] In turn, the organization's analogies illustrate that within the parental imagination gay children appeared to be shifting from political radicals, as they were often perceived by parents during the liberation period, to problem children, an image that was propagated rather than denied by those parents organizing on their behalf.

But thinking of gayness in this way seemed to give gay sexuality a more precise reality or existence. Another set of metaphors developed by organized parents simply suggested that gays were a fundamental part of modern life. A pamphlet developed by Smith and others for the Pensacola Parents of Gays Society in the late 1970s featured three quotations: "If man were meant to fly, he would have been born with wings"; "The automobile will never replace the horse"; and "Homosexuals are sick, perverted persons who are a danger to the future of our society."[71] The juxtaposition of the third myth about homosexuality with the first two ridiculous and provincial statements suggested that parents of gays who had accepted their gay children were more sophisticated than those who did not. It also suggested that parents get more in step with their times: "Like the airplane, the automobile, and the railroad train, homosexuality is a part of our contemporary lifestyle."[72] Gays, then, could be safely related metaphorically to daily, accepted technological changes but not, of course, to such fraught and more specifically gendered and sexualized changes of the postwar period

such as contraception, the legalization of abortion, and sex-change operations.[73]

However, the sympathy sought by drawing on these images could not
arise if gays were seen as sexual predators or pariahs, as Anita Bryant's
supporters made them out to be, with such signs as "Don't Destroy
America for your Lust." Activist parents dealt only with gay children who
were in fact adults or at least late adolescents. During the late 1970s and
early 1980s, activist parents of gays made a conscious effort to purify these
children by suggesting that their sex lives were as familiar and staid as any
heterosexual lifestyle arrangement, even without the sexually neutral rituals
of heterosexual life, such as marriage, which at least rendered sexuality
commonplace or even desexualized the couple. Ironically, these desexualizing efforts illuminated a heterosexual interest in and voyeurism about
homosexuality at the same time that they attempted to deflect that prurience.

The earliest parental activists such as Sarah Montgomery stressed that
it was heterosexual voyeurism that sexualized gay people, challenging the
notion that gays had ever "flaunted" anything. In Montgomery's view it
was the "homophobic, straight world" that forced gays to demand their
rights and justify their sexual existence.[74] When an alarmed father called to
tell Montgomery that he had discovered his son and another young man
giving each other a bath in the family bathroom, she responded, "Well,
what's the matter with that?"[75] After he hung up on her, she realized her
views were more progressive than most. As she told the periodical the
Empty Closet, "Love is love and sex is sex, no matter how you slice it."[76]
Other activist parents of the early 1970s took a more resolute stance on the
issue of parental voyeurism. In her personal testimony, one mother
declared the injustice of gay persecution in light of the tolerance afforded
promiscuous heterosexuals. According to Mary Milam, "The girl next door
may be a tramp, promiscuously sleeping around, [not able to] identify the
father of a child she may conceive . . . but she is just 'wild.' The boy next
door may be on the make for every girl he sees . . . yet he is 'just sowing
his wild oats.'" However, in pursuing any sexual relationship at all, a gay
person would be followed by "cruel and dirty epithets."[77]

Activist parents were put in the ironic position of having to see the
shortcomings or sordid side of their own sexual culture to defend their
children, a theme that was highlighted when parents in the late 1970s
responded more explicitly to the New Right. A mother attempting to start

a parents of gays group in Calgary, Alberta, a province known then and now for its social conservatism, wrote a letter to the Manfords in 1977, recording her sense that Albertans on the whole were "heavy on a Bible under the arm publicly" but secretly "kinky heterosexuals behind the scene."[78] The implication was that homosexuality surely was not as scandalous as heterosexuality could be.

Other parents admitted their discomfort with any display of sexuality on the part of their children. This avowal was especially the case in those more introspective sources, such as memoirs of parents with gay children, and advice written to fellow parents. In a 1983 "two way survival guide" for both gay children and their heterosexual parents, Mary Borhek, a religious mother of a gay son from Eden Prairie, Minnesota, attested that homosexuality was troubling to parents because it exposed an already sensitive area, sexuality, only with an unthinkable twist. A member of the New Testament Church, an independent charismatic congregation, she found her son's revelation, in 1975, of his gay sexuality to be quite appalling. She cautioned gay children that parents simply did not *want to probe into the matter of sexuality—ours or our children's. We were raised in a simpler age, when we knew which kind of sexual behavior was accepted and which was taboo. Now our children are asking us to make major revisions in our thinking, feeling, perceiving—our understanding of being.*[79] While discussions about reproduction and the mechanics of sex had become expected matters for family discussions during the 1950s and 1960s, sexuality in its variations and emotional consequences were not necessarily on the agenda, even if some parenting literature by the 1970s had started to address the need for sexual expressiveness in general and questions of homosexuality at least in passing.[80] A discussion of the bare bones of sexuality might have been uncharted ground enough for many postwar parents, without this added dimension.[81]

But Borhek also revealed a sense of curiosity about the sexuality of gay children, emblematic of a larger heterosexual fascination with a homosexual culture often conflated with unbridled sexuality. Especially by 1980, images of gays in visual media and film were perhaps even less flattering and more sensationalized than they had been earlier, when gays were more indirectly referred to as unmentionable, largely symbolic figures. William Friedkin's 1980 movie, *Cruising*, for example, portrayed a gay serial killer with a disapproving father. The film featured a lurid gay nightlife and pornography clips of gay men's sex spliced into the scenes.[82] In the same vein,

CBS made another documentary in 1980 about homosexuals, this time called "Gay Power, Gay Politics," that showed blackened clips of men cruising in San Francisco city parks.[83] These were just some of the images and scripts for gay lives that parents might have drawn from when they conjured up gay sexuality during this period. Ironically, while gay children might have seen their parents as the representatives of an overriding heterosexual banality during these years, their parents might have seen their children as the ambassadors of a sexually exotic, uninhibited, and at times frightening world. Borhek admitted that "parents often find that what really bothers them is the idea of their child having sex with a person of the same gender. There may be a horrified curiosity (many times unacknowledged) about how they do it."[84]

Gloria Guss Back also noted a subconscious fascination with gay sex on the part of heterosexual parents, in her coping guide, *Are You Still My Mother? Are You Still My Family?* (1985). "Don't dwell too much on the sexual aspects of homosexuality," she advised parents. "Don't peer too closely into the bedroom of a Gay son or daughter—you wouldn't with a straight child, would you?"[85] These parents stressed the necessity of desexualizing their children to hold prurience at bay. Similarly, Betty Fairchild recalled her bolt of recognition when she saw that her son, heartbroken after having lost a boyfriend, must have been "really" in love and not just having "fleeting sexual encounters" with this young man and several others.[86] Ironically, only through disavowing the idea of their children as sexual beings could these parents restore some sense of feeling, beyond the purely lustful or misguided, to their gay children.

Perhaps the most devastating of heterosexual myths about homosexuality that activist parents attacked, however, was that gays were pedophiles. Borhek noted to gay children that "demeaning as it may seem, you may have to reassure your parents emphatically that you are not a child molester, nor are you going to recruit people to a same-sex orientation."[87] In organized parents literature of this period, parents noted that gay people respect children, clarifying that the majority of sexual child abuse was committed by heterosexual men.[88] This effort to clear their children's sexual record would continue for PFLAG, with even more vehemence, over time.[89]

While the image of homosexual pedophilia could be countered bluntly with the aid of statistics, parents of gays also assumed a task that was in many ways more abstract: that of portraying gays as recognizable figures in society. In this respect another PFLAG pamphlet, "About Our Children"

(1978), stressed that "gay persons establish stable longlasting relationships, work for a living, shop, watch TV, vote, and pay taxes," as if to show that their lives were in fact as bogged down by the quotidian as any heterosexual's was.[90] Borhek advised gays that one way they could assuage parental fears was to convey, as her son did, the "ordinariness" of his life with a gay partner: "They went to work in the morning and came home to the apartment at night to cook meals, wash clothes, shop, clean. They began to redecorate the apartment, doing the work themselves. They went to church on Sunday and to movies, plays, and concerts."[91] In this way, gay children could not be regarded solely as sexual beings, or even alien ones to the domestic scene. In fact, these kinds of portraits provided a more interesting corrective than perhaps even Borhek realized: parents, rather than scientific or cultural observers, were now studying and representing the lives of gays. Almost two decades earlier, in 1967, William Simon and John Gagnon had complained that those who studied deviant behavior had been "vulnerable to the temptations of a kind of intellectual hipsterism" and had therefore studied homosexuals in relation to only their most "exotic" behavior and not their more "conforming behavior." Thus there were extensive studies of homosexual "bars or taverns" but not much about the ways "the homosexual earns a living, finds a place to live, or manages relations with his family."[92] Of course, he was admonishing social science scholars when he said so, not the general public, but it seems Borhek was taking up and advocating her own kind of social science here through self-help.

In challenging myths about their children, however, parents also had to shed myths about themselves, including cultural stories and images of the parent figures of gays. Most centrally, psychology needed to be disputed if parents were to feel that they had not made significant mistakes. This effort was particularly true for mothers, often pathologized as overbearing. Marlene Fanta Shyer, for example, raised her gay son during the 1960s and 1970s in suburban Larchmont, New York, which she considered "an untouched freeze-frame" in an era of "sit-ins, peace marches, militant demonstrations, flag burning and riots."[93] Reflecting on her son's early years, Shyer owned that at one point she firmly believed his "sissy" qualities had developed because he had spent so much time "in the house with the feminine trio of mother, sister and housekeeper." As if to show how ridiculous she now found this idea, she noted in her memoir, *Not Like Other Boys*, that this "was the way we were thinking then, when we were also frying chicken in butter and sunbathing all summer because we thought suntans were glamorous and healthy."[94] The wisdom of these homophobic ideas had now gone the way of other petty, conventional wisdoms, strikingly those about domestic matters and health, as though homophobia was something of an old wives' tale in the household too.

Mary Borhek also ultimately came to discredit those psychoanalysts that she respected before she learned her son was gay. In her earlier 1979 memoir, *My Son Eric*, she appeared to be in a dialogue with those ideas of family life deeply engrained in her from having read psychoanalysis. She assured herself that she had neither "bathed Eric when he was eleven years old [as] Eric had banished me from the bathroom when he was four or five." Nor had she "allowed him to crawl into bed with me." Thus she concluded that she had not castrated Eric. She also had not seduced him by "undress[ing] in front of him. Tom's and my lovemaking had not been flaunted before the children: it had taken place behind closed doors."[95] Because Borhek had not committed any of these notorious mistakes of the overbearing mother, she rejected the very tenets of psychology when it came to homosexuality. Similarly, Gloria Guss Back began to feel resentful of ever having paid heed to these inherited wisdoms about homosexuality, from psychology or even religion. Parents of gays were "forced to take another look at old shibboleths. Why should ancient, musty writings turn us against our own children?"[96]

Yet these efforts to cast off ideas that might have hampered a relationship between gay children and their parents did not detract from significant awkwardness in approaching gay children and talking intimately. Another function of the parents movement, then, was simply to provide advice on how to handle emotions and intimate interactions. The 1983 pamphlet "Can We Understand?" revealed a central tenet of the early PFLAG movement: "If you did not know [about your child's gayness], you would never really know your child. A large part of his or her life would be kept secret from you, and you would never really know the whole human being."[97] This emphasis on family intimacy curiously recalls the gay liberation and lesbian feminist insistence that parents and children could not truly know each other without knowing about their children's sexuality. Parents would come to accentuate the same stance to other parents within the context of their own movement.

And yet there were fundamental differences in the tenor of the intimacy that PFLAG proposed and the one that their children had requested in the preceding decade. Parents of gay liberationists and in particular lesbian feminists seemed at times intrigued by the very prospect of talking intimately with gay children, who had broken some barriers simply by coming out. In turn, gay children seemed to alter parents' ideas about sexuality and even heterosexual sensibility. Having a gay child come out seemed to make it easier for some parents to give voice to certain private, intimate matters such as their own relationship dissatisfactions. Of course, this was not true of all parents and remained a kernel of an impetus for many, even among fairly tolerant and progressive parents such as the lesbian poet's mother. Nonetheless, gay children seemed to awaken some interest in parents not just about gays but about sexual diversity and problems within heterosexual relations. This was not a curiosity that PFLAG sought to reinforce. In part, the reason for this was simply that PFLAG was an organized movement offering a model of family interactions, one that was often in the position of responding to the New Right. Thus the group could hardly trumpet the idea of making parents more tolerant about sexual nonconformity, as these ideas would simply verify the New Right idea that the boundaries between homosexuality and heterosexuality were perilously slipping away. In a sense, PFLAG needed to restore an image of sexual innocence to childhood, one that was being torn down even in the heterosexual world, as contemporary children knew more than they did in any previous eras about sexuality.[98]

By the late 1970s and early 1980s, then, the incipient PFLAG movement was also buttressed by an increasing popular impetus to discuss personal family matters that hitherto had not been given much public circulation. These were not limited to sexuality but included depression, mental illness, wife abuse, and incest, within published personal accounts, films, scholarly studies, and in increasing media attention.[99] The diminished discretion surrounding these issues owed something not just to the sexual liberation movements preceding this decade, but to the popularity of the self-help movements of the late 1970s and early 1980s. Rejecting a medical model, self-help recommended peer care for individuals suffering from mental, addiction, or family problems, among others.[100] However, as the need for anonymous hot lines shows, inhibitions and social stigma remained quite entrenched.[101] There were still stories that people dared not tell, even in the late twentieth century, and help was needed about how to approach their telling. Accordingly, another PFLAG flyer of the late 1970s, "How to Come Out to Family and Friends," gave even more specific instructions on exactly what to say upon coming out or "some things you might tell them as you

begin the meeting." Gays were told to dole out significant parental assurances: "You brought me up in the best way—you're terrific parents. I love
you."[102] This advice was not only about the revelation of gayness but simply
about how to say "I love you": the coming out "meeting" was becoming
much more scripted with parents at the heart of it.

But it was important for organized parents of gays to reassure themselves that they were terrific, and one way they could do so was to position
themselves against an imagined excommunicating family, a theme that
gained prominence as PFLAG developed into a national organization. The
notion of excommunication lurked in the literature and rhetoric of incipient PFLAG groups to such a degree that it suggests a parental need for
repentance about any impulse they might have had to reject gay children.
Through PFLAG, this impulse was to be replaced with a script of unconditional love and acceptance. When Mary Borhek found out her son Eric was
gay via a third party, she called him to say that she knew. The conversation
was strained and awkward, but among the first things she recalled saying
to her son was, "You are still my son. I won't disown you."[103] Parents could
feel noble when they did not reject their children. This was the case in a
letter of a desperate-sounding mother to Mrs. Manford in 1973. She
explained that when she found out her son was gay just a few years before,
"I didn't take it too gracefully. I didn't understand so I went thru the whole
bit, frustration, anger, refused to accept as being an irreversible thing, tears,
defeat"; however, she clarified, "but at no time was he an outcast. We
assured him he was loved . . . and he has been free to live at home."[104]

Registering this sentiment, PFLAG groups of the late 1970s and early
1980s praised as virtuous those parents who had not rejected their children.
A tribute song by Leroy Dysart, "You Did It out of Love" (1982), acknowledged the idea of excommunication in noting, "It would have been conve-
nient just to turn your head / Pretend that we were dead, not even there."
It then extolled parents for standing in the face of prejudice, particularly
when "the forces that oppose us soon will have your name / And try to
bring you shame, because you care." The chorus, however, emphasized
love, and the sacrifice that parents took on when they too became the victims of homophobia:

You didn't have to share our load, you didn't have to walk our road
But you did it out of love

You didn't have to hold our hand, you didn't have to UN-DER-
 STAND!
But you did it out of love.[105]

Organized parents in fact publicized the theme of child disowning to convey the urgency of their project. In a letter seeking to reconcile gays and
religious institutions and leaders, Adele Starr, who with her husband, Larry,
had started a Los Angeles parents' group in 1976 and was central in the
formation of the national organization, wrote a letter to clergy members in
1985, urging them to realize that "misguided parents" were resulting in the
"tragedies [of] . . . families torn apart and teenagers forced out of their
homes."[106] In this vein, PFLAG groups portrayed disowning parents as
parochial, intolerant, and cruel. The Pensacola PFLAG pamphlet, for example, used as its cover the quotation: "I would like to share a very personal
part of my life with you, Mom and Dad. . . . You see, Mom and Dad, I
want to tell you that I am a homosexual. And now I have a question: do
you still love me?"[107] A poem in the pamphlet tried to capture a mother's
feelings upon learning her son was gay:

Twenty years
of loving him
of being proud. . . . My God! Is it possible
that I let the trauma of a few
minutes wipe away
all of this?[108]

But parents often did not reach this state of acceptance without soul searching or struggle. In fact, literature during the late 1970s and early 1980s
tended to highlight parents' transformations by conveying just how
stunned and emotional they had been upon learning about their gay children, in narratives that seem almost histrionic or operatic when they are
compared to the more pragmatic and political parents movement forerunners, such as Manford and Montgomery in the early 1970s and their prede-
cessors in the Mothers of the Year during the 1950s. Yet these moments of
domestic drama served as an effective narrative strategy to impel other parents to understanding. Were these stories, then, strategic, or were they genuine recollections of these parents' emotions at the time? In *Now That You
Know* (1979), Betty Fairchild recalled upon hearing her son utter the words

"I'm homosexual" that "everything in me shrieked NO! and my mind raced idiotically . . . no grandchildren . . . awful! . . . can't be . . . what did I do wrong . . . NO!"[109] She even wished her son had gotten a girl pregnant. Confiding these initial reactions through this stream-of-consciousness technique perhaps served the purpose of heartening their readers that they too might yet have a transformation and love their gay children.

These parental memoirs are primarily written by mothers and seem shaped by traces of a long-standing tradition of women's sentimental advice and confessional literature.[110] Perhaps not coincidentally, PFLAG mothers created themselves in a parallel way to "pro-family" women of the New Right, only with a deeper need for confession. Mary Borhek's memoir about her gay son, for example, was subtitled "A Mother Struggles to Accept Her Gay Son and Discovers Herself." Borhek has noted that after her son came out to her in 1975, she kept taped recordings of her feelings about the predicament, envisioning then that she would go on to write a book about how she had successfully prayed her son straight.[111] This was not, of course, the book that she would go on to write, but this profound shift in her initial purpose of writing might have spurred on her tone of broader transformations. The inset of her memoir reads, "How Does a Woman Grow? Sometimes painfully, even violently. . . . First came the divorce from her minister husband. Then came the revelation that her son was gay. Mary Borhek cried out, faltered, fought back, and then agonizingly began to grow."[112]

Borhek's unforeseen life turmoil was all bound up with having a gay son, but having a gay son did not ease her mind about the personal problems she faced. In her guidebook on coming out, she urged gay children to take account of how their revelations might coincide with other potentially grim realities of the life cycle. Parents in midlife "may be increasingly aware of their unfulfilled dreams, their mistaken decisions and choices in the past, the things they have not done that now may never be accomplished. They begin to realize that while they used to be able to keep going strong until 1 am, now they begin to wilt at 10 or 11 pm. They find their eyes at half-mast over the evening paper. They fall asleep watching television. The french fried onion rings they used to be able to eat . . . now cause indigestion, and feet that never hurt before start aching. The signs are there: *I am getting old.*"[113] Through this somewhat suffocating domestic scene of tiredness, grumpiness, and infirmity, Borhek suggested that gay children could become emblematic of just another dream gone wrong.

In fact, as PFLAG emerged as a national movement after 1982, the idea of gay children disrupting family equilibrium was coming to the forefront. It is as though a parent's disquiet in learning that a child was gay equaled the child's own pain and struggle in coming to terms with gay sexuality. While organized parents in the early 1970s upbraided other parents for being more concerned with their own feelings or what the neighbors thought than with their own children, later literature would identify this fear as a genuine and understandable concern on the part of parents. In the PFLAG pamphlet "Can We Understand?" (1983), a section called "Parents' Concerns for Themselves" included the two subsections "Should We Tell the Family?" and "What Will the Neighbors Say?" both suggesting that parents would need to come to some level of comfort with their children's sexuality before they could garner the strength to challenge the ignorance and prejudices of others.[114] Even some of the founders of PFLAG as a national organization, Larry and Adele Starr, were quoted in the *Advocate* in 1983 as saying, "You can't really say which is the more difficult: for a parent to learn that a child is gay or for a son or daughter to come out to parents."[115] Dr. Mary Calderone, a former president of the Sexuality Information and Education Council of the United States (SIECUS), in paying tribute to the New York City parents' organization in 1982, concurred: "Like their children's own feelings on discovering their homosexuality, most parents on first learning of it feel utterly alone and without support."[116]

The tension and uneasiness between the idea of what children appeared to be—heterosexual—and what they really were—gay—deepened during these years. One manifestation was the anxious metaphor of the child's gayness as a child's death. In this understanding, discovering that they had a gay child would feel like a death to parents, at least until the moment that parents came to terms with it. David and Shirley Switzer's book, *Parents of the Homosexual* (1980), geared toward Christians, suggested in a chapter titled "We've Lost Our Child" that it was common "for parents initially to experience the fact of their daughter's/son's homosexuality as if that person had died. . . . [P]arents experience the revelation as a death: the loss of the valued person whom they thought and felt they had [as a daughter or son]."[117] This book is empathetic to parental grief, even as its central purpose is to convince parents to love their children in spite of their sexuality.

But PFLAG adopted this rhetoric as well. In fact, PFLAG literature emphasized Elisabeth Kübler-Ross's stages of grief as ones that parents

would go through when they found out their children were gay. The 1984
PFLAG publication "Read This before Coming Out to Your Parents"
affirmed that many parents would see their children's orientations as a
temporary loss, "almost a death, of the son or daughter they have known
and loved" and suggested they would go through the phases of denial,
anger, bargaining, depression, and acceptance that Kübler-Ross had proposed of the dying.[118] This death metaphor is especially poignant when
compared to how the death metaphor for gay children came up in earlier
periods. Twenty years prior to this, in *Good Housekeeping*, a gay child was
conceived of as a reversible death. But now that organized parents were
registering a greater sense of finality about sexuality, gay children were taking on connotations of a more unalterable death that parents would have
to get used to in spite of their misgivings.

Mainstream media sources by the 1980s, too, would conceive of gay
children in the family as analogous to a child's death, and an alarming
social trend. *USA Today*, for example, recorded in 1983, "Each year more
gay young people than ever before 'come out'—and at a younger age. A
growing number of parents—stunned by this trend—are getting support
and reassurance from other parents in a national activist group," PFLAG,
which acted as a "rap group for the distraught." In this same article, a gay
activist was quoted as saying that the parents were usually "in such a state
of shock and disarray. . . . It's like this is the worst thing that can ever
happen in a family. It's like a death . . . a death of the aspirations they've
had for their child."[119] Fear of child loss was a pervasive and deeply held
theme in the 1980s, shaped by the increasing incidence of and anxiety surrounding mothers in the work force, most prominently.[120] Paula Fass shows
in her study of child kidnapping that fears of literal child loss were in a
sense marketed in this period, as a titillating fantasy of the worst imaginable
thing that could happen to a parent.[121] PFLAGers, too, shared in this sense
of child loss, even though their children, of course, had never disappeared.

Because PFLAG offered the promise that parents might get to know
their gay children, and even come to a greater parent-child intimacy, the
story of PFLAG, at least ideally, ends in transformation and rebirth. Even
disowning a gay child could be a reversible act. "Sally," a mother raising a
son during the 1970s and 1980s, who would become the subject of a 1993
PFLAG promotional video titled *With Arms That Encircle*, reflects that she
wished she could have provided more support of her son's effeminate interests when he was a boy, such as his dance lessons. She would have done so,

she felt, if she had received education about homosexuality and not been so scared about it. The video goes on to tell the story of her son's eventual estrangement from his family and his church as a young man. The commentator states that though this period of not talking caused "great disappointment and anxiety, it was also a time for transformation." And for Sally—and here the commentator smiles widely and knowingly—this time was "the beginning of acceptance." Sally then returns to tell of her first anxious PFLAG meeting and the subsequent Mother's Day, when, while she was sitting alone, still incommunicado with her son, he turned up at her door with a bouquet of flowers. He had not known that she had started going to PFLAG or that she had made progress. Clearly broken up and emotional over this memory, she does manage to say, "And that was the beginning of a totally new relationship between us. And I have to say that I look at my perfect family in an entirely different way now."[122] The commentator emphasizes that this could be the reality in anyone's family, if they simply reached out "with arms that encircle."

These often confessional stories about parents' feelings placed parents at the center of the parents of gays movement. It had always been a movement by and for parents, of course. But gradually, as PFLAG emerged as a national organization during the early 1980s, a sense of the primacy of children's needs and rights that the forerunners to PFLAG had accentuated had given way, in the movement's literature and advertising, to those of their parents. In contrast to the early organized parents who found parental self-pity to be self-indulgent, a distraction from the larger political project, later PFLAGers would come to expect and validate a need for parent-centered grief and healing through therapeutic nurturance.[123] As gay children gradually came to be seen as a potential crisis for family life, parental responses to them became more strictly focused internally and psychologically on the parental image of and investment in their children and the integrity of the family rather than a broad range of social justice and activism.

How did this ethos of parent grief come to be, when the parents movement had in fact eased the burden of having gay children through the movement's rhetoric of innate biological reality or sexual condition? A rhetoric developed to defend gay children also seemed to leave parents feeling more cognizant of and resigned to the permanence of their gay children's sexuality. Permanence was likewise a theme suggested in reformist gay activism during this period, and the parents movement had some over-

lap with these activists. John D'Emilio and Estelle Freedman have noted
that gay movements of the mid and later 1970s were more likely to have
discussed a fixed sexual orientation than the polymorphous desires characteristic of earlier gay activists.[124] Given this context, parents were less likely
to have an alternative psychological or political framework through which
to view or imagine their children's gayness. Instead of seeing their children's gayness from the perspective of civil rights and attempting to change
their children's political reality, by the end of the 1970s, the thrust of the
parents movement became more about urging its members, and hostile
outsiders, to see that these children were really and definitively gay. The
activist vision and focus on children was replaced by a therapeutic movement of sorts.

Critics of this period have charged the politicization of the personal
during the 1970s with the potential for overwhelming self-absorption, an
"apolitical interiority," as Donald Freedheim called it.[125] North American
society in the 1970s was quite conscious of the self and, as Irene Taviss
Thomson notes, a society with a growing therapeutic ethos that one must
"work" at intimacy.[126] Was the desire for social change becoming replaced
by a desire for self-realization, as Christopher Lasch charged, even among
the parents of gays movement? Were parents forced into a position primarily of sentiment, of dismay and outrage, given the level of vitriol against
gays that the New Right offered? Or were these parents actually having a
far more intimate realization about their children's inner worlds that earlier
parents had failed to register, and thus they needed to develop strategies to
teach each other about intimacy? The later group of parents might have
been the first to look on their children as unequivocally gay, especially as
PFLAG emerged as a national organization after 1982.

The baldness of their children's gayness, coupled with a sense of siege
that parents might have felt in the wake of the New Right's ideas about
gays and family life, combined to leave the parents of gays movement in a
profoundly paradoxical spot. As parents increasingly acknowledged the
reality of their children's sexuality, they sounded more dramatic and less
practical about their feelings, and perhaps more saddened and less reassured. As parents called for more intimacy between parents and children,
they increasingly offered a rigid coming-out script that foreclosed the spontaneous mutual exploration of those feelings. As parents disavowed any
traces of family influence on their children's sexuality, they repudiated the
influence of the family within the context of a movement whose very pur-

pose was to affirm the position of parents in the family lives of gays. And yet the parents movement and the literature that it spawned were also intended to give voice to and channel an array of confusing and contradictory feelings about these gay children. Whatever else they were in the parents' rhetoric, gay children were now undeniably real.

5

"Every Generation Has Its War"

WHEN THE AIDS activist group AIDS Coalition to Unleash Power (ACT-UP) staged street-theater-oriented protests in the later 1980s, one of their iconographic Ronald Reagan posters asked the question, "What If Your Son Gets Sick?"[1] The question was deliberately provocative, of course, part of the ongoing needling about the president's son's sexuality that was present in both gay-activist and gay-humor sources, but it also had a more somber underlying intention: gay men dying from AIDS were indeed sons who would be mourned by their parents, even in traditional families.[2] In a society that increasingly reinforced polarities between the so-called innocent victims of the disease and the presumably immoral ones, the simple idea that those dying from AIDS were family members was a poignant one.

When AIDS first became known in the early 1980s, it was deemed purely a gay disease. Doctors at the UCLA Medical Center and in New York City were puzzled that young gay men in their twenties and thirties were dying with pneumocystis pneumonia (PCP), an infection normally only seen in transplant or cancer patients. Some were suffering with a particularly virulent strain of Kaposi's sarcoma (KS), a disfiguring skin cancer characterized by purple and brown lesions, previously only seen in aging Mediterranean men, and even then considered not to be life threatening.[3] These patients all showed a lowering of their immune function, their bodies unable to ward off even typically harmless infections. Doctors first referred to these symptoms as gay related immune disorder (GRID) and only called the condition acquired immunodeficiency syndrome (AIDS) after the Centers for Disease Control renamed the epidemic in 1982. Before human immunodeficiency virus (HIV) transmission became understood in 1984, early theories about the disease suggested that gay men contracted it through an immune overload that was the consequence of spending sleepless nights at gay bars and discothèques, inhaling poppers, and having promiscuous sex.[4] Early media reports followed suit by calling the disease the "Gay Plague."[5]

AIDS casualties multiplied rapidly throughout the 1980s. By 1984, 5,600 Americans had died of AIDS, and by 1988 the number was almost ten times that figure, nearly 50,000.[6] The case load also grew tremendously throughout the 1980s: it was 225 at the end of 1981, jumping to 1,400 by 1983, 15,000 by 1985, and 40,000 by 1987. By 1990, more than 100,000 people in the United States had died of AIDS, and the majority were gay men.[7] The great majority of these deaths were young men between the ages of 25 and 44.[8] The disease spread rapidly within urban centers, most notably New York City, San Francisco, and Los Angeles. In Canada, where AIDS was initially seen as an American disease, AIDS cases multiplied first in major cities such as Montreal and Vancouver. After the mid-1980s, however, the disease made its way to other North American cities and rural areas.[9]

Throughout the 1980s, AIDS had become a potent part of the politics and sensibility of the American culture wars, the acrimonious divisions between social conservatives and traditionalists on the one hand, and social liberals and pluralists on the other, in the late twentieth-century United States. Especially as the Cold War waned, attention became focused on domestic issues, relations between American family members, and sexuality as it reflected the national character. The body was often the site of these conflicts; controversy surrounded not just gay sexuality but also abortion, pornography, and sex education.[10] Within the public imagination, AIDS added a dimension of a frightening, visible disease to an already entrenched New Right notion that homosexuality was unnatural. As Reagan-era surgeon general C. Everett Koop noted, the disease was marked by mystery, fear, and the unknown.[11] Those gay men who contracted it especially during the early part of the decade were seen as abstract or alien figures who suffered, as a 1985 *Newsweek* article suggested, "months to live with no place to die."[12]

Many observers of the AIDS epidemic have thus characterized the disease as one that united gay men and lesbians as peers within volunteer care networks, bringing the notion of chosen families—of partners and friends—to the forefront. And yet this disease also overlapped the social lives, experiences, and cultures of gay men and their families of origin. The family emerged in metaphors and images within gay activist rhetoric, figured in public health advertising and gay fiction, and appeared in personal testimonies and correspondence. Throughout the 1980s, gay men who suffered with this disease and their families often felt a powerful sense of isolation: they may have felt abandoned by indifferent politicians, alienated by callous images in visual and print media sources, and discriminated against by a fearful health care system. The understanding of this discrimination allowed parents to feel a sense of gay rejection firsthand, placing them closer to their gay children and intensifying the relationships—often ambivalently but nonetheless recognizably—between them and their gay sons. Simply by virtue of its being such a visible, horrific, and unrecoverable disease, the entire family often witnessed and wrote about AIDS, including siblings and grandparents, as well as parents. The observations of parallel generations and extended family bring a different but nonetheless powerful set of perceptions to family members with this disease. Family relationships in the face of AIDS even prompted a collective reimagination of ideas of care, nurturance, family love, and primal bonds. Amid the disease, conceptions of family life shifted from companionate, reciprocally emotional ones to more practical, protective units.

That AIDS was first named gay related immune deficiency syndrome indicates the extent to which it was perceived, at first by the medical community and then more broadly, as a disease inherently related to gay sexuality, often conceived strictly as anal sex.[13] This was an interpretation that some family members embraced as well, persisting in folklore, even after 1984 when the virus was named and understood better. Charles (Chasen) Gaver, a performance artist living with AIDS in Washington, chose to tell his father and siblings, living in the small town of Adrian, Michigan, about his illness in 1987. Gaver's artistry and lifestyle had long set him apart from his family. Though he worked as a paralegal at the Federal Trade Commission, he was also a successful performance poet, receiving one of the first grants awarded to an artist dealing with gay subject matter from the Commission on Arts and Humanities, in Washington, D.C., and having his performances reviewed in the *Washington Post*. After he contracted AIDS, Gaver performed poems about his experiences with the disease. He also kept a careful diary of his illness and preserved clippings and correspondence about it between 1987 and his death in 1989, calling these collections the *Fever Journal.*

At first, some members of his family were ignorant and fearful about his disease, and these fears seemed bound up with a squeamishness about his sexuality. When his sister Jill and brother-in-law John came for a visit, Gaver noted that "John had a case of 'AIDS paranoia' and claimed he got crabs from my apartment. His sister, a former nurse (who thinks you can get AIDS just from looking cross-eyed at someone), advised John to disinfect all his clothes in Quell and A-200 when he returned to Michigan. Real dumb!" He noted that John's attitude was particularly "disturbing . . . especially since he's 'family.' "[14] While polls of Americans in the mid-1980s showed that many still believed one could become infected with AIDS through coughs or handshakes, John's paranoia seems more informed by homophobia than illness: if he truly were worried simply about getting sick, perhaps he would not have been so concerned that he had "crabs," which does imply a transmission fear based on sexual rather than more routine contact.[15]

AIDS in the family brought gay sexuality and gay existence—real and imaginary—to the forefront. A short story by Sherman Yellin, "An Early Frost," which was to become the first movie to dramatize AIDS on network television in 1985, portrayed the tense, fraught relationship between a heterosexual father, a well-to-do businessman in New England, and his gay son, Mike, a lawyer in Chicago living with his partner. Coming out to his parents poses an insurmountable barrier. He tells them both that he is gay and has AIDS only when it cannot be put off any longer, after he becomes ill with a vicious strain of pneumonia. When he tries to touch his father to comfort him after his revelation, however, his father draws back as if to punch his son, only to be restrained by the mother. His father silences any conversation on the topic: "I heard you," he says. "That you're homosexual, that you have this . . . disease." In fact, his father can scarcely bring himself to say the word "gay," and when he does, it is as if the word tastes awful and he has to get it out of his mouth quickly: "He's a . . . what do they call it now, *gay?*"[16]

Parental portraits at times highlighted a more general male voyeurism and queasiness about gay sex, one that seemed to suggest, as playwright Tony Kushner said, gay men deserved to die simply for having sex with each other.[17] Paul Reed created a father who embodies this perspective in his 1984 book *Facing It,* one of the first AIDS novels in North America.

This father already considered his gay son, Andy, "his greatest disappoint-ment."[18] He could not abide his wife's mentioning his son's "disgusting illness," but on the other hand, "[h]e wasn't surprised; he knew the sorts of vile things that queers did—fucking strangers in alleys, sucking every cock that comes along, in bus stations, public parks, anywhere they could satisfy their groping lusts for men's flesh. And there was worse, he knew . . . it was no wonder Andy was sick. The whole subject made him nau-seous."[19] The uneasiness here seemed to go beyond gay sex and reach into a revulsion about sexuality and bodies in general, one that was grafted onto his gay son and his imagined sexual practices.

This gay writer's creation of a homophobic father evoked a condemna-tion of sodomy that saw a wider circulation during the 1980s. Conservative writer and commentator William F. Buckley called up a prurient image of gay sex when he announced that every gay man with AIDS should have a tattoo declaring his disease "on the buttocks to prevent the victimization of other homosexuals."[20] Supreme Court judges reinforced the idea of sod-omy as unnatural in the 1986 *Bowers v. Hardwick* case by upholding the Georgia sodomy statute, one of many state statutes prohibiting sodomy still on the books that was overturned only in 2003.[21] Michael Hardwick had been arrested for having sex with another man in his own bedroom; the Supreme Court justified this invasion of privacy for an act of consensual sodomy on the grounds that not all private acts at home between family members could be protected, placing sodomy on the same plane as crimes such as murder and incest. Upholding Hardwick's conviction, the Supreme Court ruling said that this sexual behavior had been denounced by "millen-nia of moral teaching." Was this idea of sodomy informed by AIDS, as well as these teachings?[22]

The connotations of anal sex and promiscuity discomfited some parents and seemed to taint the unqualified sympathy they might have offered were the disease "just" cancer or a more morally neutral one. As Susan Sontag has pointed out, however, even cancer has been a disease fraught with inter-pretations of negligence: at times, individuals with cancer have been seen as self-indulgent and irresponsible about their health, perhaps reflecting a distinctly American view of health as an individual rather than a collective or state responsibility.[23] AIDS was especially vulnerable to the charge of individual neglect or irresponsibility. By the mid-1980s, mainstream Amer-ican media sources and political culture had started distinguishing between "innocent" victims of the disease, such as newborns and recipients of HIV-contaminated blood transfusions, and "willful" perpetrators of the disease, such as gay men or drug users.[24] Portraits of the "innocents"—especially hemophiliacs and children—were careful to show them as ingenuous, asexual beings. By contrast, portraits of gay men and drug users often showed them in urban settings, clustered together anonymously in bars, as if they had no daily life outside of promiscuity and certainly no families.[25] As Douglas Crimp argued in his analysis of representations of individuals with AIDS, these people were often displayed as "safely within the boundaries of their private tragedies."[26]

These interpretations of the sufferers of this disease also pervaded family life and were apparent in the desire to understand the origins of illness within a gay son. Postulating the cause of disease and attributing a moral narrative to disease were not unique to AIDS, and this might have been particularly the case during the 1980s when North American exercise and nutrition habits came under a sharper scrutiny.[27] However, AIDS seemed to demand of parents that they defend their sons from promiscuity. Barbara Peabody, a mother who would go on to found the Mothers of AIDS Patients (MAP) organization in San Diego, reflected that her son had not "led an especially promiscuous life," and as far as she knew only had two lovers. However, she supposed "it was possible" that his sex life had been more active than she had imagined it. But "[e]ven so, [she] would never reject him, especially now."[28]

These assurances of their sons' innocence at times seem reminiscent of PFLAG rhetoric about the child's lack of choice in being gay, only here parents affirmed that their children did not choose to be sick. BettyClare Moffatt wrote a memoir combined with advice literature for families with sons with AIDS. Here she included a section written by her mother to give a grandparent's perspective. This grandmother recalled feeling that her grandson, Michael, "would not . . . join that category of people most susceptible to AIDS!"[29] She knew well that AIDS was a "disease fraught with social stigma" and that if she told her friends that she had a grandson with AIDS, they would first want to know, "Is he a homosexual?"[30] Religion played a role in her acceptance, however; she reminded herself that Christ had "walked with lepers," a group of people who had also, from a Christian standpoint, led sinful lives that needed forgiving.[31] Ultimately, she advised grandparents not to "recoil from that grandchild who has contracted AIDS. He is still the same little boy . . . who came running joyfully into your arms to show off his Superman suit, the same little boy who used to play games with you, whose dimples and shining dark eyes made any day brighter and more blessed."[32]

This disquiet about how sons got AIDS appeared even in portraits of idealized, accepting families. The 1993 AIDS film *Philadelphia* attempted to show parallels between gay and racial discrimination, perhaps to make gays a recognizable topic for mainstream North Americans. The central character, Andrew Beckett, has a loving and supportive family of parents, sisters, brothers, in-laws, nieces, and nephews. They are there for him in his court case against the law firm that has fired him for having AIDS. Still, when the defendant lawyer interrogates him on the stand about an anonymous sexual encounter he had had in a gay male pornography theater, his mother looks down in shame, the only such moment in the film. It is not clear whether Andrew and his partner had a strictly monogamous relationship or if they considered this encounter the definite source of AIDS.[33] But the mention of her son's anonymous sexual encounter does give this mother pause. The movie seems to say that the young man's disease and death could all have been prevented had he not indulged himself that one time, a theme perpetuated even in some gay cultural sources, such as Randy Shilts's journalistic account, *And the Band Played On*. This work angrily portrayed the flight attendant Gaetan Dugas, the notorious "Patient Zero," as a reckless, promiscuous sociopath perceived to have spread AIDS around North America.[34]

For some parents, the notion of individual responsibility was not irrelevant, even in the face of their own children dying. The desire to attribute blame to their sons' perceived promiscuity did not preclude sympathy for their sickness, though it certainly precipitated a reevaluation of the sexual revolution. One mother, Beverly Barbo, pointed out in the first page of her memoir about her son, Tim: "Why is my son dying? Because he made some bad choices a few years ago, one of which resulted in the disease AIDS, and AIDS related cancer, Kaposi's Sarcoma, is killing him."[35] Though Barbo was religious, her family had accepted their son's sexuality. The "bad choices" she referred to were not her son's "choice" to be gay but his choice of sexual partners. She believed that when her son first moved to California, from his tiny hometown of Lindsborg, Kansas, he must have experienced the culture shock of gay acceptance, and it was in this situation that she felt "sexual excesses do occur."[36] It is not clear, though, if her son had in fact been "excessive" or if he simply had had unprotected sex, unaware of the risk. Another memoirist, Ardath H. Rodale, seemed haunted by how her son's AIDS death could have been avoided. Like Barbo, she noted that her son, David, had grown up amid an ethos that seemed to say, "Enjoy sex to the fullest. . . . People were encouraged to experiment with the latest ideas. There were suggested positions for having sex that I never heard of before— never even imagined! People throughout the media winked an eye at, even openly approved of, multiple partners."[37] Careful to set herself apart from these sensibilities, she noted that she was brought up with more "Victorian attitudes," and having sex in her day was not "a function of getting acquainted as it often is nowadays!" In her view, these more liberal sexual mores had led the younger generation only "into anguish."[38]

This perception had its adherents in the gay world as well. Some prominent gay observers, most notably Michael Callen, criticized what they saw as the sexual revolution's excesses and the joys of an unfettered gay sexuality during the 1970s, the kind of hedonistic, postliberation gay mood that novelist Andrew Holleran gave voice to in his 1978 novel, *Dancer from the Dance*. He perceived an emptiness to gay life: most of Holleran's dancers— gay men in bars, in discothèques—are preoccupied with beauty, clothes, and anonymous sex and appear to be shallow and emotionally absent.[39] These observations of gay sexual practices of course prompted bitter debates among gay men about the legitimacy of casual sex in the face of AIDS. In cities with large gay populations, many wondered if commercial establishments such as baths and gay bars should be closed.[40]

Though Rodale made oblique references to her son's sexual partners as the probable cause of his death, she did not blame a perceived gay lifestyle. Instead, most of the book is devoted to memories of his innocence. The picture to emerge is similar to the icon of the innocent victim, a particularly potent image when another locus of the culture wars was simply the innocence of children more generally, or, as historian Steven Mintz put it, advocates of a "protected" childhood versus a "prepared" childhood.[41] Even beyond this, because a central site of contention of the culture wars was between subscribers to what historian Robert Collins calls "a transcendent moral authority" and those who sought secular authorities, it was in fact quite powerful to bestow a gay son with an air of transcendence or religiosity.[42] Rodale wrote that David had been a "good little boy, with a deep, wonderful chuckle," who wrote plays, was gentle with animals, and was "peace loving."[43] She even appeared to conceive of her son as a cultural type or a separate category of person: her dedication was to "all the Davids, and those who love them." These representations gave gay sons an abstract quality as an eternally loving and affable family member, even as they acknowledged, albeit haltingly, a sexuality that made their difference from parents striking.

Even with attempts to distance gay sons from promiscuity, AIDS made gay sex more real, if only as an acknowledged method of transmission. This complicated PFLAG's response to the parents of gay sons. If the rhetoric of organized parents had made gay children real, it had nonetheless severed sexuality from these children. Now gay sexuality also needed to be recognized. Moreover, AIDS challenged the PFLAG metaphor of gay as condition. If gay children already had the condition of being gay, then what was AIDS? For Mary Borhek, gay sons with AIDS appeared to have two unfortunate diseases. She instructed gay sons with AIDS that they must tell their parents that they are gay first, and let that sink in, as this announcement in itself would cause "enough grief . . . without having to deal with further cause of grief." As she warned HIV-positive gay men: "if you don't tell them you are gay, in the event of your death you will present them with an agonizing triple blow: their child has died; they discover that their child was gay; and they discover that he died of AIDS. . . . Not only do the parents lose their child to death; they also lose the child they thought they had, so that even the memory of him as they thought he was eludes them."[44]

A powerful underlying suggestion here, one that contradicts the PFLAG mandate about truly knowing their children, is that parents might not want to know their children, or might prefer their fantasies of what their children are. Only when these were absolutely impossible to maintain—as they would be in the face of AIDS—should gay children think about disrupting "the child they thought they had" and even here acknowledge their parents' grief and pain above their own. Cheryl L. West created a mother who felt something similar in her play *Before It Hits Home*, about an African American jazz musician, Wendal, and his family's response to his illness. His mother was furious when she found out her son had AIDS and was preoccupied with how he "got it." When Wendal tries to tell his father the next morning, his revelation is cut off by his mother, who tells him to "shut up. Just shut up. Don't say a word. I heard enough from you last night to last me a lifetime."[45]

For some parents, like Wendal's mother, the boundary between the revelation of gayness and a fatal disease was itself blurry. Coming out about gay sexuality and AIDS were both monumental and at times foreboding moments in parental representations of family life. Two other PFLAG and

AIDS activist parents, Bernie and Sylvie Goldstaub, were moved to publish an account that urged parents of gay sons to love their children. Their son, Mark Goldstaub, a publicist for entertainers in New York City, had revealed his sexuality on his father's birthday in 1979, introducing what he had to say with, as Mrs. Goldstaub recalled it, "I love you both, and God knows, I wish I could spare you the agony I know you must both feel at this moment."[46] By 1986, Mark had been diagnosed with AIDS, but, doing well on the then new drug azidothymidine (AZT), he did not reveal his disease to his parents until a year later, when his health had started to deteriorate. Mrs. Goldstaub recalled her son using almost the very words he had when he approached them about his sexuality: "Mom, Dad, I love you both. I wish with all my heart I could spare you this, but the time has come for me to tell you."[47] Had he truly said this, or was the moment so staggering to Mrs. Goldstaub that the words simply appeared the same in her memory? Was gayness such a menacing revelation, until it was trumped by something much more immense—and tragic—still?

From the perspective of their parents, gay men with AIDS also seemed to inhabit an unseen and unknown world of viruses, and, especially in the epidemic's early years, uncertain means of transmission. Cartoonist Howard Cruse, who was noted for combining both satire and brutal realism in his comic strips, evoked these early AIDS fears in his 1983 stream-of-consciousness story, "Safe Sex." The panels here depict many different scenarios of AIDS in American life, such as an immigrant from Haiti—stereotyped as primary carriers of HIV—being stamped with a message "Presumed Sick until Proven Well."[48] In one scenario, a mother serves her son at a holiday dinner wearing long rubber gloves and a surgical mask, and her son asks her, "Been watching a lot of TV news recently, Mom?"[49] If humor about AIDS was sparse during these years, the hysteria surrounding AIDS infection might sometimes be fodder for satire.[50] However, even as late as 1993, when the dangers of AIDS transmission were well known and reinforced many times by the media and public health advertising campaigns, PFLAG advice literature to families noted that AIDS could not be easily transferred and that there is "no reason to fear you are catching AIDS by being in the same room with someone who has AIDS, or by using the same linens, or kitchen utensils after proper washing. There is no reason to believe that AIDS is spread by casual household contact."[51] Such advice was meant to calm caregivers and those sharing domestic space with their gay sons. That this hesitancy could last until the early 1990s attests to the level

Figure 7. Cartoon in *Christopher Street*, 1983. Copyright 1983 by Howard Cruse; courtesy of Howard Cruse, www.howardcruse.com.

of uncertainty about the underlying presence of disease and the unknown entities that carried it.

Quite commonly, especially during the early 1980s, the hospital experience itself reinforced the idea that AIDS might be contagious, amplifying the idea of plague, which, as Susan Sontag famously noted, had become AIDS's central metaphor.[52] Before it was widely known that the disease was virus based, hospitals confined AIDS patients to isolation zones, hospital workers refused to clean their rooms, and funeral workers refused to embalm their bodies.[53] These realities compounded the already deeply ingrained social prejudices against gays and shaped parental interactions with their dying sons. In her memoir, Barbara Peabody recounted how distressed she felt when she had to visit her twenty-eight-year-old son at

New York's St. Vincent's Hospital in an isolation room. When she and her husband left this zone, they took off their "masks and gloves and stuffed them into the bag labeled 'Infectious Waste.' The yellow gowns go into 'Infectious Linens.'" Her experiences are reminiscent of one major artistic response to AIDS, choreographer Bill T. Jones's ballet *Absence*, in which the dancers were wrapped in bed clothes borrowed from his dead partner and his lover's hospital robes, as if to save these fragments of loved ones that otherwise would have been destroyed.[54] Such hospital precautions, even when in place to protect the person with AIDS as much as the parents, made Mrs. Peabody feel that she was visiting a leper.[55] Her former husband, a doctor, was grateful that he could treat his son during his seizures—common as AIDS progresses—because he knew that an "ambulance crew might have panicked at the prospect of treating an AIDS victim."[56]

Gay men with AIDS often had to educate their own family members on this score and at times endure their ignorance. In one of the first AIDS plays for a mainstream audience, William Hoffman's *As Is*, a dying gay man, Rich, receives a visit from his brother, with whom he has a distant relationship. The brother apologizes for not having visited earlier. By this point Rich is dispirited and almost grimly amused by the extensive contraptions his brother has donned simply to stand by his bedside. As he deadpans to his brother, "Unless you're planning to come into intimate contact with me or my body fluids, none of that shit you have on is necessary."[57]

At times families were placed in the complicated circumstance of fearing contamination and the physicality of the disease and yet wishing to show their loved ones compassion. Perhaps these fears attest to the success of public health advertising campaigns throughout the twentieth century, which, as medical historian Nancy Tomes says, were so successful in evoking an invisible world of germs that individuals grew constantly wary.[58] It would indeed be hard for family members not to pay heed to the place AIDS held in the public imagination as potentially more deadly than scientists had imagined. The visual and news media did little to dispel these thoughts, particularly when magazines, newspapers, radio, and television began reporting on AIDS more regularly after 1983.[59] Geraldo Rivera claimed on the ABC program *20/20* in 1983 that the nation's "entire blood supply" could be infected with AIDS, and even more respectable sources such as the *Journal of the American Medical Association* said the same year that AIDS could in fact be spread through casual contact.[60] Gay men feared that they might be contagious to those around them.[61]

Basic acts of caring for someone with AIDS, then, could be fraught with fear. This was true for Marie Blackwell's family, who cared for her brother, Chet. Blackwell wrote up her family's story for the African American women's general interest magazine *Essence* in 1985. Here she made it clear that Chet's gayness was firmly a part of their family lore and was never questioned. Chet "never had the pressure of having to 'break it to the family' [because] his being gay or acting sort of feminine" was what they considered a fundamental part of his personality. Mrs. Blackwell even told her son, "If you have to mess around with men, then go and find yourself a rich one."[62] Chet was diagnosed with AIDS in 1983, a time when her family felt "totally ignorant about the extent of AIDS contagiousness." Thus, when they brought him home to care for him, Chet was not allowed in the family kitchen, and they were wary of touching any food that they had left for him in his room. Blackwell often turned him down "with the excuse of being on a diet. He always looked very disappointed when I didn't eat his offerings." She became desperate to find ways to make her brother feel less contaminated and yet still care for him in a way that necessitated intimate contact and gestures, such as sharing food.

In this family, fears about AIDS and its prognosis also reflected a degree of mistrust of the medical profession. When Chet would have moments of feeling somewhat better, his mother would say, as if to convince herself, that he was "getting better. I knew those stupid-ass doctors didn't know what they were talking about. . . . All you have to do is eat a lot of food and be around people who love you. Those doctors just want to experiment."[63] The idea of hospitals as alien institutions was becoming quite engrained in the late twentieth-century United States, one that prompted theologian Paul Ramsey to ask that doctors treat "the patient as person" in 1970.[64] A notion of doctor distrust, however, might have been particularly prevalent for African American families, owing to the greater public awareness during this period of a history of medical experimentation on African Americans, most notably the legacy of the Tuskegee experiments during the Public Health Service syphilis study in the 1930s and 1940s. Cheryl L. West provides an example of this when her protagonist, Wendal, is told by a white doctor that he is indeed HIV positive. Wendal responds, "You telling me I got bad blood . . . well now . . . remember ol' Tuskegee? I recall you told 'em they had bad blood too . . . and then watched 'em rot to death. Ya'll got a history of this bad blood shit, don't you?"[65] This medical history specific to African Americans compounded a more general shift in public consciousness that regarded doctors with suspicion.[66]

The physicality of AIDS went far beyond connotations and hints of contamination, however. Those with full-blown AIDS became shockingly disfigured. They suffered from violent fevers, coughing, incontinence, and dementia, looks and smells and ailments that were well beyond the world of unseen germs. As would be true in Blackwell's family, many family members felt devastated by the emaciating quality of the disease, by how waxen, sallow, and skeletal their family members had become. Charles Gaver, who was fond of drawing doodles to illustrate his points in his letters, once closed with a picture that he labeled "Death Mask," or his reflection that he saw in the bathroom tile one evening at about 2 AM.[67] These physical symptoms were understandably shocking and painful for family members to behold in their loved ones. Michael Lassell's poem from the perspective of a brother of a gay man with AIDS, "How to Watch Your Brother Die," is written in the imperative tense, the narrator trying to reassure himself about being a witness to something so unimaginable: "Try not to be shocked that he already looks like / a cadaver."[68]

The face of those suffering with AIDS could be ravaged by the purple-brown lesions of KS, as though gay men with AIDS carried the visual lacerations and markings of a perceived nonascetic life. Even an experienced physician such as Elisabeth Kübler-Ross, who had worked previously with syphilis patients in Africa, a disease whose ulcerations could terribly disfigure the face, found it trying to behold an AIDS patient scarred with KS lesions.[69] She wrote of a young man with AIDS who had been estranged from his family, seeking one last visit home before he died. He confided to Ross that he had wondered, upon seeing his mother come out to greet him from the front porch, "what would happen if she really saw the purple lesions on his face? [Would she] stop and hesitate? [Would she] put her arms down and stop a few feet before they would hug each other?"[70]

Though in this case the man's mother did not respond as he feared, the anxiety about appearing grotesque was salient for many within their families. Striking in these accounts is that siblings seem more willing to admit to a revulsion about the physical aspects of the disease, perhaps because of the simple familial fact that they had not provided the material care for their siblings that parents had over the years. Writing about her brother, Montreal painter Nick Palazzo, Marie Palazzo said that she felt cruel because she could scarcely bear to behold him during the final stages of his

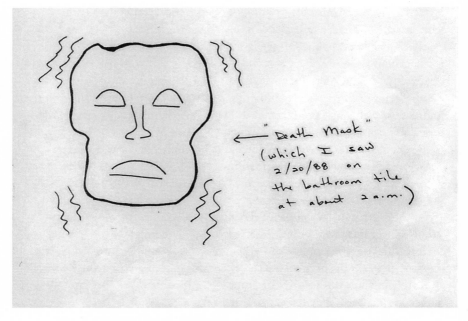

Figure 8. Charles Gaver's drawing of a "Death Mask," 1988.

disease. During his dying years, her brother had produced a series of paintings in which he drew himself as something half-skeleton and half-human;
it was called "The Disappearing Series." Marie Palazzo acknowledged that
"AIDS deforms. I don't want to remember my brother looking like he did
then—he used to be so good-looking—but I can't get that vision out of my
mind. It still haunts me."[71]

However, even AIDS advice books for parents recognized that such feelings of repugnance were quite common. Betty Fairchild advised parents not
to "put off a visit for fear of what your child will look like. Most people
with AIDS want more than anything else for their parents to be there, and
to know that Mom and Dad love them no matter what they look like. Keep
in mind that your child is already extremely aware of and sensitive about
his loss of good looks." She then advised parents to maintain physical relationships with their sons: "[Y]our willingness to look at him, to embrace
him, hold his hands and kiss him, and to be at ease with him, will convey
even without words how much you love him."[72]

There is some universal character to observing a loved one with disease, because the observers are always in some sense on the periphery, outside of the prolonged and painful suffering. Yet what is specific to this crisis is that the family members of gay men with AIDS were already somewhat peripheral as gay sons. Gay sexuality was often hidden from parents, at least for some portion of time. In the words of BettyClare Moffatt, reflecting on her then estranged son, Michael, the disease "had combined with the hiddenness of his life, the aloneness, too."[73] Her feeling resonated with media portraits that reinforced the idea of mysterious diseases for mysterious sons.[74] In one sense, the universal aspects of disease and suffering seemed to make their gay sons more familiar and knowable to parents, or at least more concrete. Yet in another sense this particular disease seemed to mark gay sons with another layer of abstraction, reinforcing the sense that parents were only the observers of their sons' veiled and obscure gay lives. Though her son did not develop AIDS until 1989, Bobbie Stasey recalled in her memoir that when her son came out to her in 1981, she became preoccupied with thoughts of a gay disease. Interspersed through her son's coming-out conversation as she recounted it is her stream of consciousness: "*A disease is killing homosexuals. A mysterious disease killing homosexuals.*"[75] Just as gay men throughout the 1980s were starting to perceive and represent an interconnection between gay sex and death, parents appeared to be doing the same.[76]

At times parents finessed their son's illnesses, so that their children did not die of this mysterious disease associated almost solely with homosexuals, but instead died of Hodgkin's disease or meningitis or an unspecified lengthy illness. Some parents reasoned that this misrepresentation of their children's illnesses seemed necessary to protect the family. Ann Des Rosiers, whose son had come home to Worcester, Massachusetts, to die, reflected that in her small city, "everything is hush-hush . . . and that's how we had to live it."[77] For this family the AIDS Commemorative Quilt became an essential way of expressing pride in their son and grief for him and acknowledging that they had indeed cared for him during his slow death. One of the purposes of the AIDS Quilt, subtitled the NAMES Project, was to give a name, or a reality, to those who had died from AIDS, one often denied within published death notices or newspaper obituaries. Yet even the AIDS Quilt's organizers received letters that urged them to keep a gay man's name anonymous, because it would contradict parents' stories about how their sons had died.[78]

Some parents lied about their sons' diseases as a way to gain empathy for their family's suffering. Michael Stone faced the unique position of being one of the first teenagers to die with AIDS, at the age of nineteen, in 1984.[79] At the time, the Stone family, according to their father, "told everybody at work it was Hodgkin's disease." He felt that, if he had said AIDS, "everyone focuses on AIDS and the homosexuality and not on the person."[80] In making up another disease, this father felt that he could in effect give his son the grief that he deserved. He was not amiss in thinking he might not receive sympathy if his son had died from AIDS. Even AIDS funerals had become sites of antigay protests: mourners had been spat upon, derided, and reminded of biblical condemnations of gays during the services.[81] There was even violence against those "innocent" victims of the disease: Ryan White was run out of his small town of Kokomo, Indiana, after a bullet had been fired into his family's living room, and the Ray family, whose hemophiliac sons had all contracted AIDS, had had their house burned down in Arcadia, Florida, in 1986.[82] The fabricated illnesses need to be considered in this context of profound stigma and even physical violence. Surgeon General C. Everett Koop said that a new word needed to be coined for homophobia during these years because homophobia was simply not strong enough to capture the hatred he had witnessed.[83] Thus discretion about children's illnesses could reflect a basic desire for dignity and protection and not solely parental shame.

This discretion, however, added a layer of isolation to parents' grief because AIDS became, in the words of philosopher Judith Butler, a "publicly ungrievable loss."[84] Jean Baker, who lost her son to AIDS, sought acknowledgment of her grief from a community of family sufferers. She recalled in her memoir that after her son died she developed a preoccupation with reading obituaries, hoping for some connection to those who had endured the same sorrow she had. She would take note of the "death of a man, particularly between the ages of about twenty-five and forty or possibly even older, who was unmarried; whose survivors included parents, siblings, nieces, and nephews, but no spouse and no children; whose death was unexplained; and who was often involved in some creative field."[85] As she aptly observed, AIDS had a particularly devastating impact on the North American artistic community: gone were artists Keith Haring, David Wojnarowicz, and Robert Mapplethorpe and writers Craig Harris and Essex Hemphill, among others.[86] These kinds of descriptions would "immediately alert me to think that maybe this unknown person was gay, like my son,

and maybe this person had died from AIDS, like my son."[87] The community of grief that Baker sought was only found through these subtle messages, akin to the gay cultural codes of earlier decades, only here with the
tragic spin that they came about through a gay death.[88]

The community of fellow sufferers was at times so elusive that family
members of sons dying with AIDS sought one through identification with
collective sufferings of the past. For Barbara Peabody, AIDS was a genocide
rather than a randomly cruel biological phenomenon, and thus she felt
some affinity for witnesses to the Holocaust. After having seen a placard at
a demonstration declaring AIDS "God's pest control," Peabody noted that
some "sincere Christians" felt AIDS to be a "'final solution,' as the gas
chambers were for the Jews."[89] It was not a coincidence that ACT-UP organizers chose an inverted pink triangle as their symbol, to evoke the badge
sewn onto the uniforms of gay prisoners in Nazi concentration camps, or
that activists took up metaphors of war to describe what was happening to
gay people during this period.[90] This metaphor was not invoked cavalierly:
using the Holocaust to convey ultimate suffering served to give a feeling of
reality to family grief and pain. Some perceived the striking physical simi-
larities between AIDS bodies and concentration camp victims. In the words
of Peabody, who made this comparison, both were "gaunt, knobby, emaciated . . . weak from malnourishment." What really struck her was what she
called "an AIDS face." An AIDS face was "prematurely aged. Men of 30
appear years older, the skin stretched tight over skin and jawbone. . . . The
eyes are torturous, sunk deep into their bone-ridged hollows."[91] These
World War II analogies were also common in artistic responses to AIDS. In
his print "Prophylaxis: Blind Admonition," Michael Tidmus juxtaposed an
image of a baby doll and a little boy against a mushroom cloud, with Hit-
ler's face hovering in the background, inscribed with the words "AIDS
Baby: (Born 1951)."[92] AIDS babies were, of course, a group deemed innocent victims of the disease; in this photo, the innocents were adult gay men
born soon after World War II. AIDS was producing a culture of suffering
inflected with Holocaust imagery. Looking to the Holocaust for a verifica-
tion of suffering was not unlike Jean Baker's motivations in scanning the
obituaries.

In late twentieth-century North America, however, the dying were often
hidden, or at least removed from public view, placed within clinical atmo-
spheres of hospitals and quickly disposed of in morgues and graves.[93] Reticence about the dying, moreover, is not unique to AIDS. And yet this

Figure 9. Michael Tidmus, "Prophylaxis: Blind Admonition," 1993. Courtesy of Michael Tidmus.

particular historical moment of the experience of death could be said to have collided with a collective gay craving for family acknowledgment and care. This longing was a theme in philosopher/photographer Duane Michals's haunting AIDS photograph and narrative poem, "The Father Prepares His Dead Son for Burial" (1991). Lying on a mattress on the floor, the son in the photo appears too perfectly poised to be sleeping, but too robust to be dead. The room appears somewhat filthy, with spattered walls, dirty carpets, and scraps on the floor, yet the son lies sheathed in a white, translucent sheet, his face and body form apparent, prepared for burial by his father. The father had washed his son's body

slowly, deliberately, looking hard at him
for the last time.
He touches him with oil, carefully as if not to awaken him.

In a scene of squalor, the father has cleansed his son most meticulously for his death. But in performing this loving ritual the father "begins to quiver with grief," and this escalates into a "terrible shout of anguish."[94] The odd juxtaposition of both alive and dead here suggests a yearning for these kinds of parental caring rituals expressed throughout a child's lifetime: sleeping and dreaming, as opposed to oblivious and dead.

Organizations responding to the AIDS crisis had taken into account this kind of longing and insisted that a son's dying could become a moment of profound family intimacy that was so elusive in this photo. During the mid-1980s, PFLAG had developed an HIV/AIDS Family Support Project, and it was joined by other groups, including several independent organizations, such as Mothers of AIDS Patients (MAP), that provided support in various cities.[95] Though the PFLAG Family Support Project had warned parents about the discrimination they might face in exposing their sons' illnesses, ultimately the organization cautioned against reticence, because "[t]he silence may . . . feel like a betrayal of their loved one and lead to feelings of worry and guilt. . . . [Moreover,] the bereaved loses an important avenue for recovery—talking about the loved one."[96]

This idea of family closeness through open discussions about the disease was taken up in public health advertising campaigns as a way to encourage AIDS knowledge. "Ojos Que No Ven" ("Eyes That Fail to See"), produced in 1987 by the Instituto de la Raza, a community-based nonprofit organization in San Francisco, was one such ad, specifically targeting the city's Chicano community. In general, Latinos in the United States had been particularly hard hit by AIDS; in 1990, they represented 27 percent of all cumulative AIDS deaths.[97] In this series of realist photo captions, an unsuspecting mother comes home early from work to find her son, Manuel, and another young man making out on her couch. In subsequent captions, they sit down to talk about all of this. When Manuel's sister, Isabel, arrives home, she wants to know just what the scene is all about. Manuel explains that he has just told his mother that he is gay. Shocked, Isabel insists that it cannot be and then, in her unthinking haste, tells her brother that she is glad that their father is already dead, otherwise this would kill him. Horrified by this comment, the mother reaffirms that Manuel is, above all, fam-

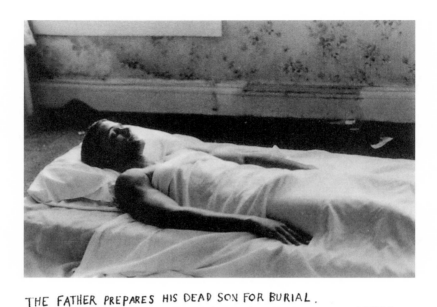

THE FATHER PREPARES HIS DEAD SON FOR BURIAL.
HE WASHES HIS BODY SLOWLY DELIBERATELY, LOOKING HARD AT HIM
    FOR THE LAST TIME.
  HE TOUCHES HIM WITH OIL, CAREFULLY AS IF NOT TO AWAKEN HIM.
THE FATHER LEANS TO HIS SON'S EAR AND WHISPERS SOMETHING.
  HE WRAPS HIM IN COTTON LIKE A CHILD ASLEEP AND EMBRACES HIM
      THEN THE FATHER BEGINS TO QUIVER WITH GRIEF.
    AND THE VIBRATION OF HIS MOVEMENT BECOMES A SOUND,
    LIKE A DEEP MOAN THAT GROWS LOUDER AND LOUDER
      INTO A TERRIBLE SHOUT OF ANGUISH.

Figure 10. Duane Michals, "The Father Prepares His Dead Son for Burial," 1991. Copyright Duane Michals. Courtesy Pace/MacGill Gallery, New York.

ily. But Isabel remains wary and cross, saying that the next thing he would probably confess was that he had AIDS. When Isabel later approaches Manuel to apologize for her rash response, the conversation becomes chatty and chummy, with Manuel even protectively telling his sister that she too should practice safe sex. Isabel is grateful for both the information and the ability to talk about sex openly like this with her brother, because she had not yet been able to do so with her mother. Likewise, the mother is relieved and heartened to return home to find her son and daughter laughing and joking together, and even more relieved to know that her son had been working at an AIDS Information Line. She then initiates a conversation with her daughter about sexuality.[98]

As this portrait shows, AIDS was increasingly seen as a threat to heterosexuals, and gays had something to teach them about the disease. After 1985 especially, mainstream visual and news media insisted, as *Life* magazine declared during this year, that "no one is safe from AIDS."[99] The Instituto de la Raza's ad showed a marked difference from earlier, more judgmental public health advertisements showing gays and bisexuals passing the disease to unsuspecting wives and other heterosexuals.[100] By contrast, the Instituto's 1987 ad showed AIDS surfacing in the context of familial relationships. Though many Chicano writers have described the difficulties and uncertainties of being gay within a culture that often views homosexuality as a violation of *la familia*, the Instituto's ad shows that an ideal of family strength within Chicano communities could be harnessed for a communal effort at AIDS prevention, shaped by a reconciliation between gays and heterosexuals, as represented by this mother and son.[101]

Despite portraits like this one, the acute hostility to gays and AIDS sufferers continued throughout the 1980s and became an explicit part of the New Right view of moral problems in contemporary life. The slow responses of both the Reagan and Bush administrations to the AIDS crisis appeared to all but condone the suffering of individuals with AIDS and their families. Ronald Reagan did not discuss AIDS publicly until a speech in 1987.[102] North Carolina Republican senator Jesse Helms proposed quarantining people with AIDS and staunchly opposed bills allocating money to AIDS research; he declared on the Senate floor in 1987 that every case of AIDS could be traced back to a homosexual act.[103] "The poor homosexuals," conservative columnist and Reagan speech writer Patrick Buchanan wrote most infamously in 1983, "[t]hey have declared war on nature, and now nature is exacting an awful retribution."[104] Religious commentators such as Jerry Falwell placed a picture of a white family wearing surgical masks on the cover of his *Moral Majority Report* with the headline "Homosexual Diseases Threaten American Families."[105]

These conservatives' emphasis on morality and family contrasted cruelly with their treatment of gay men with AIDS and their families. In her memoir, Jean Baker indicted Presidents Reagan and Bush, who could "barely bring themselves to say the word AIDS." She believed that the administrations' "callous [response] affected all those who have suffered and died

Figure 11. Instituto de la Raza, advertisement, 1987. Image courtesy of the Division of Rare and Manuscript Collections, Cornell University Libraries. Permission to publish courtesy of the Instituto Familiar de la Raza.

En casa de Doña Rosa, se ha desatado una tormenta. Lo que vió al entrar a su casa la ha destrozado. En esos momentos entra Isabel.

¿Qué está pasando aquí?

¿Porqué estás llorando mamá?

Es bueno que lo sepas tú también de una vez. Acabo de confesarle a mamá que soy homosexual.

¡¡¡Qué!!! Tú, un . . . ¡¡¡No, no puede ser!!! ¡Qué bueno que papa está muerto sino esto lo mataría de vergüenza!

¡Isabel! ¡Te callas por favor! Ante todo, Manuel es tu hermano.

Manuél, ¿porqué no me dijiste antes?

En casa de Doña Rosa, Isabel trata de concentrarse en sus estudios pero no puede. El pensar en su comportamiento del día anterior la perturba. En esos momentos entra su hermano, Manuél, y se dirije a tomar un vaso de leche del refrigerador.

Manuél, ¿me perdonas por lo de ayer? No me porté como hermana.

¡Te voy a estrangular, es lo que voy a hacer! ¡No corras!

Como no te voy a perdonar Flaca, pero sí te vuelves a portar así, la próxima vez que traigas a tu novio me pongo un vestido!

¿Con esos bigotes? Ni de broma te la cree.

Hablando de tu novio, Isa, tú tienes relaciones con él?

Sí, yo no veo nada de malo en eso y me estoy protegiendo con la pastilla.

¡Pero eso no te protege del SIDA!

¡Pero el no es gay! ¡Ay que bruta soy!

Olvidalo, mira Isabel, yo trabajo en una línea de información del SIDA. He aprendido mucho. Sobretodo que el virus no discrimina. Agarra parejo. Todos tenemos que cuidarnos.

Me gusta hablar contigo así Meme. Con mamá nunca he podido.

Haz la prueba. A la mejor te sorprende.

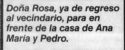

Doña Rosa, ya de regreso al vecindario, para en frente de la casa de Ana María y Pedro.

Doña Rosa, ¡qué sorpresa! Pásele.

Solo quería darte estos folletos sobre el SIDA que me acaban de regalar.

Las risas de sus hijos reciben a Doña Rosa al entrar a su casa.

Así me gusta verlos.

Mamá, ¿sabías que Meme trabaja en una línea de información del SIDA?

¿De veras hijo? Me quitas un peso de encima porque eso quiere decir que tú te sabes cuidar.

¿Me dejas a solas con tu hermana? Necesito hablar con ella.

Sí mamá.

Doña Rosa y Isabel entablan una conversación íntima, franca y sin rodeos.

Isabel, hace mucho tiempo que debí hablar contigo como debe hacerlo toda madre con su hija. Tú ya eres una señorita, y es importante que sepas que las relaciones sexuales, a la vez que son algo muy bello, también pueden traer consecuencias desagradables . . .

from the disease and those who love them."[106] Ultimately, she felt that many AIDS deaths were needless ones: "Vast numbers of young gay men, including my son Gary, may have become infected simply because they did not know of the existence of a sexually transmitted virus that could kill them and because they were not given the information, soon enough, that could have helped save their lives. . . . I often picture Gary and his friends, young and strong, striding happily through the bustling streets of Manhattan, laughing, partaking of the city's excitement and promise, thinking their lives are ahead of them, and all the while living, unknowingly, on the edge of disaster."[107] Her criticisms echoed a larger branch of gay activism, such as Larry Kramer's well-noted journalistic piece, "1112 and Counting" in the *New York Native*, which emphasized that even if a cure could not have been found early, information and warnings most certainly could have been circulated much earlier than they were.[108]

Abandoned by politicians, gay men and their families also depicted the medical system as having failed them. Parents and sons were flabbergasted by the cost of drugs such as AZT, particularly when the drug first began its testing during 1986 and 1987. Not only did the drug cost as much as ten thousand dollars a year, putting it out of reach of those without medical insurance or Medicaid, but its side effects could be ghastly.[109] Some parents thus became resolute activists demanding changes in the health care system. Ann Baker, for example, wrote a letter to President George H. W. Bush in 1989 that she then published in the *PWA (Persons with AIDS) Coalition Newsline*. She and her husband had come to Washington to commemorate the AIDS death of their son, Curtis. Sixty thousand people were doing the same in a candlelight procession around the Lincoln Memorial. However, she was disappointed that the president and his family were not among them. In her letter, she established herself and her family as decent, law-abiding citizens whose sons had served in the Vietnam War. As she saw it, the president too was a "family man, good husband, good father, and good grandfather," and yet he was "supposed to represent the Father of our country."

The most concrete demand of this letter was to ask for better health care for people with AIDS by calling their care a basic civil right. Federal health care funding in general had suffered during the 1980s: Reagan's health policies had been to limit public expenditure on Medicare and Medicaid for the elderly and the poor and to give local governments greater responsibility for these matters.[110] Not until 1987 did Congress, in response to protests about the high costs of AZT, give money to states to offset costs.[111] And it was not until 1990 that Congress passed the Ryan White Comprehensive Care Act, which provided funds toward planning and services for people with AIDS.[112] Mrs. Baker noted that she had seen firsthand "how much these people have to pay to stay alive (if that's what you can call it) for two years tops." She was "only one mother who has suffered and will go on suffering the pain of the loss of my beautiful son." Her final appeal to the president was, "Please help all of humanity all around the world by making sure that the pharmaceutical companies don't make great amounts of money on these people who have to live with a death sentence."[113]

The plain fact that AIDS sufferers were indeed family members always underlay these activist petitions: they were pleas for recognition as much as they called for support or assistance. Ann Baker stressed it over and over: she was the mother of a son who died with this disease. It was a recognition that AIDS activists, through such organizations as ACT-UP, sought as well. Drawing on an idea of participatory democracy and activist street theater and art, Larry Kramer founded ACT-UP in New York City in 1987.[114] Other groups soon appeared in Los Angeles and many other American cities, as well as Canadian ones such as Vancouver.[115] Taking up the artistic and advertising skills of its members, the group began to stage imaginative, dramatic, militant demonstrations.[116] ACT-UP's first political funeral took place on election day in 1992, when 250 members carried the emaciated corpse of Mark Lowe Fisher, a New York architect, to the Bush-Quayle campaign headquarters in New York City's midtown. Protestors held up a banner that read, "Mark Lowe Fisher, 1953–92, Murder by George Bush," while chanting, "George Bush, you can't hide, we charge you with genocide."[117] Before he died, Mark Lowe Fisher had issued a statement about his prospective public funeral. The statement became an ACT-UP advertisement titled "Bury Me Furiously." Here Fisher explained that he did not want a "discreet memorial service." He understood that "our friends and families need to mourn. But we also understand that we are dying because of a government and health care system that couldn't care less." Acknowledging that his funeral was going to "shock people," he wanted, nevertheless, "to show the reality of my death, to display my body in public; I want the public to bear witness. We are not just spiraling statistics; we are people who have lives, who have purpose, who have lovers, friends, and families."[118] Did it take a grisly, shocking protest simply to underscore the reality of AIDS sufferers and the basic claim that they, too, had loved ones?

There was a kind of surreal, nightmarish quality about living with and caring for a loved one with AIDS in the context of a broader culture that scarcely acknowledged the mass grief that the epidemic had produced, preferring to focus instead upon its risks or prurient voyeurism regarding gay sex. Family members and partners of gay men with AIDS seemed to be part of a war that nobody else recognized or experienced as a part of their daily lives, hence the importance of efforts at self-publishing memoirs of sons who died with AIDS or seeing them memorialized in the AIDS Quilt. In an article on AIDS writing in *Christopher Street*, writer and editor Michael Denneny wrote that his life had become a "surrealistic series of medical disasters, hospital vigils, and memorial services [while] everyday life went on as if nothing were happening."[119] He wrote of Annie Dillard's advice to writers in a recent issue of the *New York Times Book Review*, to write as if you were dying, "for an audience consisting solely of terminal patients." Yet she had not "imagine[d] that a whole generation of writers might be" already living out this metaphor.[120] Denneny and other observers of AIDS, through the loss of loved ones, were forced to live out St. Paul's lament in the Bible, "I die daily."[121]

Horrific as the disease was, it did offer sons and their parents a unique parallel experience. A generation of gay baby boomers was now witnessing the kinds of mass deaths normally reserved for those in old age. In a letter to his father when his partner was dying, Robert John Florence wrote, "I sure know what it's like to be surrounded by people who are sick & dying, as you mentioned in your letter about the mobile home park. Several friends have died recently & my intimate friend of five years has been in the hospital eight times so far this year."[122] AIDS also could put sons closer to the calamities that their parents had seen in their own time and of their parents' collective memories as experienced through illness. Writer James Edwin Parker's mother scarcely mentioned her son's involvement with men or sexuality, though she did know about it.[123] He felt that she must have been "somewhat aghast to think of the number of sexual partners I had, especially with people dropping dead of pneumonia and KS and other AIDS related diseases." Still, she appeared to feel a kinship with her son, seen through the lens of her past grief. When her son found out a friend was dying of AIDS, she offered, "I went through a similar thing, you know, with the war . . . the end result was the same: young men dying. Every generation has its war. You have to fight them when they happen."[124]

Parents also remembered the shame and stigma of sickness, a recognition that might have been particularly true for adults who came of age in the 1930s and 1940s, when the humanity of the sick was not so readily seen, before Elisabeth Kübler-Ross's groundbreaking work on the experience of the dying had become a part of medical school curricula and before the advent of the hospice movement in the 1960s and 1970s.[125] Political activist Dean Lechner's parents knew the mark of disgrace of sickness all too well, particularly contagious sickness, as they had a son who died of polio in the 1950s. Polio had been blamed on uncleanliness in the literal sense: parents were urged to keep their homes spotless and to observe proper nutrition.[126] The state health department had nailed a sign to this family's front door, to tell the public to keep away. This experience had fortified them to speak up against anyone in their small farming town of Waseca, Minnesota, who might shun their son who was dying from AIDS. He was living in San Francisco, but his parents and siblings invited him home to die there. As his sister addressed him, "Dogs go off to die . . . and you're no dog. . . . You're a son; you're a brother. And you are loved."[127] As these testimonies suggest, much as AIDS could evoke apathy and even repugnance among heterosexual observers, it could also evoke sympathy for suffering, both for individual family members and for gays as a besieged minority who faced intolerable suffering.[128]

Like this son who came home to die in rural Minnesota, the two Americas, one rural and seemingly unsophisticated and homophobic, and the other urban and at least on the surface cosmopolitan and diverse, were, like the disparate generations and sexual sensibilities, meeting one another through AIDS.[129] *Farm Journal* commented upon this phenomenon in 1991 with its feature article, "Back to the Farm to Die: Rural America Is about to Be Blindsided by the AIDS Epidemic."[130] Nevertheless, shocking examples of discrimination had occurred against gays in these rural contexts, such as Kokomo, Indiana, and even PFLAG literature felt the need to warn parents in rural areas that taking in their loved ones could result in violence.[131] Nonetheless, these areas could also be sites of a loyalty and fierce embrace of anyone once their own. Wayne Schow, the father of a gay son living in Pocatello, Idaho, embraced his son's return home when he started ailing with AIDS. Still, he could not help but notice that there seemed to be some profound disjuncture between his son's death and his rural social circumstance. He saw Pocatello, where he worked as an English professor and where his son had grown up, as a "comfortable place . . . sheltered from the ills that beset contemporary urban life. Here you generally expect life to be kind." When his son, Brad, came home to die, he reflected that his brutal, slow death was "not the sort of thing that should have happened in southern Idaho. The cultural geography is altogether wrong."[132]

To be sure, some gay men felt an ambivalence about this prospect of returning home to die, and even toward the home itself. Charles Gaver could not bear rural Michigan, finding that the place produced a feeling of "confinement, limitation, and drabness." He referred to the town where his father and sister lived as "that prejudice Adrian."[133] He had arranged for his death and his funeral in Washington. Similarly, in his personal essay, "Kentucky 55 South: A Visit with Dad," writer, actor, and activist James Carroll Pickett felt a simultaneous pull toward and distaste for the rural Kentucky farm where he had grown up. Living in Los Angeles, he had visited his father at home, to talk about his impending death. While he and his father appeared to grow closer during the visit, he was emphatic with his father that his ashes be spread over the Pacific and that he did not, in any circumstance, wish to be returned to Kentucky.[134] Rosalind Solomon captured this ambivalence about the home and parents in an arresting photograph that became part of her series "Portraits in the Time of AIDS." Here a son and parents pose in a backyard with a fence, shrubs, and garden. In the foreground, the son appears somewhat defiant or fed up with arms folded, and a resigned yet daring expression. His parents, hovering behind him, seem hardly posed at all, but almost awkwardly placed in the photograph, as if momentarily in the way of the picture. Not only are they distant from their son, but aged, tired, old-fashioned, and detached from the scene, looking away from both their son and the photographer. The overall impression of the photograph is disjuncture and a feeling of disorientation. Yet the son's resolute stance suggests a need or perhaps a right to be rooted in families.[135]

Ambivalence about the family relationship became particularly urgent in the face of a child's actual death. Representations about sons coming home to die have been criticized as moments of forced reconciliation, which deny any of the nuances of the family relationship and give parents a primacy in their children's lives that they neither felt nor deserved.[136] Douglas Crimp has illuminated the material circumstances of this forced homecoming, which sometimes occurred only when individuals with AIDS

Figure 12. Rosalind Solomon, "Untitled," 1987. © 1987 Rosalind Solomon.

did not have medical insurance or disability benefits to stay on their own, a point that embodies a larger one that gay activists made about representations of AIDS, that they often did not depict and ignored the larger social contexts of AIDS suffering.[137] The 1991 movie *Our Sons* evokes this theme of the domesticity of dying and a desire to represent a reconciliation between parents and children. The story is of two mothers who both had some emotional distance from their gay sons. One of the mother characters, who had disowned her son for being gay when he was seventeen years old, reaches some sort of rapprochement with him on his deathbed. After her son dies, this mother takes her son's coffin home from San Diego to Arkansas, even though she had not been present in her son's life for years and had yelled at him in the hospital that he had brought the disease on himself and was dying from "what he is."[138] The relationship is quite forced here, with a suggestion that no matter how horribly parents treated their gay children, they nonetheless had the right to their children in their dying moments and ownership over the child's body and memory. Understandably, gay observers protested these kinds of portraits, seeking recognition of the acts of care that community members had provided and noting the extreme vulnerability of gay relationships in the face of a lover's death, when parents could simply trump that connection.[139]

But moments of love and reconciliation, and even moments of anger and estrangement, are seldom as uncomplicated as they are portrayed in Hollywood films or even gay activist sources. The claim to family and home was also one that gay men made and represented, even if done cautiously. This feeling is captured in a haunting 1987 photograph by Billy Howard, which shows a mother holding a large, framed photo of her deceased son in a living room. The living room has a middle-aged feel to it, with lace curtains, a velvet couch, flowered straight-back chair, a carpet, a plant, and a doll figurine. The sorrowful mother is lovingly holding her son's picture, as though hugging it, which heightens the accompanying "Conversations with my Son," especially her recorded words of June 13, 1986: "What do you want me to do, my son?"[140] Howard's photograph can be read as another visual demonstration of parental ownership, a mother who, whatever her relationship with her son during his life, was clearly there for him during his death and now had guardianship over his memory. The large photograph of her son could be said to inscribe him forever, and without choice, in the family home, trapped in a daunting picture frame, surrounded by his mother's tastes and will. And yet it could also represent an affirmation of love between mother and son, something that could nonetheless have the same ambivalence as the gay memoirist who in 1961 recalled hating his parents' tacky kitchen and chandelier yet craved the love and comfort that it seemed, as a fragment of parental domesticity, to represent.

One of the attractions that drew gay sons home was not simply the care and nurturing offered there but the memory, prospect, or hope of it. This yearning is not the same as the simple, Hallmark moments of long-denied family reconciliation and harmony that AIDS movies and television seemed so keen to represent, but nonetheless suggests a powerful, sometimes submerged fantasy of family intimacy, one that was not defined by knowing

"Conversations with my Son"

May, 1985 – "Mother, don't worry. It's just a virus. I'll be O.K. I always have and I always will."

October, 1985 – "Mom, I was given the AIDS test today and the results will be ready on the job."

October 20, 1985 – "Mom, the results show that I have AIDS."

October 22, 1985 – "You know Mom, I have good news! the doctor says I don't have AIDS. What I have is A.R.C."

November, 1985 – "Mom, when I get well there are a lot of things that I will do differently."

December, 1985 – "No, Mother, I don't want you to come. Save your money."

January, 1986 – "Mom, can you come? I'm scared."

February, 1986 – "Mom, I'm coming home."

May, 1986 – "Mother, I'm buying my car this weekend."

June 3, 1986 – "Things are not working out too well."

June 13, 1986 – "What do you want me to do, my son?"

"Oh, yes Mom – I want lots and lots of flowers!"

Ricardo M. Plera

Figure 13. Photograph by Billy Howard, 1989. Courtesy of Billy Howard from his book *Epitaphs for the Living: Words and Images in the Time of AIDS.*

children's inner worlds or understanding their feelings, but perhaps by a more basic kind of family love and the material aspects of care. Before the AIDS crisis struck, gay liberation and lesbian feminist movements had also reevaluated the meanings of family love to include open communication, an understanding of inner lives, a recognition of a breadth of sexual experiences and choices, and mutual confidences. A sense of emotional reciprocity between parents and children was paramount for them. AIDS, however, established an esteem of the nurturing qualities often associated with motherly love. If gay activists and writers had in previous decades rejected the quotidian as aspects of the conformist nuclear family and the oppressive character of the day to day, a new ethos was taking shape during the AIDS crisis that suggested an embrace of domesticity and an idea of caring as an opportunity rather than a burden: material care became its own kind of emotional authenticity and even a spiritual act of witnessing. In this sense, the family was reenvisioned so as to resemble an earlier sort of family constellation, based on reciprocal practical obligations rather than reciprocal sentiment, only in the AIDS crisis these practical obligations were not economic but physical and quotidian. The family ideal that gays sought could now be marked by a sense of service that was the source of affection.

Sue Halpern evoked this sensibility when writing about the Chris Brownlie AIDS Hospice in Los Angeles, where she observed a mother ritualistically bringing meals for her ailing thirty-two-year-old son that he would never eat. Halpern reflected that the "dailiness of [family life was] that which gives love its openings."[141] This sense was not limited to the families she observed at the hospice. A sense of renewed parenting surfaced during the AIDS crisis between parents and gay sons. Gaver felt that his father had become a quiet, daily presence that was extremely comforting to him. He wrote that "although he's not one to say much, I can really feel the caring when I see him (like at Christmas) and talk to him on the phone."[142] This sort of interaction was certainly a departure from his earlier relationship with his father. His father had expressed his wariness about his son's poetry performances in 1977 because "according to the article [in the *Washington Post*], you use a lot of props and act like a queer or whatever it is—I just don't understand."[143] But they had reached some understanding during his son's illness, even comparing the pills that they had to take for their various ailments.[144]

Michael Williams also felt that his father offered a pacifying presence. Williams was an environmentalist living in California, and he wrote letters to his sister and his father during his partner's and his own sickness with AIDS. Feeling destitute and hopeless in 1989, Williams wrote to his father to break the tough news that he was going to start taking AZT. "Since it is probably my last good opportunity to begin AZT, and since the FDA won't sanction any of the other reasonable alternatives at a reasonable speed so that my insurance company would have to cover them, I will probably start taking it next week," he explained. "I am very upset about the whole mess. . . . [I]f I didn't feel that my real task is showing the world that it is silly to flush my life down the drain as they are doing, I would do something very drastic and sensational, like inject the virus into some prominent bigot, and tell them they've got a few years to promote the search for a cure. I am in a state of shock, fighting depression."[145]

Williams's father was quite taciturn in his letters and generally wrote in an unvarnished way. He stated candidly to his son in response, "Very distressed about your health. Your letter of 16 April caused me to cry. Still, better I know now, than be terribly surprised later. We have nice weather today."[146] In this context, a comment about the weather, one that had been such a prominent symbol of the emotional poverty of family talk within gay liberation sources, was a valued gesture of small talk. Here the daily observation seemed to reinforce some commonality between father and son, or shared humanity, and implicitly challenge the idea that closeness can only be achieved through mutual confidences. Williams and his father shared an interest in gardening, and in the same letter his father told him that he had started to see some yields from his spring garden—"a few spuds, some garlic."[147] When Michael developed terrible stomach cramps as a side effect of AZT, his father again expressed his concern through their shared interest in gardening: "Are there any herbs you would use to help your stomach cope with AZT? Will close for now and to Post Office. Love, Dad."[148]

Fathers were perhaps cherished for this reticence more than mothers were, and the expectations of a more expressive or effusive nurturing might have been higher for mothers. In her book on AIDS, Elisabeth Kübler-Ross described mothers who, she felt, took on the most difficult physical duties of caring, bringing their sons home, cleaning up after them, providing their medication, and being on call all through their sons' sleepless, feverish nights, having little reprieve from their caring obligations. Ross saw these tasks as particular to the feminine domestic sphere.[149] Public health advertising generated by gays themselves played on this notion of an idealized

Figure 14. "L.A. Cares . . . like a Mother," 1985. Courtesy of the Los Angeles Gay and Lesbian Center. Image Courtesy of the Division and Rare and Manuscript Collections, Cornell University Libraries. Permission to publish courtesy of the Los Angeles Gay and Lesbian Center.

mother figure as well, there to help gay men in times of crisis. One billboard advertisement in Los Angeles, for example, shown throughout the mid and later 1980s, produced by the Los Angeles Gay and Lesbian Community Services Center, featured the actress Zelda Rubinstein as a matronly-looking woman flanked by shirtless gay men. The slogan read, "Play Safely. L.A. Cares . . . like a mother."[150]

Fittingly, the AIDS advice that PFLAG had now started to dispense not only concerned emotional intimacy with one's gay child through talking about personal issues but also included a prominent component on the material aspects of care, often directed at mothers, who were presumed to take on these tasks. In the PFLAG "Family Support Guide," the authors gave substantial attention to the physical comfort of sons with AIDS who were receiving care in the home, including the necessity of changing the bed clothes, ways to cope with spiking fevers, and the kinds of massages that might offer comfort.[151] This advice pamphlet, subtitled "A Need for Constant Love," reminded that an unequivocal embrace of gay children was reflected in this care. The authors noted that sons with AIDS "are usually more isolated and have fewer visitors than most patients. They are also touched less and may be in need of more caring physical contact. Remember, they are dealing with more psychological pain than others with terminal illness. Quiet conversations with loved ones in familiar surroundings are encouraged."[152] In this portrait, the family's functions seemed parallel to an extremely caring nurse.

Gay men certainly looked to their peers to provide this kind of care, as well, and they did, creating their own caring structures and organizations, recognizing the value of widespread intimacy and caring in the face of disease. The Gay Men's Health Crisis (GMHC) formed in 1981 in New York City, and it drew together volunteers to help care for the sick and the dying in a buddy system, a relationship beautifully portrayed in David Leavitt's novella, *Saturn Street*.[153] The Shanti Project in San Francisco, an organization that predated AIDS, as well as the AIDS Project of Los Angeles (APLA) performed similar functions, assuring gays that they were not without committed and caring individuals in families by design, a kinship strategy that anthropologist Kath Weston has suggested is a particularly poignant one for gays.[154] Moreover, AIDS tended to mobilize gay men as well as lesbians, who at times brought expertise from their own public health care ventures.[155]

One mobilizing factor within these peer communities of care was rejection by the family of origin, a fear that gay culture and community organizations alike addressed. David Summers, who was to become a founding member of the PWA (Persons with AIDS) Coalition, recognized that it was not possible for all AIDS sufferers to go home. His mother suggested that he not come back to their Texas home after he was diagnosed in 1984, and he protested her shallow preoccupation with propriety. "How dare you tell me not to come home because I'll make everyone uncomfortable," he wrote. "What an incredibly selfish attitude to take. I have a serious disease, Mom. Maybe even fatal. . . . When you say I would *make everyone uncomfortable* by coming to Texas, what you are really saying to me is *What will the neighbors say?* And I thought you were stronger than that."[156] Another 1990 caregiver's guide for people with AIDS assumed that AIDS patients did not have biological family support and could only get this support within the community itself.[157] In her memoir about caring for her friend, Mike, Amy Hoffman wrote a stunning rebuke to the overvaluation of biological families over chosen families. She claimed that her friend's "real family," as her mother referred to them, were "a bunch of ill-matched people living in too small a space, making each other miserable." It was his "fake family" who performed all of the caring in the midst of his disease.[158] A nurse at Sloan-Kettering became a member of the GMHC upon witnessing the suffering of some familyless patients with AIDS. In her solicitation

of support for the GMHC, she wrote of an AIDS patient named Robert
who had told her that his family was ashamed of him for having the disease.
She phoned his mother to try and intervene and to "explain how desper-
ately Robert needed her," and the mother hung up on her.[159] In turn, Mr.
and Mrs. Goldstaub were moved to write their book on unconditional love
because of the stories they had heard of rejecting parents. Bernie Goldstaub,
a music professor, had already composed a tribute to their son titled "Vene-
tian Echoes." In their book they made a specific appeal to families who
disowned their gay sons who were sick and dying from AIDS: *"Don't Do
That to Your Child during the Most Needed Time of His or Her Life! This IS
Your Very Own Flesh and Blood!"*[160]

Despite these stories of family rejection, the nurturing and care that gay
peers offered to each other nonetheless was suffused with a familial sensibility, and perhaps reflects a token of a family connection or a longing for
one. When his partner was dying, Michael Williams was ashamed to admit
to his best friend, Bonnie, that he found caring for him draining and that
he had wondered what it would have been like to lead a more conventional
life, caring for children of his own rather than a partner his own age. Bonnie
was quite emphatic in her response, revealing the boredom she felt at times
when taking care of her children and telling him that taking care of a tod-
dler simply did not compare to taking care of a grown man. His partner,
after all, was a man of over thirty years old, who had contributed so much
and was certainly "worth" a child.[161] These comparisons between families
of origins and families of friends were implicit in AIDS advice sources,
though the hierarchy between the two was resisted. Even generic advice
pamphlets on caring for those dying from AIDS assured friends that they
were instrumental to the caring process and that friends could also be "part
of the family."[162] Organizations such as the GMHC did not presuppose that
parents were absent from the lives of their dying gay sons altogether. In
fact, one function of the GMHC was to blend the "chosen" families with
the biological. In a collection of personal stories for the GMHC, one man
wrote about his lover's mother, who had moved from Florida to New York
City to be with them. He did not know "what [they would have done]
without Nick's mother, Nita. Through this crisis, the three of us have
bonded to become a new kind of family."[163] A PFLAG advice pamphlet to
families caring for a son with AIDS tried to encourage this sort of family
blending as well. It reassured parents that even if they lived far apart from
their sons, their sons most likely had "developed an extended family com-

prised of a number of relationships." This pamphlet told the story of a mother who traveled from the East Coast to see her son in California, finding the presence of these friends "very reassuring."[164]

PFLAG itself encouraged a family reassessment, not to see the superiority of a biological or a chosen family, but to unite the two for a more effective family. At the PFLAG National Convention in 1991, Anne Serabian, whose son had died of AIDS in 1985, made a heartfelt speech. She hoped that by 1991 parents were beyond the shame and sense of disgrace she had felt when her son had succumbed less than a decade before. In his illness and death, she relied on young people, feeling that their generation was not so preoccupied with the stigma of a disease contracted sexually.[165] Her feeling exemplified a broader generational strategy on the part of parents of gay sons during this period. The 1992 advice book *After You Say Goodbye: When Someone You Love Dies of AIDS* advised families to honor their sons' friendships and relationships as a healing strategy in the wake of death.[166] Similarly, after her son, Jimmy, died, Bobbie Stasey turned to his friends, who shared their stories about Jimmy with her. "Look what families cut themselves off from when they cut themselves off from their son's friends," she reflected. "There's a part of him they'll *never* know if they don't know his gay friends."[167]

For some parents, the reembrace of the caring role could also become a reevaluation of gay sexuality, or their perceptions of gays. Before this epidemic was made known, PFLAG had asked parents to transform their homophobic attitudes. AIDS caused these parents to come to terms with a much more profound sense of regret about how they had treated their gay children before the onset of their disease. In a PFLAG advertisement, Betty Holloran, whose son had died of AIDS, told a story of reconciliation with her son through the disease. She admitted that when their son told them about his gayness, she was "sorry to say . . . we were shocked and upset."[168] However, during his three-year struggle with AIDS, she "learned to love and accept him as a gay man," they became very close, and he died in the family home.[169] Again, PFLAG provided a venue for parental repentance, and for stories of transformation, but it is difficult to disentangle whose fantasy of family reconciliation this represents, exactly: was this a deeply felt, collective, parental one? A somewhat forced gesture toward conventional family life? An acknowledgment that these parents thought their sons would have hoped for?

When Jean Baker reflected on the death of her son, she could not quite imagine that she had ever experienced her son's gayness as remotely tragic and issued a poignant challenge to an interpretation of a child's gayness as a child's loss. "How strangely insignificant [now] seemed the fact of his gayness," she said. "How difficult to believe I had ever thought his being gay was a tragedy. Being gay is not the tragedy; what is tragic is that any parent can reject a child simply because the child is gay. And, of course, the death of one's child is the ultimate tragedy."[170] As her testimony suggests, AIDS changed how gay sons and their parents imagined each other and changed their expectations of each other.

As a disease and social phenomenon, AIDS brought about a more intense parental repentance for not having given their children unconditional love, something that was tested most rigorously in the face of this disease. Even as AIDS made gay sexuality more vivid and highlighted a chasm between gays and heterosexuals, it also emphasized the importance of parental care. Thus the AIDS crisis helped to shift the tenor of gay perceptions of the meanings of family love, shaping an often conflicted but nonetheless present gay fantasy of family intimacy. The disease substantially altered expectations of nurturing from parents and the value attached to their caring roles. In both gay culture and the culture of parents observing their sons, a new relationship to family and domesticity was taking form.[171]

EPILOGUE

Mom, Dad, I'm Gay

B Y THE 1980s and early 1990s, gays were starting to envision themselves as enduring, if contested, family members. Images proliferated
of gays revealing their sexuality to their parents, bringing their partners home to meet their parents, and participating in family events. The
desire for family integration appeared throughout gay advice literature and
gave inspiration to gay and parental confessional stories alike. Increasingly,
gays seemed to be embracing domesticity and the expressions of interiority
that it offered.

This impetus for family integration, however, was a long-standing one,
just as the fear of family banishment was never far from the surface. During
the immediate postwar period, gays devised strategies to maintain both
their gay identities and their family membership through discretion. During
the late 1960s and early 1970s, those gays who had adopted a liberation
perspective largely abandoned discretion, claiming a more unequivocal recognition from heterosexual society, which included their families. This
demand encompassed a substantial critique of the stunted emotional
expression that heterosexual society, nuclear families, domesticity, and their
own parents represented. Paradoxically, the very vehemence of this critique
also seemed to suggest a longing for family to which the gay culture of this
period also gave expression. In seeking to expand the possibilities for family
intimacy, lesbian feminists embraced this liberation analysis as well but felt
an even greater ambivalence, as antifamily ideas contradicted the movement's ethos of womanly intimacy and mother-daughter love. In turn, the
AIDS crisis suggested a profound reimagination of family care and nurturance. Postwar families had come to be seen as places of emotional intimacy
through self-revelation between its members, a demand that gays themselves increasingly sought throughout the 1960s and 1970s. But it was also

gays who troubled this demand for emotional intimacy in the renewed respect for basic acts of familial care that the AIDS crisis engendered, one that saw gays returning to the family fold both literally and figuratively.

In the wake of the AIDS crisis, however, these sentiments became supplemented by a conception of intimacy characterized by both material care and understanding and empathy, one that seems to fuse the desires of liberation cultures with AIDS caring values. Could basic care and primal love be combined with an understanding of inner lives? Could the family of origin have an unequivocal place in the chosen family? This was not an unqualified fantasy for gays, and a substantial ambivalence remained as the family of origin seemed to become more omnipresent in gay lives, perhaps more so than many gays had ever hoped for or envisioned.

Parents, too, held an array of confusing feelings about their gay children during the postwar period. During the immediate postwar period, they were prompted to view gay sexuality as a psychological phase or a consequence of psychological immaturity; during the liberation period, they tended to see it as a political or ideological phase or a consequence of an experimental, exhibitionistic youth culture. Seeing children as "really" gay, as some parents increasingly did through parental organizing and writing, necessitated understanding a child's lost connection to parents: any commonality through a heterosexual sensibility was now irrevocable. In turn, the AIDS crisis tended to highlight gay sexuality and gay existence even as it suggested a committed form of family caring that was not concerned with sexuality.

By the end of the century, what had definitively changed in parents' expectations of gay children and in gay children's expectations of their family lives was the ritual of coming out. Gays could no longer live a life of discretion, a life without an increasingly formalized and scripted coming out to their families. A fully developed, mature PFLAG organization was deeply implicated in establishing the necessity of the coming-out moment for the sanctity of both parents and gay children. By 1988, PFLAG had nearly two hundred local groups and was making gains within smaller, rural areas; the national organization had relocated from Denver to Washington, where it now had an executive director and staff. During these years PFLAG developed a more formalized advertising campaign in which the organization tried to make families with gay children conventional or normal. One way they did so was by making these families white. One telling PFLAG advertisement, which served as an invitation to PFLAG's annual

dinner in New York City in 1986, titled "We Are Family!" featured the
Norman Rockwell painting "Freedom from Want" (1943). The painting
shows a white family at a holiday turkey dinner, a mother/grandmother
ready to hand out the fixings, and several young people at the table.[1] In this
version, however, the image is gayed up by showing two young men and
two young women making eyes at each other from across the table.[2] The
desire to portray the families of gays as utterly conventional, white, and
even Christian seemed to preclude nonwhite organizational images, or even
nonwhite member parents.[3]

The very kind of rhetoric emphasizing conventional families with gay
children also applied to PFLAG political activism, which took on an even
more intensely inward, familial dimension during these years. As PFLAG
developed more committees and task forces on specific issues, the organization received greater publicity for these efforts. Former PFLAG president
Paulette Goodman's series of letters to then first lady Barbara Bush in 1989
received perhaps the most attention of any PFLAG action during this
period.

While twenty-five years ago Jeanne Manford had written to the president, as both a mother and a citizen, Goodman now wrote to the wife of
the president, "mother to mother." Goodman emphasized that PFLAG had
"lifted the veil of ignorance [to learn that] our gay and lesbian children are
fine, responsible, contributing members of our communities. They deserve
our love and support." Still, she identified the most central oppression
faced by gays as the tumult they faced within their own families: "Families
are often overwhelmed when confronted by the issue of homosexuality.
The suffering we experience due to our prejudice toward gay men and
lesbians is unnecessary and disrupts family life. . . . We and our gay loved
ones would certainly appreciate a kinder and gentler America." Taking up
George Bush's clichéd slogan, Goodman then asked Mrs. Bush to show
"the human face of homosexuality [by helping PFLAG] to dispel the
myths." Soliciting "positive words" from those who were "important and
respected in government [could stop] violence and hysteria in our society."
She praised Mrs. Bush for being a "powerful role model as a mother and
grandmother" and for being "loving and compassionate," and thus having
the power to "help heal the wounds" of gays and their families.[4] In this
letter, Goodman's emphasis was not civil rights, as Manford's had been,
but instead the vital roles of gays within the family.

This letter was premised almost solely on motherly devotion, and Mrs.

Figure 15. PFLAG advertisement, 1986. Courtesy of the IGIC Collection, Manuscripts and Archives Division, the New York Public Library, Astor, Lenox, and Tilden Foundations.

Bush could do no other than respond in kind. Her brief note affirmed the principle of equality and commended Mrs. Goodman for being a "caring parent" who loved her child and spoke with "compassion for all gay Americans and their families."[5] But this simple and rather noncommittal response was enough to generate some controversy and pressure for Mrs. Bush to rescind her comments.[6] Betty Fairchild urged her not to do so, writing her back and telling her of the urgent need for family support, because "families continue to suffer needlessly," and the work of the organization "reunited [them] in love and understanding."[7] PFLAGers were in the unique position of pronouncing, as signs read in early 1990s gay pride parades, that "prejudice and bigotry are not family values."[8] The deepening conservative rhetoric about family values had provided a family framework for activism that left room for this intensely personal kind of political plea.

The notion that gay children and parents had encountered and withstood homophobia prompted a sense of mutual victimhood. Parents were not only blameless in causing gayness, but there was also a sense emerging among gay children during this period that parents were not to be held accountable for homophobia. This trend was made manifest in the burgeoning rituals surrounding the act of coming out to family members during these years. These coming outs had originally been an aspect of the liberation cultures of the late 1960s and early 1970s, only then they were often performed in a political context. By contrast, the family coming outs of the 1980s and 1990s seemed much more internal in purpose, encompassing feelings of self-worth and self-fulfillment. Rob Eichberg offered this plea in his advice on coming out in 1990: "[Coming out] is . . . the first step in liberating yourself to be a whole, complete, and powerful adult—the authority figure in your own life. Withholding the truth from others, as well as from yourself, generally leads to depression and feelings of powerlessness."[9] He even encouraged gays to come out to parents who were already dead, by writing them a letter or even taking this letter to the parents' graveside and reading it aloud to them.[10] These revelations reflect a narrated, confessional self emerging during these years, as well as a sentimental culture of coming-out.

The recognition that parents might have their own pain and difficulties with the revelation, which PFLAG insisted be recognized, seemed to have permeated even the revelations that gays made to their families within intimate contexts. UCLA doctor and diarist Robert Kevess was quite self-conscious about his coming out to his mother in 1989. He wrote in his diary about the buildup to writing his mother and carefully composed the letter he would send her in New York City, even selecting the PFLAG materials to send along with it. He included a copy of the coming-out letter in his diary, telling his mother that it was necessary for him to tell her because "we simply cannot have a good relationship without you being aware of it." Assuring her that she was a terrific mother, he also allowed her time for all of this to sink in. "Mom, I don't expect you to understand all of this right away," he assured her. "You are of a generation which has had much less tolerance for non-traditional lifestyles, especially that of gay people." The only thing he asked from his mother was that "unless you have positive things to say," he would rather that she "wait 2 weeks before talking to me about the contents of this letter. I certainly wouldn't want you to say things that you might later regret. Take two weeks, think it over, and call."[11] The two weeks allotted seemed to be for the raw, potentially painful emotional reaction that his mother would presumably have, before she had time for thoughtful meditation or to read over the PFLAG materials. In a published collection of coming-out letters of 1988, several other authors made a similar suggestion to their parents. "Alan," aged forty-two, told his parents that this was "the most emotional letter that a son or daughter could write to his parents" and that he thought it might be "easier on all of us if you both had a chance to read this and 'mull' it over before we eventually sit down and talk about it."[12] Even if coming out was a significant life moment, it was not an entirely spontaneous one, on either side.

The very idea that parents would need to take time before talking to their children suggests a fear of an irrational parental response and the desire to control it, as well as a somewhat mechanistic quality to these revelations: they might have been sparked by an inner imperative, but they were managed after that. Even if they did hear these initial reactions, gay writers made great allowances for their parents' homophobia. Rachel Pepper was living in Chicago while her parents were living in Canada, and she came out to them over the Christmas holidays in 1988. She was working for Chicago's *Outlines* magazine at the time and published her musings on this parental confrontation there. Their reactions were quite severe: they swore a lot at her, and her father told her that homosexuality was "bringing down the modern western world." They told her that they "no longer wanted to be a part of [her] world" and that they were "no longer proud of who [she] was." They even suggested that she just invented being a lesbian to hurt them or that she had some unresolved psychological issues from her youth. Though their "remarks hurt badly," she knew that "my parents need time to work through the shock I've given them. And I love them enough not to push them. In time, they'll deal with it, in their own way."[13]

These parental interactions departed quite dramatically from the unrepentant style of coming out of the liberation period and almost seemed a throwback to the early postwar period, in which many gay writers simply expected that their parents would be terribly upset. However, there was one crucial difference here. These revelations presumed the transformation of parents. An NGTF pamphlet of the early 1980s, "About Coming Out," suggested that even though the revelation could "surprise, anger, or upset," gays should not "react angrily or defensively" because the "initial reaction may not be the long-term one." What gays needed to do was give parents "time to adjust and to comprehend the new information about you. Don't expect or demand immediate acceptance."[14]

The idea of familial embrace of gay sexuality, partners, and gay sensibility was in fact illusory for many gays writing in this period. For Susan Chen, a first-generation Chinese woman, the narratives of transformation that circulated about PFLAG parents contrasted starkly with how her family had reacted to her sexuality. In 1988, she was a sophomore in college, and her parents found out that she was in a relationship with a woman. Her father told her in Mandarin, "You step on my heart."[15] In turn, "[s]ome of my non-Asian friends suggested that I just respond with, 'Forget it; if they don't accept me it's not my problem. I'll just continue with my life as I please, and ignore them.'" Yet, even at her angriest moments, "I could only maintain that attitude for a short period of time. Then the guilt returned. Besides I loved them very much. Despite feelings of bitterness . . . I knew everything I had came from my parents. They had done so much for me and I owed much to them in return."[16] Chen's story speaks to a different assessment of parental obligation between gay children of immigrant families and nonimmigrant ones, as well as a greater attention to parental shame.[17] Despite her fear that "Asian parents just didn't become PFLAG parents," she hoped to see her parents join the organization and "march in a huge gay and lesbian parade."[18]

The idea of parental duty was particularly pronounced for Chen, but this notion was still very much in place within a broader consciousness of gays, perhaps more so than it was for heterosexual children. Twenty years after Barbara Stephens had given her indignant testimony about having to take on the financial and caring burdens of her aging parents, Glenn Wein, a writer for *Christopher Street*, wrote in 1985 that gay children are still the children upon whom parents depend when they need help as they grow older and their health diminishes, even when these parents refused to acknowledge their children's sexuality.[19] Had the pain and alienation of being gay, as well as the experience of witnessing the AIDS epidemic, produced a kind of empathy with aging parents who were marginal and somewhat alien now themselves? And could this empathy for parents become a gay political strategy? Journalist and essayist William Dubay thought so. Writing in *Christopher Street* in 1985, he thought that a new direction for gay liberation could be found in returning to the family of origin and cultivating an understanding between the two sexual sensibilities.[20] At virtually the same moment that family sociologist Judith Stacey, in her study of late twentieth-century American families, *Brave New Families*, was writing that the family was an "ideological concept that imposes mythical homogeneity on the diverse means by which people organize their intimate relationships . . . distort[ing] and [devaluing a] rich variety of kinship stories," Dubay in fact seemed to be drawing from a much older, early nineteenth-century family ideal, in which adult children could stay with their parents indefinitely.[21] These sentiments pose questions about how much parents and children had truly let go of one another in the late twentieth century: perhaps gays responded uniquely to a deep yearning for ever-intact families that never fully left family consciousness, even from within white, middle-class family constellations that are said to be so individualistic. In turn, perhaps fantasies of gay banishment did in fact express a broader, underlying fear of family breakup and a larger, basic sadness of children growing up and moving away from their homes and their family pasts. In a sense, gays were seeking to become the recovered orphans that all adult children, from the vantage point of the late twentieth century, were.

And yet these two journalists evoke a complex family situation in which family selves but not gay selves were acknowledged. This kind of family accommodation was inherently contradictory, and it bred equally contradictory gay responses and interpretations. Not all gays assumed their family roles cheerfully when their gay selves were shunted to the side. Poet and performance artist Essex Hemphill wrote an arresting poem from the perspective of a gay man who appears to have only a duty-oriented presence within his family. In "Commitments" he writes, "I will always be there": in the family photographs, he will be "smiling / among siblings, parents /

nieces and nephews." While the children in these photos are held by parents,

> [m]y arms are empty, or around
> the shoulders of unsuspecting aunts
> expecting to throw rice at me someday . . .
> I am always there
> for critical emergencies,
> graduations,
> the middle of the night.
> I am the invisible son.
> In the family photos . . .
> I smile as I serve my duty.[22]

There is a hollowness to his family existence, almost like the flat, plastic figure he appears to be in the photograph. The poem seems to comment on the barrenness of family duty, even family care, without the accompanying closeness that would come through an understanding of gay selfhood.

Gay cultural expressions about the family took into account both Hemphill's feelings of a fragmentary, unsatisfying presence in family life and a desire to become more fully connected with the rites of the family during the 1980s and 1990s. Even gay cartoons and humor appeared to recognize that the family might be simultaneously alienating and accepting, that it might combine many elements of oppression and love.[23] In these cartoons gay partners were being brought home to the parents and gays were mingling with their families in kitchens, living rooms, and house porches, interactions seldom depicted in the gay cartoons of even slightly earlier eras.[24] The finality of gayness during this period seemed to combine with a sense of finality about the family's presence. The children were gay whether parents liked it or not, and the parents were going to have some part in the lives of those children whether the children wanted it or not.

During this period, gays also gave a more intensive consideration to what it would mean to have their parents' unconditional acceptance, a prospect that itself bred some ambivalent feelings. In the short story "Territory," David Leavitt imagined the mother of a gay son who had been in touch with PFLAG the day after her son came out to her and was also a chapter president. She and her friends would drive their "station wagons to San Francisco, set[ting] up their card tables in front of the Bulldog Baths,

Figure 16. Cartoon from *Hey, Mom, Guess What!* 1993.

the Liberty Baths, pass[ing] out literature to men in leather and denim who were loath to admit they even had mothers." She gave her son, Neil, a sophomore in college living in San Francisco, "pamphlets detailing the dangers of bathhouses and back rooms, enemas and poppers, wordless sex in alleyways." These acts of caring did not make Neil feel particularly comfortable or accepted, but more violated: "He winced at the thought that she knew all his sexual secrets, and vowed to move to the East Coast to escape her."[25] Neil starts to feel quite discomfited by this apparent pride in her son. He detects that it is somewhat disingenuous, or at least more hesitant than his mother avows. She tells her son that one has to "be brave to feel such pride."[26] She bristles about affectionate displays between her son and her son's partner, though she does not admit this forthrightly.[27] She claims to be "very tolerant, very understanding," but she "can only take so much."[28]

This mother symbolized the gay privacy that had to be ceded when suddenly an older generation of heterosexuals began to participate in gay culture. The impetus to get parents to acknowledge and understand gay

Figure 17. Cartoon from *Hey, Mom, Guess What!* 1993.

children's private lives bred, at the same time, a parental right to know about, comment upon, and probe a gay child's sexuality and set up a dialogue that was all the more intensely personal. Parents had a new entitlement to their gay children's private lives.

To be sure, parents in previous decades speculated about their children's growing up and the "causes" of their sexuality—and got upset about it— but the expectation that parents and children should talk over these matters was becoming much more pronounced in the 1980s and early 1990s. These trends were highlighted in parental "coming outs" about their gay children, in memoirs and other confessionals, encouraged perhaps by a tell-all biography genre particularly prevalent at this time.[29]

In her reflection for the 1987 collection *Different Daughters: A Book by Mothers of Lesbians*, Deborah, a forty-six-year-old cardiology technician living in suburban New Jersey, attempted to understand her twenty-four-year-old daughter's lesbianism. Deborah wrote wistfully that as a teenager her daughter, Melissa, had been "popular and beautiful and went out with a zillion boys." But when her daughter turned sixteen, "I started to notice how much she talked about a certain friend of hers. I noticed that she ignored her boyfriend in order to spend time with this friend. I joked with her that she might be gay, but basically I just thought she was behaving strangely." This sense of something awry turned to a focus on Melissa's fantasy life. When her daughter turned eighteen, Deborah noticed that Melissa "developed an obsession about the TV program *Cagney and Lacey*" and had a "thing" for Cagney.[30] When Melissa came out to her mother, Deborah justified her hostility by the pain she felt. After her daughter came home with her first girlfriend, Deborah recorded that she felt "tense and angry and was quite nasty and short tempered with her. I knew this was bad behavior, but I couldn't stop myself. I didn't feel guilty because I was so mad at her. . . . [S]he was . . . changing. She started looking totally different. Out went the hair dye and the make up. . . . I missed the other Melissa, because that's the one I knew."[31] Yet after she and her daughter had talked about Melissa's childhood, and her girlhood crushes, Deborah "realize[d] that [Melissa] kept many of her feelings to herself." Even after admitting that she had disparaged her daughter, she still expected her daughter to have shared her feelings: "I feel badly that we couldn't talk when she was growing up."[32] Striking in this account is how Deborah recounted Melissa's progression toward being a lesbian as a gradual realization in Deborah's own life. It came through a scrutiny of something as intangible as her daughter's interests—her "obsessions" or fantasy life—and the more concrete manifestations such as her appearance.[33] The surveillance of her daughter's affective life was quite broad.

Linda Alcoff has written about the ways that visual media during this period contributed to a feeling of spectacle surrounding confessional stories at the same time that it contributed to greater visibility.[34] Gay confessionals were certainly taken up as spectacle during these years, particularly in the venue of television talk shows. Donahue was particularly fond of gays as a topic, and Geraldo Rivera, Sally Jesse Raphael, and Oprah Winfrey all featured gay-themed shows during this period, including one *Oprah* in 1993 on "parents who can't deal with the fact that their children are gay."[35] Oprah used this show both to reconcile estranged parents and their gay children and to dispel myths about gays to a somewhat unsure audience. At the beginning of the show, she held up a photograph of a young woman named Nicole, who then had long hair and wore makeup. She juxtaposed it with another photo of a young woman with a shaved head and more of a butch look, saying that this is what Nicole looked like now. Nicole had told her mother she was gay, and it was "tearing her [mother's] heart out right now."

The show centered around this mother and daughter pair, as well as an estranged mother and son, and several members of the audience claiming to be in the same situation. Nicole's mother, Karen, had coiffed hair and lots of makeup and cried liberally as she spoke. Her daughter, in turn, seemed to be in physical pain whenever her mother spoke, wincing and rolling her eyes at many of the things her mother said. This mother told Oprah that she was not "opposed to people being gay"—which prompted an audible sigh from her daughter's corner—but "as a mother, I had an expectation that my daughter would walk down the aisle just like everybody else, get married, have babies." Taking up, consciously or not, some of the very words PFLAG had apportioned to this parental moment of sadness, Oprah said, "So you grieve the loss of the daughter you thought you had." The mother affirmed that this was so.

Here too a gay daughter's private life had given way to a mother's casting about for explanations of the origins of her sexuality. As the mother said to Oprah, "I had certain reasons to believe that maybe she was a victim at one time." At this, Oprah raised her eyebrows and asked, "Meaning? Somebody molested her?" The mother said, "Something happened. I don't know. It's never been talked about and it's never been brought out." The daughter shook her head furiously and pronounced, "I *never* was a victim. I don't know what any of that is about." Oprah tried to bridge the confrontation by suggesting, again in the vein of PFLAG, that gayness simply existed and one could not be victimized into it. When the mother said that she was not "opposed" to gayness, Oprah said, "That to me is like saying, I'm not opposed to people being black, but I'd prefer they . . ." "No!" the mother exclaimed, not letting Oprah finish the analogy. Seeing that this had embarrassed the mother, Oprah explained her response: "I only said that, though, Karen, because I think . . . you're born gay, and that's what you are. . . . I always say, you know, it's like going in a field of clovers. Most of them are three leaved, sometimes there's a four-leaf clover. And I always think, oh, that's a gay clover. [laughter and applause from the audience] It's a gay clover!"

Despite this greater visibility, including sympathetic images of gays who had some family role or presence like this one, the 1980s and early 1990s were also in many ways a bleak era for gays. Reported violence against gays

increased, particularly against gay youth, as did gay suicide.[36] There had
been a 200 percent increase in reported antigay violence between 1985 and
1988 alone.[37] Perhaps these acts of violence were also the unintentional,
tragic consequences of gay visibility, and coming out younger, and were
even pervading family life in the wake of a more widespread acknowledgment of gay existence. If gay children could not be talked out of it, and
nothing could be attributed with blame, then what parental response was
there to this knowledge? There was acceptance, of course, as PFLAG advocated, but there was also resignation, disbelief, and even punishment. One
twenty-seven-year-old woman wrote to the Boston Woman's Health Collective in 1990, recalling that, as a known lesbian in Newton, Massachusetts,
high school had been a "living hell" for her and that her family members
had been "very hostile and cruel." She had been away from her family for
seven years, and she had "no one to talk to about my fears and feelings. I
don't know the Ts or any bus roots [sic] to any facilities where I can go."[38]
This kind of stark and brutal response to gay children did not go unheeded
in the gay cultural expressions of this period. One poignant example is the
series of comic books by Ivan Velez Jr., published during the late 1980s by
the Hetrick-Martin Institute, a New York City group that tried to ensure
the protection of gay young people by providing services and public education. These comics portray gay high school kids living in Queens, New
York, who endure teasing and cruelty at the hands of their peers, doctors,
teachers, and, most prominently, their parents. The reality of the young
people portrayed here is isolation, suicidal thoughts, and daily, relentless
violence, from both outside sources and their families.[39]

Perhaps discretion as a strategy, then, might still have been useful even
for the gays of this generation, for protection from the thoughts, fantasies,
and the violence of families, as well as from other observing heterosexuals.
But discretion was a scarcely acknowledged strategy or value, even within
the gay culture of this period. Spurred on by Queer Nation, an activist
group that had emerged from ACT-UP in 1990 to combat homophobia,
gay activism increasingly esteemed the coming-out moment. One Queer
Nation advertisement proclaimed, "Your Closet Is Your Coffin."[40] As this
poster bluntly declared, keeping sexuality private could be conceived as a
kind of violence in itself.[41] A debate ensued about the ethics of outing public
figures within the gay press and, more generally, about the value of being
out.[42]

In the face of these emerging trends, filmmaker and playwright Arch

Brown, writing for *About Town*, a gay entertainment magazine, reflected that since Stonewall "mostly what has been lost is that special feeling of belonging to a secret subculture, having its own language, style, mores, and anonymity." In his view, gays had forfeited "subtle things that belonged to us and no one else. The most obvious being language. Words like 'Gay' and 'Camp' could be safely used in front of straight friends and in fact whole conversations could go on in public that were essentially private between those who 'understood.' "[43] In this vein, Elizabeth Kennedy has recorded a lesbian interview correspondent's feeling that there was also a sense of excitement in having a secret, a feeling that being gay was something unique and special.[44] It is as though these gays were permitted to experience a realm outside of existing social structures—and perhaps thereby closer to a feeling of suspended time or transcendence that romantic love promotes—where parents and broader social obligations did not really infringe.[45]

By the late 1980s and the early 1990s, gays experienced and represented an obligation to confess, and telling the family became a central, necessary stage of self-revelation. In the process, gays had gone from secret to known, even formalized, selves. The selves that could once be considered purely personal in the early postwar period had become more expressly political during the liberation period, and then, during the AIDS crisis and in this most recent period, public. Parents could not help but register these changes. What they may have once considered simply an abstraction—gay life—was now claiming an undeniable presence in family spheres.

But families did not simply come along and intrude on gay privacy. The preoccupation with parents, including past life with them and the desire for attachment to them, were long present in gay culture, and the family hovered over the lives of gays even when gay sexuality was not precisely known, declared, or discussed. The embrace and symbolization of the family were also always hesitant and uneven, both at moments of profound gay radicalism and in this period of increased mainstream integration. Families were recognized as collections of people who protected its members from loneliness but who also made them lonely, who modeled social possibilities and ways of love and intimacy both for what gays might seek and for what they might reject. Even now, noble, model families are considered to be idealized versions of acceptance, family love, and domesticity that many gays did not think they had—but were not sure they truly wanted either. In turn, what gays owed their parents and vice versa was ever present and remained a pronounced dilemma as these decades progressed, not one that had slipped away from family considerations altogether. The fact that gays like William Dubay would contemplate a liberation strategy within family obligations to parents shows most strikingly the persistent notion of responsibility and indebtedness as a kinship strategy.

What does seem irretrievable in gay culture and in gay representation more broadly, even in the day-to-day interactions of letter writing and diary keeping, are those screened, nebulous allusions to gayness within the family. Gays once bred a culture about their relationships to the family that was expressed largely metaphorically, materially, and deeply inwardly, even within the realm of fantasy. These representations became displaced by more direct portraits: the coming-out statement "Mom, Dad, I'm gay" was absolutely direct and concrete. The need to live a double life of sorts that had once shaped a set of gay writings that straddled family roles and gay roles had given way to writings and a gay expressive culture less enshrouded in symbolism and increasingly informed by autobiographical reflection and revelation. Where once James Baldwin created a character who could imagine gay life only as a series of rumors and fleeting images, as though the very idea lacked a firm definition and contour but was almost a kind of agitating moment in his mind, gay stories had now become coherent, even routine narratives, drained of their fearfulness and yet blunted in their intensity and emotion. Perhaps these stories once had to be told through fiction of necessity, whether in writing or simply fabrications in daily life: now they were truths and real-life narratives. The way that gay secrets have been shared has had a dramatic impact on postwar culture no less so than family life: the possibilities for revelation of all aspects of selfhood were enhanced while the possibilities for the imaginative expression of gay selfhood were diminished.

Gay intimate writings, culture, and politics, and the dynamics within them, were not solely the consequences of a more far-reaching disavowal of discretion in the postwar period, or even a companionate family's emphasis on revelation, however. Gays—and their parents—had fueled this larger trend as well. To be sure, broad political and cultural developments, and new emotional contexts, shaped this disavowal and emphasis as well, including the valorization of the personal within the vast range of liberation movements, the willingness to talk openly about and question political causes and wars, the search for new experiences to mine in the arts, the disappointment in and restlessness surrounding intimate mores and conventions within middle-class family life, and the value placed on empathy.

Yet a central source of the drift toward self-revelation was also simply the internal curiosity of postwar families, one that was especially pronounced when the children were gay. The changing shape of gay culture and politics created a world in which opportunities for privacy are scant, the personal is named and talked about, and selves are known, as though the companionate family's central question, "Who are you?" had had a definitive response—"Let me tell you"—and become grafted onto the larger culture.

NOTES

Introduction

1. Elsa Gidlow, *Elsa: I Come with My Songs; The Autobiography of Elsa Gidlow* (San Francisco: Druid Heights, 1986), 301 and 302.

2. Ibid., 303.

3. Ibid., 305.

4. Ibid., 301.

5. In her analysis of Gidlow and Liz Boyer Reinstein, Elizabeth Kennedy suggested that for segments of the upper class during the 1920s and 1930s, and for the artistic circle in which Gidlow traveled, all sexuality was deemed a strictly personal matter. Thus, in this context, a lesbian relationship might be viewed as parallel to a heterosexual affair and "graciously ignored." See Kennedy, "But We Would Never Talk about It: The Structures of Lesbian Discretion in South Dakota, 1928–1933," in Ellen Lewin, ed., *Inventing Lesbian Cultures in America* (Boston: Beacon, 1996), 15–39, here 38.

6. See Kath Weston, *Families We Choose: Lesbians, Gays and Kinship* (New York: Columbia University Press, 1991), 35. See also Ellen Lewin, *Lesbian Mothers: Accounts of Gender in American Culture* (Ithaca, N.Y.: Cornell University Press, 1993); and Katherine Arnup, *Lesbian Parenting: Living with Pride and Prejudice* (Charlottetown, P.E.I.: Gynergy Books, 1995). See also Ellen Herman, "All in the Family: Lesbian Motherhood Meets Unpopular Psychology in a Dysfunctional Era," in Lewin, ed., *Inventing Lesbian Cultures in America*, 83–104.

7. Much of this gay historiography has been social history or history with an ethnographic approach. On the public presence of gays within commercial establishments and political activist circles, see, for example, John D'Emilio's work of the postwar period, *Sexual Politics, Sexual Communities: The Making of a Homosexual Minority in the United States, 1940–1970* (1983; repr., Chicago: University of Chicago Press, 1998), as well as Gary Kinsman's *The Regulation of Desire: Sexuality in Canada* (Montreal: Black Rose, 1987), which looks at gays as civil rights activists, in a study of sexual regulation and resistance in Canada from the colonial period through the postwar era. David Johnson looks at the postwar discrimination of gays in *The Lavender Scare: The Cold War Persecution of Gays and Lesbians in the Federal Government* (Chicago: University of Chicago Press, 2004), while Allan Berube and Paul Jackson have both explored the gay social presence in the World War II military in the United States and

Canada, respectively. See Berube's *Coming Out under Fire: The History of Gay Men and Women in World War II* (New York: Penguin, 1991) and Jackson's *One of the Boys: Homosexuality in the Military during World War II* (Montreal: McGill-Queen's University Press, 2004). For gay community studies, see Brett Beemyn, ed. *Creating a Place for Ourselves: Lesbian, Gay, and Bisexual Community Histories* (New York: Routledge, 1997). One full-length study to have emerged from this work is Marc Stein's *City of Sisterly and Brotherly Loves: Lesbian and Gay Philadelphia, 1945–1972* (Chicago: University of Chicago Press, 2000). Finally, see John D'Emilio and Estelle Freedman, *Intimate Matters: A History of Sexuality in America* (1988; repr., Chicago: University of Chicago Press, 1997), esp. 288–95.

8. On homosexuality in the colonial era, see Richard Godbeer, "Sodomy in New England," in Kathy Peiss, ed., *Major Problems in the History of American Sexuality: Documents and Essays* (Boston: Houghton Mifflin, 2002), 92–105. The literature on same-sex friendship in the antebellum period is extensive, but see, for example, Carroll Smith-Rosenberg, "The Female World of Love and Ritual," and Karen Hansen, "An Erotic Friendship between Two African-American Women," both also anthologized in Peiss, *Major Problems*, 201–36. See also Jonathan Katz, "Coming to Terms: Conceptualizing Men's Erotic and Affectional Relations in the United States, 1820–1892," in Martin Duberman, ed., *A Queer World: The Center for Lesbian and Gay Studies Reader* (New York: New York University Press, 1996), 216–35.

9. George Chauncey has shown a viable gay culture well before World War II in *Gay New York: Gender, Urban Culture, and the Making of the Gay Male World, 1890–1940* (New York: Basic Books, 1994). Elizabeth Kennedy and Madeline Davis have done the same for the working-class lesbian community living in Buffalo, New York. See *Boots of Leather, Slippers of Gold: The History of a Lesbian Community* (New York: Penguin, 1993), which looks at the 1930s to the 1960s. These works show how gay communities formed by claiming public spaces for socializing and performing. The bifurcation between public and private is not rigid in these works. Kennedy's interview correspondents, for example, talked about how they negotiated their family relationships (see 57). She also shows that black lesbian life in particular featured house parties (see 36, 42, and 123–31).

10. John D'Emilio, "Capitalism and Gay Identity," in Henry Abelove, Michele Aina Barale, and David M. Halperin, eds., *The Lesbian and Gay Studies Reader* (New York: Routledge, 1993), 467–76.

11. See, for example, Margaret Cruikshank, *The Gay and Lesbian Liberation Movement* (New York: Routledge, 1992); and Deborah Goleman Wolf, *The Lesbian Community* (Berkeley: University of California Press, 1979).

12. Intellectual historian William Graebner notes that it is not a coincidence that 1940s films employed the technique of the flashback to convey, not moments of pleasure or nostalgia, but moments of terror, inflected by larger memories of World War II. See William Graebner, *Age of Doubt: American Thought and Culture in the 1940s* (Boston: Twayne, 1991), 53.

13. It is important to note here that kinship styles vary drastically. For example, to mitigate the severity of racism, African American families sometimes have blended nuclear families with extended families of grandparents, aunts and uncles, and friends in child rearing. Carol Stack notes that this was particularly the case for black families living on welfare. See her famous study of an African American community in a small, midwestern city, *All Our Kin: Strategies for Survival in a Black Community* (New York: Harper and Row, 1974), 49ff. But, as Veronica Strong-Boag notes in her history of adoption in Canada, relatives and neighbors of any race have long taken on parental roles during times of economic insecurity especially. See Strong-Boag, *Finding Families, Finding Ourselves: English Canada Encounters Adoption, from the Nineteenth Century to the 1990s* (Don Mills, Ontario: Oxford University Press, 2006), 11. On the domus in Italian Harlem serving as a theater of self-revelation, see Robert Orsi, *The Madonna of 115th Street: Faith and Community in Italian Harlem, 1880–1950* (New Haven, Conn.: Yale University Press, 1985), 85.

14. See Elaine Tyler May, *Barren in the Promised Land: Childless Americans and the Pursuit of Happiness* (New York: Basic Books, 1995), 139. Here she cites the existence of family station wagons, family theme parks, family sitcoms, and the like.

15. Arlene Skolnick, *Embattled Paradise: The American Family in an Age of Uncertainty* (New York: Basic Books, 1991), xviii. See also Tamara Hareven, "Family Time and Historical Time." *Daedalus* (Spring 1977): 57–70. The process to companionate family styles was a gradual one, however. Joseph E. Illick notes that, between the mid to late nineteenth century, the family, which had once served several functions, among them economic and educational, was already becoming restricted to emotion and nurture. See Joseph E. Illick, *American Childhoods* (Philadelphia: University of Pennsylvania Press, 2002), 69.

16. See Steven Mintz and Susan Kellogg, *Domestic Revolutions: A Social History of American Family Life* (New York: Free Press, 1988), 132–75. On parental investment, see Kristina Orfali, Chiara Saraceno, Ingeborg Weber-Kellermann, and Elaine Tyler May, "Nations of Families," in Antoine Prost and Gerard Vincent, eds., *Riddles of Identity in Modern Times*, 5 eds. Phillipe Aries and Georges Duby, *History of Private Life* (Cambridge, Mass.: Harvard University Press, 1991), 415–539, here 490ff. See also John N. Edwards, "The Future of the Family Revisited," in Joann S. and Jack R. DeLora, eds., *Intimate Life Styles: Marriage and Its Alternatives* (Pacific Palisades, Calif.: Goodyear, 1972), 348–57; and Sharon Hays, *Cultural Contradictions of Motherhood* (New Haven, Conn.: Yale University Press, 1996), 45 and 46.

17. On this theme, see Steven Mintz, *Huck's Raft: A History of American Childhood* (Cambridge, Mass.: Harvard University Press, 2006), 273.

18. This was the case even with the validation of introspection and family analysis provoked by psychology's ascent in the immediate postwar years and by self-help movements in the later postwar years. Lynn Jamieson, *Intimacy: Personal Relationships in Modern Societies* (Malden, Mass.: Polity Press, 1998), 41. I should note that, even in the early twentieth century, traditional expectations that children would contribute to

the family kitty endured, and there were ongoing tensions between children as economic or emotional contributors. Ellen Herman notes that "love and labor were not opposites in this world where the meanings of childhood and family were in transition." See Herman, *Kinship by Design: A History of Adoption in the Modern United States* (Chicago: University of Chicago Press, 2008), 26–27.

19. Hilde Bruch, *Don't Be Afraid of Your Child: A Guide for Perplexed Parents* (New York: Farrar, Straus and Young, 1952), 64.

20. On children as their parents' better selves, see Paula Fass and Mary Ann Mason, *Childhood in America* (New York: New York University Press, 2000), 1.

21. On young men and women leaving behind their families (and rural areas) to seek work in the industrial cities of the United States, see Karen Halttunen, *Confidence Men and Painted Women: A Study of Middle-Class Culture in America, 1830–1870* (New Haven, Conn.: Yale University Press, 1982), 1. For a fascinating discussion of family leave-taking, see two articles in Steven Noll and James Trent, eds., *Mental Retardation in America: A Historical Reader* (New York: New York University Press, 2004): Penny L. Richards, "Beside Her Sat Her Idiot Child," 65–84, and Janice Brockley, "Rearing the Child Who Never Grew: Ideologies of Parenting and Intellectual Disability in American History," 130–64. Both argue that children with intellectual disabilities were seen as boons of sorts during the nineteenth century, as they were emblematic of children who would stay with their parents indefinitely. On the dramatization of the orphan in nineteenth-century culture, see Julie Berebitsky, *Like Our Very Own: Adoption and the Changing Culture of Motherhood, 1851–1950* (Lawrence: University Press of Kansas, 2000), 53ff.

22. See again Chauncey's *Gay New York*. See, for example, 35–36, on the bachelor subculture, and 271, on gays moving to the city.

23. Miriam G. Reumann notes, for example, that the war promoted discussions about sexual "aberrations" such as divorce, promiscuity, and homosexuality and whether they would endure beyond World War II. See Miriam G. Reumann, *American Sexual Character: Sex, Gender, and National Identity in the Kinsey Reports* (Berkeley: University of California Press, 2005), 5.

24. Many of my sources, for example, came from gay community archives. For a discussion of grassroots archives and their competition with institutional archives, see Ann Cvetkovich, *An Archive of Feelings: Trauma, Sexuality, and Lesbian Public Cultures* (Durham, N.C.: Duke University Press, 2003), 244–51.

Chapter 1

1. Letter, October 12, 1945, "Gay Scrapbook," 1–13, at 2, William Wilmer Billings Papers, Gay and Lesbian Center, San Francisco Public Library, San Francisco, Calif.

2. Ibid., 4.

3. Ibid., 5.

4. Ibid., 6.

5. Ibid., 5 and 7.

6. Ibid., 8.

7. Ibid., 10–11. I should note that Billings also would go on to become one of the founding members of San Francisco's Council on Religion and the Homosexual in 1965.

8. On World War II and the legacy of its rumors, see Ralph Rosnow and Gary Alan Fine, *Rumor and Gossip: The Social Psychology of Hearsay* (New York: Elsevier, 1976).

9. See Berube, *Coming Out under Fire*, 15, 37–38, 57. See also Ellen Herman, *The Romance of American Psychology: Political Culture in the Age of Experts* (Berkeley: University of California Press, 1995), 89. On a more fearless sexual experimental dynamic to emerge in the face of World War II, see Mintz and Kellogg, *Domestic Revolutions*, 154ff.

10. See Elaine Tyler May, *Homeward Bound: American Families in the Cold War Era* (New York: Basic Books, 1988), 70–71.

11. On this, see Kenneth D. Rose, *Myth and the Greatest Generation: A Social History of Americans during World War II* (New York: Routledge, 2008), 68.

12. The term "companionate marriage" was coined by Ben Lindsey in his book with the same title. See *Companionate Marriage* (New York: Boni and Liveright, 1927). For a definition of the companionate family, see again Skolnick, *Embattled Paradise*, xviii. Finally, see Viviana A. Zelizer, *Pricing the Priceless Child: The Changing Social Value of Children* (New York: Basic Books, 1985); and see May, *Homeward Bound*, 38ff.

13. On these trends, see Mintz and Kellogg, *Domestic Revolutions*, 114, 178ff.

14. William Billings, letter, October 12, 1945, 11.

15. Ibid., 12.

16. Ibid., 13.

17. On camp as an aspect of military culture, see Berube, *Coming Out Under Fire*, 67–71. See also Leila Rupp, *A Desired Past: A Short History of Same Sex Love in America* (Chicago: University of Chicago Press, 1999), 138. For a more thorough discussion of camp, see Susan Sontag's noted 1964 essay "Notes on Camp," in *Against Interpretation and Other Essays* (New York: Farrar, Straus and Giroux, 1966), 275–93.

18. See Sigmund Freud, *Three Essays on the Theory of Sexuality*, (1905); repr., ed. James Strachey (New York: Basic Books, 1962), 11, 12, 73. On the theme of rehabilitation and self-alteration in the postwar period, see David Serlin, *Replaceable You: Engineering the Body in Postwar America* (Chicago: University of Chicago Press, 2004), 33.

19. On this, see Freud, *Three Essays on the Theory of Sexuality*, 6–11. On homosexuality as a life phase and universal bisexuality, see Ronald Bayer, *Homosexuality and American Psychiatry: The Politics of Diagnosis* (New York: Basic Books, 1981), 22–25. Finally, see an early American disciple of Freud's, A. B. Brill, *Psychoanalysis: Its Theories and Practical Applications* (1912); repr., (New York: Arno Press, 1972).

20. See Sigmund Freud, "A Letter from Freud," *American Journal of Psychiatry* (April 1951): 786.

21. On the observation of homosexuality in the military, see Berube, *Coming Out under Fire*, 15–16, 20–21. See also D'Emilio, *Sexual Politics, Sexual Communities*, 45. For observations about mental instability, see Mintz, *Huck's Raft*, 262ff.. On gays in the Canadian military, see Kinsman, *Regulation of Desire*, 150–53.

22. On American interpretations of Freud, see Henry Abelove, "Freud, Male Homosexuality, and the Americans," in Abelove et al., eds., *The Lesbian and Gay Studies Reader*, 381–93. Some of the American analysts to depart from Freud included Sandor Rado, who highlighted unhealthy parenting in the creation of homosexuals in "An Adaptational View of Sexual Behavior," in Paul Hoch and Joseph Zubin, eds., *Psychosexual Development in Health and Diseases: The Proceedings of the 38th Annual Meeting of the American Psychopathological Association Held in New York City, June 1948* (New York: Grune and Stratton, 1949).

23. For details on homosexuality's appearance in the initial *DSM* and its revisions, see Bayer, *Homosexuality and American Psychiatry*, 39–40.

24. For parenting types in Freud, see Freud, *Three Essays on the Theory of Sexuality*, 12. Freudian writings on sons and mothers emphasized the oedipal struggle more than the type of the overbearing mother. On this, see Alan P. Bell, Martin S. Weinberg, and Sue Kiefer Hammersmith, eds., *Sexual Preference: Its Development in Men and Women* (Bloomington: Indiana University Press, 1981). For American psychiatry's response of domineering mothers and distant mothers, see Bayer, *Homosexuality and American Psychiatry*, 29–31. According to Bayer, these American analysts would gain more prominence in the 1960s, following the work of those who split from Freud in the 1950s at Columbia University's Psychoanalytic Clinic for Training and Research. Examples of those American analysts to reject a hereditary view of homosexuality include Gordon Westwood, *Society and the Homosexual* (New York: E. P. Dutton, 1953); Daniel Cappon, *Toward an Understanding of Homosexuality* (Englewood Cliffs, N.J.: Prentice Hall, 1965); Frank Merriman, *The Making of a Homosexual* (Los Lunas, N.M.: Edea Books, 1966); and Irving Bieber, *Homosexuality: A Psychoanalytic Study of Male Homosexuals* (New York: Basic Books, 1962).

25. Herman, *Romance of American Psychology*, 112.

26. Robert Leach Journals, vol. 24, 4th day, 26th, 1950, p. 189, Robert J. Leach Papers, box 1, 7609, Division of Rare and Manuscript Collections, Cornell University Library, Cornell University, Ithaca, N.Y.

27. Letter to mother, August 3, 1950, pp. 1 and 2, Robert Leach Papers, box 6, file 3.

28. Letter to son, August 20, 1950, 1, Robert Leach Papers, box 5, file 37.

29. Letter to mother, September 6, 1950, pp. 2 and 3, Robert Leach Papers, box 6, file 3.

30. See Philip Wylie, "Common Women," chap. 11 in *Generation of Vipers* (New York: Rinehart and Co., 1942), 184–204. See also Mauree Applegate, *Everybody's Business: Our Children* (Evanston, Ill.: Row, Peterson, and Company, 1952), on the problems bred by the "smother-mother."

31. Letter to son, March 18, 1945, Robert Leach Papers, box 5, file 11. On earlier twentieth-century parenting styles, see Don Humachek, *Encounters with the Self* (New York: Harcourt, Brace, Jovanovich, 1992), 208; and Tommie J. Hamner and Pauline H. Turner, *Parenting in Contemporary Society* (Englewood Cliffs, N.J.: Prentice Hall, 1985), 18.

32. Letter to mother, September 6, 1950, 3, Robert Leach Papers, box 6, file 3.

33. Letter to son, September 19, 1950, 1, Robert Leach Papers, box 5, file 37.

34. Ibid., 2.

35. Ibid., 2 and 3.

36. Ibid., 3.

37. On the value of privacy in Victorian families, see Mintz and Kellogg, *Domestic Revolutions*, 90.

38. Letter to son, October 1, 1950, 2, Robert Leach Papers, box 5, file 37.

39. On the intellectual response to conformity and the popularity culture of this period, see Stephen J. Whitfield, *The Culture of the Cold War* (Baltimore: Johns Hopkins University Press, 1991), 182ff. See also Thomas Blass's biography of Stanley Milgram for themes concerning social experimentation and conformity versus nonconformity, *The Man Who Shocked the World: The Life and Legacy of Stanley Milgram* (New York: Basic Books, 2004).

40. On Arendt's thoughts on the masses, see Wilfred M. McClay, *The Masterless: Self and Society in Modern America* (Chapel Hill: University of North Carolina Press, 1994), 221.

41. On Mailer and postwar conceptions of masculinity, see Robert J. Corber, *Homosexuality in Cold War America: Resistance and the Crisis of Masculinity* (Durham, N.C.: Duke University Press, 1997), 46. His essay "The White Negro" was published in 1957. On the Beats, see Maurice Isserman and Michael Kazin, *America Divided: The Civil War of the 1960s* (New York: Oxford University Press, 2004), 154, and for the Beat perspective on sexuality and homosexuality, see Christopher Gair, *The American Counterculture* (Edinburgh, U.K.: Edinburgh University Press, 2007), 39ff.

42. Martin Meeker, *Contacts Desired: Gay and Lesbian Communications and Community, 1940s–1970s* (Chicago: University of Chicago Press, 2006), 83.

43. On this, see Jeffrey Escoffier, "Homosexuality and the Sociological Imagination: The 1950s and 1960s," in Duberman, ed., *A Queer World*, 248–61.

44. Robert Lindner, *Must You Conform?* (New York: Holt, Rinehart, and Winston, 1956), 32 and 11.

45. See Bruno Bettelheim, *The Informed Heart: Autonomy in a Mass Age* (New York: Free Press, 1960), 137. See, for example, Wilfred M. McClay's discussion of Bruno Bettelheim's essay "Individual and Mass Behavior in Extreme Situations," in *Masterless*, 230ff. On "inner-" and "other-" directedness, see David Riesman, *The Lonely Crowd: A Study of the Changing American Character* (New Haven, Conn.: Yale University Press, 1950), esp. 109ff and 126ff. It is possible to have another, more positive reading of the other-directedness that Riesman suggested was prevalent in

American society, though the negative one tended to be the dominant interpretation of the time. On the popularization of existential philosophers in this period, see Julius E. Heuscher, *Psychology, Folklore, Creativity, and the Human Dilemma* (Springfield, Ill.: Charles C. Thomas, 2003), 344ff; on Sartre and authenticity, see Jean-Paul Sartre in Wade Baskin, ed., *The Philosophy of Existentialism* (New York: Philosophical Library, 1965). Finally, see Howard Brick, "Authenticity and Artifice," in *Age of Contradiction: American Thought and Culture in the 1960s* (New York: Twayne, 1998), 66–87, esp. 68.

46. On this, see McClay, *Masterless*, 270. See also George Lipsitz, *Class and Culture in Cold War America* (New York: Praeger, 1981), 175ff (on film noir) and 195ff (on rock music).

47. "Reflections on My Journal," 1952, 53, Robert Leach Papers, box 3, file 28.

48. Beth Bailey, *Sex in the Heartland* (Cambridge, Mass.: Harvard University Press, 1999), 54–55.

49. "Reflections on My Journal," 1959, 2, Robert Leach Papers, box 4, file 7.

50. On homosexuality as a retreat from the requirements of the masculine role in this period, see Barbara Ehrenreich, *The Hearts of Men: American Dreams and the Flight from Commitment* (New York: Anchor/Doubleday Press, 1983), 25.

51. On the deviance of childlessness, see Elaine Tyler May, "Pushing the Limits, 1940–1961," in Nancy Cott, ed., *No Small Courage: A History of Women in the United States* (New York: Oxford University Press, 2000), 473–528, here 519–20. For household zoning regulations in Canada, see Kinsman, *Regulation of Desire*, 226; in the United States, see Gwendolyn Wright, *Building the Dream: A Social History of Housing in America* (New York: Pantheon Books, 1981) on "neighborhood character," 247–48.

52. See Lyn Pedersen (Jim Kepner), "The Importance of Being Different," reprint from *ONE*, 1954, in Mark Blasius and Shane Phelan, eds., *We Are Everywhere: A Historical Source Book of Gay and Lesbian Politics* (New York: Routledge, 1997), 320–23; and also Hollister Barnes (Dorr Legg), "I Am Glad I Am a Homosexual," from *ONE*, 1958, in Blasius and Phelan, eds., *We Are Everywhere*, 323–26.

53. See Barbara Stephens, "A Plea for Integration," *Ladder* 1 (May 1957): 17–18, here 17.

54. On the "silent generation," see Lewis Perry, *Intellectual Life in America* (New York: Franklin Watts, 1984), 420.

55. On these laws, see Estelle Freedman, "Uncontrolled Desires: The Response to the Sexual Psychopath, 1920–1960," *Journal of American History* 74 (June 1987): 83–106, here 84. In Canada, throughout the 1950s, male homosexual acts were also against the law; gross indecency, which extended to female homosexuality and oral sex, were both punishable by five years' imprisonment. For details, see Neil Miller, *Out of the Past: Gay and Lesbian History from 1869 to the Present* (New York: Vintage, 1995), 295.

56. On gay teachers in the twentieth century, see Jackie Blount, *Fit to Teach: Same Sex Desire, Gender and School Work in the Twentieth Century* (Albany: SUNY Press, 2005), 43.

57. Freedman, "Uncontrolled Desires," 102.

58. On the figure of the homosexual child molester, see Kinsman, *Regulation of Desire*, 152; and D'Emilio and Freedman, *Intimate Matters*, 215. On the conflation of the category of homosexual with those of pervert and psychopath, see again Freedman, "Uncontrolled Desires," 103–4. Finally, on the notion of homosexual recruitment, see Johnson, *Lavender Scare*, 57.

59. Mrs. Billings's letter to the *Denver Post*, May 23, 1955, "Gay Scrapbook," 2, William Billings Collection.

60. On harassment in gay bars, see D'Emilio and Freedman, *Intimate Matters*, 294; and D'Emilio, *Sexual Politics, Sexual Communities*, 14–15. On police crackdowns and harassment in lesbian bars, see Elizabeth Kennedy and Madeline Davis's oral history of lesbians in Buffalo during the pre- and postwar periods, *Boots of Leather, Slippers of Gold*. See also Lynn Fernie's film, *Forbidden Love*, 84 min., National Film Board of Canada, Montreal, 1992.

61. On Rustin's arrest, see John D'Emilio's biography, *Lost Prophet: The Life and Times of Bayard Rustin* (New York: Free Press, 2003), 191–92.

62. See "I Am a Homosexual," the reprint of a letter of a young gay man forced to come out to his parents because of police entrapment, in the *Mattachine Review* 6 (June 1960): 20–23. *Mattachine Review* often republished this as an informational pamphlet, "What to Do If You're Arrested," during its run in the 1950s and 1960s.

63. See "A Minneapolis Father Discovers His Son's Homosexuality," *Mattachine Review* (May–June 1955): 24–30, reprinted from the *Minneapolis Star*.

64. Diary entry, July 1, 1955, 22b, Marge McDonald Papers, 87–7, Lesbian Herstory Archives, Brooklyn, N.Y.

65. Diary entry, April 22, 1956, 86, Marge McDonald Papers.

66. Diary entry, November 7, 1959, 684, Marge McDonald Papers.

67. Ibid., 685b.

68. Ibid., 687.

69. See Elliot Valenstein, *Great and Desperate Cures: The Rise and Decline of Psychosurgery and Other Radical Treatments for Mental Illness* (New York: Basic Books, 1986), 253 and 291, and also *The Psychosurgery Debate: Scientific, Legal, and Ethical Perspectives* (San Francisco: W. H. Freeman, 1980). On the greater administration of lobotomies and electroconvulsive shock treatments to women, see Nancy Tomes, "Female Histories of Psychiatry," in Mark S. Micale and Roy Porter, eds., *Discovering the History of Psychiatry* (New York: Oxford University Press, 1994), 348–83, here 375.

70. Marshall McLuhan, an early media theorist, for example, emphasized the notion of numbness or automation that might result before electronic media. See *Understanding the Media: The Extensions of Man* (New York: McGraw-Hill, 1964), 47 and 346. The motif of catatonia was likewise prevalent in 1950s alien invasion films. For a discussion, see Patrick Lucanio, *Them or Us: Archetypal Interpretations of 50s Alien Invasion Films* (Bloomington: Indiana University Press, 1987).

71. As Andrea Tone points out, the 1950s was, in many respects, the golden age

of applied science in the United States. And yet all of the accomplishments of laboratory research, including, as she notes, the invention of the atomic bomb and the discovery of new drugs such as antibiotics and antidepressants, were not unambiguously hailed inventions. In fact, Americans questioned the ethics of both science and scientists. Andrea Tone, *The Age of Anxiety: A History of America's Turbulent Affair with Tranquilizers* (New York: Basic Books, 2009), 81. On the morality of science in the postwar period, see David A. Hollinger, *Science, Jews, and Secular Culture: Studies in Mid-Twentieth-Century American Intellectual History* (Princeton, N.J.: Princeton University Press, 1996), 164. See also Priscilla Wald's analysis of *The Body Snatchers* and *Invasion of the Body Snatchers*, in *Contagious: Cultures, Carriers, and the Outbreak Narrative* (Durham, N.C.: Duke University Press, 2008), 159ff. William Graebner also notes that Alfred Kinsey was widely depicted as being an overly rational scientist who reduced human emotion to the question of animal sexual outlets. See Graebner, *Age of Doubt*, 128.

72. On the censure of gay publications and FBI surveillance, see Rodger Streitmatter, *Unspeakable: The Rise of the Gay and Lesbian Press in America* (Boston: Faber and Faber, 1995), 3 and 32–33; and D'Emilio, *Sexual Politics, Sexual Communities*, 115. See also D'Emilio and Freedman, *Intimate Matters*, 282–87.

73. Meeker, *Contacts Desired*, 35.

74. Although there are no specific statistics on the class and race of the readership and membership of these homophile organizations, both periodicals appear to have had a predominantly white and middle-class composition. One clue is the *Ladder*'s readership survey in 1958, wherein it was found that their women readers earned more than triple the average salary for women: $4,200 as opposed to $1,310, suggesting a strong middle-class base. See Streitmatter, *Unspeakable*, 42.

75. See reprint of the Institute of Social Ethics, "An Introduction to the Homophile Movement," part 3, "Activities of the Organizations," 15, Julie Lee Papers, 79–7, Lesbian Herstory Archives.

76. See, for example, "Will I Ever Be Able to Face the World Again?" *Mattachine Review* 4 (April 1958): 36. This ad was run several times in different variations. See also Toronto's *Gay* 1 (June 1964): 9.

77. Historians have only a limited portrait of just how many gays really were rejected by their parents during this era (or any other for that matter). Elizabeth Kennedy, in her oral history of Buffalo lesbians between the 1930s and 1950s, asked her interview subjects about their family's reactions and found that these varied from beatings to begrudging acceptances. As she wrote, "[N]one were completely rejected by their immediate families, nor were any warmly accepted." See Kennedy and Davis, *Boots of Leather, Slippers of Gold*, 57.

78. See advertisement in the *Mattachine Review* 7 (September 1961): 15. "The Rejected" was written by John W. Reavis Jr. and produced by him and Irving Saraf as a National Educational Television Presentation for KQED Channel 9, San Francisco. See transcript, September 11, 1961, KQED, 525 9th Street, San Francisco 3, Calif.

79. See Ken Burns, "'The Homosexual Faces a Challenge': A Speech to the Third Annual Convention of the Mattachine Society," reprinted in Blasius and Phelan, eds., *We Are Everywhere*, 285–89, here 287; also in *Mattachine Review* 2 (August 1956): 20 and 25–27.

80. These studies were published in 1948 and 1953, respectively. On Kinsey's findings for men, see D'Emilio and Freedman, *Intimate Matters*, 291–92; for women, see 295. Also on women, see Cruikshank, *Gay and Lesbian Liberation Movement*, 34. More generally, see Jennifer Terry, *An American Obsession: Science, Medicine, and Homosexuality in Modern Society* (Chicago: University of Chicago Press, 1999), 299ff. Finally, see Reumann, *American Sexual Character*, esp. chap. 5, 165–98.

81. See Edmund Bergler, *1000 Homosexuals: Conspiracy of Silence, or Curing and Deglamorizing Homosexuals?* (Paterson, N.J.: Pageant Books, 1959), 213. Edmund Bergler and William S. Kroger also rejected a Kinseyan idea of a continuum of sexuality. See their *Kinsey's Myth of Female Sexuality: The Medical Facts* (New York: Grune and Stratton, 1954).

82. On pulps, see Joye Zimet, *The Art of Lesbian Pulp Fiction, 1949–1969* (New York: Viking, 1999); and Michael Bronski, *Pulp Friction: Uncovering the Golden Age of Gay Male Pulps* (New York: St. Martin's Press, 2003). See also Fernie, *Forbidden Love*. Finally, see Suzanna Danuta Walters, "'As Her Hand Crept Slowly Up her Thigh': Ann Bannon and the Politics of Pulp," *Social Text* 23 (Fall–Winter 1989): 83–101.

83. Ben Travis, *The Strange Ones* (Boston: Beacon, 1959).

84. See Gore Vidal, *The City and the Pillar* (1948) ; repr., (New York: Ballantine, 1965), 15.

85. Mrs. Leah Gailey, "A Mother Gives an Answer: What Can I Do?" *Mattachine Review* 4 (May 1958): 5–8, here 7.

86. Anne Fredericks, "One Parent's Reaction," *Ladder* 5 (August 1961): 4–7, here 6.

87. Mrs. L. R. Maxwell, "Just between Us Mothers," *Mattachine Review* 3 (June 1957): 20–22, here 20.

88. Ibid., 21.

89. Warren Susman has argued that middle-class families felt ashamed at the degree to which their accustomed way of life shattered and changed. See Warren Susman, ed., *Culture and Commitment, 1929–1945* (New York: George Braziller, 1973), 11–15. See also Lawrence Levine, *Unpredictable Past: Explorations in American Cultural History* (New York: Oxford University Press, 1993), 209. On the loss of family privacy that this era entailed, see Perry R. Duis, "No Time for Privacy: World War II and Chicago's Families," in Lewis Erenberg and Susan Hirsch, *The War in American Culture: Society and Consciousness during World War II* (Chicago: University of Chicago Press, 1996), 17–46. On women learning toughness, see Laura Hapke, *Daughters of the Great Depression: Women, Work, and Fiction in the American 1930s* (Athens: University of Georgia Press, 1995), 104.

90. For her analysis of twentieth-century women's magazines such as *Good House-*

keeping and the *Ladies Home Journal*, see Nancy Walker, *Shaping Our Mothers' World: American Women's Magazines* (Jackson: University of Mississippi Press, 2000).

91. D'Emilio, *Sexual Politics, Sexual Communities*, 115.

92. For background on Laura Hobson's novel and her own family situation, see Nan Robertson, "For the Parents of Homosexuals," *San Francisco Examiner Chronicle*, September 25, 1975, William Billings Collection. Hobson was a successful novelist who had written about the torment of anti-Semitism in her work *Gentleman's Agreement* (1950).

93. Laura Z. Hobson, *Consenting Adult* (New York: Doubleday, 1975), 4 and 5.

94. James Baldwin, *Giovanni's Room* (New York: Laurel, 1956), 15.

95. Established in 1930, the Motion Picture Production Code referred to the code of untreatable topics, such as sexual perversion, by which the motion picture industry regulated itself. The code was not abolished until 1968. For gay depictions in movies, see Vito Russo, *The Celluloid Closet: Homosexuality in the Movies* (New York: Harper and Row, 1981).

96. Hobson, *Consenting Adult*, 104.

97. For context on a more pervasive sense of discretion in the earlier half of the twentieth century and its gradual demise from a cultural perspective, see Rochelle Gurstein, *The Repeal of Reticence: A History of America's Cultural and Legal Struggles over Free Speech, Obscenity, Sexual Liberation, and Modern Art* (New York: Hill and Wang, 1996), 209ff.

98. Mary Meigs, *Lily Briscoe: A Self-Portrait; An Autobiography of Mary Meigs* (Vancouver: Talonbooks, 1981), 67.

99. On McCarthy and gays, see D'Emilio, *Sexual Politics, Sexual Communities*, 40ff and 52ff; and Johnson, *Lavender Scare*, 73. On anticommunism in Canada, see Kinsman, *Regulation of Desire*, 115ff and 179–81. See also Gary Kinsman, Dieter K. Buse, and Mercedes Steedman, eds., *Whose National Security? Canadian State Surveillance and the Creation of Enemies* (Toronto: Between the Lines, 2000).

100. Meigs, *Lily Briscoe*, 67.

101. Ibid., 69.

102. Diary entry, September 6, 1950, 2, Robert Leach Papers, box 6, file 3.

103. "Reflections on My Journal," 1950, 28, Robert Leach Papers, box 3, file 26.

104. From chapter 21 of Donald Webster Cory, *The Homosexual in America* (New York: Greenberg, 1951), 230. Cory would later go on to defend cures of homosexuality in his 1965 introduction to Albert Ellis's *Homosexuality: Its Causes and Cure* (New York: Lyle and Stuart, 1965). Nonetheless, he was at the forefront of a psychological movement that suggested society was responsible for the neuroses that seemed to be a part of gayness. See, for example, Alfred A. Gross, *Strangers in Our Midst* (Washington, D.C.: Public Affairs Press, 1961), esp. chap. 3, "Society Is the Patient," 53–67; and prior to that, Evelyn Hooker's groundbreaking 1954 work summarized in Bayer, *Homosexuality and American Psychiatry*, 50–53; Charlotte Patterson and Anthony D'Augelli, *Lesbian, Gay, and Bisexual Identities over the Lifespan: Psychological Perspec-*

tives (New York: Oxford University Press, 1995), 2; and finally, "A Preliminary Analysis of Group Behavior of Homosexuals," *One Institute Quarterly* (Winter 1959): 26–32.

105. See Alice LaVere, "Emotions That Destroy Your Health and Personality," Don Lucas Collection (1997–25), box 8, file 6, "Homophile Organizations: Mattachine Society," Gay, Lesbian, Bisexual, and Transgendered Historical Society of Northern California, San Francisco.

106. In her famous essay on nineteenth-century women's relationships, Carroll Smith-Rosenberg evokes a moment when closeness was, in fact, bolstered by such confidences and sharing of secrets. But I argue that this sensibility does not last, or at least gets interrupted, especially during the Depression and war eras. See Carroll Smith-Rosenberg, "The Female World of Love and Ritual: Relations between Women in Nineteenth-Century America," in *Disorderly Conduct: Visions of Gender in Victorian America* (New York: Knopf, 1985), 11–53.

107. Letter to son, May 12, 1952, 1, Robert Leach Papers, box 5, file 39.

108. Letter to son, August 29, 1952, 1, Robert Leach Papers, box 5, file 39.

109. Letter to son, October 20, 1952, 1, Robert Leach Papers, box 5, file 39.

110. Letter to son, October 25, 1952, 1, Robert Leach Papers, box 5, file 39.

111. Letter to son, November 7, 1952, 1, Robert Leach Papers, box 5, file 39.

112. Letter to son, November 7, 1952, 1, Robert Leach Papers, box 5, file 39, and letter to mother, November 11, 1952, 1, box 5, file 7.

113. Ann Aldrich, *We, Too, Must Love* (Greenwich, Conn.: Gold Medal Books, 1958), 54.

114. Diary entry, March 17, 1956, 80b, Marge McDonald Papers.

115. Diary entry, July 21, 1959, 647b, Marge McDonald Papers.

116. On lesbian butch-femme roles in this period, see Kennedy and Davis, *Boots of Leather, Slippers of Gold.* On the importance and consequences of female cross-dressing in the 1950s, see Lillian Faderman and Stuart Timmons, *Gay L.A.: A History of Sexual Outlaws, Power Politics and Lipstick Lesbians* (New York: Basic Books, 2006), 94–96.

117. Diary entry, August 12, 1955, 41b, Marge McDonald Papers.

118. Ibid., 41b and 42.

119. Ibid., 42.

120. See Vin Packer (who also wrote as Ann Aldrich), *Whisper His Sin* (Greenwich, Conn.: Fawcett Gold Medal, 1954), and *The Evil Friendship* (Greenwich, Conn.: Fawcett Gold Medal, 1958).

121. Diary entry, November 18, 1959, 689b, Marge McDonald Papers.

122. Diary entry, June 13, 1959, 590b, Marge McDonald Papers.

123. This story is in Johnson, *Lavender Scare*, 119.

124. On military hunches, see Berube, *Coming Out under Fire*, 21.

125. See Valerie Korinek, "'Don't Let Your Girlfriends Ruin Your Marriage': Lesbian Imagery in *Chatelaine* Magazine 1950–69," in Veronica Strong-Boag, Mona Glea-

son, and Adele Perry, eds., *Rethinking Canada: The Promise of Women's History* (Toronto: Oxford University Press, 2002), 334–52.

126. On the plummeting marriage age in the 1950s, see D'Emilio and Freedman, *Intimate Matters*, 261; and Joseph Kett, *Rites of Passage: Adolescence in America, 1790–Present* (New York: Basic Books, 1977), 265.

127. D'Emilio and Freedman, *Intimate Matters*, 288–89; and D'Emilio, *Sexual Politics, Sexual Communities*, 27–29. See also May, *Homeward Bound*, 71–72. May points out that, although enlisted women could have been dismissed for being lesbian, few were. Berube shows that it was not until near the end of the war that directives were issued aimed at excluding lesbians from the armed forces. See Berube, *Coming Out under Fire*, 28–29. However, on women who were investigated for lesbianism and asked to spend time in a psychiatric hospital, see Emily Yellin, *Our Mothers' War: American Women at Home and at the Front during World War II* (New York: Free Press, 2004), 321ff. On an investigation launched into WAC because of the complaint of a mother that WAC had "homosexuals and sex maniacs," see Rose, *Myth and the Greatest Generation*, 150.

128. Letter from Smitty to Dotty, October 5, 1960, 3, "Correspondence 1960s," Dorothee Gore Papers, series 1, box 1, folder 13, Manuscript and Archives Division, the New York Public Library, Astor, Lenox, and Tilden Foundations. Library, New York.

129. Ibid., 3–4.

130. Ibid., 4.

131. See again D'Emilio, "Capitalism and Gay Identity," 467–76. In turn, Elizabeth Kennedy has shown that, particularly in lesbian contexts, the house party and meetings in the home were integral to the formation of gay identities. See Kennedy and Davis, *Boots of Leather, Slippers of Gold*, 53, for example.

132. On the desire for domestic space, see Lizabeth Cohen, *A Consumers' Republic: The Politics of Mass Consumption* (New York: Alfred A. Knopf, 2003), 73; Paul Lineberger and Bruce Tucker, *The New Individualists: The Generation after the Organization Man* (New York: HarperCollins, 1991), 127; and see Duis, "No Time for Privacy," 17–46. On bedrooms, see Wright, *Building the Dream*, 254. See also Donald G. Wetherell and Irene R.A. Kmet, *Homes in Alberta: Building, Trends, and Design, 1870–1967* (Edmonton: University of Alberta Press, 1991), 246 and 261.

133. On the importance of high schools to the institutionalization of heterosexuality in the postwar period, see Susan K. Cahn, *Sexual Reckonings: Southern Girls in a Troubling Age* (Cambridge, Mass.: Harvard University Press, 2007), 215.

134. While it has been suggested by some historians that the post-Freudian age valued a natural expression of the sexual interests of the child and regarded suppression as something to cause individual and social problems such as insanity, this interest in expressive communication about sexuality did not necessarily apply to gays. See Sterling Fishman, "A History of Childhood Sexuality," *Journal of Contemporary History* 17 (1982): 269–83.

135. Paul Monette, *Becoming a Man: Half a Life Story* (San Francisco: Harper, 1992), 29.

136. Arnie Kantrowitz, *Under the Rainbow: Growing Up Gay* (New York: William and Morrow, 1977), 34. Kantrowitz would go on to become a gay rights activist and also an English professor.

137. Ibid., 35.

138. The emergence of the juvenile delinquent as a cultural and legal concept during this period had instilled some fear in North American society over troublesome youths and adolescent crimes wherein hypermasculine, manly boys were the most suspect. On the connections between mesomorphy/muscularity and delinquency, see Seymour Halleck, *Psychiatry and the Dilemmas of Crime: A Study of Causes, Punishment, and Treatment* (New York: Harper and Row, 1967), 117. A worry over rough play and its degenerating to delinquency also might have set apart gentle play. See Harry Manuel Shulman, *Juvenile Delinquency in American Society* (New York: Harper and Brothers, 1960), 262. Also see Ronald D. Cohen, "The Delinquents: Censorship and Youth Culture in Recent U.S. History," *History of Education Quarterly* 37 (Fall 1997): 251–70. Finally, on the often contradictory experience of psychoanalysis for gays, see Eli Zaretsky, *Secrets of the Soul: A Social and Cultural History of Psychoanalysis* (New York: Knopf, 2004), 299.

139. Kantrowitz, *Under the Rainbow*, 35.

140. Alice T. Friedman has suggested a notion of women as the caretakers of family privacy in *Women and the Making of the Modern House* (New York: Harry N. Abrams, 1998), 150.

141. Kantrowitz, *Under the Rainbow*, 23 and 29.

142. It was not until the 1960s, for instance, that doctors in both the United States and Canada instituted gender identity programs to teach proper gender roles to children and parents or established gender identity clinics. See Kinsman, *Regulation of Desire*, 200. Joanne Meyerowitz links this development to the widespread reportage of transsexuals in the North American news media, including the renowned former soldier Christine Jorgensen, in *How Sex Changed: A History of Transsexuals in the United States* (Cambridge, Mass.: Harvard University Press, 2002). She points out that, during the early 1960s, psychiatrists attempted to refine the concept of gender identity (see 115ff). Finally, for her interpretation of flexibility within gender roles of the 1950s, see Jessica Weiss, *To Have and to Hold: Marriage, the Baby Boom, and Social Change* (Chicago: University of Chicago Press, 2000), 86–90.

143. On camp's origins within the family context, see Mark Booth, "Mummy Is the Root of All Evil," in *Camp* (New York: Quartet Books, 1983), 85–116. Camp reflected broader systems of gay codes and cues of sissy figures within popular, mainstream movie culture of the 1930s, for example, that would become a code for "gay." On gay codes, cues, style, language, and folklore in the pre–World War II period, see Chauncey, *Gay New York*, for example, 64. While many of the gay publications of the

1950s and early 1960s reflect a homophile sensibility rather than a camp one, the more culture-oriented gay periodicals during these years embraced elements of camp.

144. *Two* was a bimonthly magazine starting in 1964 (lasting eleven issues, until 1966) that included humor, interest pieces, and physique pictures. For details, see Kinsman, *Regulation of Desire*, 248. In fact, the two major Canadian homophile-era periodicals, *Two* and *Gay*, both came under criticism for not being serious enough. Canadian periodicals were not as affiliated with large homophile organizations to support their agendas and relied entirely on ads, subscriptions, and newsstand sales to keep afloat.

145. *Two* 11 (July–August 1966): 33. "Wolf Cubs" was the Canadian/British term for the Baden-Powell children's organization that preceded the Scouts.

146. *Drum* ran between 1964 and 1969. It was cheerful in tone and tended to celebrate gay culture. For details, see Rupp, *Desired Past*, 166; and Stein, *City of Sisterly and Brotherly Loves*, 232ff. Similar in scope and content, *Tangents* ran between 1965 and 1970.

147. Cartoon by Michael Waltrip in *Tangents* 1 (August 1966): 29.

148. Cartoon by Herb Green in *Drum: Sex in Perspective* 4 (October 1964): 12.

149. Richard McCann, "My Mother's Clothes: The School of Beauty and Shame," in Dean Kostos and Eugene Grygo, eds., *Mama's Boy: Gay Men Write about Their Mothers* (New York: Painted Leaf Press, 2000), 141–60, here 151. (This story has been reprinted many times and was first published in 1986).

150. On the displacement of fathers during the Depression, see Ralph La Rossa, *The Modernization of Fatherhood: A Social and Political History* (Chicago: University of Chicago Press, 1997), 19. On the decline of masculine power within the family during the postwar period, see Reumann, *American Sexual Character*, 70.

151. On masculine domesticity, see Robert Rutherdale, "Fatherhood and Masculine Domesticity during the Baby Boom: Consumption and Leisure in Advertising and Life Stories," in Lori Chambers and Edgar-Andre Montigny, *Family Matters: Papers in Post-Confederate Canadian Family History* (Toronto: Canadian Scholars' Press, 1998), 309–33. See also Weiss, *To Have and to Hold*, 42 and 85–86. On television fathers, see Nina C. Leibman, *Living Room Lectures: The 50s Family in Film and Television* (Austin: University of Texas Press, 1995), 256–59.

152. McCann, "My Mother's Clothes," 152.

153. See May, *Homeward Bound*, 14, on the idea of containment. On women's sexuality specifically, see 61ff., and on gay sexuality, see 95ff.

154. On this individualistic post–World War II family climate, see Donald K. Freedheim and Associate Editor Herbert J. Freudenberger, eds., *History of Psychotherapy: A Century of Change* (Washington, D.C.: American Psychiatric Association, 1992), 50–51. And on the newness and unfamiliar terrain of these middle-class family structures to flourish in the postwar period, see Weiss, *To Have and to Hold*.

155. See Bieber, *Homosexuality*, 90 and 45, respectively. In its January 1966 edition, *Time* also embraced this family configuration in an article titled "The Homosex-

ual in America"; for a discussion, see Eric Marcus, *Making History: The Struggle for Gay and Lesbian Equal Rights 1945–90; An Oral History* (New York: HarperCollins, 1992), 90. On the emasculation of fathers in the modern family, see Cappon, *Toward an Understanding of Homosexuality*, 10.

156. In some postwar studies, such as Frank S. Caprio's and Judd Marmor's, the authors suggested that women became lesbians when their fathers encouraged masculine pursuits and tomboy natures. See Frank S. Caprio, *Female Homosexuality: A Psychodynamic Study of Lesbianism* (New York: Citadel, 1954), 121 and 132–39; and see May E. Romm, "Sexuality and Homosexuality in Women," in Judd Marmor, *Sexual Inversion: The Multiple Roots of Homosexuality* (New York: Basic Books, 1965).

157. See Marvin Drellich, "New Findings from Psychoanalytic Research on Homosexuality," *New York Mattachine Newsletter* (March 1961): 4.

158. I am thinking here, for example, of stories appearing in Cheever's 1958 collection *The Housebreaker of Shady Hill and Other Stories* (New York: Harper and Brothers, 1958), particularly the story, "The Worm in the Apple," of the desire to see a downside to the seemingly too perfect, happy family, the Crutchmans. See *The Stories of John Cheever* (New York: Ballantine, 1980), 338–42.

159. For details on *Good Housekeeping*, see Walker, *Shaping Our Mothers' World*, 27. This magazine advised women on the practicalities of homemaking, food, clothing, physical appearance, and the emotional sanctity of the family.

160. Lester David, "'Our Son Was Different': When a Mother Discovers the Agonizing Truth," *Good Housekeeping*, January 1966, 51–125, here 51.

161. Ibid., 114.

162. Ibid., 51.

163. Ibid., 113 and 114.

164. Ibid., 120.

165. Ibid., 121.

166. Ibid., 120.

167. On this reaction, see Susan Bordo, *The Male Body: A New Look at Men in Public and Private* (New York: Farrar, Straus and Giroux, 1999), 121. See also Ehrenreich, *Hearts of Men*, 44–50.

168. David, "'Our Son Was Different,'" 122.

169. Ibid., 123.

170. Ibid., 125.

171. See, for example, *Gay* (January 1965): 14. For details on *Gay*, see Donald McLeod, *A Brief History of Gay: Canada's First Gay Tabloid, 1964–66* (Toronto: Homewood, 2003).

172. See *Gay* (January 1965): 12.

173. Images of gay domesticity during this period included the early 1960s paintings of British painter David Hockney (who resided for a period in Los Angeles) such as *Domestic Scene, Los Angeles* (1963). For more on representations of gay domesticity, see Kenneth E. Silver, "Master Bedrooms, Master Narratives: Home, Homosexuality,

and Post War Art," in Christopher Reed, ed., *Not at Home: The Suppression of Domesticity in Modern Art and Architecture* (London: Thames and Hudson, 1996), 206–21, here 217.

174. Bill T. Jones with Peggy Gillespie, *Last Night on Earth* (New York: Pantheon Books, 1995), 38.

175. Ibid., 43. For a discussion of lynchings of African American men who had been accused of raping white women, see William F. Pinar, *Gender of Racial Politics and Violence in America: Lynching, Prison, Rape, and the Crisis of Masculinity* (New York: Peter Lang, 2001). Also see D'Emilio and Freedman, *Intimate Matters*, 217–21.

176. See Caprio, *Female Homosexuality*, particularly his chapter "Autobiographical Confessions," 244–69.

177. Ann Aldrich, *We Two Won't Last* (Greenwich, Conn.: Gold Medal, 1963), 103.

178. On child-specific fantasy lives encouraged by children's toys and children's television shows in the postwar period, see Gary Cross, *Kids' Stuff: Toys and the Changing World of American Childhood* (Cambridge, Mass.: Harvard University Press, 1997). On the exclusivity of youth culture in the postwar period, see Ken Plummer, "Intimate Citizenship and the Culture of Sexual Story Telling," in Jeffrey Weeks and Janet Holland, eds., *Sexual Cultures: Community, Values and Intimacy* (New York: St. Martin's Press, 1996), 34–52, here 40.

179. "Correspondence, Autobiography re. *Lesbian/Woman*, 1972–79," letter, "Dear Del and Phyl," October 29, 1973, 3 (of 4), Del Martin and Phyllis Lyon Papers, 93–13, box 22, file 22, Gay, Lesbian, Bisexual and Transgendered Historical Society of Northern California, San Francisco.

180. Glen H. Elder suggested that women who hailed from deprived families during the Depression were more likely, as adults, to pour the intensity of their emotions and creativity into their families, including providing for their children. See his *Children of the Great Depression: Social Change in Life Experience* (Chicago: University of Chicago Press, 1974). On the 1950s domestic consumer economy, see Dale Carter, "Evasive Action: War, Peace, and Security in the 50s," in Dale Carter, ed., *Cracking the Ike Age: Aspects of 50s America* (Aarhus, Denmark: Aarhus University Press, 1992), 35–56, here 39–40; and see Cohen, *Consumers' Republic*, on credit and borrowing specifically, see 123. Civilian consumption was particularly strong in the United States by the early 1960s, and an expansion of consumer credit helped this trend. See Robert Guttmann, *How Credit Shapes the Economy: The U.S. in a Global System* (Armonk, N.Y.: M. E. Sharpe, 1994), 140; and David E. Shi, *The Simple Life: Plain Living and High Thinking in American Culture* (New York: Oxford University Press, 1985), 249–50.

181. Karla Jay, "First Love," in Joan Larkin, ed., *A Woman Like That: Lesbian and Bisexual Writers Tell Their Coming-Out Stories* (New York: Perennial, 1999), 28–41, here 29. With Allen Young, Karla Jay edited *Out of the Closets: Voices of Gay Liberation* (New York: Douglas, 1972), *After You're Out: Personal Experiences of Gay Men and*

Lesbian Women (New York: Quick Fox, 1975), and *Lavender Culture* (New York: Jove, 1979). An English professor at Pace University in New York, she also has written several other books.

182. Jay, "First Love," 28.

183. Ibid., 29.

184. On the stock theme of the tomboy in lesbian memoirs from this period and more recently, see Lynne Yamaguchi and Karen Barber, eds., *Tomboys: Tales of Dyke Derring-Do* (Los Angeles: Alyson, 1992). See also "Correspondence, Autobiography re. *Lesbian/Woman*, 1972–79," box 22, file 22, and "Correspondence, Young Women, 1972–79," box 24, file 5, Del Martin and Phyllis Lyon Papers.

185. See Terri de la Pena, "Blunt Cuts and Permanent Conditions," in Nisa Donnelly, ed., *Mom: Candid Memoirs by Lesbians about the First Woman in Their Life* (Los Angeles: Alyson, 1998), 111–32, here 126. De la Pena would go on to write the novels *Margins* (Seattle: Seal Press, 1992) and *Latin Satins* (Seattle: Seal Press, 1994), both focusing on gay and Chicana experiences.

186. De la Pena, "Blunt Cuts," 115.

187. See Albert Camarillo, *Chicanos in California: A History of Mexican Americans in California* (San Francisco: Boyd and Fraser, 1984), 74.

188. On the domestic ideals of the postwar period, see Betty G. Farrell, *Family: The Making of an Idea, an Institution and a Controversy in American Culture* (Boulder, Colo.: Westview Press, 1999), 108ff. I use "baby boom" to refer to the sustained births in the postwar period until about 1964, in the United States and Canada. Baby boom parents—a relatively small cohort—were born in the 1930s, rearing their children, the products of youthful postwar marriages, in the 1950s and early 1960s. For details and statistics on the American baby boom, see Landon Y. Jones, *Great Expectations: America and the Baby Boom Generation* (New York: Coward, McCann, and Geoghegan, 1980); for similar information on the Canadian baby boom, see Doug Owram, *Born at the Right Time: A History of the Baby Boom Generation* (Toronto: University of Toronto Press, 1996). On "democratic" child rearing, see Edward K. Spann, *Democracy's Children: The Young Rebels of the 1960s and the Power of Ideals* (Wilmington, Del.: Scholarly Resources, 2003), on the "New Domesticity" of the postwar period, 77ff. See also Erik Erikson, *Youth: Change and Challenge* (New York: Basic Books, 1961); and Erich Fromm, *Escape From Freedom* (1941); repr., (New York: Holt, Rinehart, and Winston, 1965). See also Mintz, *Huck's Raft*, 262ff. Finally, see Benjamin Spock, *The Common Sense Book of Baby and Child Care* (1946); repr., (New York: Duell, Sloan, and Pearce, 1957). On Dr. Spock parenting styles, see Philip Slater, *The Pursuit of Loneliness: American Culture at the Breaking Point* (Boston: Beacon Press, 1976), 59ff. See also Katherine Arnup, *Education for Motherhood: Advice for Mothers in Twentieth Century Canada* (Toronto: University of Toronto Press, 1994), 55.

189. Alan Helms, *Young Man from the Provinces: A Gay Life before Stonewall* (New York: Avon, 1995), 52. For details on physique magazines, often gay male magazines masquerading as fitness magazines, see Kinsman, *Regulation of Desire*, 248.

190. See Joanne Meyerowitz, *Women Adrift: Independent Wage Earners in Chicago, 1880–1930* (Chicago: University of Chicago Press, 1988). On the expansion of credit and social assistance programs in the Canadian context, see Alison Prentice, Paula Bourne, Gail Cuthbert Brandt, Beth Light, Wendy Mitchinson, and Naomi Black, eds., *Canadian Women: A History* (Toronto: Harcourt and Brace, 1996), 380. In the United States, see Michael J. Rosenfeld, *The Age of Independence: Interracial Unions, Same-Sex Unions and the Changing American Family* (Cambridge, Mass.: Harvard University Press, 2007), 36.

191. Dorothy Lyle, "The Family and Money Injustice," *Ladder* 10 (March 1966): 21–22, here 21.

192. Ibid., 22.

193. Del Martin and Phyllis Lyon, *Lesbian/Woman* (San Francisco: Glide, 1972), 212.

194. See "Parents' Reaction," *Mattachine Review* 8 (October 1962): 21–23.

195. See Jess Stearn, *The Sixth Man: A Startling Investigation Revealing That One Man in Six Is a Homosexual* (New York: Doubleday, 1961), 240. For details on the popular reception of this work, see D'Emilio, *Sexual Politics, Sexual Communities*, 139.

196. Stern, *Sixth Man*, 246.

197. On the expression "my son, the doctor," see Mariam K. Slater, "My Son the Doctor: Aspects of Mobility among American Jews," *American Sociological Review* 34 (June 1969): 359–74.

198. See Gay Publishing Company Papers, box 1, file 53, 7442, Division of Rare and Manuscript Collections, Cornell University Library, (in reference to the collection "My Son, the Daughter," Washington, D.C.: Guild Book Service, P.O. Box 7410, Franklin Station, Washington, D.C., 1964).

199. See Philip Bockman, "Fishing Practice," in Patrick Merla, ed., *Boys Like Us: Gay Writers Tell Their Coming-Out Stories* (New York: Avon Books, 1996), 73–81, here 77.

200. *Mattachine Review* (November–December 1955): 6–9. Nan Alamilla Boyd notes that the Mattachine Society did not really promote itself as a homosexual organization per se, but an organization open to "anyone interested in the condition of the homosexual." See her *Wide Open Town: A History of Queer San Francisco to 1965* (Berkeley: University of California Press, 2003), 177. By 1964, Canada's homophile movement had gained some ground as well, with the formation of the Association of Social Knowledge (ASK). For details, see Kinsman, *Regulation of Desire*, 236–46.

201. Christopher Nealon, *Foundlings: Lesbian and Gay Emotion before Stonewall* (Durham, N.C.: Duke University Press, 2001), 5.

202. On this, see Terry H. Anderson's discussion of figures such as Dick Gregory, Joe McDonald, and Ken Kesey in *The Movement and the Sixties* (New York: Oxford University Press, 1995), 142.

203. Kirsten Fermaglich, *American Dreams and Nazi Nightmares: Early Holocaust*

Consciousness in Liberal America, 1957–1965 (Lebanon, N.H.: Brandeis University Press, 2006), 4–8.

Chapter 2

1. Letter, "Darling," n.d. 1950, 1, Barbara Deming Papers, box 12, folder 215, series 2, MC 408, Schlesinger Library Archives, Radcliffe Institute for Advanced Study, Harvard University, Cambridge, Mass..

2. Letter, "Dearest Mother," April 30, 1969, 1, Barbara Deming Papers, box 12, folder 215.

3. Letter, "Very Dear Mother," July 17, 1974, 1, Barbara Deming Papers, box 12, folder 215.

4. The term "counterculture" was popularized by Theodore Roszak in his *The Making of a Counter Culture: Reflections on the Technocratic Society and Its Youthful Opposition* (New York: Doubleday, 1968). I am using it to encompass a broad range of political, social, and cultural dissent and oppositional stances. See also Doug Rossinow, "The Revolution Is about Our Lives: The New Left's Counterculture," in Peter Braunstein and Michael William Doyle, eds., *Imagine Nation: The American Counterculture of the 1960s and '70s* (New York: Routledge, 2002), 99–124, here 110. On gay liberation and the antiwar movement, see Charles Thorpe, "Anti-War Protests," Charles Thorpe Papers, box 1, folder 8, Harvey Milk Archives, Scott Smith Collection, James C. Hormel Gay and Lesbian Center, San Francisco Public Library, San Francisco, Calif. Finally, on the Black Power movement and its relation to gays specifically, see Devin W. Carbado, Dwight McBride and Donald Weise, *Black Like Us: A Century of Lesbian, Gay, and Bisexual African American Fiction* (San Francisco: Cleis Press, 2002), 113.

5. For an interpretation of the Stonewall riots, see the introduction to Martin Duberman, Martha Vicinus, and George Chauncey eds., *Hidden from History: Reclaiming the Gay and Lesbian Past* (New York: New American Library, 1989), 4ff. For Canadian legal reforms, which actually only legalized sexual acts between consenting adults in privacy but were broadly interpreted as the legalization of homosexuality, see Kinsman, *Regulation of Desire*, 142, 164. For Pierre Trudeau's impact on gay liberation in Canada and the United States, see Donald McLeod, *Lesbian and Gay Liberation in Canada: A Selected Annotated Chronology, 1964–75* (Toronto: ECW/Homewood Press, 1996).

6. On the mythologizing of Stonewall as a momentous marker for gay history, see Elizabeth Kennedy, "Telling Tales: Oral History and the Construction of Pre-Stonewall Lesbian History," *Radical History Review* (Spring 1995): 58–80.

7. For details, see Toby Marotta, *The Politics of Homosexuality: How Lesbians and Gay Men Have Made Themselves a Political and Social Force in Modern America* (Boston: Houghton Mifflin, 1981), 88ff.

8. As a gay code, "coming out" had formerly meant, in the earlier part of the twentieth century, coming out to one's gay peers. As George Chauncey has written of

the 1930s, gays were coming out *into* a gay world rather than coming out of the closet. See *Gay New York*, 7–8.

9. On the street-theater-like quality of protests and demonstrations that might have encouraged this idea of performance, see David Steigerwald, *The Sixties and the End of Modern America* (New York: St. Martin's Press, 1995), particularly his analysis of the Living Theatre and the Guerilla Theatre (160ff).

10. On the public curiosity about hippies in both the United States and Canada, see Owram, *Born at the Right Time*, 186. See also Susan Douglas, *Where the Girls Are: Growing Up Female with the Mass Media* (New York: Random House, 1994), 109.

11. See, for example, James DiGiacomo and Edward Wakin, *We Were Never Their Age* (New York: Holt, Rinehart and Winston, 1972), an advice manual for parents on their children's rebellion. See also Lewis Feuer, *The Conflict of Generations: The Character and Significance of Student Movements* (New York: Basic Books, 1969). Theodore Roszak has pointed to the force of market segmentation and the expansion of higher education as contributors to this sensibility of age consciousness. See *Making of a Counter Culture*, 27.

12. See again Steigerwald, *Sixties and the End of Modern America*, 257. Here he cites sociologist Mirra Komarovsky, who studied working-class families during the 1960s.

13. Ibid., 33. On Agnew and permissive parenting, see Benjamin Spock, *A Better World for Our Children: Rebuilding American Family Values* (Bethesda, Md.: National Press Books, 1994), 32. Dr. Spock wrote a defense of his parenting theory of "permissiveness" in "Don't Blame Me!" *Look Magazine* (1971): 36–38. Notably, the attacks on Dr. Spock also might have been politically motivated; in 1972, he became a candidate of the National People's Party, a coalition of ten small independent state political parties dedicated to cooperation, feminism, and world peace. On Spock, student activists, and the reactions of Agnew, see also Barbara Ehrenreich and Deirdre English, *For Her Own Good: 150 Years of the Experts' Advice to Women* (Garden City, N.Y.: Doubleday, 1978), 236. For more on fears of postwar maternal overindulgences, see Hays, *Cultural Contradictions of Motherhood*, 47–49.

14. On this, see Eugene T. Grendlin, "A Philosophical Critique of Narcissism: The Significance of the Awareness Movement," in David Michael Levin, ed., *Pathologies of the Modern Self: Postmodern Studies on Narcissism, Schizophrenia, and Depression* (New York: New York University Press, 1987), 251–304, here 253.

15. Richard Farson, *The Future of the Family* (New York: Family Service Association of America, 1969), 57.

16. Lynn Hunt has written about the context of empathy developed in the eighteenth century owing to a new appreciation of the inner lives of others, in this case through new ways of reading and seeing developed during that time. See Lynn Hunt, *Inventing Human Rights: A History* (New York: W. W. Norton, 2007).

17. See, most famously, Smith-Rosenberg, "Female World of Love and Ritual," 27–55.

18. Letter, "Dearest Bobbie," November 10, 1957, 2 and 3, Barbara Deming Papers, box 12, folder 213.

19. For a discussion of turn-of-the-century and modern notions of privacy see Gurstein, *Repeal of Reticence*, in particular her discussion of the prying, muckraking journalism of the Gilded Age as a violation of privacy (36ff and 149).

20. In the face of the intrusions into private life due to the development of rapid means of communication, lawyers Louis Brandeis and Samuel Warren most famously defended privacy as a right in the 1890s, conceiving it as the right to be let alone and the protection of an inviolate personality. On this, see Jed Rubenfeld, "The Right to Privacy," *Harvard Law Review* 102 (February 1989): 737–807.

21. Letter, "Dearest Bobbie," July 20, 1974, 1, Barbara Deming Papers, box 12, folder 215.

22. Ibid., 3 and 4.

23. Ibid., 3.

24. For these poems, see Anne Sexton, *Love Poems* (New York: Oxford University Press, 1969), 33 and 12. See also her 1972 work, *The Book of Folly* (Boston: Houghton Mifflin, 1972).

25. I say "renewed" here because T. J. Jackson Lears has suggested that a sense of the American carnivalesque had once, even if only fleetingly, existed in American culture. On this, see T. J. Jackson Lears, "Reconsidering Abundance: A Plea for Ambiguity," in Susan Strasser, Charles McGovern, and Matthias Judt, eds., *Getting and Spending: European and American Consumer Societies in the Twentieth Century* (Cambridge, U.K.: Cambridge University Press, 1998), 449–66, here 452.

26. On early twentieth-century confessional cultures, see Roland Marchand, *Advertising the American Dream: Making Way for Modernity, 1920–1940* (Berkeley: University of California Press, 1985), 53ff. On the radical intelligentsia and its openness about sexuality during the 1910s, see Christine Stansell, "Talking about Sex: Early-Twentieth-Century Radicals and Moral Confessions," in Karen Halttunen and Lewis Perry, eds., *Moral Problems in American Life: New Perspectives on Cultural History* (Ithaca, N.Y.: Cornell University Press, 1998), 283–307.

27. On the New Journalists who assumed a literary model in the 1960s, among them Thomas Wolfe but also Joan Didion, Norman Mailer, and Hunter Thompson, see Richard Campbell, *60 Minutes and the News: A Mythology for Middle America* (Urbana and Chicago: University of Illinois Press, 1991), 20–21. See also Christopher Lasch's treatment of confession and its interpenetration with fiction in *The Culture of Narcissism: American Life in an Age of Diminishing Expectations* (New York: Norton, 1979), 48–49.

28. Letter, "Dearest Bobbie," July 20, 1974, 3, Barbara Deming Papers, box 12, folder 215.

29. See Lasch, *Culture of Narcissism*, 33ffE, 66, and 151. In a similar critique, Richard Sennett argued in *The Fall of Public Man* (Toronto: Vintage, 1974) that the public world stage had been overtaken by a private psychic scene and an ideology of

intimacy that ultimately harmed both that individual and society. On Friedan, see Debra Michaels, "From Consciousness Expansion to Consciousness Raising: Feminism and the Countercultural Politics of the Self," in David Farber, ed., *The 60s: From Memory to History* (Chapel Hill: University of North Carolina Press, 1994), 41–68, here 51. See also Janann Sherman, ed., *Interviews with Betty Friedan* (Jackson: University of Mississippi Press, 2002), on Friedan's naming her more radical sisters "bra-burning, anti-man, politics of the orgasm school" types, see xiii; on navel gazing and the "lavender menace," see 61.

30. Callen was to write a booklet, with Richard Berkowitz and Joseph Sonnabend, *How to Have Sex in an Epidemic* (News from the Front Publications: 1983) and *Surviving AIDS* (New York: HarperCollins, 1990).

31. Letter, "Dear Mom & Dad," November 7, 1979, 1 (of 4), Michael Callen Papers, 010, Lesbian and Gay Community Services Center, National Archive of Lesbian and Gay History, New York.

32. Ibid., 2.

33. Ibid., 4.

34. Letter, "Dear Mike," November 13, 1979, 1 (of 4), Michael Callen Papers.

35. Ibid., 2.

36. On this theme of gays' moving from exhibits to subjects in the larger popular culture, see Larry Gross's commentary in *Off the Straight and Narrow: Lesbians, Gays, Bisexuals, and Television*, directed by Katherine Sender (Northampton, Mass.: Media Education Foundation, 1998), as well as *Further Off the Straight and Narrow: New Gay Visibility on Television, 1998–2006* (Northampton, Mass.: Media Education Foundation, 2006).

37. For another example of a family letter in this vein, see Merv Walker, "The Family: 'Don't Shut Us Out of Your Life,'" *Body Politic* 20 (October 1975): 12–13.

38. There is an extensive literature on Vietnam and the psychological disorders it bred, including Jacob P. Lindy, *Vietnam: A Casebook* (New York: Brunner/Mazel, 1988); Herbert Hendin and Ann Pollinger Haas, *Wounds of War: The Psychological Aftermath of Combat in Vietnam* (New York: Basic Books, 1984); and Richard K. Kulka, B. Kathleen Jordan, Daniel Weiss, and John A. Fairbank, eds., *Trauma and the Vietnam War Generation: Report of Findings from the National Vietnam Veterans Readjustment Study* (New York: Brunner/Mazel, 1990). On Vietnam and World War II, see John P. Wilson, Zev Hurel, and Boaz Kahana, eds., *Human Adaptation to Extreme Stress: From the Holocaust to Vietnam* (New York: Plenum, 1988), 171–92 and 357–75.

39. On divorce in this period, see James T. Patterson, *Grand Expectations* (New York: Oxford University Press, 1996), 671–72.

40. See Martha Shelley, "Gay Is Good," *Gay Flames* pamphlet 1 (New York, 1970), 2 (of 4). For details on these New York City produced pamphlets, see Streitmatter, *Unspeakable*, 127–28.

41. "Dear Dad," December 17, 1979, 3 (of 6), Michael Callen Papers.

42. On this question, see Christopher Hobson's critique of his mother's notions of privacy advanced in her novel. Hobson, *Consenting Adult.* See "What It Is Like to Be the Mother of a Homosexual," 13 (of 16), in Harry Langhorne Papers, 7304, box 2, file 9, Division of Rare and Manuscript Collections, Cornell University Library, Ithaca, N.Y.

43. Brass would go on to become a playwright, writing the plays *All Men* (performed in 1987 and 1988 in New York City, Chicago, and Los Angeles) and *Men Living with Each Other,* as well as his earlier articles for *COME OUT!* magazine.

44. "Notes on Correspondence with Family," Perry Brass Papers, 7329, box 1, file 58, Division of Rare and Manuscript Collections, Cornell University Library, Ithaca, N.Y.

45. "Mother: Helen Brass," letter to Perry, February 22, 1973, 1, 2, and 3, Perry Brass Papers, box 4, file 8.

46. See Hilary Radner and Moya Luckett, eds., *Swinging Single: Representing Sexuality in the 1960s* (Minneapolis, MN: University of Minnesota Press, 1999), esp. Leerom Medovi's portrait of the Yippies, "A Yippie-Panther Dream," 137–78, here 153–54.

47. Indeed, it should be noted that some sexual liberation writers were explicitly hostile to gay liberation. See Bailey, *Sex in the Heartland,* 137.

48. See D'Emilio and Freedman, *Intimate Matters,* 338–39.

49. See D'Emilio's discussion of *Redrup v. New York* (1967) in *Sexual Politics, Sexual Communities,* 133.

50. See Norm Winski, *The Homosexual Revolt* (Canoga Park, Calif.: Viceroy Books, 1967).

51. Started in 1967, the *Advocate* catered to a gay sensibility rooted in consumerism, including reports on movies, fashion, furniture, and the bar scene. By 1969, the *Los Angeles Advocate* had a circulation of 23,000 during its second year, doubling the circulation of any publication before it. It was to become the *Advocate* in 1970. See Streitmatter, *Unspeakable,* 83.

52. Cartoon by J. Lawrence in the *Los Angeles Advocate,* March 1969, 5.

53. Cartoon by "Shawn" in the *Los Angeles Advocate,* September 1969, 25.

54. Some examples were *Come Out!* magazine, a periodical that evolved from the leaflets the Gay Liberation Front handed out after the Stonewall riots; *Gay Liberator;* and the 1970s series of "Gay Flames" pamphlets. For details, see Streitmatter, *Unspeakable,* 127ff.

55. On student participation in gay liberation, see Marcus, *Making History,* 228. John D'Emilio and Estelle Freedman note that "with the range of penalties that exposure promised to homosexuals, it was radical youth, contemptuous of the rewards that American society offered for conformity, who were more likely to rally to the banner of gay liberation." See *Intimate Matters,* 322.

56. On student protests of the late 1960s and early 1970s, see Steigerwald, *Sixties and the End of Modern America,* 146ff; and Christopher Lasch, "The Agony of the

American Left," in Leonard Freedman, ed., *Issues of the Seventies* (Belmont, Calif.: Wadsworth, 1970), 520–23. For specific accounts of the student protests and riots at Harvard, see William E. Leuchtenburg, *A Troubled Feast: American Society since 1945* (Boston: Little, Brown, and Co., 1983), 177; and for Columbia's student revolt of 1968, see Diana Trilling, "On the Steps of Low Library," in *We Must March, My Darlings* (New York: Harcourt, Brace, Jovanovich, 1977), 77–153; finally, on Columbia and Berkeley, see Paul Sann, *American Panorama* (New York: Crown, 1979), 252ff.

57. See Paul Goodman, *The Moral Ambiguity of America* (Toronto: CBC Publications, 1966), 25.

58. On the generational differences in interpretations of the Vietnam War, see the letters between Allen Ginsberg and his father, Louis, in Michael Schumacher, ed., *Family Business: Selected Letters between a Father and Son* (New York: Bloomsbury, 2001).

59. Erika Doss has shown that the bodily performance art of this period also asked spectators to pose questions to themselves about the meanings of voyeurism, given this increased attention to the bodies of war victims. See Erika Doss, *Twentieth-Century American Art* (New York: Oxford University Press, 2002), 173ff.

60. See James Seaton, *Cultural Conservatism, Political Liberalism: From Criticism to Cultural Studies* (Ann Arbor: University of Michigan Press, 1996), 74.

61. For the Port Huron statement, see Robert Marcus, ed., *How Many Roads? Recent America in Perspective* (New York: Holt, Rinehart, and Winston, 1972), 170–76. For details on the GLF and the New Left, see Mark Blasius's and Shane Phelan's commentary in *We Are Everywhere*, 377ff. On the New Left's attempt to allay a sense of banality, see Rossinow, "Revolution Is about Our lives," 113. Finally, see Doug Rossinow's book, *The Politics of Authenticity: Liberalism, Christianity and the New Left in America* (New York: Columbia University Press, 1998).

62. See Jerry Rubin, *We Are Everywhere* (New York: Harper and Row, 1971), 159.

63. See Laurence Veysey, *The Communal Experience: Anarchist and Mystical Counter Cultures in America* (New York: Harper and Row, 1973), 185–87. See also Bailey, *Sex in the Heartland*, 141.

64. On gay liberation and women's liberation, see Alice Echols, "Nothing Distant about It: Women's Liberation and 60s Radicalism," in David Farber, ed., *The 60s: From Memory to History* , 149–74. See also Dennis Altman's discussion in *Coming Out in the Seventies* (Boston: Alyson, 1979), 51. On women's liberation and stifling gender roles within the nuclear family, see Peggy Morton, "A Woman's Work Is Never Done," *Leviathan* 2 (May 1970): 32–37. On women's liberation more broadly, see the essays in the anthology of women's liberation writings, Robin Morgan, ed., *Sisterhood Is Powerful* (New York: Random House, 1970). See also *Notes from the Second Year: Women's Liberation; Major Writings of the Radical Feminists* (New York: Radical Feminism, 1970).

65. See Rosenfeld, *Age of Independence*, 66.

66. See "The Family and Gay Oppression," *Come Out Fighting: The Newspaper of the Lavender and Red Union*, April 1977, 4 and 5, here 5.

67. For the "Here I Am, MOM" photo, see, for example, the cover of the *Lesbian Tide* 1 (June 1972).

68. On Red Butterfly, see Marotta, *Politics of Homosexuality*, 124. Red Butterfly, "The Institutions of Repression," *Gay Oppression: A Radical Analysis* (New York City: Red Butterfly, 1969), 5.

69. For other gay critiques of gender roles, see A. N. Diaman, "On Sex Roles," and Guy Nassberg "Revolutionary Love: An Introduction to Liberation," *Gay Flames* pamphlet no. 11 (1970): 4. See also Carl Wittman, "Gay Manifesto," *Gay Flames* pamphlet no. 9 (1970): 4.

70. This cartoon was run, for example, in the *Mattachine New Times* 1 (October 1975): 11. While the *Body Politic* was produced in Toronto, much of its circulation was in the United States. See Streitmatter, *Unspeakable*, 212.

71. On the countercultural rejection of cultures of abundance during this period, see Shi, *Simple Life*.

72. Joan Larkin, "Rhyme of My Inheritance," from *Housework* (1975), reprinted in Carl Morse and Joan Larkin, eds., *Gay and Lesbian Poetry in Our Time: An Anthology* (New York: St Martin's Press, 1988), 219.

73. Ibid., 220.

74. On SUPA and its American interconnections, see Bryan D. Palmer, *Canada's 1960s: The Ironies of Identities in a Rebellious Era* (Toronto: University of Toronto Press, 2009), 258ff.

75. On the formation of the CYC, see ibid., 274. For broader details on Canadian student activism during these years, see Myrna Kostash, *Long Way From Home: The Story of the 60s Generation in Canada* (Toronto: James and Lorimer, 1980). See also Cyril Levitt, *Children of Privilege: Student Revolt in the Sixties; A Study of Student Movements in Canada, the U.S., and Germany* (Toronto: University of Toronto Press, 1984).

76. On the Canadian critique of American cultural imperialism in Canada, see J. L. Granatstein, "War, Cold War, and Canadian Dependency," in Joseph Tulchin, ed., *Hemispheric Perspectives of the U.S.: Papers from the New World Conference* (Westport, Conn.: Greenwood Press, 1975), 241–57. For a view within a feminist lesbian periodical, see "USA & Canada," *Other Woman* 1 (March 1973): 13 and 16.

77. See Amerigo Marras, "Hetero-burbia," *Body Politic* 7 (Winter 1973): 5.

78. Here it is important to note that Canadian postwar suburbs were much more varied socioeconomically than American ones, and yet there were still these continuities of feeling. See Gillian Mitchell, *The North American Folk Music Revival: Nation and Identity in the United States and Canada, 1945–1980* (Aldershot, Hampshire, Eng.: Ashgate, 2007), 89.

79. Betty Friedan, *The Feminine Mystique* (New York: W. W. Norton, 1963).

Chapter 12 is titled "Progressive Dehumanization: The Comfortable Concentration Camp," 282–309.

80. This poem was censored after its first publication. See the commentary of Richard Ellmann and Robert O'Clair, editors of *The Norton Anthology of Modern Poetry* (New York: W. W. Norton, 1988), 1209.

81. See Wylie, *Generation of Vipers*, and Hans Sebald, *Momism: The Silent Disease of America* (Chicago: Nelson-Hall, 1976), which evoked a generation of bored, career-frustrated housewives who placed all of their life-sucking energy into the baby-boom generation.

82. B. I. Groach, "Mothers in Agony," *Closetary Comix* (series), *Empty Closet* 45 (December 1974): 7. For a similar example, see "Media Injection," *Empty Closet* 61 (May 1976): 8.

83. On misogyny within the American cartooning tradition, see Mary F. Corey, *The World through a Monocle: The New Yorker at Midcentury* (Cambridge, Mass.: Harvard University Press, 1999); and Stephen Becker, *Comic Art in America: A Social History of the Funnies, Political Cartoons, Magazine Humor, Sporting Cartoons, and Animated Cartoons* (New York: Simon and Schuster, 1959).

84. On this idea, see Gary Cross, *An All Consuming Century: Why Commercialism Won in Modern America* (New York: Columbia University Press, 2000), 166.

85. See *Focus* 2 (February 1971): 2.

86. The countercultural rejection of traditional psychiatry involved the embrace of psychiatrists who took an antiauthoritarian approach to mental illness and curing. R. D. Laing was one such psychiatrist. He was instrumental in establishing residences where psychosis could be lived through rather than immediately treated. See R. D. Laing, *The Politics of Experience* (London: Penguin, 1967). The publication of books such as Thomas Szasz, *The Myth of Mental Illness: Foundations of a Theory of Personal Conduct* (1961; repr., New York: Harper and Row, 1974); and Ken Kesey, *One Flew Over the Cuckoo's Nest* (1962); repr., (New York: Viking Press, 1973) also bolstered this trend in their questioning of what they perceived as spirit-crushing psychiatric treatments.

87. At the 1971 annual meeting of the American Psychiatric Association in Washington, D.C., Frank Kameny and other gay liberationists grabbed the microphone and declared war against psychiatry. For an account, see Vern L. Bullough, ed., *Before Stonewall: Activists for Gay and Lesbian Rights in Historical Context* (Binghamton, N.Y.: Harrington Park Press, 2002), 214.

88. Many works continued to uphold the ideas of Irving Bieber and other American psychoanalysts that gay liberation tried to revoke. See, for example, Marcel T. Saghir and Eli Robins, *Male and Female Homosexuality: A Comprehensive Investigation* (Baltimore: Williams and Wilkins, 1973). On harbingers of child homosexuality, see Peter and Barbara Wyden, *Growing Up Straight: What Every Thoughtful Parent Should Know about Homosexuality* (New York: Signet, 1968).

89. On the shift in sodomy laws, see D'Emilio and Freedman, *Intimate Matters,* 324.

90. On this, see Charles Silverstein, "The Origin of the Gay Psychotherapy Movement," in Duberman, ed., *A Queer World,* 358–80.

91. Satya Klein, "The Heterosexual World: An Anthropological Study," *Vector: The Gay Experience* 11 (October 1975): 55.

92. Ibid., 56. Such pieces were becoming a widespread source of humor in gay periodicals during these years. For example, *Sisters,* the magazine of the San Francisco DOB, ran a similar piece titled "The Heterosexual" that parodied their warped family environments. See *Sisters* (July 1973): 3–4.

93. Kohut was particularly concerned with a capacity for empathy and introspection, also prominent foci of gay liberationists and lesbian feminists during this period. See his *The Restoration of the Self* (New York: International Universities Press, 1977); for a broader selection, see *The Search for the Self* (New York: International Universities Press, 1978). For a discussion, see Freedheim et al., *A History of Psychotherapy,* 51. See also Zaretsky, *Secrets of the Soul,* 314ff., for a discussion of Kohut's reevaluation of narcissism and the development of the psychology of the self.

94. On the probing of gay personal experience and its parallels to psychoanalysis, see Terry, *American Obsession,* 376.

95. Dick Michaels, "The World Is My Ashtray," *Los Angeles Advocate* 1 (December 1967): 7 (of 8).

96. See Howard Brown, *Familiar Faces, Hidden Lives: The Story of Homosexual Men in America Today* (New York: Harcourt, Brace, Jovanovich, 1976), 68.

97. John Knoebel, "Words on Mother," from New York City's "effeminist" gay periodical, for self-described effeminate gay male radicals, *Faggotry* (1972): 22–24, here 24.

98. I will expand on the shifting standards of women's appearance in my next chapter, but for now see Lois W. Banner, *American Beauty* (New York: Knopf, 1983), 285ff.

99. Lisa Fenton, "The Radical Home Haircut," *Lesbian Voices* 4, no. 1 (1979): 13 (of 14). This lesbian periodical was from San Jose, California.

100. On the hair and dress of Vietnam War protestors, see interview with homophile activist Barbara Gittings in Marcus, *Making History,* 124.

101. See Medovi, "Yippie-Panther Dream," 154. On the importance of long hair as a gay code, see John Murphy, *Homosexual Liberation: A Personal View* (New York: Praeger, 1971), 14. And for a historical look at gay men's fashions in Britain and the United States, see Shaun Cole, *Don We Now Our Gay Apparel: Gay Men's Dress in the Twentieth Century* (Oxford: Berg, 2000), 89.

102. Diaries, June 5, 1971, Mike Hippler Papers, 90–12, box 3, Gay and Lesbian Historical Society of Northern California, San Francisco. Hippler would go on to write a biography of air force sergeant and gay rights leader Leonard Matlovich.

103. For details, see Joshua Freeman, "Hardhats: Construction Workers, Manli-

ness, and the 1970 Pro War Demonstration," *Journal of Social History* (Summer 1993): 725–37. See also William E. Leuchtenberg's account in *Troubled Feast*, 247.

104. See the entry on the "New Left" in Mari-Jo Buhle, Paul Buhle, and Dan Georgakas, eds., *Encyclopedia of the American Left* (New York: Garland, 1990), 517–23, here 519.

105. Patterson, *Grand Expectations*, 699.

106. See the reprint of Kennan's speech in *Democracy and the Student Left* (New York: Bantam, 1968), 3–18. See also Martin Duberman's response essay of this period, "On Misunderstanding Student Rebels," in Harold Jaffe and John Tytell, eds., *The American Experience: A Radical Reader* (New York: Harper and Row, 1970), 162–76, here 164.

107. On this theme, see Richard Dyer, *The Culture of Queers* (New York: Routledge, 2002). On the inherent "queerness" of the student and counterculture revolt during this period, see Ian Lekus, "Losing Our Kids: Queer Perspectives on the Chicago Conspiracy Trial," in John McMillian and Paul Buhle, eds., *The New Left Revisited* (Philadelphia: Temple, 2003), 199–213. Finally, see Ronald D. Cohen, "The Delinquents: Censorship and Youth Culture in Recent American History," *History of Education Quarterly* 37 (Fall 1997): 251–70.

108. Emily Rubin Weiner, "Wow, I'll really be uptight if my family sees this," *Come Out!* 2 (Winter 1972), n.p.

109. In Karen Duder's work on lesbians and their parents in Ontario between the 1920s and 1960s, she suggests that many families might have believed homosexuality existed only as an abstraction, but not within their own families. She argues that this sense was to change as more visible lesbian communities emerged. See Karen Duder, " 'That Repulsive Abnormal Creature I Heard of in That Book': Lesbians and Families in Ontario, 1920–1965," in Lori Chambers and Edgar-Andre Montigny, eds., *Ontario since Confederation: A Reader* (Toronto: University of Toronto Press, 2000), 260–83.

110. Letter, "Dearest Mother," June 17, 1977, William Cannicott Olson Papers, box 6, Duke University, Rare Book, Manuscript, and Special Collections Library, Durham, N.C.

111. Letter, "Dearest Mother," July 7, 1976, 2 of 2, William Cannicott Olson Papers, box 5.

112. [112] Letter, "Dearest Mother and all," June 16, 1977, 1 of 2, William Cannicott Olson Papers, box 5.

113. Letter, "Dear Bob," July 24, 1975, 2 of 2, William Cannicott Olson Papers, box 5.

114. Letter, "Dearest Mother and all," July 2, 1976, 1 of 2, William Cannicott Olson Papers, box 5.

115. John D'Emilio notes that before 1969 about fifty gay organizations existed; after 1973, there were more than eight hundred gay groups in America. See "Gay Politics and Community in San Francisco since World War II," in Martin Duberman

et al., eds., *Hidden from History: Reclaiming the Gay and Lesbian Past*, 456–73, here 466.

116. Jeanne Cordova, "How to Come Out without Being Thrown Out," in Karla Jay and Allen Young, eds., *After You're Out: Personal Experiences of Gay Men and Lesbian Women*, 89–95, here 90.

117. Ibid., 91.

118. Ibid., 92.

119. Ibid., 94.

120. See, for example, Lilly Hansen, "Should Your Parents Know?" *GAY* 9 (March 29, 1970): 15. See also the unrepentant coming-out letters published in *Spectre* 3 (July–August 1971): 4–6; and *Lesbian Voices* 1 (September 1975): 16–17. For gay men, see *Body Politic* 19 (July–August 1975): 18.

121. Robert Burke, "Coming Out!" *Vector*, May 1973, 27–30, here 28.

122. *Lesbian Tide*, September 1971, 7. For a blunt statement of family excommunication, see also "On Being a Lesbian," *Lesbian Connection* 2 (December 1976): 11.

123. B. I. Groach, *Closetary Comix*, *Empty Closet* 43 (October 1974): 6.

124. On Lee's self-identification as a nonpolitical lesbian, see "Correspondence re. Lesbian/Woman," letter from Julie Lee to Martin and Lyon, "Dear Del and Phyl," May 17, 1971, 1 and 2, Del Martin and Phyllis Lyon Papers, box 22, file 24. Many lesbians were critical of her, viewing any form of counseling as inherently elitist and coercive, merely enhancing the power of the counselor. In an issue of the lesbian periodical *Albatross* in October 1975 (21–27), Julie Lee was satirized and given the name "Jewel Elitist." For a more positive assessment of Julie Lee's advice, see George Weinberg, "Julie Lee Rhymes with DOB," *GAY* (April 12, 1971): 5.

125. Martin and Lyon, *Lesbian/Woman*, 174.

126. Ibid., 213.

127. Letter from Anonymous to Julie Lee, August 27, 1972, 2, Julie Lee Papers.

128. Letter from "Sal" to Julie Lee, February 1973, 1 (of 2), Julie Lee Papers.

129. Letter from "Emily" to Julie Lee, December 20, 1972, 2 (of 4), Julie Lee Papers.

130. Ibid., 3.

131. On this idea of lesbian feminist communities as substitute families, see Duder, "'That Repulsive Abnormal Creature I Heard of in that Book.'"

132. Letter to "Emily" from Julie Lee, January 11, 1973, 1 (of 2), Julie Lee Papers.

133. Letter to Anonymous from Julie Lee, August 10, 1972, Julie Lee Papers.

134. See "The Well of Possibility," *GAY* 24 (July 20, 1970): 15. For details on *GAY*, see Streitmatter, *Unspeakable*, 126–28.

135. Letter to Julie Lee from "Liza," February 16, 1971, 3, Julie Lee Papers.

136. Letter to Julie Lee from "Liza," April 29, 1971, Julie Lee Papers.

137. Letter to Julie Lee from "Liza," August 15, 1971, 1 (of 2) , Julie Lee Papers.

138. See D'Emilio and Freedman, *Intimate Matters*, 324. See also George

Chauncey, *Why Marriage? The History Shaping Today's Debate over Gay Equality* (New York: Basic Books, 2004), 37.

139. The novels that Duplechan wrote with Rousseau as a protagonist include *Eight Days a Week* (Boston: Alyson, 1985), *Blackbird* (New York: St. Martin's Press, 1986), and *Captain Swing* (Boston: Alyson, 1992). Duplechan spent his high school years in Lancaster, California, the same "rednecky town" that Duplechan portrays in Blackbird. Duplechan has recorded that his real life coming out was very similar to the one he depicted in this novel. See Stuart Timmons, "Larry Duplechan: Coming Out, Friendship, and Romance," *Advocate* 533 (September 12, 1989): 62–63.

140. The Third World Gay Revolution platform and program drafted in 1970 criticized heterosexual masculinity within white, Afro-American, and Latino communities, and patriarchy within the family. For the Third World Gay Revolution platform and program drafted in September 1970, see the reprint in the *Detroit Gay Liberator* (February 1971): 6. In a 1970 essay, Black Panther founder Huey Newton recognized gays as an oppressed group facing a comparable struggle to African Americans to counteract the idea of homosexuality as a white man's sickness, offered by Eldridge Cleaver, for example. See Neil Miller's discussion of Leroi Jones and Eldridge Cleaver in *Out of the Past*, 373. See also Marotta, *Politics of Homosexuality*, 128. Finally, see Cleaver's work itself, *Soul on Ice* (New York: Dell, 1968), 103.

141. Duplechan, *Blackbird*, 83.

142. Ibid., 151.

143. Ibid., 152.

144. Ibid., 154.

145. Ibid., 155.

146. Dick Leitsch, "Turning On To Daddy" in *GAY* (March 15, 1970): 8.

147. On Leitsch, see Dudley Clendinen and Adam Nagourney, *Out for Good: The Struggle to Build a Gay Rights Movement in America* (New York: Touchstone, 1999), 24ff.

148. On *GAY* and the GAA, see Streitmatter, *Unspeakable*, 128.

149. See, for example, the *Empty Closet's* features on Jeanne Manford, the first PFLAG mother in "Gays in the Family," in 61 (May 1976): 6 and 7; and also Regina Kahney, "Sarah Montgomery: Everybody's Favorite Mother" (January 1977): 6–9. New York's *GAY* featured on its front cover in 1972 "Parent Defends Gay Son's Right to Teach," in 84 (September 4, 1972), as well as a cover feature of its vol. 4, no. 100 (April 23, 1973) issue, "Parents of Gays Organizing." See also Randy Wicker's interview with early activist Sarah Montgomery, "A Conversation with Sarah Montgomery, Grandma Lib," in *GAY* 5 (March 1974): 6, 7, 15. I will discuss these figures and their portrayal more in my chapter on PFLAG and its origins.

150. See Del Martin's 1970 piece (first published in the *Advocate* during October of that year), "If That's All There Is." For a reprint, see Blasius and Phelan, *We Are Everywhere*, 352–55. See also Marotta, *Politics of Homosexuality*, 53ff and 237ff; and D'Emilio, "Gay Politics and Community in San Francisco since World War II," 467.

151. In Anita Cornwell's *A Soul Sister's Notebook* (1972), for example, she discussed seeing race as a primary identity in her analysis of violence against African Americans during 1972. "The bullets don't give a damn whether I sleep with a woman or man," she declared. See Anita Cornwell, "From a Soul Sister's Notebook," (1972), reprint in Blasius and Phelan, *We Are Everywhere*, 364–66. For details on Cornwell, see Stein, *City of Sisterly and Brotherly Loves*, 344–45.

152. Martin Duberman, *Midlife Queer: Biography of a Decade, 1971–1981* (New York: Scribner, 1996), 94–95.

Chapter 3

1. On sexism in the gay male movement, see Marotta, *Politics of Homosexuality*, 234, 239. Marotta mentions the somewhat transient attempts to form specific women-only groups within gay liberation such as the Gay Women's Liberation Front, a group of twelve women led by Deni Corello in 1971–72 (p. 275). See also Clendinen and Nagourney, *Out for Good*, 85ff. In the Canadian context, where the conflict between lesbians and gay men was often less severe, see Gillean Chase, "Gay Pride? Week," in the Montreal lesbian periodical, *Long Time Coming* 2 (December 1974). For a more vehement portrait in the American context, see Nancy Tucker, "F—— You, 'Brothers'! or Yet Another Woman Leaves the Gay Liberation Movement," *Ladder* 15 (August–September 1971): 52 and 53.

2. Minnie Bruce Pratt made these comments at the ALMS Conference in New York City on Saturday, May 10, 2008, but she has also written about her sense of having been deceived in *Rebellion: Essays, 1980–1991* (Ithaca, N.Y.: Firebrand Books, 1991), 11, 15, 57, and 123. Pratt was born in 1946 in Selma, Alabama, and she attended a segregated high school and the University of Alabama in Tuscaloosa. On this, see Joan Nestle, "The Will to Remember: The Lesbian Herstory Archives of New York," *Feminist Review* 34 (Spring 1990): 86–94, here 87.

3. Elisabeth Lasch-Quinn, "Liberation Therapeutics: From Moral Renewal to Consciousness Raising," in Jonathan B. Imber, ed., *Therapeutic Culture: Triumph and Defeat* (New Brunswick, N.J.: Transaction, 2004), 3–18, here 5.

4. James L. Nolan quotes Jean Bethke Elshtain on this transformation from citizen to therapeutic selfhood. See his *The Therapeutic State: Justifying Government at Century's End* (New York University Press, 1998), 6.

5. Lauren Berlant, *The Female Complaint: The Unfinished Business of Sentimentality in American Culture* (Durham, N.C.: Duke University Press, 2008), 234.

6. As a counterbalance to Lasch, a more positive assessment of the political uses of self-fulfillment is in Peter Clecak's *America's Quest for the Ideal Self: Dissent and Fulfillment in the 60s and 70s* (New York: Oxford University Press, 1983), for example, 107.

7. See Lasch, *Culture of Narcissism*, 26 and 102, on the narcissistic inability to identify with the past.

8. See Charlotte Bunch, "What Every Lesbian Should Know," *Furies* (January

1972): 40, a periodical of a Washington lesbian collective. See Radicalesbians, "The Woman-Identified Woman," in Karla Jay and Allen Young, eds., *Out of the Closets: Voices of Gay and Lesbian Liberation* (New York: Quick Fox, 1972), 156. For another critique in this vein, see Rita Mae Brown, "The Shape of Things to Come," in Nancy Myron and Charlotte Bunch, eds., *Lesbianism and the Women's Movement* (Baltimore: Diana Press, 1975), 70–73.

9. By the beginning of the 1970s, hundreds of women's groups existed within major American and Canadian cities. On the altercations between heterosexual and lesbian women within American women's liberation groups, see Dana Heller, *Cross Purposes: Lesbians, Feminists, and the Limits of Alliance* (Bloomington: Indiana University Press, 1997), and Nancy Myron and Charlotte Bunch, *Lesbianism and the Women's Movement* (Baltimore: Diana Press, 1975). See also D'Emilio and Freedman, *Intimate Matters*, 316. Finally, see Charlotte Bunch's essay, originally published in 1975, "Not for Lesbians Only," in *Passionate Politics: Feminist Theory in Action, 1968–1986* (New York: St. Martin's Press, 1987), 174–81. For the Canadian context, see Nancy Adamson, Linda Briskin, and Margaret McPhail, eds., *Feminists Organizing for Change: The Contemporary Women's Movement in Canada* (Toronto: Oxford University Press, 1988), 116; and Naomi Black, "The Second Wave," in Sandra Burt, Lorraine Code, and Lindsay Dorney, eds., *Changing Patterns: Women in Canada* (Toronto: McClelland and Stewart, 1993), 151–75. Again, these debates were not as acrimonious as they were in the United States.

10. See Charlotte Bunch, "Going Public with Our Vision," in *Passionate Politics: Feminist Theory in Action, 1968–1986*, 61–78, here 65.

11. On the institution of heterosexuality, see Cruikshank, *Gay and Lesbian Liberation Movement*, 146–52.

12. For a collection covering a range of these concerns, see the women's liberation anthology, *The New Woman: A Motive Anthology on Women's Liberation* (New York: Bobbs-Merrill, 1970).

13. Verta Taylor and Leila Rupp, "Women's Culture and Lesbian Feminist Activism: A Reconsideration of Cultural Feminism," *Signs* 19 (Autumn 1993): 32–61, here 37. See also Shane Phelan, *Identity Politics: Lesbian Feminism and the Limits of Community* (Philadelphia: Temple University Press, 1989), 43.

14. On lesbians and cultural feminism, see Lillian Faderman, *Odd Girls and Twilight Lovers*, (New York: Columbia University Press, 1991), 248–49.

15. Alice Echols, in *Daring to be Bad: Radical Feminism in America, 1967–75* (Minneapolis: University of Minnesota Press, 1989), placed lesbian feminists within the traditions of both radical and cultural feminism. On lesbian separatism, see, for example, Charlotte Bunch, "Learning from Lesbian Separatism," in Karla Jay and Allen Young, eds., *Lavender Culture*, 435; for a thorough analysis of the notion of separatism, see Jill Johnston, *Lesbian Nation* (New York: Simon and Schuster, 1973). See also Lisa Ransdell, "Lesbian Feminism and the Feminist Movement," in Jo Freeman, ed., *Women: A Feminist Perspective* (Mountain View, Calif.: Mayfield, 1995), 641–53, here

648. And finally see Bonnie Zimmerman, *The Safe Sea of Women: Lesbian Fiction, 1969–1989* (Boston: Beacon Press, 1990), 119ff. Tom Warner has noted that the concept of lesbian feminist separatism did not really take root in Canada. See *Never Going Back: A History of Queer Activism in Canada* (Toronto: University of Toronto Press, 2002), 178.

16. See Arlene Stein, *Sex and Sensibility: Stories of a Lesbian Generation* (Berkeley: University of California Press, 1997). See also Janice Raymond, *A Passion for Friends* (Boston: Beacon Press, 1986). On romantic friendships, see Faderman, *Odd Girls and Twilight Lovers*, 11ff. I should note that the extent to which these friendships actually engaged in sexual relations is disputed. See, for example, Martha Vicinus, "They Wonder to Which Sex I Belong: The Historical Roots of the Modern Lesbian Identity," *Feminist Studies* 18 (Fall 1992): 467–98.

17. See Adrienne Rich, "Compulsory Heterosexuality and Lesbian Existence," in *Blood, Bread, and Poetry: Selected Prose, 1979–1985* (New York: W. W. Norton, 1986), 23–75. This essay was first published in 1980.

18. On this, see Robert Castel, Francoise Castel, and Anne Lovell, *The Psychiatric Society*, trans. Arthur Goldhammer (New York: Columbia University Press, 1982), 234; and Jane Gerhard, *Desiring Revolution: Second Wave Feminism and the Rewriting of American Sexual Thought, 1920 to 1982* (New York: Columbia University Press, 2001), 15, 30, 51, and 69. Also, on the attribution of narcissism to lesbians, see Barbara Creed, "Lesbian Bodies: Tribades, Tomboys, and Tarts," in Liz Grosz and Elspeth Probyn, eds., *Sexy Bodies: The Strange Carnalities of Feminism* (New York: Routledge, 1995), 86–103, here 98–101. For broader feminist revisions of male-dominated psychiatry during this period, see Phyllis Chesler, "Patient and Patriarch: Women in the Psychotherapeutic Relationship," in Vivian Gornick and Barbara Moran, eds., *Woman in Sexist Society* (New York: Basic Books, 1971), 251–76. By the late 1960s, sexologists William Masters and Virginia Johnson had revised Freudian ideas about women's orgasms. On Masters and Johnson, see Roger Lewis, *Outlaws of America: The Underground Press and Its Context; Notes on a Cultural Revolution* (Harmondsworth, Eng.: Cox and Wyman, 1972), 39; see also William Masters and Virginia Johnson, *Human Sexual Response* (Boston: Little, Brown, and Company, 1966). For Freud's original ideas about women's sexuality, see Freud, *Three Essays on the Theory of Sexuality*, 73–87. For a Freudian revision, see Juliet Mitchell, *Psychoanalysis and Feminism* (Harmondsworth, Eng.: Penguin, 1975), 108. Finally, see Ehrenreich, *Hearts of Men*, 23.

19. See Anne Koedt's "Myth of the Vaginal Orgasm," in Ellen Levine and Anita Rapone, eds., *Radical Feminism* (New York: Quadrangle Books, 1973), 198–207. See also Boston Women's Health Collective, *Our Bodies, Ourselves: A Book by and for Women* (New York: Simon and Schuster, 1973), 45. On this collection's popularity, see Kathleen C. Berkeley, *The Women's Liberation Movement in America* (Westport, Conn.: Greenwood Press, 1999), 63.

20. On this oft-repeated slogan "Feminism is the theory, lesbianism is the prac-

tice," attributed to singer Ti-Grace Atkinson, see again, Taylor and Rupp, "Women's Culture and Lesbian Feminist Activism."

21. This was, of course, not the sole genre to convey coming-out stories. Alan Sinfield notes that lesbian theater during the 1970s was galvanized by the drama of the coming-out story, including theater groups such as the Lavender Cellar in Minneapolis. See *Out on Stage: Lesbian and Gay Theatre in the Twentieth Century* (New Haven, Conn.: Yale University Press, 1999), 308.

22. Bonnie Zimmerman, "The Politics of Transliteration: Lesbian Personal Narratives," *Signs* 9 (Summer 1984): 663–82, here 663 and 664.

23. See Lee Badgett, *Money, Myths, and Change: The Economic Lives of Lesbians and Gay Men* (Chicago: University of Chicago Press, 2001), 108.

24. For details on lesbian feminist periodicals, including their production and circulation outputs, see again Streitmatter, *Unspeakable*, 160ff; and see also Lynne D. Shapiro, *Write On, Woman! A Writer's Guide to U.S. Women's/Feminist/Lesbian/Alternate Press Periodicals* (New York: Lynne D. Shapiro, 1978), 14–16. Small autonomous feminist newspapers in Quebec, in particular, were to spawn some of the most famous lesbian writers of the contemporary period, such as Nicole Brossard. On this, see Prentice et al., *Canadian Women*, 389.

25. For a discussion on the outpouring of women's creativity in the seventies, see Gayle Kimball, ed., *Women's Culture: The Women's Renaissance of the Seventies* (Metuchen, N.J.: Scarecrow Press, 1981). Self-writing had gained some broader credence during the 1970s. As Marlene Schiwy points out, this decade saw the publication of Anaïs Nin's *Diary*, as well as the introduction of journal workshops at universities offered by psychologist Ira Progoff, among others. See Marlene A. Schiwy, *A Voice of Her Own: Women and the Journal Writing Journey* (New York: Simon and Schuster, 1994), 20.

26. Stansell, "Talking about Sex," 300.

27. See Lewin, *Inventing Lesbian Cultures in America*, 6.

28. See, for example, East Lansing's *Lesbian Connection* (May 1976): 9; Ann Arbor's *Leaping Lesbian* 2, no. 2 (February 1978): "Dear Mother," 7 and 8; *Leaping Lesbian* 2, no. 3 (March–April 1978): 27 and 28; California's *Lesbian Voices* 1, no. 4 (September 1975): 16–17; Chicago's *Lavender Woman* 1 (May 1972): 4.

29. *Dyke* 3 (1976) gave responses to the coming-out letters of the previous issue; this response is on p. 7, "Mother Letters."

30. This periodical was produced by five lesbian women and contained much lesbian content, although it was more broadly defined as a feminist periodical. See Nancy Adamson et al., *Feminists Organizing for Change*, 116. The *Other Woman*'s run was between 1972 and 1977.

31. *Other Woman* 3 (August 1974): 8.

32. On Parsons, see Jamieson, *Intimacy*, 3–47ff.

33. *Other Woman* 3 (August 1974): 8 (italics in original).

34. On sexual exploitation within the New Left, see the Montreal lesbian periodi-

cal *Long Time Coming* 2 (January 1975): 35, article with no name by "marychild." On sexism within SUPA, see Palmer, *Canada's 1960s*, 300. Piercey, *Small Changes* (New York: Doubleday, 1973), depicts several male characters who fit this contradictory image. See also Vivian Estellachild, "Hippie Communes," in Joann S. DeLora and Jack R. DeLora, eds., *Intimate Life Styles: Marriage and Its Alternatives*, 332–37, here 333, an essay that characterizes two kinds of men favoring the hippy alternative: "Bill C. Ph.D.," who was "too good to work with his hands" but not too good to "f——— everything that moves," and "Jim C. Variety," a "macho alcoholic" who sired lots of children but "will never be a father." Similar examples are described in Echols's *Daring to Be Bad: Radical Feminism in America 1967–75*, for example, p. 31. For a more detailed treatment of how women were treated in American New Left movements such as the Student Nonviolent Coordinating Committee (SNCC) and Students for a Democratic Society (SDS), see Sara Evans, *Personal Politics: The Roots of Women's Liberation in the Civil Rights Movement and the New Left* (New York: Vintage Books, 1979), 184–85 and 190–91. See also Rebecca Klatch's interviews in *A Generation Divided: The New Left, the New Right and the 1960s* (Berkeley and Los Angeles: University of California Press, 1999), 167ff. Finally, see D'Emilio and Freedman, *Intimate Matters*, 311.

35. Jane Alpert, a former SDSer and Weatherman member, was one such woman who tried out lesbianism after she became more feminist in orientation and had reflected upon the male exploitation in the movements. See Jane Alpert, *Growing Up Underground* (New York: Morrow, 1981).

36. Letter to Lesbian Liberation, Women's Educational Center, Cambridge, September 19, 1973, Boston Women's Health Book Collective, box 159, folder 1, Letters, 1973–74, MC 503, Schlesinger Library, Radcliffe Institute for Advanced Study, Harvard University, Cambridge, Mass.

37. Audre Lorde, *Zami: A New Spelling of My Name* (Freedom, Calif.: Crossing Press, 1982), 225.

38. "Consciousness raising" allowed women to reinterpret some of the institutions of womanhood. On lesbians and consciousness raising, see "Lesbians and the Health Care System," by the Radicalesbians Health Collective, 1971, and "A Guide to Consciousness Raising," *Lesbian Feminist* (August 1976): 3. For a more general look at women's consciousness raising, see *Ms.* (July 1972): 18, 22, 23; and see Margaret Elias, "Sisterhood Therapy," *Human Behavior* (April 1975): 31–36. Finally, see Charlotte Bunch, "A Broom of One's Own," *Passionate Politics*, 27–46; and Herman, *Romance of American Psychology*, 298.

39. Letter, December 17, 1975, 1, manuscript collection, 81–04, Lesbian Herstory Archives (hereafter cited as LHA), Brooklyn, N.Y.

40. On the idea of lesbian sex being gentle and unexploitive, see Zimmerman, *Safe Sea of Women*, 97. On the idea of lesbianism as an immature life-stage experiment, see Christina Simmons, "Companionate Marriage and the Lesbian Threat," in Kath-

ryn Kish Sklar and Thomas Dublin, eds., *Women and Power in American History: A Reader*, vol. 2 (Englewood Cliffs, N.J.: Prentice Hall, 1991), 183–94, 188.

41. Letter, April 11, 1975, 1, LHA, 81–04.

42. For Freudian thought on homosexuality as a life stage, see Freud, *Three Essays on the Theory of Sexuality*, 140.

43. Letter, November 1, 1975, 1, LHA, 81–04.

44. On the lack of affluence before the postwar period and the attitudes it engrained, see Dominick Cavallo, *A Fiction of the Past: The Sixties in American History* (New York: St. Martin's Press, 1999), 5.

45. Letter, November 12, 1975, 1, LHA, 81–04.

46. Letter, December 1, 1975, 1 (of 3), LHA, 81–04.

47. Letter, "Dear Mom & Dad," February 26, 1976, 1, LHA, 81–04.

48. On this, see Amy Gottlieb, "Mothers, Sisters, Lovers, Listen," in Maureen FitzGerald, Connie Guberman, and Margie Wolfe, eds., *Still Ain't Satisfied: Canadian Feminism Today* (Toronto: Women's Press, 1982), 234–43, here 235; and Barbara Grier and Coletta Ried, eds., *Lesbian Lives: Biographies of Women from* The Ladder (Baltimore: Diana Press, 1976), which portrays the lesbian lives of famous couples, novelists, artists, poets, and other prominent figures who were not widely known to be lesbian.

49. I am thinking not only of Rich's writing on the lesbian continuum here, which emphasizes the emotional experience of lesbianism first and foremost, but also of lesbian historiography such as, Smith-Rosenberg, "Female World of Love and Ritual."

50. Letter, "Dearest Mom," November 12, 1975, 3, LHA, 81–04.

51. On the blurring distinction between art and life in the art movements of the 1960s, and on conceptual art, see Hazel G. Warlaumont, *Advertising in the 60s: Turncoats, Traditionalists, and Waste Makers in America's Turbulent Decade* (Westport, Conn.: Praeger, 2001), 65; and Daniel Bell, *The Cultural Contradictions of Capitalism* (New York: Basic Books, 1976), 125.

52. Martha Nussbaum, *Upheavals of Thought: The Intelligence of Emotions* (Cambridge: Cambridge University Press, 2001), 25.

53. Letter from "Candy," October 8, 1973, 2, Julie Lee Papers.

54. Ibid., 4.

55. Ibid., 5.

56. Nancy Garden, *Annie on My Mind* (New York: Farrar, Straus and Giroux, 1982), 187.

57. Ibid., 188.

58. See *The Homosexuals*, 1967, produced for CBS News, narrated by Mike Wallace.

59. See the description of this article (published in January 26, 1971) in Clendinen and Nagourney, *Out for Good*, 70.

60. On the notion of recruitment, see Stacy Braukman, "'Nothing Else Matters

but Sex': Cold War Narratives of Deviance and the Search for Lesbian Teachers in Florida, 1959–1963," *Feminist Studies* 27 (Autumn 2001): 553–75, here 554.

61. Letter from "Jan," February 10, 1973, Julie Lee Papers.

62. Letter from "Jane," January 5, 1974, p. 3, Julie Lee Papers.

63. Judith Katz, "Born Queer," in Joan Larkin, ed., *A Woman Like That: Lesbian and Bisexual Writers Tell Their Coming-Out Stories*, 117–35, 129.

64. Ibid., 131.

65. On this, see Wolf, *Lesbian Community*, 85. On butch/femme articulations and rejections during this period, see Joan Nestle, "The Femme Question," in *The Persistent Desire: A Butch-Fem Reader* (Boston: Allyson, 1992), 64ff. It should be noted that at times this unisexual look seemed to overlap with a butch look, including shorter hair, jeans, work boots, plaid shirts.

66. For details on *Dyke*, see Streitmatter, *Unspeakable*, 162.

67. Penny House, "Letters from My Mother," *Dyke* (Spring 1976): 21–23, here 23. John Money had gained some notoriety throughout the later 1960s and 1970s for publishing accounts of his successful sex reassignment surgeries, most notoriously in the *Archives of Sexual Behavior*, in the "Joan/John case" of 1966, in which he felt he had successfully changed a young boy from Winnipeg, Manitoba, Bruce Reimer, into "Brenda." On this case, see John Colapinto, *As Nature Made Him: The Boy Who Was Raised as a Girl* (Toronto: HarperCollins, 2000).

68. Penny House, "Letters from My Mother," 23.

69. Diana Trilling's interview with a student at Harvard, in *We Must March, My Darlings*, 266. This interview was first published in 1971–72.

70. On this, see Susan Brownmiller, *Femininity* (New York: Simon and Schuster, 1984); and on 1970s lesbians more specifically, see Becki Ross, *The House That Jill Built: A Lesbian Nation in Formation* (Toronto: University of Toronto Press, 1995), 89. See also Wolf, *Lesbian Community* (Berkeley: University of California Press, 1979), 85. On the popularization of the notion of "the male gaze" during this period, and feminist art that rejected it, see Doss, *Twentieth Century American Art*, 184ff.

71. On feminist interpretations of biology during the 1970s, see Nelly Oudshoorn, "On Bodies, Technologies, and Feminisms," in Angela Creager, Elizabeth Lunbeck, and Londa Schiebinger, eds., *Feminism in Twentieth Century Science, Technology and Medicine* (Chicago: University of Chicago Press, 2001), 199–213.

72. See Thomas Edwards's discussion of Diana Trilling, a woman who exemplified this viewpoint, in *Over Here: Criticizing America, 1968–89* (New Brunswick, N.J.: Rutgers University Press, 1991), 92. And see Diana Trilling, "The Prisoner of Sex," in *We Must March, My Darlings*, 199–210. This essay was published in 1971. On the appearance revisions of women's liberation, see the entry on women's liberation in Buhle et al., *Encyclopedia of the American Left*, 836–838, here 838, for a description of the 1968 protest against Miss America in Atlantic City and the feminist "freedom trashcan."

73. On this generational perception, see Neil Jumonville, *Critical Crossings: The*

New York Intellectuals in Postwar America (Berkeley: University of California Press, 1991). See also Nina Roth, "The Neoconservative Backlash vs. Feminism in the 1970s and 1980s: The Case of *Commentary*," in David E. Nye and Carl Pedersen, eds., *Consumption and American Culture* (Amsterdam: VU University Press, 1991), 83–99. Finally, see George H. Nash, *The Conservative Intellectual Movement in America since 1945* (Wilmington, Del.: Intercollegiate Studies Institute, 1998).

74. Letter, December 1, 1975, 3, LHA, 81–04. This wariness of mass conformity within social movements was not the sole province of older, heterosexual women. Lesbians in this age group exhibited the same wariness: Zoe Masur, a lesbian intellectual who was middle-aged by the late 1960s, wrote in 1969 of the student movements that she felt that "their scorn for anyone or anything that doesn't agree with their lifestyle . . . is dangerous. . . . Being a strong individualist, I do not think even one person is expendable to a social movement." See Zoe Masur, diary entry, July 14, 1969, LHA, 84–28.

75. Letter, November 10, 1975, LHA, 81–04.

76. Letter, April 1975, 3, LHA, 81–04.

77. See Alice Munro's story "The Turkey Season," in *The Moons of Jupiter* (1982; repr., Markham, Ont.: Penguin, 1986) , 74. Here she says, "There are different ways women have of talking about their looks. Some women make it clear that what they do to keep themselves up is for the sake of sex, for men. Others . . . make the job out to be a kind of housekeeping, whose very difficulties they pride themselves on." On feminists accusing fellow women of vanity, see, for example, Nancy Friday, *My Mother/My Self* (New York: Delacorte Press, 1977), 19.

78. Letter, "Dear Mom and Dad," December 2, 1974, 2, LHA, 81–04,.

79. Letter, December 11, 1974, 2, LHA, 81–04.

80. On this, see again Patterson, *Grand Expectations*, 311.

81. On this, see Peter N. Carroll, *It Seemed Like Nothing Happened: The Tragedy and Promise of America in the 1970s* (New York: Holt, Rinehart, and Winston, 1982), 36 and 273.

82. Judith Ramsey, "My Daughter Is Different," *Family Circle* 10, no. 11 (1974): 14, 16, 82, 89, 90, here 82.

83. Ibid., 16.

84. For a discussion of working-class alienation from lesbian feminism, see Esther Newton's collection of essays and personal reflections, *Margaret Mead Made Me Gay: Personal Essays, Public Ideas* (Durham, N.C.: Duke University Press, 2000), 205ff. Newton, who considered herself a butch "bar dyke," felt that most middle-class put-downs of butches and femmes amounted to class stereotypes and prejudice. On this, see also Kate Brandt's interview with Dorothy Allison, "Telling Tales, Telling Truths," in *Happy Endings: Lesbian Writers Talk about Their Lives and Work* (Tallahassee, Fla..: Naiad, 1993), 9–18.

85. Ramsey, "My Daughter Is Different," 89.

86. On this, see Vivienne Louise, "Crossing That Bridge," in Julia Penelope and

Susan J. Wolfe, eds., *The Original Coming Out Stories* (Freedom, Calif.: Crossing Press, 1980), 250–67. Louise was an African American lesbian who moved from Washington, D.C., to Oakland, California, during the mid-1970s to participate in the lesbian movement there. She emphasized that the black lesbians she had known were more likely to wear a range in attire from pants and sweaters to dresses, high heels, and makeup; for them, "dress-up was the creed, with an accent on either 'standard prep' or 'in vogue,'" which was in sharp contrast to the white lesbians she had met, who were more likely to wear "jeans, flannel shirts, and soft-soled shoes." See 265.

87. From Donna Allegra, "Lavender Sheep in the Fold," in Lisa C. Moore, ed., *Does Your Mama Know? An Anthology of Black Lesbian Coming-Out Stories* (Decatur, Ga.: RedBone Press, 1997), 149–61, here 153.

88. Letter, December 17, 1975, 1, LHA, 81–04.

89. Letter with no date, "Dearest Daddy" (1975 or 1976), 2, LHA, 81–04.

90. Nonwhite lesbian feminists in particular often did not embrace separatism, recognizing a need at times to organize with men, as well as the importance of maintaining kinship ties in the face of racism. For a discussion of the relative scarcity of nonwhite lesbian feminists, see Faderman, *Odd Girls and Twilight Lovers*, 242ff., and also her "The Return of Butch and Fem: A Phenomenon of Lesbian Sexuality in the 1980s and 90s," *Journal of the History of Sexuality* 2 (April 1992): 578–96. Nonetheless, a periodical by and for lesbians of color was published in 1977. See Streitmatter, *Unspeakable*, 175, for details on *Azalea: A Magazine by Third World Lesbians*. In 1974, a group of black and Latina lesbian New Yorkers founded the Salsa Soul Sisters as an alternative to bars, which had historically been racist. Not only did this group problematize heterosexuality and homosexuality as orientations, as their white counterparts did, but they also focused on racism, employment, housing, and single lesbian parenting. See Molly McGarry and Fred Wasserman, *Becoming Visible: An Illustrated History of Lesbian and Gay Life in Twentieth-Century America* (New York: New York Public Library, Penguin Studio, 1998), 187.

91. On this matrophobia, see Adrienne Rich, *Of Woman Born* (New York: Norton, 1976), 235. On women's liberation critiques, see Caroline Lund, *The Family: Revolutionary or Oppressive Force?* (New York: Merit Pamphlet, 1971). For a poem that encapsulates this matrophobia, see Pauline B. Hart's acrostic, "Mother's Day Poem": "M is for her menopausal problems; O is for her masochistic needs; T is for her terror as she ages; H is for the help for which she pleads; E is for the emptiness her life is; R is for the roles that she has lost. Put them all together: they spell MOTHER. The ones the culture's double crossed." In Gloria Kaufman and Mary Kay Blakely, eds., *Pulling Our Own Strings: Feminist Humor and Satire* (Bloomington: Indiana University Press, 1980), 147. For a historiographical view, see Marianne Hirsch, *The Mother/Daughter Plot: Narrative, Psychoanalysis, Feminism* (Bloomington: Indiana University Press, 1989).

92. For a vivid description and recollection of "Womanhouse," see Norma

Broude and Mary D. Garrard, *The Power of Feminist Art: The American Movement of the 1970s, History and Impact* (New York: H. N. Abrams, 1994), 48–60.

93. J. David Hoeveler, *The Postmodernist Turn: American Thought and Culture in the 1970s* (Lanham, Md.: Rowman and Littlefield, 1996), 115.

94. Friedan, *Feminine Mystique*, 313.

95. Kay Silk, "Lesbian Novels in the Fifties," *Focus* (August 1973): 4.

96. It is important to mention here that the attention to domesticity during this period might have been informed by a broader 1960s and 1970s enthusiasm for "found" materials in art and the re-creation of domestic environments. On this, see Hugh Adams, *Art of the 60s* (New York: Phaidon Press, 1978), 21; and Edward Lucie-Smith, *Art in the 70s* (Oxford: Phaidon, 1980), 9.

97. On this idea, see again Weiss, *To Have and to Hold*. Weiss argues that historical work on these generations tends to overplay the sexual revolution of the young and underplay the innovations of the older generations who enjoyed a particularly high divorce rate in the 1970s and who often went back to work as older women, having married so young. See 169ff.

98. Joy Scorpio, "My Mother," *Coming Out Rage* (May 1973): 12.

99. Another poem in this vein appeared in Canadian lesbian poet Gwen Hauser's collection, *Mad about the Crazy Lady*, titled "Poem for My Mother" (Vancouver: Air Press, 1977), 48–49.

100. See, for example, "Rediscovering Anger," 21–22 in Boston Women's Health Collective, *Our Bodies, Ourselves*, in the chapter "Our Changing Sense of Self," 17–23.

101. "The Last Letter Home," *Spectre* 3 (July–August 1971): 4. For examples of a more general, disturbing anger voiced by lesbian feminists, see the Women's Gun Pamphlet trumpeted in a 1972 issue of *Lesbian Voices* 75, or the poem "I'm Tired of F——'ers F——'in Over Me" by Bev Grant in *Other Woman* 1 (May–June 1972). See also the article on the ravages of "The Heterosexual" in San Francisco's *Sisters* (July 1973): 3–4.

102. "Last Letter Home," 4.

103. Ibid., 5.

104. See *Lavender Woman* 3 (January 1974): 15.

105. Deborah Glick, "Blessed Be the Mothers of Lesbian Nation," *Gay Activist* (April 1973), n.p.

106. See *Lesbian Connection* 4 (October 1978): 6. This periodical is from East Lansing, Michigan, and was perhaps the lesbian periodical with the widest audience during the 1970s, with a bimonthly circulation of more than five thousand. On this, see Shapiro, *Write On, Woman*, 15.

107. Jo-Ellen Yale, "family dinner," *Focus* (June 1977): 1.

108. Susan MacDonald, "Coming Out: Sooner or Later," *Lesbian Feminist* (August 1976): 3.

109. Here I am thinking of Canadian women writers whose works had received some international recognition during these years, particularly Margaret Atwood, *The*

Edible Woman (Toronto: McClelland and Stewart, 1969); and Alice Munro's short story collections such as *Dance of the Happy Shades* (Toronto: McGraw-Hill Ryerson, 1968) and *Lives of Girls and Women* (Toronto: McGraw-Hill Ryerson, 1971). In the American context, I think of the poetry of Adrienne Rich, such as her 1967 collection *Snapshots of a Daughter in Law* (New York: W. W. Norton, 1967), and that of Anne Sexton, such as "Housewife" in the *Complete Poems* (Boston: Houghton Mifflin, 1981), 77. All of these portray a subtly different consciousness from men based on an introspective domestic culture, including its physical objects, its sense of time, its occasional stultification, and its possibilities.

110. Adrienne Rich, " 'When We Dead Awaken': Writing as Re-Vision," in *Arts of the Possible: Essays and Conversations* (New York: W. W. Norton, 2001), 10–30, here 23. Literary theorist Patricia Meyer Spacks has suggested in her work on autobiographies that autobiographies affirm identity. See *Imagining Self: Autobiographies and Novels in Nineteenth Century England* (Cambridge, Mass.: Harvard University Press, 1976).

111. See Sharon Malinowski and Christa Belin, eds., *The Gay and Lesbian Literary Companion* (Detroit: Visible Ink Press, 1995), 351. Also, on the public media portrayals of Millett as crazy and unattractive, see Douglas, *Where the Girls Are*, 109.

112. Letter from mother, April 11, 1975, 1, LHA, 81–04.

113. "K. Millett: Flying," document with no date, LHA, 81–04.

114. Letter, February 29, 1976, Letters to *Ms.* magazine, MC 331, box 3, Schlesinger Library, Radcliffe Institute for Advanced Study, Harvard University.

115. Letter, February 21, 1976, 1 and 2, Letters to *Ms.* magazine, MC 331, box 3, Schlesinger Library, Radcliffe Institute for Advanced Study, Harvard University.

116. On lesbian documents becoming cultural artifacts, see Nestle, "Will to Remember," 90.

117. Letter from mother, April 11, 1975, 1, LHA, 81–04.

118. This poem was included in the collection at LHA, 81–04.

119. Letter from mother, April 1975 (no exact date), 1, LHA, 81–04.

120. Ibid., 2.

121. Ibid., 3.

122. Ibid., 2.

123. See, for example, the poem "I am all things female: they call me / Mother / I am she who brings life," in *Dykes and Gorgons* 1, no. 1 (1973): 24–25. See also Florence Rush, "The Parable of Mothers and Daughters," in Phyllis Birkby, Esther Newton, Bertha Harris, Jill Johnston, and Jane O'Wyatt, eds. *A Lesbian Feminist Anthology: Amazon Expedition* (Albion, Calif.: Times Change Press, 1973), 4–11. This story conveys the sense of the womanly bond between mothers and daughters that preexisted and was destroyed by patriarchy.

124. See Nancy Chodorow, *The Reproduction of Mothering: Psychoanalysis and the Sociology of Gender* (Berkeley: University of California Press, 1978), 95. See also Marcia

Westkott, "Mothers and Daughters in the World of the Father," *Frontiers* 3, no. 2 (1978): 16–21. Finally, see Sherry Zitter, "Coming Out to Mom: Theoretical Aspects of the Mother Daughter Process," in Boston Lesbian Psychologies Collective, *Lesbian Psychologies: Explorations and* Challenges (Urbana-Champaign: University of Illinois Press, 1987), 177–94, here 178.

125. Chodorow, *Reproduction of Mothering,* 200.

126. Letter to mother, "Dearest Mom," March 17 1975, 1, LHA, 81–04. This style of communication again seemed to mirror Lasch's observation of "conversations as confession." See Lasch, *Culture of Narcissism,* 27. And on family relationships modeled after therapy, see Robert Bellah, *Habits of the Heart: Individualism and Commitment in American Life* (Berkeley: University of California Press, 1985), 121.

127. See *Gay Community News* 2 (October 12, 1974): 7. The strip is called "After Mell" by "Mike R." A national gay paper, the *Gay Community News* started in 1973 and ended in 1990.

128. Letter from mother, December 1, 1975, 2, LHA, 81–04.

129. Letter from mother, August 1, 1976, 1, LHA, 81–04.

130. Letter to mother, "Dearest Mom," March 27, 1975, 1, LHA, 81–04.

131. Mrs. O'Keefe, "Mrs. O'Keefe," in Ruth Baetz, ed., *Lesbian Crossroads: Personal Stories of Lesbian Struggles and Triumphs* (New York: William Morrow and Company, 1980), 135–39, here 135.

132. Ibid., 136.

133. On this theme of envy between mothers and daughters—that could verge into jealousy for their daughters' displacing them with female partners as the primary women in their daughters' lives, see Zitter, "Coming Out to Mom," 177–94.

134. Susan MacDonald, "On the Homefront," *Lesbian Feminist* (September–October 1976): 12.

135. Ramsey, "My Daughter Is Different," 16 and 82.

136. Ibid., 14.

137. Ibid., 16.

138. Ibid., 90.

Chapter 4

1. Julie Lee, letter to "Jane," Julie Lee Papers, January 15, 1974, 1.

2. Announcement, Parents of Gays, April 3, 1973, IGIC Ephemera, Organizations, Parents and Friends of Lesbians and Gays, MSS. and Archives Section, New York Public Library.

3. For the sake of clarity, I will be calling these parents primarily "organized parents of gays" or "activist parents" or "sympathetic parents." As the movement gathered steam between the late 1970s and early 1980s, I sometimes refer to them as "early PFLAG parents."

4. Some psychiatrists continued to oppose homosexuality as a healthy identity. In spite of the removal of homosexuality from the *DSM-IV* list of mental disorders in 1973, and a range of sympathetic psychology published in the early and mid 1970s, such as Weinberg, *Society and the Healthy Homosexual*, there remained many ambivalent treatments of homosexuality. See, for example, Martin Hoffman, *The Gay World* (1969; repr., New York: Bantam, 1973), which backed up Irving Bieber's observations about the families of homosexuals. Less ambivalently, the American Psychological Association had been deeply divided by the decision to remove homosexuality from the *DSM*. Psychologists such as Paul Cameron used his research as a way to campaign against gay civil rights. Now chair of the Family Research Institute, he and others like him still practice conversion therapy enthusiastically.

5. For an interesting discussion on this theme, see Susan Neiman, *Moral Clarity: A Guide for Grown-Up Idealists* (Orlando, Fla.: Houghton Mifflin Harcourt, 2008), 17.

6. On the structurelessness of the GLF versus the structure of the GAA, see Marotta's chapter on the GAA in *Politics of Homosexuality*, 145ff. See also his descriptions of GAA zaps, 178ff. And see Clendinen and Nagourney, *Out for Good*, 189ff.

7. Jim Gallagher, "How She Accepted Her Homosexual Son," *San Francisco Examiner*, July 10, 1973. Leonore Acanfora in fact became an early mother activist who defended her gay son's right to teach in Pennsylvania during the early 1970s.

8. Wicker, "Conversation with Sarah Montgomery," 6.

9. Kahney, "Sarah Montgomery," 7.

10. Maureen Oddone, "Moving Out of Another Closet," *Advocate* 241 (May 17, 1978): 18–19, here 19.

11. "Parents of Gay People of the Greater Bay Area," 1978, Jeanne Manford Papers, box 1, file 6, Correspondence 1978, IGIC, Manuscripts and Archives Division, the New York Public Library, Astor, Lenox and Tilden Foundations.

12. Troy Perry, *The Lord Is My Shepherd and He Knows I'm Gay: The Autobiography of the Rev. Troy D. Perry* (Los Angeles: Nash, 1972), foreword by Mrs. Edith Allen Perry, 2.

13. Jean Smith, "What Parents of Gay Children Fear Most Is Their Children," *Insight: A Quarterly of Gay Catholic Opinion* (Winter 1977): 15.

14. Betty Fairchild, *Parents of Gays* (Washington, D.C.: Parents of Gays, 1975), 2.

15. Ibid., 6.

16. Ibid., 2, of "The 'No-Magic-Answer' List."

17. Wicker, "Conversation with Sara Montgomery," 6. Montgomery even took part in the National Gay Task Force's (NGTF) campaigns to encourage gays to support their own people. In an advertisement appearing in the NGTF journal, *It's Time*, throughout the mid and later 1970s, titled "To All Closet Gays," she urged gays to give money to their cause. "I certainly do not wish to intrude on anyone's life," she said, "but I see a great need . . . and [appeal] to all gays who are well off to help your

beautiful and valiant young gays to carry on their fight against ignorance and bigotry." See *It's Time* 1 (June–July 1975): 2.

18. "Parents of Gays and Lesbians Speak Out," 1977, PFLAG Collection, 7616, Division of Rare and Manuscripts Collection, Cornell University Library, Ithaca, N.Y.

19. On this, see D'Emilio and Freedman, *Intimate Matters*, 323–24. See also "How Gay Is Gay?" *Time Magazine*, April 23, 1979, 72–77.

20. Letter, "Dear President Ford," August 18, 1974, 1, Jeanne Manford Papers, box 1, file 1.

21. Ibid., 2.

22. On Queens as the "Middle America" of New York, see John Paul Hudson, "My Son Is Gay," *Advocate* 112 (May 23, 1973): 2.

23. See Judy Klemesrud, "For Homosexuals, It's Getting Less Difficult to Tell Parents," *New York Times*, September 1, 1972, 32. See Douglas Sarff, "'Parents of Gays' Help Others Understand," *Newswest*, August 7, 1975, n.p.

24. This 1973 letter to "Mrs. Jones" has been reproduced in several places; see, for example, *Homosexual Counseling Journal* 2 (January 1975): 26–33, here 28. For originals, see February 14, 1973, Jeanne Manford Papers, box 1, file 1, Correspondence, 1972–74.

25. "Dear Mr. Kilpatrick," June 6, 1977, 1, Jeanne Manford Papers, box 1, file 4, Correspondence 1977.

26. See Rebecca Klatch, "The Two Worlds of Women of the New Right," in Louise A. Tilly and Patricia Gurin, eds., *Women, Politics, and Change* (New York: Russell Sage Foundation, 1990), 529–52, here 529–30. See also Alan Crawford, *Thunder on the Right: The New Right and the Politics of Resentment* (New York: Pantheon, 1980), 166. See also Hoeveler, *Postmodernist Turn*, 141.

27. See both Bruce Schulman, *The Seventies: The Great Shift in American Culture, Society, and Politics* (New York: Free Press, 2001); and Dan Carter, *The Politics of Rage: George Wallace, The Origins of the New Conservatism, and the Transformation of American Politics* (New York: Simon and Schuster, 1995). And see David Steigerwald, *Sixties and the End of Modern America*, 243.

28. See Susan Sontag, *AIDS and Its Metaphors* (New York: Farrar, Straus and Giroux, 1988), 63.

29. On this, see Tom Kemp, *The Climax of Capitalism: The U.S. Economy in the Twentieth Century* (London: Longman, 1990); and Leonard Silk, ed., *The U.S. and the World Economy: The Postwar Years* (New York: Arno Press, 1976). On Canada's economy during these years, see Kenneth Norrie and Doug Owram, *A History of the Canadian Economy* (Toronto: Harcourt and Brace, 1991).

30. Nancy Walker has an intriguing argument about 1950s nostalgia in *Shaping Our Mothers' World*. She argues that the 1950s nostalgia was in fact a product of the 1950s, not the 1970s, during a time when many families realized a disparity between what their socioeconomic reality was and desires that the pop culture promoted. See 18. For more interpretations of 1950s nostalgia, see Stephanie Koontz, *The Way We*

Never Were: American Families and the Nostalgia Trap (New York: Basic Books, 1992). On 1950s nostalgia in popular culture, see Elsebeth Harup, "Bridge over Troubled Water: Nostalgia for the 50s in Movies of the Seventies and Eighties," in Dale Carter, ed., *Cracking the Ike Age: Aspects of 50s America*, 56–76.

31. On laissez-faire conservatives versus social conservatives, see Klatch, "Two Worlds of Women of the New Right," 540, and her book, *Women of the New Right* (Philadelphia: Temple University Press, 1987).

32. Lauren Berlant, *The Queen of America Goes to Washington City: Essays on Sex and Citizenship* (Durham, N.C.: Duke University Press, 1997), 3. On the establishment of no-fault divorces and the legalization of abortion and their impacts, see Steven Mintz, "Regulating the American Family," in Joseph M. Hawes and Elizabeth I. Nybakken, eds., *Family and Society in American History* (Urbana: University of Illinois Press, 2001), 9–31; and Carolyn Johnston, *Sexual Power: Feminism and the Family in America* (Tuscaloosa: University of Alabama Press, 2002), 273–76. Between 1960 and 1980, the divorce rate was up by more than 200 percent, there was a rising incidence of premarital sex, a rise of cohabitation between men and women, and a more widespread embrace of birth control. D'Emilio and Freedman, *Intimate Matters*, 334–35E. See also Carroll, *It Seemed Like Nothing Happened*, 268–69. While no-fault divorce had swept Canada and the United States in the early 1970s, abortions were hotly contested in both countries, despite legal changes in Canada, in 1969, when contraception was legalized, allowing abortions under some restricted conditions, and despite *Roe v. Wade* in 1973 in the United States.

33. On American Protestant conservatism, see Sharon Linzey Georgianna, *The Moral Majority and Fundamentalism: Plausibility and Dissonance* (Queenston, Ont.: Edwin Mellen Press, 1989), 35–36. On the New Right's emphasis on issues related to sexuality and the family, see Barbara Ehrenreich, "Family Feud on the Left," *Nation*, March 13, 1982, cover and 303–6. See also Kenneth Heineman, *God Is a Conservative: Religion, Politics, and Morality in Contemporary America* (New York: New York University Press, 1998), 7–8.

34. See Klatch, "Two Worlds of Women of the New Right," 534, and *Women of the New Right*, 47.

35. On the bread dough that Phyllis Schlafly made, see Kathleen C. Berkeley, *The Women's Liberation in America* (Westport, Conn.: Greenwood Press, 1999), 85.

36. See Johnston, *Sexual Power*, 277. See also Schulman, *Seventies*, 170 and 187. On issues of family values and their relatively minor presence within Canadian political rhetoric, see, for example, Paul Mazar, "Gay and Lesbian Rights in Canada: A Comparative Study," *International Journal of Public Administration* 25, no. 1 (2002): 45–63. On the Canadian antigay and "pro-family" movement of the 1980s, please see "It's All in the Family," *Body Politic*, no. 133 (December 1986): 11. On Canadian REAL (Realistic, Equal, Active for Life) Women (formed in 1983), which, like their American New Right counterparts, had a Christian base and opposed the social changes of the 1970s that had some bearing on family life such as abortion, no-fault

divorce, publicly funded day care, and legal rights to gays, see Prentice et al., *Canadian Women*, 452.

37. "Anita Bryant's Letter to Her Supporters," "Newsletters from Outside NYC," Jeanne Manford Papers, IGIC, box 2, file 4.

38. Schulman, *Seventies*, 232; see also B. Drummond Ayres Jr., "Miami Debate over Rights of Homosexuals Directs Wide Attention to a National Issue," *New York Times*, May 10, 1977, 18. And see Clendinen and Nagourney, *Out for Good*, 299ff.

39. See Carroll, *It Seemed Like Nothing Happened*, 291.

40. See "Anita Bryant Defeats Miami Gay Rights Ordinance," 1978, in Walter Williams and Yolanda Retter, eds., *Gay and Lesbian Rights in the U.S.: A Documentary History* (Westport, Conn.: Greenwood Press, 2003), 143. This was taken from an interview Anita Bryant had done with *Playboy* in 1978.

41. This image was in Bill Doubleday and J. E. Myers, "First 'Week of Dialogue' Set for October 22–28," *It's Time: Newsletter of the National Gay Task Force* 5 (October 1978): 1–3.

42. On the Briggs Initiative, see D'Emilio, "Gay Politics and Community in San Francisco since World War II," 468–69. And see Clendinen and Nagourney, *Out for Good*, 376ff.

43. For a portrait of Dan White's defense, see Emily Mann, "Execution of Justice," in Don Shewey, ed., *Out Front: Contemporary Gay and Lesbian Plays* (New York: Grove Press, 1988), 149–220, here 162. And see D'Emilio, "Gay Politics and Community in San Francisco since World War II," 470–71.

44. See David Rothenberg, "Another Voice," *Gaysweek* 83 (September 25, 1978): 19.

45. For a discussion on waning gay radicalism in favor of reformist strategies, see Miller, *Out of the Past*, 422ff., as well as McGarry and Wasserman, *Becoming Visible*, 167ff. See also Daniel Harris's lament of increasing commercialization in the gay world, an inadvertent consequence he perceived of gay liberation, in his *The Rise and Fall of Gay Culture* (New York: Ballantine Books, 1997). The dispersal of the gay liberation movement mirrored the dispersal of the New Left into academics, labor organizations, and so on. On this, see Steigerwald, *Sixties and the End of Modern America*, 147.

46. See the interview with Morty Manford in Eric Marcus, *Making History: The Struggle for Gay and Lesbian Equal Rights: 1945–1990: An Oral History* (New York: HarperCollins, 1992), 211, and see also 257 for a discussion of the dispersal of gay liberation's youth contingent.

47. For details on the shift from the GAA to the NGTF in 1973, see again Marotta, *Politics of Homosexuality*, 320ff. The NGTF was joined by other groups such as the National Coalition for Black Lesbians and Gays (1978), and the Human Rights Campaign Fund (1980). See Marcus, *Making Gay History*, 172.

48. For a discussion of the "We ARE Your Children!" campaign, see the organization's press release of June 13, 1977. For some gay responses, see David Rothenberg,

"Family Defense: The Contradictions," *Long Island Connection,* April 25–May 9, 1984, sec. 1, 37.

49. See *It's Time: Newsletter of the National Gay Task Force* 5 (October 1978): 1–3.

50. Betty Fairchild, "For Parents of Gays: A Fresh Perspective," in Betty Berzon and Robert Leighton, eds., *Positively Gay* (Millbrae, Calif.: Celestial Arts, 1979), 101–12, here 103–4.

51. Terry, *American Obsession,* 373.

52. "Accepting Your Gay or Lesbian Child: Parents Share Their Stories" (Boulder, Colo.: Sounds Time Recordings, 1990), audiotape, 90-A122, PFLAG Collection, Cornell University Library.

53. Essay, "Parents of Lesbians of Gay Men Protest the Persecution," 1 (of 4), IGIC Ephemera, PFLAG.

54. On sexologists' interpretations of homosexuality as inherent, see Regina Kunzel, *Criminal Intimacy: Prison and the Uneven History of Modern American Sexuality* (Chicago: University of Chicago Press, 2008), 50.

55. Ann Landers, "Parents Shouldn't Reject Homosexual Son," *Pensacola News Journal,* September 8, 1977; and Jean Smith, "Dear Ann Landers," September 8, 1977, Jeanne Manford Papers, box 1, file 4, "Correspondence: 1977."

56. Abigail Van Buren, "Don't Blame Yourself," *Choice* (August 14, 1981): 59.

57. This cultural practice of trying to evoke a reader's empathy through something horrific was also a technique of sentimental fiction in nineteenth-century America. See Shirley Samuels's discussion of *Uncle Tom's Cabin* in *The Culture of Sentiment: Race, Gender and Sentimentality* (New York: Oxford University Press, 1992), 4.

58. On the murder of Robert Hillsborough, see Clendinen and Nagourney, *Out for Good,* 319.

59. On the low sales of her book, see Streitmatter, *Unspeakable,* 219. And on Johnny Carson's making jokes at Bryant's expense, see Clendinen and Nagourney, *Out for Good,* 329.

60. Jean Smith, "Parents of Gays vs. Anita," June 1, 1977, Jeanne Manford Papers, box 1, file 4, "Correspondence: 1977."

61. On the Children's Aid Society as a kind of child-saving society, see Paula Fass, *Kidnapped: Child Abduction in America* (New York: Oxford University Press, 1997), 43.

62. Jean Smith, "The Key to the Closet: Dedicated to the Gay Community of Pensacola—For Helping Me to Understand," May 26, 1978, Third Annual Florida Gay Conference, Tallahassee, Fla., Jeanne Manford Papers, box 2, folder 5, "Non PFLAG Newsletters."

63. Larry Gross has argued that television representations of queer people as victims are often the precursor to seeing them as human. See his commentary in *Further off the Straight and Narrow: New Gay Visibility on Television, 1998–2006,* dir. Katherine Sender (Northampton, Mass.: Media Education Foundation, 2006).

64. Essay, "Parents of Lesbians of Gay Men Protest the Persecution," 2, IGIC Ephemera, PFLAG.

65. "Dear Mr. Tanno," September 12, 1977, 2 (of 2), Jeanne Manford Papers, box 1, file 4, "Correspondence 1977."

66. For PFLAG's shared mandate with groups such as Alcoholics Anonymous and Overeaters Anonymous, see Public Affairs Pamphlet no. 559, by Elizabeth Ogg, "Partners in Coping: Groups for Self and Mutual Help" (New York: Public Affairs Committee, 1978); and Dali Castro, "We Love Our Gay Children Too," *Parents of Gays National Newsletter* 1 (April 1980): S4. On the rise of Alcoholics Anonymous and other support groups dating from the 1930s, see Robert M. Collins, *Transforming America: Politics and Culture in the Reagan Years* (New York: Columbia University Press, 2007), 156.

67. Sandra Rivard, "Listen World! My Son Is Gay. Accept Him—Please," *Living*, February 26, 1976, D.

68. See Jo Brans, *Mother, I Have Something to Tell You* (New York: Doubleday, 1987).

69. Ellie Grossman, "Groups That Want to Help," 1979, Jeanne Manford Papers, box 1, file 13, Clippings.

70. In her study of the history of adoption, Ellen Herman has shown that kinship by design contrasted starkly to and was in tension with the elements of chance and mystery that were seen to characterize biological families. See Herman, *Kinship by Design*, 14.

71. "If Man Were Meant to Fly . . .," 1–10, here 1 (Anderson, S.C.: Orthodox-Catholic Church, n.d.), Jeanne Manford Papers, box 2, file 12, Publications.

72. Ibid., 3.

73. On the dangers of new reproductive technologies and sex changes, see, for example, Robert and Anna Francoeur, *The Future of Sexual Relations* (Englewood Cliffs, N.J.: Prentice Hall, 1974).

74. Kahney, "Sarah Montgomery," 7.

75. Ibid., 7.

76. Ibid., 9.

77. Mary C. Milam, "My Son Is Gay," 1973, 1, Jeanne Manford Papers, box 1, file 1, "Correspondence: 1972–74."

78. Letter to "Jules Manford," September 5, 1977, 2, Jeanne Manford Papers, box 1, file 4, "Correspondence: 1977."

79. Mary Borhek, *Coming Out to Parents: A Two Way Survival Guide for Lesbians and Gay Men and Their Parents* (Cleveland: Pilgrim Press, 1983), 17.

80. On parents' talking to their children about sex during the postwar period, see, for example, Sol Gordon and Irving R. Dickman, *Sex Education: The Parents' Role*, Public Affairs Pamphlet no. 549 (New York, 1977), 18–19; as well as other more popular works such as Arkady Leokum, *Tell Me Why: Answers to Questions Children Ask about Love, Sex, and Babies* (New York: Grosset and Dunlap, 1974), which included a

section of questions on homosexuality such as, "How do homosexuals have sex?" and "What makes a person a homosexual?"

81. In fact, a survey of high school youth in the early 1980s found that almost half had learned nothing about sex—presumably heterosexual sex—from their parents. D'Emilio and Freedman, *Intimate Matters*, 341.

82. The Gay and Lesbian Alliance against Defamation had formed by 1985, primarily spurred on by sensationalized AIDS coverage during the early 1980s but also as an agency that would monitor media and pop culture portrayals of gays in song lyrics and mainstream movies, for example. It was presaged by a huge gay outcry against the movie *Cruising*.

83. On the CBS News report, see Clendinen and Nagourney, *Out for Good*, 449.

84. Borhek, *Coming Out to Parents*, 117.

85. Gloria Guss Back, *Are You Still My Mother? Are You Still My Family?* (New York: Warner Books, 1985), 230.

86. Fairchild, "For Parents of Gays," 106.

87. Borhek, *Coming Out to Parents*, 73.

88. See, for example, Parents and Friends of Gays, "About Our Children" (Los Angeles, 1978), 5; see also Helaine Lovett Michaels, "When Your Child Is Gay—The Shock and the Acceptance," *Single Parent* (November 1981): 20–23, here 23; see also "Did You 'Myth' This One?" Jeanne Manford Papers, box 2, file 3, "Newsletters: NYC PFLAG."

89. The organization took a particularly firm stance against the North American Man Boy Love Association (NAMBLA). One PFLAG group even withdrew from the Community Council of Long Island over NAMBLA's admission to their scene. On this, see *Long Island Connection*, August 17–31, 1983, sec. 1, 15. By 1993, PFLAG had issued a press statement denouncing NAMBLA outright. See "Press Statement: PFLAG Denounces NAMBLA and Sexual Exploitation of Children," PFLAG Collection, box 43, Cornell University Library.

90. Parents and Friends of Gays, "About Our Children," 4.

91. Borhek, *Coming Out to Parents*, 70.

92. William Simon and John H. Gagnon, "Femininity in the Lesbian Community," *Social Problems* 15 (Autumn 1967): 212–21, here 213.

93. Marlene Fanta Shyer and Christopher Shyer, *Not Like Other Boys: Growing Up Gay; A Mother and Son Look Back* (Boston: Houghton Mifflin, 1996), 20.

94. Ibid., 57.

95. Mary Borhek, *My Son Eric* (New York City: Pilgrim Press, 1979), 76.

96. Back, *Are You Still My Mother?* 95.

97. "Can We Understand?" (New York City Parents of Lesbians and Gay Men, 1983), 6, PFLAG Collection, Cornell University Library, Ithaca, N.Y.

98. On this idea, see Fass and Mason, *Childhood in America*, 7.

99. I am thinking here of memoirs of mental illness such as Joanne Greenberg, *I Never Promised You a Rose Garden* (1964; repr., New York: New American Library,

1976); memoirs of incest such as Charlotte Vale Allen, *Daddy's Girl* (Toronto: McClelland and Stewart, 1980); or Katherine Brady, *Father's Days: A True Story of Incest* (New York: Seaview, 1979); and a large outpouring of feminist studies of wife abuse such as Del Martin, *Battered Wives* (San Francisco: Glide, 1976); and the documentaries *Loved, Honoured, and Bruised* (Montreal: National Film Board of Canada, 1982) and *Wife Beating* (New York: National Broadcasting, 1977). In the visual media, Phil Donahue's groundbreaking exposé talk show opened up the forum to previously undiscussed issues, with topics such as "Women Who Love Porn" in 1975. In the 1980s, he did a number of shows on gays including "From Gay to Straight: Conversion Therapy," "Gay Characters on TV" (1984), and "Lesbian Nuns" (1985).

100. On self-help movements and their origins, see Alan Gartner and Frank Riessman, *The Self-Help Revolution* (New York: Human Sciences, 1974). See also Ogg, "Partners in Coping," which discussed the Alcoholics Anonymous movement (which actually had its origins in the 1930s but became more mainstream in the 1970s, with spin-off organizations for the families of alcoholics), the group SHARE (Self-Help Action and Rap Experience), Parents without Partners (PWP) founded in 1957, and other parental support groups for parents who had children with learning disabilities, physical handicaps, and emotional problems.

101. On this, see Gerard Vincent, "A History of Secrets?" in Antoine Prost and Gerard Vincent, eds., *A History of Private Life*, vol. 5, 145–231, here 167.

102. "How to Come Out to Family and Friends," Parents and Friends of Gays Information, Los Angeles, n.d., Jeanne Manford Papers, box 1, file 10.

103. Borhek, *My Son Eric*, 30.

104. "Dear Sir," February 5, 1973, 1, Jeanne Manford Papers, box 1, file 9, "Correspondence: 1970s."

105. For these song lyrics, see *PFG San Francisco Newsletter*, November 1984, 3. To listen to this song, see the PFLAG audiotape, "Accepting *Your* Gay or Lesbian Child."

106. "Dear Member of the Clergy," January 25, 1985, IGIC Ephemera, PFLAG, Federation of Parents and Friends of Lesbians and Gays.

107. "If Man Were Meant to Fly . . .," 1–10, here 5 (Anderson, S.C.: Orthodox-Catholic Church, n.d.), Jeanne Manford Papers, box 2, file 12, Publications.

108. Ibid., 6.

109. See Betty Fairchild and Nancy Hayward, *Now That You Know* (1979; repr., San Diego: Harcourt Brace, 1998), 4.

110. On women's sentimental culture, see Lori Merish, *Sentimental Materialism: Gender, Commodity, and Culture in Nineteenth-Century American Literature* (Durham, N.C.: Duke University Press, 2000), 79; and see Andrew Burstein, *Sentimental Democracy: The Evolution of America's Romantic Self-Image* (New York: Hill and Wang, 1999). See Donald K. Freedheim's discussion of the American self in the nineteenth century in his introduction to Freedheim et al., *History of Psychotherapy*, 33.

111. I am getting this bit of history from Borhek's biographical statement on www.lgbtran.org, in the Religious Archives Network.

112. This inset is from the edition of *My Son Eric* published in 1979 by Pilgrim Press.

113. Borhek, *Coming Out to Parents*, 13.

114. "Can We Understand?" 6.

115. Charles Faber, "Parents and Friends and an Organization to Support Them," *Advocate* 359 (January 6, 1983): 22.

116. This is in the newsletters from the NYC Parents of Lesbians and Gay Men, "Mary Calderone Salutes Parents of Gays on Their Ninth Anniversary," January 31, 1982, Lenox Hill Station, New York.

117. David and Shirley Switzer, *Parents of the Homosexual* (Philadelphia: Westminster Press, Christian Care Books, Help for Living Today, 1980), 25.

118. See T. H. Sauerman, "Read This before Coming Out to Parents" (PFLAG, 1984), 6. These are the very phases Kübler-Ross noted in her dying parents; see Elisabeth Kübler-Ross, *On Death and Dying: What the Dying Have to Teach Doctors, Nurses, Clergy, and Families* (New York: Touchstone, 1969).

119. Marilyn Elias, "Gay Children, Sad Parents, and Help for Them Both," *USA Today*, January 31, 1983, D8.

120. For particular 1980s concerns about family life, including the increasing trend of mothers working, see Koontz, *Way We Never Were*, 149. See also Elaine Tyler May, "Myths and Realities of the American Family," in Prost and Vincent, eds., *History of Private Life*, vol. 5, 539–95, here 589. On working mothers and social change at the popular level, see B. Hazen and Deborah Calvin Borgo, *Why Can't You Stay Home with Me?* (New York: Golden Books, 1986); and Jeanne Deschamps Stanton, *Being All Things: How to Be a Wife, Lover, Boss, and Mother (and Still Be Yourself)* (New York: Doubleday, 1988).

121. See again Fass, *Kidnapped*, 8 and 245.

122. *With Arms That Encircle*, PFLAG, Wichita, Kansas, 1993.

123. On self-help's function for this sense of nurturance, see Eva S. Moskowitz, *In Therapy We Trust: America's Obsession with Self-Fulfillment* (Baltimore: Johns Hopkins University Press, 2001). See especially her chapter "Feelings: Expressing the Self, 1970–1980," 218–44.

124. See D'Emilio and Freedman, *Intimate Matters*, 323.

125. See Freedheim, *History of Psychotherapy*, 32. This thought was backed up by Philip Rieff in his work, *The Triumph of the Therapeutic: Uses of Faith after Freud* (1966; repr., New York: Penguin, 1973), and of course Lasch, *Culture of Narcissism*.

126. See Irene Taviss Thomson, *In Conflict No Longer: Self and Society in Contemporary America* (Oxford: Rowman and Littlefield, 2000), 70. She cites such works as Robert J. Ringer, *Looking Out for Number One* (1977), and Mildred Newman and Bernard Berkowitz, *How to Be Your Own Best Friend* (1971). Family intimacy also was a popular theme of the commercial press. I am thinking particularly here of the failure

of intimacy with men, in books such as Steven Naifeh and Gregory White Smith, *Why Can't Men Open Up? Overcoming Men's Fear of Intimacy* (New York: Clarkson Potter, 1984).

Chapter 5

1. See, for example, the picture graphics in Douglas Crimp, ed., *AIDS: Cultural Analysis, Cultural Activism* (Cambridge, Mass.: MIT Press, 1988). Another ACT-UP Ronald Reagan poster congratulated him on the "undeclared war" in the country where the enemy was identified by "the color of their skins[,] the size of their bank accounts[, and] the objects of their love." "Congratulations, Ronald W. Reagan," Robert Garcia Papers, #7574, box 3, file 14.

2. See, for example, *Gay Comix* 6 (Winter 1985): back cover. This chapter will deal exclusively with gay men who contracted AIDS, rather than lesbians, because the lesbians who became sick with AIDS often got it through means other than same-sex activity.

3. Miller, *Out of the Past*, 439.

4. James Curran, "The CDC and the Investigation of the Epidemiology of AIDS," in Victoria A. Harden and John Parascandola, eds., *AIDS: The Public Debate* (Amsterdam: IOS Press, 1995), 19–29, here 23. See also James Kinsella, *Covering the Plague: AIDS and the American Media* (New Brunswick, N.J.: Rutgers University Press, 1989), 19. See also Anthony S. Fauci, "AIDS: Reflections on the Past, Considerations for the Future," in Victoria A. Harden and John Parascandola, eds., *AIDS and the Public Debate*, 67–73; and Steven Epstein, *Impure Science: AIDS, Activism and the Politics of Knowledge* (Berkeley: University of California Press, 1996), 46–48. Epidemiologists paid particular attention to those gay men with multiple partners. See Steven Epstein, *Impure Science*, 49; and Paula A. Treichler, "AIDS, Homophobia, and Biomedical Discourse: An Epidemic of Signification," in Douglas Crimp, ed., *AIDS: Cultural Analysis, Cultural Activism*, 48. See also Ronald Bayer and Gerald Oppenheimer, *AIDS Doctors: Voices from the Epidemic* (New York: Oxford University Press, 2000), 56.

5. See Dennis Altman, *AIDS in the Mind of America* (Garden City, N.Y.: Doubleday, 1986), 17. *Discover* magazine pronounced AIDS the "fatal price" one could pay for anal sex. On this article, by John Langone, "AIDS: The Latest Scientific Facts," *Discover*, December 1985, 40–41, see Allan M. Brandt, "AIDS: From Social History to Social Policy," in Elizabeth Fee and Daniel Fox, eds., *AIDS: The Burdens of History* (Berkeley: University of California Press, 1988), 147–71.

6. These statistics are from Sean Wilentz, *The Age of Reagan: A History, 1974–2008* (New York: HarperCollins, 2008), 186.

7. The case load statistics are from D'Emilio and Freedman, *Intimate Matters*, 354. The 1990 statistic is from Marcus, *Making History*, 405. For Canadian statistics, see David Spurgeon, *Understanding AIDS: A Canadian Strategy* (Toronto: Key Porter, 1988). By 1988, there were 1,765 cases in Canada.

8. Bayer and Oppenheimer, *AIDS Doctors*, 171.

9. Jacques Bourque, "AIDS: Where's It Left Us?" *Angles* (Vancouver), May 1986, 11.

10. See James Davison Hunter, *Before the Shooting Begins: Searching for Democracy in America's Culture War* (New York: Free Press, 1994), 3; and Collins, *Transforming America*, 171.

11. C. Everett Koop, "The Early Days of AIDS as I Remember Them," in Victoria A. Harden and John Parascandola, eds., *AIDS and the Public Debate*, 9–19, here 18.

12. See Jean Seligmann and Nikki Finke Greenburg, "Only Months to Live and No Place to Die: The Tragic Odyssey of a Victim Turned Pariah," *Newsweek*, August 12, 1985, 26, part of the larger article by Matt Clark and Mariana Gosnell et al., "AIDS," in this issue, 20–27. This story tells of thirty-two-year-old Robert Doyle, a former construction worker, whose parents had died and whose siblings were estranged from him. He was discharged from both his job and his hospital, completely destitute and alone with no place to die. It is important to note that health researchers tended to replicate this notion of familyless AIDS sufferers, not just the general public. Nina Glick Schiller concluded that the health researchers she studied did not believe that people with AIDS had families. See Nina Glick Schiller, "The Invisible Women: Caregiving and AIDS," in Karen V. Hansen and Anita Ilta Garey, eds., *Families in the U.S.: Kinship and Domestic Politics* (Philadelphia: Temple University Press, 1998), 539–56, here 554.

13. On the attribution of AIDS to anal sex and to gay lifestyle, such as inhaled drugs or "poppers," see Fauci, "AIDS: Reflections on the Past," 68.

14. Fever Journal, October 1987–June 1988, diary entry, November 17, 1987, Charles Gaven Papers, 7575, box 1, file 22, Division of Rare and Manuscript Collections, Cornell University Library, Ithaca, N.Y.

15. On the polls, see Epstein, *Impure Science*, 96; and see Brandt, "AIDS: From Social History to Social Policy," 153, for a *New York Times* poll in 1985 that showed the widely perceived sources of social contact transmission.

16. I am quoting from the TV movie of *An Early Frost*, rather than the short story; the movie version was run on NBC-TV on November 11, 1985. The teleplay was by Daniel Lipman and Ron Cowen.

17. This comment was in an interview with Patrick Pacheco, "Tony Kushner Speaks Out on AIDS, Angels, Activism and Sex in the 90s," in Tony Kushner, *Angels in America*, part 1, *Millennium Approaches* (New York: Theatre Communications Group, 1992), 15–26, here 22.

18. Paul Reed, *Facing It: A Novel of AIDS* (San Francisco: Gay Sunshine Press, 1984), 153.

19. Ibid., 154.

20. Buckley was quoted in Crimp, *AIDS: Cultural Analysis, Cultural Activism*, 8.

21. By 1983, twenty-three states still had statutes condemning sodomy. See David B. Goodstein, "Our Sweet 16th: Remembering 1967," in *Advocate* 377 (September 29, 1983): 30–36, here 30.

22. For an analysis of the idea of privacy and how it was taken up in the *Bowers v. Hardwick* case, see Rubenfeld, "Right to Privacy," esp. 747–48. See also McGarry and Wasserman, *Becoming Visible*, 28–29. Finally, see Simon LeVay and Elisabeth Nonas, *City of Friends: A Portrait of the Gay and Lesbian Community in America* (Cambridge, Mass.: MIT Press, 1995), 273; and Clendinen and Nagourney, *Out for Good*, 534ff.

23. Sontag, *AIDS and Its Metaphors*, 25. On this sensibility of illness as character flaw, see Altman, *AIDS in the Mind of America*, 14. And on the theme of individual versus collective responsibility, see Dennis Altman, "Legitimation through Disaster: AIDS and the Gay Movement," in Elizabeth Fee and Daniel Fox, eds., *AIDS: The Burdens of History*, 301–16, here 336.

24. Dennis Altman attributes this division to *New York Times* journalist Robin Henig for an article she wrote about "innocent bystanders" in 1983 called "AIDS: A New Disease's Deadly Odyssey," *New York Times Magazine*, February 6, 1983, 36. See Altman, *AIDS in the Mind of America*, 74. See also Brandt's discussion in "AIDS: From Social History to Social Policy," 165.

25. On media portraits, see Timothy E. Cook and David C. Colby, "The Mass-Mediated Epidemic: The Politics of AIDS on the Nightly Network News," in Elizabeth Fee and Daniel Fox, eds., *AIDS: The Making of a Chronic Disease* (Berkeley: University of California Press, 1992), 84–122.

26. See Douglas Crimp, "Portraits of People with AIDS," in Lawrence Grossberg, Cary Nelson, and Paula A. Treichler, eds., *Cultural Studies* (New York: Routledge, 1992), 117–33, here 120.

27. On speculation about the moral logic of chronic disease, see Jason Szabo, *Incurable and Intolerable: Chronic Disease and Slow Death in Nineteenth-Century France* (New Brunswick, N.J.: Rutgers University Press, 2009), 58. The 1980s saw a spate of popular books on nutrition and exercise habits, as well as official reports from the surgeon general about nutrition. See also Prost and Vincent, eds., *History of Private Life: Riddles of Identity in Modern Times*, vol. 5, 85ff. Finally, see Patterson, *Grand Expectations*, 713.

28. Barbara Peabody, *The Screaming Room: A Mother's Journal of Her Son's Struggle with AIDS; A True Story of Love, Dedication, and Courage* (San Diego: Oak Tree, 1986), 25.

29. BettyClare Moffatt, *When Someone You Love Has AIDS: A Book of Hope for Family and Friends* (New York: Plume, 1986), 76.

30. Ibid., 78.

31. Ibid., 79.

32. Ibid., 80.

33. *Philadelphia*, dir. Jonathan Demme, 1993.

34. On the vilification of Patient Zero, see Douglas Crimp, "How to Have Promiscuity in an Epidemic," in Douglas Crimp, ed., *AIDS: Cultural Analysis, Cultural Activism*, 237–70, here 242.

35. Beverly Barbo, *The Walking Wounded: A Mother's True Story of Her Son's Homosexuality and His Eventual AIDS Related Death* (Lindsborg, Kans.: Carlsons, 1987), 1.

36. Ibid., 73.

37. Ardath H. Rodale, *Climbing toward the Light: A Journey of Growth, Understanding, and Love* (Emmaus, Pa.: Good Spirit Press, 1989), 180.

38. Ibid., 181.

39. See Callen, *Surviving AIDS*, 4. On debates surrounding the validity of free love in the face of AIDS, see D'Emilio and Freedman, *Intimate Matters*, 355.

40. See Clendinen and Nagourney, *Out for Good*, 515ff.

41. See Mintz, *Huck's Raft*, viii.

42. Collins, *Transforming America*, 179.

43. Rodale, *Climbing toward the Light*, 58–59. The David chapter is 58–73.

44. Borhek, *Coming Out to Parents*, 238.

45. Cheryl L. West, *Before It Hits Home* (New York: Dramatists Play Service, 1993), 57.

46. Sylvia Goldstaub, *Unconditional Love: "Mom! Dad! Love Me! Please!"* (Boca Raton, Fla.: Cool Hand Communications, 1993), 124, Goldstaub Family Papers, 7567, box 1, file 39, Division of Rare and Manuscript Collections, Cornell University Library, Ithaca, N.Y.

47. Ibid., 21.

48. Haitians continued to be stigmatized as disease carriers throughout the 1980s and even in 1990 were barred from being blood donors in Miami. On this, see James Harvey Young, "AIDS and the FDA," in Victoria A. Harden and John Parascandola, eds., *AIDS and the Public Debate*, 47–66, here 48; and see Altman, *AIDS in the Mind of America*, 58. Finally, see Epstein, *Impure Science*, 66; and Sheldon H. Landesman, "The Haitian Connection," in Kevin Cahill, ed., *The AIDS Epidemic* (New York: St. Martin's Press, 1983), 28–37.

49. *Christopher Street* 79, vol. 7, no. 7 (1983): 5. This series of cartoons originally appeared in *Gay Comix* 3.

50. Some have argued that camp was revived in the face of AIDS. See, for example, David Roman's discussion of the play *Pouf Positive*, in *Performance, Gay Culture, and AIDS* (Bloomington: Indiana University Press, 1998), 87–88. Humorous portraits of AIDS were controversial, particularly in this period, given that some of these were homophobic, done by heterosexual cartoonists. One by Steve Benson aired in the *Arizona Republic* in 1983 depicted two frail, sickly men in a hospital bed dying, with a Mother Nature hovering above them saying, "I told you it's not nice to fool mother nature!" The cartoon drew a negative reaction both from readers and from the Washington Post Writers Group. See "Bad Taste and Bad Manners: Benson's Bomb," *Advocate* 373 (August 3, 1983): 18. For a nonhomophobic AIDS comic of realism, see a strip of the *PWA Coalition Newsline* in the late 1980s, "AIDS: Another Interesting Day Starts," by Sal Melito. For debate regarding the appropriateness of AIDS humor, see

the discussion in Edmund White's autobiography, *Edmund White: The Burning World*, by Stephen Barber (London: Picador, 1999), 149ff. On AIDS jokes, see John Rechy, "AIDS Mysteries and Hidden Dangers," *Advocate* 383–84 (December 22, 1983): 31. Finally, see Treichler, "AIDS, Homophobia and Biomedical Discourse," 67. My sense is that the phenomenon of AIDS humor was more prevalent after its transformation into a chronic disease, in the early 1990s. See, for example, Steven Moore's 1993 routine in the "Out There!" comedy series "Drop Dead Gorgeous."

51. Selections from "HIV/AIDS Family Support Packet," 1993, 12, PFLAG Collection, box 43, file 47, Cornell University Library. These campaigns promoting savviness and AIDS awareness were produced in large numbers by gay activist organizations such as ACT-UP. For some of ACT-UP's art and posters with information on the actual way AIDS could be spread, see Ted Gott, *Don't Leave Me This Way: Art in the Age of AIDS* (Melbourne: Thames and Hudson, 1994), for Keith Haring's poster, "Ignorance = Fear," 68; for ACT-UP San Francisco's portrait, "Clark Wants Dick: Dick Wants Condoms," 156; and for Gran Fury's photograph, "Kissing Doesn't Kill: Greed and Indifference Do." For other campaigns such as Niki de Saint Phalle's posters in her "Plague" series in 1986, see Niki de Saint Phalle, *My Art, My Dreams*, ed. Carla Schulz-Hoffmann (Munich: Prestel, 2003), 118–19.

52. See Douglas A. Feldman and Julia Wang Miller, *The AIDS Crisis: A Documentary History* (Westport, Conn.: Greenwood Press, 1998), 135.

53. Before the advent of specific AIDS hospices in 1987, many long-term care facilities refused to take AIDS patients. On the emergence of AIDS hospices, see Feldman and Miller, *AIDS Crisis*, 242; and Daniel Fox, "AIDS and American Health Policy," in Elizabeth Fee and Daniel Fox, eds., *AIDS: The Burdens of History*, 316–43, here 335. On doctors' duties to those patients who posed them risk, particularly blood bank personnel, lab technicians, and IV teams, see Sydney M. Finegold, "Protecting Health Personnel," in Kevin Cahill, ed., *The AIDS Epidemic*, 125; and Bayer and Oppenheimer, *AIDS Doctors*, 64.

54. On this ballet, see Richard Golstein, "The Impact of AIDS on American Culture," in Victoria A. Harden and John Parascandola, eds., *AIDS and the Public Debate*, 132–36, here 135. Many of the dancers in his piece already had full-blown AIDS and hence needed no makeup to portray KS lesions. See also Douglas Sadownick, "The Dancer Speaks Out: New Directions, New Candor," *Advocate* 545 (February 27, 1990): 38.

55. Peabody, *Screaming Room*, 18. For details on hospital isolation in the early 1990s, see Larry Josephs, "The Harrowing Plunge," Cornell University AIDS Action Records, 51/1/2746, box 1, folder 16, *New York Times Magazine*, November 11, 1990, 38–43, here 41, in Division of Rare and Manuscript Collections, Cornell University Library, Ithaca, N.Y. AIDS activists such as Larry Kramer recalled that even the Sloan-Kettering Hospital in New York City, which specialized in skin cancer, treated its patients like lepers. Larry Kramer, "1112 and Counting," *Reports from the Holocaust:*

The Making of an AIDS Activist (New York: St. Martin's Press, 1989), 38–51, here 38. This famous piece was first published in the *New York Native*, March 14–27, 1983.

56. Walter O. VomLehn, "A Doctor's AIDS Heartbreak: 'Well, Dad, I Finally Have It,'" *Medical Economics*, December 23, 1985, 48–53, here 51–52.

57. William M. Hoffman, *As Is* (New York: Vintage Books, 1985), 77.

58. See Nancy Tomes, *The Gospel of Germs: Men, Women and the Microbe in American Life* (Cambridge, Mass.: Harvard University Press, 1998), 2.

59. On the media explosion during the summer of 1983, see David Black, *The Plague Years: A Chronicle of AIDS, the Epidemic of Our Times* (New York: Simon and Schuster, 1985), 191ff.

60. See Streitmatter, *Unspeakable*, 261.

61. For a vivid portrait, see Jameson Currier's novel, *Where the Rainbow Ends* (Woodstock, NY: Overlook Press, 1998), esp. 123–24.

62. Marie Blackwell, "AIDS in the Family," *Essence*, August 1985, 56 and 105–8, here 56.

63. Ibid., 106.

64. See Paul Ramsey, *The Patient as Person* (New Haven: Yale University Press, 1970). On this theme, see Suzanne E. and James Hatty, *The Disordered Body: Epidemic Disease and Cultural Transformation* (Albany, N.Y.: SUNY Press, 1999), 15.

65. West, *Before It Hits Home*, 20.

66. On Tuskegee, see Sander L. Gilman, "AIDS and Syphilis: The Iconography of Disease," in Douglas Crimp, ed., *AIDS: Cultural Analysis, Cultural Activism*, 87–107, here 100; and see James H. Jones, *Bad Blood: The Tuskegee Syphilis Experiment* (New York: Free Press, 1981). On doctor suspicion, see Bayer and Oppenheimer, *AIDS Doctors*, 6.

67. "Dear Family and Friends," February 19, 1988, 5 (of 5), Charles Gaver Papers, box 1, file 23.

68. Michael Lassell, "How to Watch Your Brother Die," in Carl Morse and Joan Larkin, eds., *Gay and Lesbian Poetry of Our Time* (New York: St. Martin's Press, 1988), 224.

69. For visual representations of KS lesions, see Rosalind Solomon's photographs in her series *Portraits in the Time of AIDS* (New York: New York University, Grey Art Gallery, 1988), I, VI, XII, XXVI. See also Mark I. Chester, "Robert Chesley—KS Portraits with Harddick and Superman Spandex #3 and #5," from "Diary of a Thought Criminal, 1990–91," gelatin silver photographs in Gott's compilation, *Don't Leave Me This Way*, 226.

70. Elisabeth Kübler-Ross, *AIDS: The Ultimate Challenge* (New York: Macmillan, 1987), 23.

71. Mary Melfi, ed., *Painting Moments: Art, AIDS, and Nick Palazzo* (Toronto: Guernica, 1998), 41.

72. Fairchild and Hayward, *Now That You Know*. This is the third edition of her

book; the chapter on AIDS from which I quote was added in 1989 and updated in 1998. See 247.

73. Moffatt, *When Someone You Love Has AIDS*, 5.

74. On this, see Kinsella, *Covering the Plague*, esp. 76 and 136, on the oblique terms in which gay sex was discussed.

75. Bobbie Stasey, *Just Hold Me While I Cry: A Mother's Life-Enriching Reflections on Her Family's Emotional Journey through AIDS* (Albuquerque, N.Mex.: Elysian Hills, 1993), 12.

76. In his 1992 photograph "Tigger," Bill Bytsura expressed this sense by showing a gay man kissing a hooded skeleton. This photo is in Gott, *Don't Leave Me This Way*, 58. See also Liz Grosz, "Animal Sex: Libido as Desire and Death," in Liz Grosz and Elspeth Probyn, eds., *Sexy Bodies: The Strange Carnalities of Feminism*, 278–99, here 297. She notes that AIDS safe-sex advertising itself tried to reassure gay men that sex did not have to be boring if it was safe, as if to suggest that "one need not court danger and possible death in the search for an ultimate sexual high." Gay sex had traditionally been associated with danger, with the threat of violence and police intervention, for example, and this might have, at least subconsciously, lent some added charge to gay sexuality. This interconnection between sex and death seems embedded more broadly in postwar culture as well: I am thinking of poems such as the violently charged sex poems of writers Sylvia Plath and Ann Sexton as well as Leonard Cohen and Irving Layton.

77. Cindy Ruskin, "Taking Up Needles and Thread to Honor the Dead Helps AIDS Survivors Patch Up Their Lives," *People Weekly*, October 12, 1987, 42–49, here 44.

78. Cindy Ruskin, *The Quilt: Stories from the NAMES Project* (New York: Pocket Books, 1988), 78.

79. Between 1980 and 1984, only about three dozen teenagers in America had contracted the disease. Steven Petrow, *Dancing against the Darkness: A Journey through America in the Age of AIDS* (Lexington, Mass.: Lexington Books, 1990), 16.

80. Ibid., 182.

81. For context on public displays of shunning mourners and homophobia at the hands of workers, see Paul Monette's account of the homophobia of the cemetery employees he encountered in *Last Watch of the Night: Essays Too Personal and Otherwise* (New York: Harcourt Brace and Company, 1994), 109. On the fear of funeral undertakers and hospital workers, see also Altman, *AIDS in the Mind of America*, 62–63. For more on funeral directors, see Anne Aaron and Iben Browning, *The Economic Impact of AIDS* (Albuquerque, N.Mex.: Sapiens Press, 1988), 28.

82. For details, see PFLAG's Family Support Project. By 1987, PFLAG had established the Family Support Project to help those living with family members with AIDS. They found family reticence understandable in light of this violence. See "Family Support Project," PFLAG Collection, box 5, file 4, Cornell University Library. On the Ray family specifically, see Gilman, "AIDS and Syphilis," 105. Ryan White's family was

invited to Cicero, Indiana, after they left Kokomo. On White, see Feldman and Miller, *AIDS Crisis*, 113; and see Tomes, *Gospel of Germs*, 256.

83. See Koop, "Early Days of AIDS as I Remember Them," 15–16.

84. Judith Butler, *Antigone's Claim: Kinship between Life and Death* (New York: Columbia University Press, 1998), 24.

85. Jean Baker, *Family Secrets: Gay Sons, A Mother's Story* (New York: Harrington Park Press, 1998), 5.

86. On losses to the art world, see Doss, *Twentieth-Century American Art*, 223.

87. Baker, *Family Secrets*, 5.

88. On the silence about AIDS within obituaries, see Peter Nardi, "AIDS and Obituaries: The Perception of Stigma in the Press," in Michelle Cochrane, ed., *When AIDS Began: San Francisco and the Making of an Epidemic* (New York: Routledge, 2004), 159–68.

89. Peabody, *Screaming Room*, 153.

90. On the metaphors of war in AIDS activism, see Michael S. Sherry, "The Language of War in AIDS Discourse," in Timothy F. Murphy and Suzanne Poirier, eds., *Writing AIDS: Gay Literature, Language, and Analysis* (New York: Columbia University Press, 1993), 39–53, here 40.

91. Peabody, *Screaming Room*, 154.

92. Michael Tidmus, "Prophylaxis: Blind Admonition," from "From a Life: Selections Gay and Grave," 1993, in Gott, *Don't Leave Me This Way*, 227.

93. See Philippe Aries's social history of death and dying, *Western Attitudes toward Death: From the Middle Ages to the Present* (Baltimore: Johns Hopkins University Press, 1974), 87. He cites that between the 1930s and the 1950s the home was displaced as the site of death in favor of lonely hospital deaths. On the growing privacy of the death experience, see also David Dempsey, *The Way We Die: An Investigation of Death and Dying in America Today* (New York: Macmillan, 1975), 124ff. Finally, see Sherwin Nuland, *How We Die: Reflections on Life's Final Chapter* (New York: Alfred A. Knopf, 1993).

94. Duane Michals, "The Father Prepares His Dead Son for Burial," 1991, gelatin silver photograph, reproduced in Gott, *Don't Leave Me This Way*, 130.

95. On these organizations, see Sharon McDonald, "Tender Loving Care," *Advocate* 515 (January 3, 1989): 52–53.

96. Kitsy Schoen and Ellie Schindelman, "AIDS and Bereavement," 16 (of 19), AIDS Work Collection, 7324, box 8, file "PFLAG," Division of Rare and Manuscript Collections, Cornell University Library, Ithaca, N.Y.

97. Blasius and Phelan, *We Are Everywhere*, 635.

98. Excerpt from "Una Fotonovela Completa: 'Ojos Que No Ven: Una historia de hoy . . . de nuestras vidas y la realidad del SIDA!'" (San Francisco: Instituto de la Raza, 1987), 3 and 4, box 12, file 51, James M. Foster Papers, 7439, Division of Rare and Manuscript Collections, Cornell University Library, Ithaca, N.Y.

99. For an analysis of the *Life* article, see Kinsella, *Covering the Plague*, 265. On

this, see Crimp, "How to Have Promiscuity in an Epidemic," 262; as well as Brandt, "AIDS: From Social History to Social Policy," 212. See also Cook and Colby, "Mass-Mediated Epidemic," 110.

100. For an example of one such ad, see Robert Garcia Papers, box 3, file 21. In this New York City Health Department advertisement, a husband brings home to his unsuspecting wife "a quart of milk, a loaf of bread, and a case of AIDS."

101. See Tomas Almaguer, "Chicano Men: A Cartography of Homosexual Identity and Behavior," in Henry Abelove, Michele Aina Barale, and David M. Halperin, eds., *The Lesbian and Gay Study Reader* (New York: Routledge, 1993), 255–73. See also Cherrie Moraga's discussion in *Loving in the War Years* (Boston: South End, 1983), v, 99, 102.

102. Altman, *AIDS in the Mind of America*, 118. James Kinsella mentions a 1985 press conference in which Reagan expressed sympathy with parents whose children went to school with other kids with AIDS. See *Covering the Plague*, 266.

103. Altman, *AIDS in the Mind of America*, 63–67. On quarantining efforts, including a 1986 ballot proposition in California to quarantine HIV-infected citizens, see Feldman and Miller, *AIDS Crisis*, 22; Epstein, *Impure Science*, 52; and Crimp, *AIDS: Cultural Analysis, Cultural Activism*, 8, as well as his essay "How to Have Promiscuity in an Epidemic," 262. See also Ronald Bayer, *Private Acts, Social Consequences: AIDS and the Politics of Public Health* (New Brunswick, N.J.: Rutgers University Press, 1989), 169.

104. See reference in David Gelman and Pamela Abramson, "AIDS," *Newsweek*, August 12, 1985, 20–29, here 20; this comment was originally quoted in "Mother Nature Getting Even," *Seattle Post Intelligencer*, May 25, 1983, 1–15, according to Streitmatter in *Unspeakable*, 261. See also Kenneth MacKinnon, *The Politics of Popular Representation: Reagan, Thatcher, AIDS and the Movies* (London: Associated University Presses, 1992), 164.

105. See Toby Johnson, "AIDS and Moral Issues: Will Sexual Liberation Survive?" *Advocate* 379 (October 27, 1983): 24; Miller, *Out of the Past*, 51; and D'Emilio and Freedman, *Intimate Matters*, 354.

106. Baker, *Family Secrets*, 188.

107. Ibid., 192.

108. This was a piece that Kramer wrote in the *New York Native* on March 13, 1983. For an account of the piece, see Kinsella, *Covering the Plague*, 34; and for the piece itself, see Blasius and Phelan, *We Are Everywhere*, 578–86. Kramer also noted that it took an entire year before the *New England Journal of Medicine* would even publish doctors' observations when they first saw AIDS symptoms in 1980. See Larry Kramer, "An Open Letter to Richard Dunne and the GMHC," 602, from the *New York Native*, 1987, reprinted in Blasius and Phelan, *We Are Everywhere*, 601–9. See also Epstein, *Impure Science*, 45.

109. On the drug's side effects of anemia, headaches, nausea, insomnia, and muscle pains, see Peter Arno and Karyn Feiden, *Against the Odds: The Story of AIDS Drug*

Development, Politics, and Profits (New York: HarperCollins, 1992), 18, and see 84, for hospitalization costs, which ranged between thirteen and sixteen thousand dollars. For details on how AZT functions, see Cindy Patton, *Sex and Germs: The Politics of AIDS* (Montreal: Black Rose Books, 1986), 99. Finally, see Bayer and Oppenheimer, *AIDS Doctors*, 134; and Norman Daniels, *Seeking Fair Treatment: From the AIDS Epidemic to National Health Care Reform* (New York: Oxford University Press, 1985), 9, 20, 84.

110. Altman, *AIDS in the Mind of America*, 121.

111. Fox, "AIDS and American Health Policy," 335.

112. See Feldman and Miller, *AIDS Crisis*, 161; and Daniel M. Fox, "The Politics of HIV Infection," in Daniel Fox and Elizabeth Fee, eds., *AIDS: The Making of a Chronic Disease*, 125–43, here 137 and 138. This act coincided with the Americans with Disabilities Act that gave antidiscrimination protection to people with AIDS.

113. Ann Baker, "A Mother's Cry for Help," *PWA Coalition Newsline* 49 (November 1989): 23.

114. On the founding, see Clendinen and Nagourney, *Out for Good*, 547ff.

115. D'Emilio and Freedman, *Intimate Matters*, 367.

116. Epstein, *Impure Science*, 1–2, 9, and 11. A prominent demonstration took place at the Harvard Medical School in 1988 featuring hospital gowns and fake blood. The protestors spoke against medical elitism and the overwhelming scientific attention to AZT, deemed toxic and not even satisfactory as a temporary cure.

117. See Timothy McDarrah, "An AIDS Victim Protests from beyond Grave," *New York Times*, Obituaries, November 2, 1992, n.p., and Sarah Wood, "Coffin Protest," *New York Newsday*, November 3, 1992, n.p., in ACT-UP Collection, 91–1, Lesbian Herstory Archives.

118. Mark Lowe Fisher, "Bury Me Furiously," from ACT-UP Collection, 91–1, Lesbian Herstory Archives.

119. Michael Denneny, "A Quilt of Many Colors: AIDS Writing and the Creation of Culture," *Christopher Street* 141, vol. 12, no. 9 (1989): 15–21, here 16.

120. Ibid., 18.

121. On the experience of psychic loss and separation as a parallel to St. Paul, see Norman O. Brown, *Life against Death: The Psychological Meaning of History* (Middletown, Conn.: Wesleyan University Press, 1959), 115.

122. Robert John Florence, "Coming In," *Out/Look* 2 (Fall 1989): 67–73, here 67.

123. James Edwin Parker was principally a playwright who would go on to write the play *Two Boys in Bed on a Cold Winter's Night* (1995).

124. James Edwin Parker, "Snakes, Trolls, and Drag Queens," in Dean Kostos and Eugene Grygo, eds., *Mama's Boy: Gay Men Write about Their Mothers*, 99–109, here 106.

125. On these themes and Kübler-Ross's impact, see Michele Catherine Gantois Chaban, *The Life Work of Dr. Elisabeth Kübler-Ross and Its Impact on the Death Awareness Movement* (Lewiston, N.Y.: Edwin Mellen Press, 2000), 327ff.

126. See Charles Rosenberg, "Disease and Social Order in America," in Elizabeth Fee and Daniel Fox, eds., *AIDS: The Burdens of History*, 27–50, here 50.

127. Dirk Johnson, "Coming Home, with AIDS, to a Small Town," *New York Times*, November 2, 1987, A1.

128. In fact, the Group for the Advancement of Psychiatry argued that though the equation of AIDS with homosexuality led to an escalation of hateful attitudes toward homosexuality, it also provoked a "public perception of a minority group struggling valiantly with a dread disease," and in some quarters this led to the diminishment of prejudice. See Group for the Advancement of Psychiatry, *Homosexuality and the Mental Health Professions: The Impact of Bias* (Hillsdale, N.J.: Analytic Press, 2000), 4.

129. It is worth noting that the story of a gay man with rural roots who leaves home to experience an urban gay scene is an archetypal configuration of gay lives. Eric Rofes called this the story of Hank Homo, who spent his youth in the Midwest or the South, has a sexual awakening, and then moves to New York City or Los Angeles or San Francisco or Chicago. See Eric Rofes, *Reviving the Tribe: Regenerating Gay Men's Sexuality and Culture in the Ongoing Epidemic* (New York: Harrington Park Press, 1996), 155.

130. See Greg Lamp, "Back to the Farm to Die," *Farm Journal*, January 1991, 17–20.

131. On the PFLAG warnings to rural parents, see "Family Support Project," PFLAG Collection, box 5, file 4, Cornell University Library.

132. H. Wayne Schow, *Remembering Brad: On the Loss of a Son to AIDS* (Salt Lake City: Signature Books, 1995), x. Brad Schow died of AIDS in 1986. His father was also the coeditor of the book *Peculiar People: Mormons and Same-Sex Orientation* in 1993.

133. Letter to Jill, October 27, 1988, 1, Charles Gaver Papers, box 1, file 12.

134. James Carroll Pickett, "Kentucky 55 South: A Visit with Dad," in John Preston, ed., *A Member of the Family: Gay Men Write about Their Families* (New York: Dutton, 1992), 95–101, here 99. A version of this essay first appeared in *Frontiers*, October 26, 1990.

135. See Rosalind Solomon, "Untitled," from *Portraits in the Time of AIDS*, XI.

136. On this, see Larry Gross's commentary in the film *Off the Straight and Narrow: Lesbians, Gays, Bisexuals, and Television*, dir. by Katherine Sender (Northampton, Mass.: Media Education Foundation, 1998).

137. Crimp, "Portraits of People with AIDS," 127. On these themes, and the idea of breaking down the "distinction between art as representation and art as action," see T. V. Reed, *The Art of Protest: Culture and Activism from the Civil Rights Movement to the Streets of Seattle* (Minneapolis: University of Minnesota Press, 2005), 191.

138. *Our Sons*, dir. John Erman, 1991.

139. On this, see Crimp, "Portraits of People with AIDS," 118 and 121. On the vulnerability of gay relationships in the face of a partner's death, see Chauncey, *Why Marriage?* 97ff.

140. This photograph is in Billy Howard, *Epitaphs for the Living: Words and Images in the Time of AIDS* (Dallas: Southern Methodist University Press, 1989).

141. Sue Halpern, "Values Which Are Simply There," *New York Times*, May 20, 1990, Cornell University AIDS Action Collection, 51/1/2746.

142. Letter to Family and Friends, February 14, 1988, Charles Gaver Papers, box 1, file 11.

143. Firebooks: Selected Poetry and Journals 1969–83, Letter from Father, n.d. 1977, Charles Gaver Papers, box 9.

144. Journal entry, June 11, 1988, 2 (of 2), Charles Gaver Papers, box 1, file 24.

145. Letter, "Dear Dad," April 16 1989, 1 and 2, Michael Williams Papers, 7444, box 2, file 12, Division of Rare and Manuscript Collections, Cornell University Library, Ithaca, N.Y.

146. Dad to Michael, May 4, 1989, 1, Michael Williams Papers, box 2, file 13.

147. Ibid., 2.

148. Dad to Michael, January 16, 1990, Michael Williams Papers, box 2, file 18.

149. See Kübler-Ross, *AIDS: The Ultimate Challenge*, 32–33 and 35–37.

150. For representations of Rubinstein in this role, see *Time*, August 12, 1985, 47, and Scott Haller, "Fear & AIDS in Hollywood," *People*, September 23, 1985, 28–33, here 33, Michael Ellis Papers, 7615, box 2, file 22, Division of Rare and Manuscript Collections, Cornell University Library, Ithaca, N.Y.

151. David Kessler, "A Need for Constant Love," in "Family Support Guide" (1993), 9–10, box 8, file "PFLAG," AIDS Work Collection, Cornell University Library, Ithaca, N.Y.

152. Ibid., 10.

153. D'Emilio and Freedman, *Intimate Matters*, 356; and Altman, *AIDS in the Mind of America*, 83. David Leavitt's *Saturn Street* is in the collection *Arkansas: Three Novellas* (Boston: Houghton Mifflin, 1997). The GMHC also raised money for research and lobbied both state and federal governments for accessible treatments and a cure.

154. See Weston, *Families We Choose*, 35. See also Michael Helquist, "An Epidemic in the Family," *Advocate* 404 (October 2, 1984): 29 and 56; and Michael Bronski, "Death and the Erotic Imagination," in Erica Carter and Simon Watney, eds., *Taking Liberties: AIDS and Cultural Politics* (London: Serpent's Tail, 1989), 219–28, here 220. On the Shanti Project, see Gregory M. Herek and Beverly Greene, *AIDS, Identity, and Community: The HIV Epidemic and Lesbian and Gay Men* (Thousand Oaks, Calif.: Sage, 1995), 4.

155. On lesbians and caring and AIDS activism, see Cvetkovich, *Archive of Feelings*, 156–204. On the definition of health care as political issues, a particular concern of radical feminists, see again Taylor and Rupp, "Women's Culture and Lesbian Feminist Activism," 52. See also Peg Byron, "Lesbians in the Fight against AIDS," *Advocate* 457 (October 14, 1986): 48–50; and Miller, *Out of the Past*, 452. Also see Blasius and Phelan, *We Are Everywhere*, 638–41, speech given at the NGLTF town meeting for the

gay community in 1989 by Maxine Wolfe. For lesbian accounts of caring for individuals with AIDS, see Rebecca Brown, *The Gifts of the Body* (New York: Harper Perennial, 1994); and Amy Hoffman, *Hospital Time* (Durham, N.C.: Duke University Press, 1997).

156. David Summers, "Demanding Mom's Respect," 187–88, here 187, Robert Roth Papers, 7325, box 13, file 10, Division of Rare and Manuscript Collections, Cornell University Library, Ithaca, N.Y.

157. See Bill Kirkpatrick, *AIDS: Sharing the Pain; A Guide for Caregivers* (New York: Pilgrim Press, 1990), 48ff.

158. Hoffman, *Hospital Time*, 111.

159. Kay Glidden, "Dear GMHC Supporter," 1, Robert Roth Papers, box 2, file 68.

160. Goldstaub, *Unconditional Love*, 36.

161. Letter to Bonnie, April 18, 1987, box 1, file 19, and letter from Bonnie, September 4, 1987, file 20, Michael Williams Papers.

162. See, for example, "When a Friend Has AIDS," State of Florida, Dept. of Health and Rehabilitation Services, 1989, Goldstaub Family Papers, box 2, file 13.

163. From Gay Men's Health Crisis Organization (GMHC), August 1988, a letter from Dennis C. Daniel, Robert Roth Papers, box 2, file 68.

164. "HIV/AIDS Family Support Packet," 1993, 8, PFLAG Collection, box 43, file 47, Cornell University Library.

165. Anne Serabian, "Mother, Do You Know What AIDS Is?" for the PFLAG National Convention in Charlotte, N.C., box 11, PFLAG Convention Tapes, no. 91–22, PFLAG Collection, Cornell University Library.

166. Paul Kent Froman, *After You Say Goodbye: When Someone You Love Dies of AIDS* (San Francisco: Chronicle Books, 1992), 216.

167. Stasey, *Just Hold Me While I Cry*, 185.

168. Betty Holloran, "Dear Friend," 1–4, here 3, PFLAG Collection, box 43, Cornell University Library.

169. Ibid., 4.

170. Baker, *Family Secrets*, 181.

171. Here I am referring to something beyond housekeeping and the physical aspects of the home, as Nancy Walker defined domesticity: "social relationships, child rearing practices, personal well being, purchasing habits, recreation, neighborhoods, gardening, civic involvement, food preferences, health, and personal appearances." See *Shaping Our Mothers' World*, viii.

Epilogue

1. On this painting, see Warren Susman, *Culture as History: The Transformation of American Society in the Twentieth Century* (New York: Pantheon, 1984), 194.

2. IGIC Ephemera, PFLAG, "We Are Family!"

3. To be fair, PFLAG did undergo some internal questioning about why they had

failed to attract nonwhite families. PFLAG Convention topics in these years reflect these concerns. For example, in 1987, a discussion group was held on "Reaching Out to Minority Families of Gays and Lesbians" and, in 1990, "Coming Out to an Hispanic Family," which tried to take into account both PFLAG failures and the taboos within the groups they hoped would join PFLAG. See Audiotape 87–5, box 9, and Audiotape 90–29, box 11, PFLAG Collection, Cornell University Library, Ithaca, N.Y. See also Audiotape 90–38, Outreach to Families of Colour, October 14, 1990, Anaheim Convention, where a speaker speculated about the role of PFLAG in African American communities.

4. Paulette Goodman, "Dear Mrs. Bush," June 13, 1989, 1, PFLAG Collection, box 2, Cornell University Library, Ithaca, N.Y.

5. Barbara Bush, "Dear Mrs. Goodman," May 10, 1990, 1, PFLAG Collection, box 2, Cornell University Library, Ithaca, N.Y.

6. Robert Bernstein, "Family Values and Gay Rights," *New York Times*, 1990, PFLAG Collection, box 2, Cornell University Library, Ithaca, N.Y.

7. Betty Fairchild, "Dear Mrs. Bush," June 11, 1990, 1, PFLAG Collection, box 2, Cornell University Library, Ithaca, N.Y.

8. See, for example, ACT-UP Finding Aid, ACT-UP Collection, MSS. and Archives Section, New York Public Library, New York.

9. Rob Eichberg, *Coming Out, An Act of Love: An Inspiring Call to Action for Gay Men, Lesbians, and Those Who Care* (New York: Plume, 1990), 21.

10. Ibid., 159.

11. Robert Kevess diary, copy in possession of the author, October 7, 1989.

12. "Alan," in Meg Umans, ed., *Like Coming Home: Coming-Out Letters* (Austin, Tex.: Banned Books, 1988), 95–98, here 95. Other letters in this collection that were particularly sensitive to parents' feelings, giving them thinking time, include "Vivian" (age twenty-three, Arizona), 29–33; and "Harriet," 71–73.

13. Rachel Pepper, "A Coming-Out Christmas Tale," *Outlines*, January 1988, n.p.

14. National Gay Task Force, "About Coming Out" (New York: NGTF, n.d.), Kristin Gay Esterberg Papers, 7452, box 1, Division of Rare and Manuscript Collections, Cornell University Library, Ithaca, N.Y.

15. Susan Y. F. Chen, "Slowly but Surely, My Search for Family Acceptance and Community Continues" (1991), in Sharon Lim-Hing, ed., *The Very Inside: An Anthology of Writing by Asian and Pacific Islander Lesbian and Bisexual Women* (Toronto: Sister Vision, 1994), 79–84, here 79.

16. Ibid., 81.

17. Martin Hiraga, a gay Japanese American, agreed with this characterization of Asian parents. When he came out to his parents, he started his coming-out letter with the Japanese words "I, your dishonorable son, am sorry to have shamed you." See Martin Hiraga, "Rising Son: An Asian Comes Out to His Parents," *Empty Closet* 188 (December 1987–January 1988): 14 and 15. Themes of parental shame and obligation were also prominent in the collection of coming-out stories and letters by Toronto

Asian gay men, *Celebrasian: Shared Lives; An Oral History of Gay Asians* (Toronto: Gay Asians of Toronto, 1996).

18. Chen, "Slowly but Surely," 82 and 81.

19. Glenn Wein, "Gay Siblings in an Aging America," *Christopher Street* 101, vol. 9, no. 5 (1985): 26–28, here 26.

20. William H. Dubay, "You Can Go Home Again," *Christopher Street* 101, vol. 9, no. 5 (1985): 18–21.

21. See Judith Stacey, *Brave New Families: Stories of Domestic Upheaval in Late Twentieth-Century America* (New York: Basic Books, 1990), 269. In her research on adult children with mental retardation, Janice Brockley argued that nineteenth-century popular literature endorsed the idea of a few individuals never leaving their original families, while twentieth-century literature tolerated the phenomenon much less. See "Rearing the Child Who Never Grew," 138.

22. Essex Hemphill, "Commitments," in Essex Hemphill, ed., *Brother to Brother: New Writings by Black Gay Men* (Boston: Alyson, 1991), 57–58.

23. For some examples, see Gerald Donelan's cartoons, "It's a Gay Life," in *Advocate* 451 (July 22, 1986): 40 ("Mr. You're-So-Hot"); *Advocate* 402 (September 4, 1984): 29 ("All I Ask for Is Grandchildren"); *Advocate* 452 (August 5, 1986): 49 ("Maybe Your Friend Has a Brother . . ."); *Advocate* 428 (September 3, 1985): 32 ("Mom's So Happy . . ."); and *Advocate* 503 (July 19, 1988): 63 ("Please, Amy, Tell Me"). See also Tom Brady, "Life at the Closet Door," in *Baltimore Gaypaper*, September 2, 1988, 19 ("That's All Right, Dear, So Are We.")

24. For an example, see Tim Barela, "Revenge of the Yenta" (1984), in *Domesticity Isn't Pretty* (Minneapolis: Palliard Press, 1993), 26–29. And see also Shelly Roberts and Melissa K. Sweeney, illustrator, *Hey, Mom, Guess What! 150 Ways to Tell Your Mother* (San Diego: Paradigm, 1993), 136 ("And to Think Binky Ashton's Mom . . ."); 45 ("Homo Is Where the Heart Is"); and 94 (the "PFLAG Bake Sale").

25. David Leavitt, "Territory," in *Family Dancing* (New York: Alfred A. Knopf, 1984), 8.

26. Ibid., 17.

27. Ibid., 20 and 25.

28. Ibid., 25.

29. On tell-alls, see Evan Ember-Black, *Secrets in Families and Family Therapy* (New York: W. W. Norton, 1993), 30. See also Melissa Jane Hardie on scandalous memoirs, "'I Embrace the Difference': Elizabeth Taylor and the Closet," in Liz Grosz and Elspeth Probyn, eds., *Sexy Bodies: The Strange Carnalities of Feminism*, 155–71. Finally, see Jeffrey Weeks, "Intimate Citizenship and the Culture of Sexual Story Telling," in Jeffrey Weeks and Janet Holland, eds., *Sexual Cultures: Community, Values and Intimacy* (New York: St. Martin's Press, 1996), 34–52.

30. Deborah, "The Odd Man Out," in Louise Rafkin, ed., *Different Daughters: A Book by Mothers of Lesbians* (Pittsburgh, Pa.: Cleis Press, 1987), 80–83, here 80.

31. Ibid., 81.

32. Ibid., 83.

33. See also Darlene Palmer's story of her daughter in this same collection, "A Second Chance," 114–19.

34. In her case, these confessionals were incest survivor stories. Linda Alcoff, "Survivor Discourse: Transgression or Recuperation?" *Signs* 18 (Winter 1993): 260–90. For more details on television media confessional formats, see Gilbert T. Sewall, *The Eighties: A Reader* (Reading, Mass.: Addison-Wesley, 1997), esp. David Rieff's piece, "Victims All?" 349–61. For a more nuanced reading of the presence of gays on television talk shows throughout the 1980s and 1990s, see Joshua Gamson, *Freaks Talk Back: Tabloid Talk Shows and Sexual Nonconformity*. (Chicago: University of Chicago Press, 1998).

35. This *Oprah* show on parents of gays was run in 1993. The quotations I take are from a viewing of this tape at the Lesbian Herstory Archives. In 1993, Sally Jesse Raphael also featured gays on her talk show on "Lipstick Lesbians and Gorgeous Guys Who Are Gay." In 1993, Geraldo had a show on "Gay Teenagers at the High School Prom."

36. One Queer Nation advertisement for the Christmas season featured a picture of Christ saying, "I didn't say *hate* thy neighbor; so when are you going to stop beating up the queers? Season's Greetings from Queer Nation." Queer Nation Records, 93–12, box 1, GLBT Archives of Northern California, San Francisco. On gay youth, see "IPLGY (Institute for the Protection of Gay Youth): Giving Refuge to Harassed Gay Youngsters," *Advocate* 425 (July 23, 1985): 16.

37. This statistic is from Cruikshank, *Gay and Lesbian Liberation Movement*, 84. On gay bashing during the late 1980s and early 1990s, see Bronski, "Death and the Erotic Imagination," 223. See also "Gays Under Fire," *Newsweek*, September 14, 1992, 35–41. Finally, see "Speaking Out about Our Lives," *Gay Community News* 10 (January 29, 1983): 10.

38. Letters to Lesbian Liberation, Women's Educational Center, folder 13, letter, "To whom it may concern," February 20, 1990, MC 503, box 159, Schlesinger Library, Radcliffe Institute for Advanced Study, Harvard University.

39. Ivan Velez Jr., *Tales of the Closet* (New York: Hetrick-Martin Institute, 1987), See book 1, "Isolation"; book 2, "Family"; and book 3, "Violence." It is worth noting here that lesbian writings also dealt with family violence at an unprecedented rate during this period, as the realities of wife battering and incest, so prominent in the culture at large, also were discussed within lesbian-specific sources. For some lesbians, the family was a place of inherent violence, before and after they had had their coming outs, and being gay in that context just confirmed the alienation they had already felt. On this, see Julia Penelope, "Tis the Season to Be Jolly," *Lesbian Inciter* 1 (December 1985): 16–21; and the responses to "A Letter to My Dad," *Lesbian Connection* 6 (April–May 1983): 11, and in vol. 6, no 3, p. 18, and vol. 6, no. 4, p. 14. See also the pieces on incest in *Common Lives/Lesbian Lives* 2 (Winter 1981): 62–63. Finally, see Zimmerman, *Safe Sea of Women*, 213ff.

40. This poster was in Queer Nation Records, 93–2, box 1, Gay and Lesbian Historical Society of Northern California. For more details on Queer Nation, see Guy Trebay, "In Your Face," *Village Voice*, August 14, 1990, 34–39. On Queer Nation groups in Toronto and New York City, see Warner, *Never Going Back*, 252 and 259.

41. On this theme, see Elizabeth Schneider, "The Violence of Privacy," *Connecticut Law Review* 23 (Summer 1991): 973–94.

42. See Corber, *Homosexuality in Cold War America*, 194, on the outing of Malcolm Forbes and Jodie Foster. See also Lisa Duggan and Nan Hunter, *Sex Wars: Sexual Dissent and Political Culture* (New York: Routledge, 2006), 152.

43. Arch Brown, "Gay Pride, before and After," *About Town*, June 30, 1980, 4–5, here 4.

44. See Kennedy, "'But We Would Never Talk about It,'" 18; and Boyd, *Wide Open Town*, 194.

45. On queer existence outside of social structures and the extremes of feeling that queer experience can promote, see Heather Love, *Feeling Backward: Loss and the Politics of Queer History* (Cambridge, Mass.: Harvard University Press, 2007), 142.

SELECTED BIBLIOGRAPHY

Manuscripts

ACT-UP Collection. 91-1. Lesbian Herstory Archives, Brooklyn, N.Y.

ACT-UP Collection. MSS. and Archives Section, New York Public Library.

AIDS Work Collection. 7324. Cornell University Library, Division of Rare and Manuscript Collections, Ithaca, N.Y.

Barbara Deming Papers. MC 408. Schlesinger Library Archives, Cambridge, Mass.

Boston Women's Health Book Collective. MC 503. Schlesinger Library Archives, Radcliffe Institute for Advanced Study, Harvard University, Cambridge, Mass.

Charles Gaver Papers. 7575. Cornell University Library, Division of Rare and Manuscript Collections, Ithaca, N.Y.

Charles Thorpe Papers. Harvey Milk Archives, Scott Smith Collection, James C. Hormel Gay and Lesbian Center, San Francisco Public Library.

Cornell University AIDS Action Records. 1/1/2746. Cornell University, Division of Rare and Manuscripts Collection, Ithaca, N.Y.

Del Martin and Phyllis Lyon Papers. 93-13. Gay, Lesbian, Bisexual and Transgendered Historical Society of Northern California, San Francisco.

Don Lucas Collection. 1997-25. Gay, Lesbian, Bisexual, and Transgendered Historical Society of Northern California, San Francisco.

Dorothee Gore Papers. MSS. and Archives Section, New York Public Library.

Goldstaub Family Papers. Cornell University Library, Division of Rare and Manuscript Collections, Ithaca, N.Y.

Harry Langhorne Papers. 7304. Cornell University Library, Division of Rare and Manuscript Collections, Ithaca, N.Y.

IGIC Ephemera. Organizations, Parents and Friends of Lesbians and Gays. MSS. and Archives Section, New York Public Library.

James M. Foster Papers. 7439. Cornell University Library, Division of Rare and Manuscript Collections, Ithaca, N.Y.

Jeanne Manford Papers. IGIC. MSS. and Archives Section, New York Public Library.

Julie Lee Papers. Serial 79-7. Lesbian Herstory Archives, Brooklyn, N.Y.

Kristin Gay Esterberg Papers. 7452. Cornell University Library, Division of Rare and Manuscript Collections, Ithaca, N.Y.

Manuscript Collection. Serial 81-04. Lesbian Herstory Archives, Brooklyn, N.Y.

Marge McDonald Papers. Serial 87-7. Lesbian Herstory Archives, Brooklyn, N.Y.

Michael Callen Papers. 010. Lesbian and Gay Community Services Center, National Archive of Lesbian and Gay History, New York.

Michael Ellis Papers. 7615. Cornell University Library, Division of Rare and Manuscript Collections, Ithaca, N.Y.

Michael Williams Papers. 7444. Cornell University Library, Division of Rare and Manuscript Collections, Ithaca, N.Y.

Mike Hippler Papers. Gay, Lesbian, Bisexual, and Transgendered Historical Society of Northern California, San Francisco.

Ms. magazine. Letters. MC 331. Schlesinger Library Archives, Cambridge, Mass.

Perry Brass Papers. 7329. Cornell University, Division of Rare and Manuscript Collections, Ithaca, N.Y.

PFLAG Collection. 7616. Cornell University Library, Division of Rare and Manuscripts Collections, Ithaca, N.Y.

Queer Nation Records. 93-12. Gay, Lesbian, Bisexual, and Transgendered Archives of Northern California, San Francisco.

Robert Garcia Papers. 7574. Cornell University Library, Division of Rare and Manuscript Collections, Ithaca, N.Y.

Robert Kevess diary, copy in possession of the author.

Robert Leach Papers. 7609. Cornell University Library, Division of Rare and Manuscript Collections, Ithaca, N.Y.

Robert Roth Papers. 7325. Cornell University Library, Division of Rare and Manuscript Collections, Ithaca, N.Y.

William Billings Collection. GLC 35. Harvey Milk Archives, Scott Smith Collection, James C. Hormel Gay and Lesbian Center, San Francisco Public Library.

William Cannicott Olson Papers. Rare Book, Manuscript, and Special Collections Library, Duke University, Durham, N.C.

Zoe Masur Papers. Serial 84-28. Lesbian Herstory Archives, Brooklyn, N.Y.

Books, Articles, and Pamphlets

Allison, Dorothy. "Telling Tales, Telling Truths." In Kate Brandt, ed., *Happy Endings: Lesbian Writers Talk about Their Lives and Work.* Tallahassee, Fla.: Naiad, 1993, 9–18.

Ava. "How Do You Judge Me?" *Lesbian Connection* 4 (October 1978): 6.

Ayres, B. Drummond. "Miami Debate over Rights of Homosexuals Directs Wide Attention to a National Issue." *New York Times,* May 10, 1977, 18.

"Bad Taste and Bad Manners: Benson's Bomb." *Advocate* 373 (August 3, 1983): 18.

Baker, Ann. "A Mother's Cry for Help." *PWA Coalition Newsline* 49 (November 1989): 23.

Barnes, Hollister (Dorr Legg). "I Am Glad I Am a Homosexual." From *ONE,* 1958, in Mark Blasius and Shane Phelan, eds., *We Are Everywhere: A Historical Source Book of Gay and Lesbian Politics.* New York: Routledge, 1997, 323–26.

Bergler, Edmund. *1000 Homosexuals: Conspiracy of Silence, or Curing and Deglamorizing Homosexuals?* Paterson, N.J.: Pageant Books, 1959.

————, and William S. Kroger. *Kinsey's Myth of Female Sexuality: The Medical Facts.* New York: Grune and Stratton, 1954.

Bieber, Irving. *Homosexuality: A Psychoanalytic Study of Male Homosexuals.* New York: Basic Books, 1962.

Blackwell, Marie. "AIDS in the Family." *Essence,* August 1985, 56, 105–8.

Borhek, Mary. *Coming Out to Parents: A Two Way Survival Guide for Lesbians and Gay Men and Their Parents.* Cleveland: Pilgrim Press, 1983.

Bourque, Jacques. "AIDS: Where's It Left Us?" *Angles,* May 1986, 11.

Brans, Jo. *Mother, I Have Something to Tell You.* New York: Doubleday, 1987.

Brown, Arch. "Gay Pride, Before and After." *About Town,* June 30, 1980, 4–5.

Brown, Howard. *Familiar Faces, Hidden Lives: The Story of Homosexual Men in America Today.* New York: Harcourt, Brace, Jovanovich, 1976.

Brown, Rita Mae. "The Shape of Things to Come." In Nancy Myron and Charlotte Bunch, eds., *Lesbianism and the Women's Movement.* Baltimore: Diana Press, 1975, 70–73.

Bunch, Charlotte. *Passionate Politics: Feminist Theory in Action, 1968–1986.* 1975. Reprint, New York: St. Martin's Press, 1987.

————. "What Every Lesbian Should Know." *Furies,* January 1972, 40.

Burke, Robert. "Coming Out!" *Vector,* May 1973, 27–30.

Burns, Ken. "'The Homosexual Faces a Challenge': A Speech to the Third Annual Convention of the Mattachine Society." *Mattachine Review* 2 (August 1956): 20 and 25–27.

Byron, Peg. "Lesbians in the Fight against AIDS." *Advocate* 457 (October 14, 1986): 48–50.

Callen, Michael. *Surviving AIDS.* New York: HarperCollins, 1990.

Cappon, Daniel. *Toward an Understanding of Homosexuality.* Englewood Cliffs, N.J.: Prentice Hall, 1965.

Caprio, Frank S. *Female Homosexuality: A Psychodynamic Study of Lesbianism.* New York: Citadel, 1954.

Castro, Dali. "We Love Our Gay Children Too." *Parents of Gays National Newsletter* 1 (April 1980): S4.

Chase, Gillean. "Gay Pride? Week." *Long Time Coming* 2 (December 1974): n.p.

"Consciousness Raising." *Ms.,* July 1972, 18, 22, 23.

Cordova, Jeanne. "How to Come Out without Being Thrown Out." In Karla Jay and Allen Young, eds., *After You're Out: Personal Experiences of Gay Men and Lesbian Women.* New York: Quick Fox, 1975, 89–95.

Cornwell, Anita. "From a Soul Sister's Notebook." In Mark Blasius and Shane Phelan, eds., *We Are Everywhere: An Historical Source Book of Gay and Lesbian Politics.* New York: Routledge, 1997, 364–66.

Cory, Donald Webster. *The Homosexual in America.* New York: Greenberg, 1951.

David, Lester. "'Our Son Was Different': When a Mother Discovers the Agonizing Truth." *Good Housekeeping,* January 1966, 51–125.

"Dear Mother." *Leaping Lesbian* 2 (February 1978): 7 and 8.

Denneny, Michael. "A Quilt of Many Colors: AIDS Writing and the Creation of Culture." *Christopher Street* 12, no. 9, issue 141 (1989): 15–21.

Diaman, A. N. "On Sex Roles." In Guy Nassberg, ed., *Gay Flames* pamphlet no. 11 "Revolutionary Love: An Introduction to Liberation," 1970, 4.

Drellich, Marvin. "New Findings from Psychoanalytic Research on Homosexuality." *New York Mattachine Newsletter* (March 1961): 4.

Dubay, William H. "You Can Go Home Again." *Christopher Street* 9, no. 5, issue 101 (1985): 18–21.

Ehrenreich, Barbara. "Family Feud on the Left." *Nation,* March 13, 1982, cover and 303–6.

Eichberg, Rob. *Coming Out, An Act of Love: An Inspiring Call to Action for Gay Men, Lesbians, and Those Who Care.* New York: Plume, 1990.

Elias, Margaret. "Sisterhood Therapy." *Human Behavior,* April 1975, 31–36.

Elias, Marilyn. "Gay Children, Sad Parents, and Help for Them Both." *USA Today,* January 31, 1983, D8.

Ellis, Albert. *Homosexuality: Its Causes and Cure.* New York: Lyle and Stuart, 1965.

Faber, Charles. "Parents and Friends and an Organization to Support Them." *Advocate* 359 (January 6, 1983): 22–23.

Fairchild, Betty. "For Parents of Gays: A Fresh Perspective." In Betty Berzon and Robert Leighton, eds., *Positively Gay.* Millbrae, Calif.: Celestial Arts, 1979, 101–12.

———. *Parents of Gays.* Washington, D.C.: Parents of Gays, 1975.

———, and Nancy Hayward. *Now That You Know: A Parents' Guide to Understanding Their Gay and Lesbian Children.* 1979. Reprint, San Diego,Calif.: Harcourt Brace, 1998.

"The Family and Gay Oppression." *Come Out Fighting: The Newspaper of the Lavender and Red Union* 20 (April 1977): 4 and 5.

Fenton, Lisa. "The Radical Home Haircut." *Lesbian Voices* 4, no. 1 (1979): 13–14.

Florence, Robert John. "Coming In." *Out/Look* 2 (Fall 1989): 67–73.

Francoeur, Robert, and Anna Francoeur. *The Future of Sexual Relations.* Englewood Cliffs, N.J.: Prentice Hall, 1974.

Fredericks, Anne. "One Parent's Reaction." *Ladder* 5 (August 1961): 4–7.

Freud, Sigmund. "A Letter from Freud." *American Journal of Psychiatry* (April 1951): 786.

Froman, Paul Kent. *After You Say Goodbye: When Someone You Love Dies of AIDS.* San Francisco: Chronicle Books, 1992.

Gailey, Leah. "A Mother Gives an Answer: What Can I Do?" *Mattachine Review* 4 (May 1958): 5–8.

Gallagher, Jim. "How She Accepted Her Homosexual Son." *San Francisco Examiner,* July 10, 1973, n.p.

Gay Asians of Toronto. *Celebrasian: Shared Lives; An Oral History of Gay Asians.* Toronto: Gay Asians of Toronto, 1996.

"Gays in the Family." *Empty Closet* 61 (May 1976): 6 and 7.

"Gays under Fire." *Newsweek,* September 14, 1992, 35–41.

Gelman, David, and Pamela Abramson. "AIDS." *Newsweek,* August 12, 1985, 20–29.

Glick, Deborah. "Blessed Be the Mothers of the Lesbian Nation." *Gay Activist,* April 1973, n.p.

Goodstein, David B. "Our Sweet 16th: Remembering 1967." *Advocate* 377 (September 29, 1983): 30–36.

Gordon, Sol, and Irving R. Dickman, *Sex Education: The Parents' Role.* Public Affairs Pamphlet no. 549. New York, 1977.

Gottlieb, Amy. "Mothers, Sisters, Lovers, Listen." In Maureen FitzGerald, Connie Guberman, and Margie Wolfe, eds., *Still Ain't Satisfied: Canadian Feminism Today.* Toronto: Women's Press, 1982, 234–43.

Grant, Bev. "I'm Tired of F——'ers F——'in over Me." *Other Woman* 1 (May–June 1972): n.p.

Grier, Barbara, and Coletta Ried, eds. *Lesbian Lives: Biographies of Women from* The Ladder. Baltimore: Diana Press, 1976.

Gross, Alfred A. *Strangers in Our Midst.* Washington, D.C.: Public Affairs Press, 1961.

"A Guide to Consciousness Raising." *Lesbian Feminist,* August 1976, 3.

Haller, Scott. "Fear and AIDS in Hollywood." *People,* September 23, 1985, 28–33.

Hansen, Lilly. "Should Your Parents Know?" *GAY* 9 (March 29, 1970): 15.

Harris, Daniel. *The Rise and Fall of Gay Culture.* New York: Ballantine Books, 1997.

"Have You Ever . . ." *Lesbian Tide,* September 1971, 7.

Helquist, Michael. "An Epidemic in the Family." *Advocate* 404 (October 2, 1984): 29 and 56.

"The Heterosexual." *Sisters,* July 1973, 3–4.

Hiraga, Martin. "Rising Son: An Asian Comes Out to His Parents." *Empty Closet* 188 (December 1987–January 1988): 14 and 15.

Hoffman, Martin. *The Gay World.* New York: Bantam, 1969.

House, Penny. "Letters from My Mother." *Dyke,* Spring 1976, 21–23.

"How Gay Is Gay?" *Time,* April 23, 1979, 72–77.

Hudson, John Paul. "My Son Is Gay." *Advocate* 112 (May 23, 1973): 2.

"Incest." *Common Lives/Lesbian Lives* 2 (Winter 1981): 62–63.

Institute for the Protection of Gay Youth. "Giving Refuge to Harassed Gay Youngsters." *Advocate* 425 (July 23, 1985): 16.

"It's All in the Family." *Body Politic,* December 1986, 11.

"Jewel Elitist." *Albatross,* October 1975, 21–27.

Johnson, Dirk. "Coming Home, with AIDS, to a Small Town." *New York Times,* November 2, 1987, A1.

Johnston, Jill. *Lesbian Nation.* New York: Simon and Schuster, 1973.

Josephs, Larry. "The Harrowing Plunge." *New York Times Magazine*, November 11, 1990, 38–43.

Kahney, Regina. "Sarah Montgomery: Everybody's Favorite Mother." *Empty Closet*, January 1977, 6–9.

Klein, Satya. "The Heterosexual World: An Anthropological Study." *Vector: The Gay Experience* 11 (October 1975): 55.

Klemesrud, Judy. "For Homosexuals, It's Getting Less Difficult to Tell Parents." *New York Times*, September 1, 1972, 32.

Knoebel, John. "Words on Mother." *Faggotry*, 1972, 22–24.

Kramer, Larry. "1112 and Counting." *Reports from the Holocaust: The Making of an AIDS Activist*. New York: St. Martin's Press, 1989, 33–51.

———. "An Open Letter to Richard Dunne and the GMHC." 1987. In Mark Blasius and Shane Phelan, eds., *We Are Everywhere: A Historical Source Book of Gay and Lesbian Politics*. New York: Routledge, 1997, 601–9.

Kübler-Ross, Elisabeth. *AIDS: The Ultimate Challenge*. New York: Macmillan, 1987.

Lamp, Greg. "Back to the Farm to Die: Rural America Is about to Be Blindsided by the AIDS Epidemic." *Farm Journal*, January 1991, 17–20.

"The Last Letter Home." *Spectre* 3 (July–August, 1971): 4–6.

Leitsch, Dick. "Turning On to Daddy." *GAY* (March 15, 1970): 8.

"A Letter to My Dad." *Lesbian Connection* 6 (April–May 1983): 11.

"Letters." *Body Politic* 19 (July–August 1975): 18.

"Letters." *Lavender Woman* 1 (May 1972): 4.

"Letters." *Leaping Lesbian* 2 (March–April 1978): 27 and 28.

"Letters." *Lesbian Connection* (May 1976): 9.

"Letters." *Lesbian Voices* 1 (September 1975): 16–17.

Linda. "Letter to Mother." *Other Woman* 3 (August 1974): 8.

Louise, Vivienne. "Crossing That Bridge." In Julia Penelope and Susan J. Wolfe, eds., *The Original Coming Out Stories*. Freedom, Calif.: Crossing Press, 1980, 250–67.

Lund, Caroline. *The Family: Revolutionary or Oppressive Force?* New York: Merit Pamphlet, 1971.

Lyle, Dorothy. "The Family and Money Injustice." *Ladder* 10 (March 1966): 21–22.

MacDonald, Susan. "Coming Out: Sooner or Later." *Lesbian Feminist*, August 1976, 3.

Manford, Jeanne. "Letter to Mrs. Jones." *Homosexual Counseling Journal* 2 (January 1975): 26–33.

Marmor, Judd. *Sexual Inversion: The Multiple Roots of Homosexuality*. New York: Basic Books, 1965.

Marras, Amerigo. "Hetero-Burbia." *Body Politic* 7 (Winter 1973): 5.

Martin, Del. "If That's All There Is." In Mark Blasius and Shane Phelan, eds., *We Are Everywhere: A Historical Source Book of Gay and Lesbian Politics*. New York: Routledge, 1997, 352–55.

———, and Phyllis Lyon. *Lesbian/Woman*. San Francisco: Glide, 1972.

"Marychild." *Long Time Coming* 2 (January 1975): 35.

Maxwell, L. R. "Just between Us Mothers." *Mattachine Review* 3 (June 1957): 20–22.

McDonald, Sharon. "Tender Loving Care." *Advocate* 515 (January 3, 1989): 52–53.

Melfi, Mary, ed. *Painting Moments: Art, AIDS, and Nick Palazzo.* Toronto: Guernica, 1998.

Merriman, Frank. *The Making of a Homosexual.* Los Lunas, N.M.: Edea Books, 1966.

Michaels, Dick. "The World Is My Ashtray." *Los Angeles Advocate* 1 (December 1967): 7–8.

Michaels, Helaine Lovett. "When Your Child Is Gay: The Shock and the Acceptance." *Single Parent,* November 1981, 20–23.

"A Minneapolis Father Discovers Homosexuality." *Mattachine Review* (May–June 1955): 24–30.

Monette, Paul. *Last Watch of the Night: Essays Too Personal and Otherwise.* New York: Harcourt Brace and Company, 1994.

Montgomery, Sara. "To All Closet Gays." *It's Time* 1 (June–July 1975): 2.

Moraga, Cherrie. *Loving in the War Years.* Boston: South End, 1983.

"Mother Letters." *Dyke* 3 (1976): 7.

Murphy, John. *Homosexual Liberation: A Personal View.* New York: Praeger, 1971.

Myron, Nancy, and Charlotte Bunch. *Lesbianism and the Women's Movement.* Baltimore: Diana Press, 1975.

Oddone, Maureen. "Moving Out of Another Closet." *Advocate* 241 (May 17, 1978): 18–19.

Ogg, Elizabeth. "Partners in Coping: Groups for Self and Mutual Help." Public Affairs Pamphlet no. 559. New York: Public Affairs Committee, 1978.

"On Being a Lesbian." *Lesbian Connection* 2 (December 1976): 11.

"Parent Defends Gay Son's Right to Teach." *GAY* 84 (September 4, 1972): cover.

"Parents of Gays Organizing." *GAY* 100 (April 23, 1973): cover.

"Parents' Reaction." *Mattachine Review* 8 (October 1962): 21–23.

Pedersen, Lyn (Jim Kepner). "The Importance of Being Different." Reprint from *ONE,* 1954, in Mark Blasius and Shane Phelan, eds., *We Are Everywhere: A Historical Source Book of Gay and Lesbian Politics.* New York: Routledge, 1997, 320–23.

Penelope, Julia. "Tis the Season to Be Jolly." *Lesbian Inciter* 1 (December 1985): 16–21.

Pepper, Rachel. "A Coming-Out Christmas Tale." *Outlines,* January 1988, n.p.

"A Preliminary Analysis of Group Behavior of Homosexuals." *One Institute Quarterly* (Winter 1959): 26–32.

Radicalesbians. "The Woman-Identified Woman." In Karla Jay and Allen Young, eds., *Out of the Closets: Voices of Gay and Lesbian Liberation.* New York: Quick Fox, 1972, 156.

Ramsey, Judith. "My Daughter Is Different." *Family Circle,* 1974, 14, 16, 82, 89, 90.

Ransdell, Lisa. "Lesbian Feminism and the Feminist Movement." In Jo Freeman, ed., *Women: A Feminist Perspective.* Mountain View, Calif.: Mayfield, 1995, 641–53.

Rechy, John. "AIDS Mysteries and Hidden Dangers." *Advocate* 383–84 (December 22, 1983): 31.

Red Butterfly. "The Institutions of Repression." In *Gay Oppression: A Radical Analysis.* New York: Red Butterfly, 1969, 5.

Rich, Adrienne. "Compulsory Heterosexuality and Lesbian Existence." In *Blood, Bread, and Poetry: Selected Prose, 1979–1985* (New York: W. W. Norton, 1986), 23–75.

Rivard, Sandra. "Listen World! My Son Is Gay. Accept Him—Please." *Living*, February 26, 1976, D.

Rothenberg, David. "Another Voice." *Gaysweek* 83 (September 25, 1978): 19.

———. "Family Defense: The Contradictions." *Long Island Connection*, April 25–May 9, 1984, 37.

Rush, Florence. "The Parable of Mothers and Daughters." In Phyllis Birkby, Esther Newton, Bertha Harris, Jill Johnston, and Jane O'Wyatt, eds., *A Lesbian Feminist Anthology: Amazon Expedition*. Albion, Calif.: Times Change Press, 1973, 4–11.

Ruskin, Cindy. *The Quilt: Stories from the NAMES Project.* New York: Pocket Books, 1988.

———. "Taking Up Needles and Thread to Honor the Dead Helps AIDS Survivors Patch Up Their Lives." *People Weekly*, October 12, 1987, 42–49.

Sadownick, Douglas. "The Dancer Speaks Out: New Directions, New Candor." *Advocate* 545 (February 27, 1990): 38.

Saghir, Marcel T., and Eli Robins. *Male and Female Homosexuality: A Comprehensive Investigation*. Baltimore: Williams and Wilkins, 1973.

Sarff, Douglas. "'Parents of Gays' Help Others Understand." *Newswest*, August 7, 1975, n.p.

Seligmann, Jean, and Nikki Finke Greenburg. "Only Months to Live and No Place to Die: The Tragic Odyssey of a Victim Turned Pariah." *Newsweek*, August 12, 1985, 26.

Shelley, Martha. "Gay Is Good." *Gay Flames* pamphlet no. 1. New York, 1970, 1–4.

Silk, Kay. "Lesbian Novels in the Fifties." *Focus*, August 1973, 4–5.

Smith, Jean. "What Parents of Gay Children Fear Most Is Their Children." *Insight: A Quarterly of Gay Catholic Opinion* (Winter 1977): 15–16.

"Speaking Out about Our Lives." *Gay Community News* 10 (January 29, 1983): 10.

Stearn, Jess. *The Grapevine*. New York: Doubleday, 1964.

———. *The Sixth Man: A Startling Investigation Revealing That One Man in Six Is a Homosexual*. New York: Doubleday, 1961.

Stephens, Barbara. "A Plea for Integration." *Ladder* 1 (May 1957): 17–18.

Switzer, David, and Shirley Switzer. *Parents of the Homosexual*. Philadelphia: Westminster Press, Christian Care Books, Help for Living Today, 1980.

"Third World Gay Revolution Platform and Program, 1970." *Detroit Gay Liberator*, February 1971, 6.

Timmons, Stuart. "Larry Duplechan: Coming Out, Friendship, and Romance." *Advocate* 533 (September 12,1989): 62–63.

Trebay, Guy. "In Your Face." *Village Voice,* August 14, 1990, 34–39.

Tucker, Nancy. "F——You, 'Brothers'! or Yet Another Woman Leaves the Gay Liberation Movement." *Ladder* 15 (August–September 1971): 52 and 53.

Umans, Meg, ed. *Like Coming Home: Coming-Out Letters.* Austin, Tex.: Banned Books, 1988.

"USA & Canada." *Other Woman* 1 (March 1973): 13–16.

Van Buren, Abigail. "Don't Blame Yourself." *Choice,* August 14, 1981, 59.

VomLehn, Walter O. "A Doctor's AIDS Heartbreak: 'Well, Dad, I Finally Have It.'" *Medical Economics*, December 23, 1985, 48–53.

Walker, Merv. "The Family: 'Don't Shut Us Out of Your Life,'" *Body Politic* 20 (October 1975): 12–13.

"We ARE Your Children." *It's Time: Newsletter of the National Gay Task Force* 5 (October 1978): 1–3.

Wein, Glenn. "Gay Siblings in an Aging America." *Christopher Street* 101, vol. 9, no. 5 (1985): 26–28.

Weinberg, George. "Julie Lee Rhymes with DOB." *GAY* (April 12, 1971): 5.

———. *Society and the Healthy Homosexual.* New York: St. Martin's Press, 1972.

"The Well of Possibility." *GAY* 24 (July 20, 1970): 15.

Westwood, Gordon. *Society and the Homosexual.* New York: E. P. Dutton, 1953.

Wicker, Randy. "A Conversation with Sarah Montgomery, Grandma Lib." *GAY* 5 (March 1974): 6, 7, 15.

Wittman, Carl. "Gay Manifesto." *Gay Flames* pamphlet no. 9, 1970, 4.

Women's Liberation. *The New Woman: A Motive Anthology on Women's Liberation.* New York: Bobbs-Merrill Co., 1970.

Wyden, Peter, and Barbara Wyden. *Growing Up Straight: What Every Thoughtful Parent Should Know about Homosexuality.* New York: Signet, 1968.

Memoirs, Novels, Poetry, Plays, and Reminiscences

Aldrich, Ann (Vin Packer). *We, Too, Must Love.* Greenwich, Conn.: Gold Medal Books, 1958.

———. *We Two Won't Last.* Greenwich, Conn.: Gold Medal Books, 1963.

Allegra, Donna. "Lavender Sheep in the Fold." In Lisa C. Moore, ed., *Does Your Mama Know? An Anthology of Black Lesbian Coming-Out Stories* (Decatur, Ga.: RedBone Press, 1997), 149–61.

Atwood, Margaret. *The Edible Woman.* Toronto: McClelland and Stewart, 1969.

Back, Gloria Guss. *Are You Still My Mother? Are You Still My Family?* New York: Warner Books, 1985.

Baker, Jean. *Family Secrets: Gay Sons, A Mother's Story.* New York: Harrington Park Press, 1998.

Baldwin, James. *Giovanni's Room.* New York: Laurel, 1956.

Barbo, Beverly. *The Walking Wounded: A Mother's True Story of Her Son's Homosexuality and His Eventual AIDS Related Death.* Lindsborg, Kans.: Carlsons, 1987.

Bockman, Philip. "Fishing Practice." In Patrick Merla, ed., *Boys Like Us: Gay Writers Tell Their Coming-Out Stories.* New York: Avon Books, 1996, 73–81.

Borhek, Mary. *My Son Eric.* New York: Pilgrim Press, 1979.

Brown, Rebecca. *The Gifts of the Body.* New York: Harper Perennial, 1994.

Bruch, Hilde. *Don't Be Afraid of Your Child: A Guide for Perplexed Parents.* New York: Farrar, Straus and Young, 1952.

Bulkin, Elly, and Joan Larkin, eds. *Lesbian Poetry: An Anthology.* Watertown, Mass.: Persephone Press, 1981.

Chen, Susan Y. F. "Slowly but Surely, My Search for Family Acceptance and Community Continues." In Sharon Lim-Hing, ed., *The Very Inside: An Anthology of Writing by Asian and Pacific Islander Lesbian and Bisexual Women.* Toronto: Sister Vision, 1994, 79–84.

Currier, Jameson. *Where the Rainbow Ends.* Woodstock, NY: Overlook Press, 1998.

de la Pena, Terri. "Blunt Cuts and Permanent Conditions." In Nisa Donnelly, ed., *Mom: Candid Memoirs by Lesbians about the First Woman in Their Life.* Los Angeles: Alyson Books, 1998, 111–32.

———. *Latin Satins.* Seattle: Seal Press, 1994.

———. *Margins.* Seattle: Seal Press, 1992.

Duberman, Martin. *Midlife Queer: Biography of a Decade, 1971–1981.* New York: Scribner, 1996.

Duplechan, Larry. *Blackbird.* New York: St. Martin's Press, 1986.

Ellmann, Richard, and Robert O'Clair, eds. *The Norton Anthology of Modern Poetry.* New York: W. W. Norton, 1988.

Garden, Nancy. *Annie on My Mind.* New York: Farrar, Straus and Giroux, 1982.

Gidlow, Elsa. *Elsa: I Come With My Songs; The Autobiography of Elsa Gidlow.* San Francisco: Druid Heights, 1986.

Goldstaub, Sylvia. *Unconditional Love: "Mom! Dad! Love Me! Please!"* Boca Raton, Fla.: Cool Hand Communications, 1993.

Greenberg, Joanne. *I Never Promised You a Rose Garden.* New York: New American Library, 1964.

Hauser, Gwen. *Mad about the Crazy Lady.* Vancouver: Air Press, 1977.

Helms, Alan. *Young Man from the Provinces: A Gay Life before Stonewall.* New York: Avon, 1995.

Hemphill, Essex. "Commitments." In Essex Hemphill, ed., *Brother to Brother: New Writings by Black Gay Men.* Boston: Alyson, 1991, 57–58.

Hobson, Laura Z. *Consenting Adult.* New York: Doubleday, 1975.

Hoffman, Amy. *Hospital Time.* Durham, N.C.: Duke University Press, 1997.

Hoffman, William M. *As Is.* New York: Vintage Books, 1985.

"I am all things female." *Dykes and Gorgons* 1, no. 1 (1973): 24–25.

Jay, Karla. "First Love." In Joan Larkin, ed., *A Woman Like That: Lesbian and Bisexual Writers Tell Their Coming-Out Stories*. New York: Perennial, 1999, 28–41.

Johnson, Toby. "AIDS and Moral Issues: Will Sexual Liberation Survive?" *Advocate* 379 (October 27, 1983): 24.

Kantrowitz, Arnie. *Under the Rainbow: Growing Up Gay*. New York: William and Morrow, 1977.

Katz, Judith. "Born Queer." In Joan Larkin, ed., *A Woman Like That: Lesbian and Bisexual Writers Tell Their Coming-Out Stories*. New York: Perennial, 2000, 117–35.

Kesey, Ken. *One Flew over the Cuckoo's Nest*. New York: Viking Press, 1962

Kirkpatrick, Bill. *AIDS: Sharing the Pain; A Guide for Caregivers*. New York: Pilgrim Press, 1990.

Larkin, Joan. "Rhyme of My Inheritance." In Carl Morse and Joan Larkin, eds., *Gay and Lesbian Poetry of Our Time: An Anthology*. New York: St. Martin's Press, 1988, 219–20.

Lassell, Michael. "How to Watch Your Brother Die." In Carl Morse and Joan Larkin, eds., *Gay and Lesbian Poetry of Our Time*. New York: St. Martin's Press, 1988, 224.

Leavitt, David. *Arkansas: Three Novellas*. Boston: Houghton Mifflin, 1997.

———. *Family Dancing*. New York: Alfred A. Knopf, 1984.

Lorde, Audre. *Zami: A New Spelling of My Name*. Freedom, Calif.: Crossing Press, 1982.

McCann, Richard. "My Mother's Clothes: The School of Beauty and Shame." In Dean Kostos and Eugene Grygo, eds., *Mama's Boy: Gay Men Write about Their Mothers*. New York: Painted Leaf Press, 2000, 141–60.

Meigs, Mary. *Lily Briscoe: A Self Portrait; An Autobiography of Mary Meigs*. Vancouver: Talonbooks, 1981.

Moffatt, BettyClare. *When Someone You Love Has AIDS: A Book of Hope for Family and Friends*. New York: Plume, 1986.

Monette, Paul. *Becoming a Man: Half a Life Story*. San Francisco: Harper, 1992.

Munro, Alice. *Dance of the Happy Shades*. Toronto: McGraw-Hill Ryerson, 1968.

———. *Lives of Girls and Women*. Toronto: McGraw-Hill Ryerson, 1971.

———. *The Moons of Jupiter*. Markham, Ont.: Penguin Books, 1982.

Packer, Vin (Ann Aldrich). *The Evil Friendship*. Greenwich, Conn.: Fawcett Gold Medal, 1958.

———. *Whisper His Sin*. Greenwich, Conn.: Fawcett Gold Medal, 1954.

Parker, James Edwin. "Snakes, Trolls, and Drag Queens." In Dean Kostos and Eugene Grygo, eds., *Mama's Boy: Gay Men Write about Their Mothers*. New York: Painted Leaf Press, 2000, 99–109.

Peabody, Barbara. *The Screaming Room: A Mother's Journal of Her Son's Struggle with AIDS; A True Story of Love, Dedication, and Courage*. San Diego: Oak Tree, 1986.

Perry, Troy. *The Lord Is My Shepherd and He Knows I'm Gay: The Autobiography of the Rev. Troy D. Perry*. Los Angeles: Nash, 1972.

Pickett, James Carroll. "Kentucky 55 South: A Visit with Dad." In John Preston, ed., *A Member of the Family: Gay Men Write about Their Families*. New York: Dutton, 1992, 95–101.

Piercey, Marge. *Small Changes*. New York: Doubleday, 1973.

Reed, Paul. *Facing It: A Novel of AIDS*. San Francisco: Gay Sunshine Press, 1984.

Rodale, Ardath H. *Climbing toward the Light: A Journey of Growth, Understanding, and Love*. Emmaus, Pa.: Good Spirit Press, 1989.

Rubin Weiner, Emily. "Wow I'll Really Be Uptight If My Family Sees This." *Come Out!* 2 (Winter 1972): n.p.

Schow, H. Wayne. *Remembering Brad: On the Loss of a Son to AIDS*. Salt Lake City: Signature Books, 1995.

Scorpio, Joy. "My Mother." *Coming Out Rage* (May 1973): 12.

Sexton, Anne. *The Book of Folly*. Boston: Houghton Mifflin, 1972.

———. *Complete Poems*. Boston: Houghton Mifflin, 1981.

———. *Love Poems*. New York: Oxford University Press, 1969.

Shyer, Marlene Fanta, and Christopher Shyer. *Not Like Other Boys: Growing Up Gay; A Mother and Son Look Back*. Boston: Houghton Mifflin, 1996.

Stasey, Bobbie. *Just Hold Me While I Cry: A Mother's Life-Enriching Reflections on Her Family's Emotional Journey through AIDS*. Albuquerque, N.Mex.: Elysian Hills, 1993.

Travis, Ben. *The Strange Ones*. Boston: Beacon, 1959.

Vale Allen, Charlotte. *Daddy's Girl*. Toronto: McClelland and Stewart, 1980.

Vidal, Gore. *The City and the Pillar*. New York: Ballantine, 1948.

West, Cheryl L. *Before It Hits Home*. New York: Dramatists Play Service, 1993.

Winski, Norm. *The Homosexual Revolt*. Canoga Park, Calif.: Viceroy Books, 1967.

Yale, Jo-Ellen. "family dinner." *Focus*, June 1977, 1.

Yamaguchi, Lynne, and Karen Barber, eds. *Tomboys: Tales of Dyke Derring-Do*. Los Angeles: Alyson, 1992.

Films, Television, Advertisements, and Art

Barela, Tim. "Revenge of the Yenta." In *Domesticity Isn't Pretty*. Minneapolis: Palliard Press, 1993.

Demme, Jonathan, dir. *Philadelphia*. 1993.

Erman, John, dir. *Our Sons*. 1991.

Gott, Ted. *Don't Leave Me This Way: Art in the Age of AIDS*. Melbourne: Thames and Hudson, 1994.

Hockney, David. *Domestic Scene, Los Angeles*. 1963.

Howard, Billy. *Epitaphs for the Living: Words and Images in the Time of AIDS*. Dallas: Southern Methodist University Press, 1989.

"The Homosexuals." *CBS News*. 1967.

"I Am a Homosexual." *Mattachine Review* 6 (June 1960): 20–23.

Lipman, Daniel, and Ron Cowen. *An Early Frost*. NBC Television, 1985.

Reavis, John W., Jr., and Irving Saraf. *The Rejected*. National Educational Television Presentation for KQED Channel 9, San Francisco. Transcript, September 11, 1961, KQED, San Francisco, Calif.

Roberts, Shelly, and Melissa K. Sweeney. *Hey Mom, Guess What! 150 Ways to Tell Your Mother*. San Diego: Paradigm, 1993.

Solomon, Rosalind. *Portraits in the Time of AIDS*. New York: New York University, Grey Art Gallery, 1988.

"The Rejected." *Mattachine Review* 7 (September 1961): 15.

Velez, Ivan. *Tales of the Closet*. New York: Hetrick-Martin Institute, 1987.

"Will I Ever Be Able to Face the World Again?" *Mattachine Review* 4 (April 1958): 36.

Winfrey, Oprah. "Parents Who Can't Deal with the Fact That Their Children Are Gay." *Oprah Winfrey Show*, 1993.

With Arms That Encircle. PFLAG, Wichita, Kansas, 1993.

INDEX

Italicized page numbers indicate illustrations.